Lecture Notes in Computer Science

Lecture Notes in Computer Science

Edited by G. Goos and J. Hartmanis

183

The Munich Project CIP

Volume I: The Wide Spectrum Language CIP-L

By the CIP Language Group:
F. L. Bauer, R. Berghammer, M. Broy, W. Dosch,
F. Geiselbrechtinger, R. Gnatz, E. Hangel, W. Hesse,
B. Krieg-Brückner, A. Laut, T. Matzner, B. Möller, F. Nickl,
H. Partsch, P. Pepper, K. Samelson (†), M. Wirsing
and H. Wössner

Authors

F. L. Bauer   B. Möller
R. Berghammer   H. Partsch
W. Dosch   P. Pepper
R. Gnatz   K. Samelson (†)
E. Hangel   H. Wössner
Institut für Informatik der TU München
Postfach 20 24 20, 8000 München 2

M. Broy
F. Nickl
M. Wirsing
Fakultät für Mathematik und Informatik, Universität Passau
Postfach 2540, D-8390 Passau

F. Geiselbrechtinger
Department of Computer Science, University College Dublin
Belfield, Dublin 4, Ireland

W. Hesse
Softlab GmbH
Arabellastr. 13, D-8000 München 81

B. Krieg-Brückner
Fachbereich 3, Informatik, Universität Bremen
Postfach 33 04 40, D-2800 Bremen 33

A. Laut
PCS GmbH, Periphere Computer-Systeme
Pfälzer-Wald-Str. 36, D-8000 München 90

T. Matzner
sd&m GmbH, Software Design & Management
Führichstr. 70, D-8000 München 80

CR Subject Classification (1982): D.1.0, D.2.1, D.2.4, D.3.1, D.3.3, F.3.1,
F.3.2, F.3.3

ISBN 978-3-540-15187-6   ISBN 978-3-540-39269-9 (eBook)
DOI 10.1007/978-3-540-39269-9

This book is the first of two volumes that present the main results having emerged from the project CIP - Computer-Aided, Intuition-Guided Programming - at the Technical University of Munich. The central theme of this project is program development by transformation, a methodology which is felt to become more and more important.

Whereas Volume II will contain the description, formal specification, and transformational development of a system, CIP-S, that is to assist a programmer in this methodology, the present volume gives the description and formal definition of a program development language CIP-L designed particularly for use in transformational development of programs from formal specifications. Many sources have influenced the development of this language over the past eight years, and we feel that it has now matured and consolidated to a degree that its study will be profitable to others.

Three aspects of this language appear to be of special interest:

First, the language is a *coherent wide spectrum language*. This means that it comprises a number of expressive levels ranging from predicative and algebraic specifications over applicative and procedural constructs (including parallelism) down to a machine-oriented level using jumps and pointers. However, these levels do not just form a loose collection of features; rather they are closely linked by formal transformation rules that relate the various constructs to give a coherent semantics to the entire language. Besides, these rules also give a guideline for the overall structure of the transformational development process. Since CIP-L comprises most of the essential concepts of today's programming languages in more or less similar form, the rules also provide some insight into the general structure of programming languages and programming.

The second major aspect of interest in this book is the definition of the language by the new method of *transformational semantics*. In this approach, a kernel language is distinguished as that part of the language which contains the essential semantic concepts. All other language constructs are then mapped into this kernel by formal transformation rules that allow reducing every program to an equivalent one of the kernel language. It seems remarkable that the set of rules needed for the particular language CIP-L is quite small and easy to survey; in most cases just one rule per additional language construct suffices. Thus, a transformational definition of a well-designed language is as concise as, say, a denotational one; moreover, in our opinion, it is much easier to comprehend.

As a third major aspect, CIP-L is an *abstract scheme language*. This means, first, that its formal definition works on the abstract syntax of the language. As a consequence, CIP-L allows various concrete syntactic representations, two of which, viz. an ALGOL-like and a PASCAL-like form, are given in syntax charts in an appendix. Second, CIP-L is a scheme language in that it is independent of any particular set of data structures (except the truth values); rather it comprises elaborate means for defining new data structures.

The book is organized as follows: Part 0 contains a general introduction to transformational programming and to the project CIP in particular. In Part I, the various constructs of the language are introduced informally together with examples of their place in program development. Part II, the heart of the book, then gives a description of the language in a systematic way. However, readability is considered more important than complete formality; in particular, the transformation rules are given in concrete syntax, and a number of self-evident context conditions are omitted. Finally, Part III contains a complete formal definition of the language in the same order of presentation as Part II.

Cross-references within one part are given by section numbers only; references to other parts are made by prefixing the respective section numbers with the (roman) part numbers.

We would like to express our thanks to the Deutsche Forschungsgemeinschaft who has sponsored this research within the Sonderforschungsbereich 49 "Programmiertechnik" during the past nine years. Also, we gratefully acknowledge valuable criticism of the language and of its definition by the lecturers and participants of the Marktoberdorf Summer Schools 1978 and 1981, notably by E.W. Dijkstra, D. Gries, and C.A.R. Hoare, as well as by the members of IFIP Working Group 2.1, notably by H.J. Boom, G. Goos, L.G.L.T. Meertens, S.A. Schuman, and M. Sintzoff. Particular thanks are due to R.S. Bird for pointing out a severe error in an earlier version of the semantic specification of the kernel language. Last, but by no means least, we gratefully acknowledge many helpful remarks by our colleagues C. Delgado Kloos, H. Ehler, F. Erhard, U. Hill-Samelson, A. Horsch, H. Hußmann, W. Meixner, R. Obermeier, H.-O. Riethmayer, G. Schmidt, and R. Steinbrüggen.

Munich, December 1984

The CIP Language Group

TABLE OF CONTENTS

PART 0

INTRODUCTION TO THE PROJECT CIP

'Programming is by nature a formal activity.'
Scherlis, Scott 1983

Part 0 provides a survey of the history and major aims of the project CIP from which the language CIP-L has emerged. Besides the fundamental design principles this Part also outlines the use of the language in program development following the methodology of inferential programming.

0. HISTORY OF THE PROJECT CIP

The project CIP evolved after 1968 from the attempt to find a common semantic basis for programming languages seemingly incongruent in style (cf. /Bauer 71/). 'Future programming languages, or programming languages of the future, can be the result of rational discussion among people who have ... a common basis for their reasoning' (/Bauer 73/).

It was clear that the existence of such a basis meant also that programs of different style could be transformed into each other. This, however, would include the possibility to take one (high level) program as a specification for another (low level) program. 'The result of structured programming is not just one program but a whole sequence of programs such that any one can immediately be deduced from its predecessor' (/Bauer 73/).

Thus, in 1974 the project CIP was born: Going further than mere verification of a program against a specification, an eo ipso correct program should be derived, deduced or, as we now prefer to say, *inferred* from a specification. The particular approach of CIP was to use local transformations of programs as the inference method. A local transformation rule is a rule that allows to replace program parts of a specific form by functionally equivalent program parts (cf. /Broy et al. 80/). Applying such rules may gradually transform a specification into an efficient machine-oriented program. This approach allows the programmer to make the design steps explicit and sufficiently small so that he can master their complexity. Thus the correctness of the intermediate versions (with respect to the specification) is guaranteed, and the individual design decisions are properly reflected by the applied rules ("self-documenting programming").

Abstract reference languages covering a wide spectrum of styles were to be distilled, and a system allowing mechanical manipulation of programs was to be built: CIP stands for "Computer-aided, Intuition-guided Programming". The project was outlined at the Marktoberdorf Summer School 1975 and at the 2nd International Conference on Software Engineering (cf. /Bauer 76/).

The main streams of activity in the project CIP are
- design and formal definition of a wide spectrum language CIP-L;
- design and implementation of a system CIP-S for program transformation;
- development of a methodology of inferential programming.

All three of these activities went from the beginning hand in hand, accompanied by applications in research problems and in teaching. This turned out to be very fruitful. In particular, the language design was guided and frequently corrected by the other activities. Besides, a wealth of theoretical investigations was stimulated by the project (see /Möller 84/ for a survey). A first source for methodological studies is the book "Algorithmic Language and Program Development" by F.L. Bauer and H. Wössner, Springer 1982. For the interested reader we include a bibliography of the project CIP in Appendix II.

1. A WIDE SPECTRUM LANGUAGE FOR INFERENTIAL PROGRAMMING - SURVEY OF CIP-L

The very first attempt aimed at a layered system of languages of different styles (cf. /Bauer 73/). Here, *style* means a certain level of abstraction in the formulation of a program with a specific degree of detail and a particular operational semantics. But pretty soon the separate layers were abandoned in favour of a single language covering a wide spectrum of styles. The advantages of this approach are:

- The *wide spectrum language* allows local changes of style without scrambling the whole program ('...must allow an *incremental* approach to the manipulation of program derivations' (/Scherlis, Scott 83/)[1]) and in this sense supports *incremental compilation*.
- Correspondingly, correctness considerations can be *localized*.
- The common semantic basis of the whole language gives complete freedom in the transformation process, since the language constructs "fit together".

A wide spectrum of styles is indeed necessary, since problem specification is often too distant from calculation:

- Good specifications are characterized by clarity. They are transparent and easy to understand, but utterly inefficient if viewed as a program, or not even operative at all.
- Good implementations are characterized by efficiency, however, they are generally rather hard to understand.

But clarity and efficiency are rarely achieved in *one* program. Instead, a complete derivation of a program from a specification makes it possible that clarity and efficiency *coexist* . Conceptually, such a derivation is a network of insights and design decisions, connecting a straightforward specification with an adequate implementation.

Soon it became apparent that the development of the language should go hand in hand with the analysis of program derivations: Programming is usually goal-oriented - the goal being at present a machine of the von Neumann architecture or the abstract machine defined by a compiler for such a machine, in future possibly being of somewhat different nature. While preservation of correctness means that, with respect to the mathematical semantics under consideration, initial specification and final product are equivalent, the operational semantics the user has in mind is frequently coupled in a particular way to the level of style used along the way from specification to product - Floyd-Hoare-Dijkstra semantics at the level of procedural style, flow chart semantics at the level of control-oriented style, stack-machine and term-rewriting semantics at the level of functional and logic programming.

---

[1] W. L. Scherlis and D. S. Scott make in their IFIP '83 paper /Scherlis, Scott 83/ many telling remarks that illustrate our view. As they are seemingly little influenced by the project CIP we will quote some of their formulations as those of unprejudiced observers (without referencing each time their paper).

0.1 A wide spectrum language - Survey of CIP-L

These "changes of semantic frame" are in our experience an essential part of most programmers' thought processes in establishing a program traditionally. In inferential programming they must be exhibited since they support the intuition guiding the derivation process. On the other hand, by designing the language appropriately, such changes can be expressed as formal transformation rules relating different language styles. Thus, it was a logical next step to give definitional character to the transformations: A small kernel was distilled which already contained all expressive power; the other levels were then defined relative to this kernel via transformation rules reducing all constructs to kernel constructs ("transformational semantics", cf. /Pepper 79/).

Thus, the approach of inferential programming led to the following requirements on the language:
- The language has to comprise a large number of different concepts, styles, and constructs for allowing the formulation of problem specifications and high-level programs as well as machine-oriented programs.
- During a program development certain parts of a program are gradually replaced by functionally equivalent ones using machine-oriented constructs while other parts remain unchanged. Hence, it should be allowed to mix specification constructs, high-level constructs, and machine-oriented constructs without any syntactic or semantic constraints.
- Although the language provides different styles, these styles must be closely related. As far as possible, simple syntactic transformation rules should exist for transforming programs written in a specific (sub-)style into another one. This coherence of styles should allow e.g. the transition between a system of functions in tail-recursive form and a system of procedures with jumps.
- The language definition has to provide a sufficiently formal framework in which the applied methodology of program development by transformations can be justified mathematically. This justification guarantees the correctness of a derived program with respect to the given specification.

The present volume contains the description and formal definition of the wide spectrum language L84 which was designed to meet the above criteria. Its orientation towards the von Neumann architecture suggested a call-by-value and call-time choice semantics and the primary use of strict functions (cf. I.1.1.2, I.1.1.5, II.2.1.1, II.2.1.2). A comprehensive collection of examples of the use of CIP-L can be found in /Bauer et al. 81/.

1.1. OVERALL STRUCTURE AND CONCEPTS OF CIP-L

The language provides constructs for the specification and implementation of data structures as well as constructs for the specification and implementation of control structures. Algebraic (data) types provide a means for the algebraic specification of data. They can be implemented by computation structures combining data and algorithms. Modes are described by specific types for which computation structures can be provided automatically.

Based on algebraic types and/or computation structures, programs can be specified using predicate logic, description, comprehensive choice, and fully typed set operations. Programs using these constructs are called pre-algorithmic.

Applicative programs can be formulated with the help of recursion, branching on conditions, and function abstraction and application. Guarded expressions and the finite choice allow non-deterministic applicative programs. Procedural programs are based on the classical concepts of procedures, iteration, program variables, assignments, and conditional statements. Guarded commands and the finite choice of statements allow to write non-deterministic procedural programs; labels and jumps provide the transition to the control-oriented level of machine programming.

In designing CIP-L, the following principles were found to be of paramount importance:

- There is a complete separation of control structure ("scheme language") and data structure ("algebraic types").
  - •• CIP-L is a *scheme language*:
    Programs are built over basic symbols ("identifiers") for sorts, objects, and operations. Such program terms can be manipulated independent of the actual meaning of the symbols ("program schemes") provided certain laws hold for these.
  - •• CIP-L comprises *algebraic types*:
    The identifiers for sorts, objects, and operations in a program scheme are to be interpreted by "views" of certain algebraic types, the laws of which are also used for verifying the applicability conditions of transformations. Concrete implementations of the algebraic types then associate concrete meaning with the symbols. Fundamental is the *Principle of Generation*: Every object must be generable by finitely many applications of the basic operations.

- CIP-L is a *first-order logic language*:
  In the algebraic types, first-order logic *formulas* are used as laws; in the scheme language, sequential first-order logic provides non-strict language constructs, e.g. conditional boolean operations and if-then-else-fi.

- CIP-L is a *fully typed language*:
  Different domains of objects can be distinguished ("many-sortedness"). The type-checking, i.e. the test for compatibility of formal and actual parameters of operations, can be done completely statically.

- CIP-L is an *expandable language*:
  The language has a kernel for logic and functional programming, on which all other constructs are based by definitional transformations. Relative to the mathematical semantics it has complete freedom of execution: in contrast to e.g. PROLOG, the execution is not committed

0.1.1 Overall structure of CIP-L

to the order of presentation of the clauses. The transformationally defined extensions of this kernel are

●● a full applicative language comprising declarations of objects and functions;
●● a procedural style with variables and procedures;
●● parallel programming with shared variables and conditional critical regions;
●● a control-oriented style comprising labels and jumps.

For CIP-L it can be proved that the transformational semantics for the typical constructs of the aforementioned styles agrees with the classical denotational semantics.

● CIP-L is an *abstract language* :
Both the scheme language and the language of algebraic types are *abstract* languages: From a transformational viewpoint, their external representations are irrelevant.[2]

● CIP-L is a *modular language* :
Modularity is provided by algebraic types on the specification level, and by computation structures, modules and devices (modules with internal state) on the implementation level. These constructs provide complete encapsulation.

● CIP-L is a *non-deterministic language* :
A specification may still leave freedom; certain decisions ("commitments", cf. /Scherlis, Scott 83/) are deliberately left open ("intentional vagueness"). In this way, it is often possible to develop whole families of functionally equivalent implementations. Modification can then be focussed at decision points. To allow a rigorous specification and program development even in such cases, non-determinism was to be included both in specifications and programs.

1.2. REMARKS ON WIDE SPECTRUM LANGUAGES FOR NON-CONVENTIONAL ARCHITECTURES

When the project was started, it was rather clear that program develoment would aim under practical viewpoints towards machines of the von Neumann type, including array and vector processors. This has led us also to include block structure. Reduction machines and corresponding languages, advocated by J. Backus since 1973, seemed to be far from reality. The rapid progress in the technology of solid state devices, in particular very large scale integration, have changed the situation since. Reduction machines and a variety of data flow machines are in reach. This means, however, that the semantic basis of suitable wide spectrum languages is no longer necessarily oriented towards call-by-value and smash-products, but has to take into account also call-by-expression and non-strict direct products. In particular, the incorporation of infinite

---

[2] The system CIP-S works with internal tree representations. Appendix III gives syntax diagrams for an ALGOL-like ("ALGOL 84") and a PASCAL-like ("PASCAL 84") external representation which are used side by side in Part I. In Part II we use only the ALGOL-like representation to avoid duplications. In Part I also scattered examples of LISP-like, PROLOG-like and other external representations can be found.

objects (cf. /Möller 82,85/) suggests this change. For tomorrow, we would widen the semantic basis of the CIP language and would incorporate those concepts in order to make the semantics adaptable to these needs. In addition, incorporation of operators for lazy and busy evaluation and the definition of an appropriate composition of them would lead to machine-oriented styles for reduction architectures. We consider it an open question whether more general recursion equations (accommodating a PROLOG style) should be included. It should also be investigated whether certain basic "meta"-operations of the transformation system like pattern-matching and unification should be included in the language.

2. METHODOLOGY OF PROGRAM DEVELOPMENT

CIP-L was designed as a vehicle for *inferential programming*, i.e. the process of building, manipulating, and reasoning about programs and their derivations. However, the mere use of the language does not yet produce efficient programs, nor does it make the programmer better. Also, the approach of inferential programming does not make the programmer superfluous: 'No one in near future will succeed in fully automating the programming power, and we must not waste our efforts in such an attempt. As our understanding of the process of programming improves, it is true that more aspects of it will be subject of automation - but the completely mechanical programmer is a will-o'-the-wisp'.

However, the programmer can be freed from the burden of trivial details by providing him with a support system. Moreover, such a system can enforce a certain discipline in the development process while keeping the programmer free for the essential parts of the development task.

'The good programmers are not only smarter, but they have command of a larger collection of standard programming patterns'; moreover, they are able to invent new patterns if the need arises. We call this ability intuition, and intuition is to be supplied by the user in the interactive dialogue user/system. 'The user is regarded as an extension of the system' (R. A. Kowalski). Gradually, more and more of the programmer's experience can be stored in the system in the form of transformation strategies; this establishes the knowledge-base in using it as an expert system. A system that supports inferential programming must store representations of past experiences; if programmers then find useful analogies with derivation patterns in the store, it must help them in selecting the most fruitful ones, and finally allow them to adapt the store of knowledge as needs and understanding change. In order to keep the pattern catalogues manageable in size, the system should allow every programmer to have his or her own specific knowledge base (T. Cheatham: 'Knowledge-based software assistant').

2.1. THE LEGAL PROCESS OF PROGRAMMING

Software as an industrial product should be reliable, correct with respect to its specification, and efficient with respect to a given (real or abstract) machine. This is particularly important if software is the basis for large-scale production (e.g. frozen software on chips) or if it is established under extreme responsibility for human safety or under stringent political requirements. The time is clearly ripe for the transferral of formal methods for software construction from academic to industrial environments; this observation was the main result of a recent workshop on Program Transformation and Programming Methodology (cf. /Pepper 84/).

Before a program is designed, the problem to be solved should be specified completely and precisely. Frequently, only an iterative process involving a number of approximating versions leads to such a specification, which then can be used as a *contract* between the customer and the programmer (cf. /Bauer 81/). The specification has to be as clear and understandable as possible such that the partners can whole-heartedly sign the contract. To achieve such a specification, it may very often be necessary to use implicit, descriptive, and predicative characterizations.

Taking programming to consist in *correctness-preserving transformations* of a specification into a product will help to make the contract between customer and programmer sound; it allows one to view the 'difference between specification and implementation simply as one of *degree*' .

2.2. THE ECONOMICAL PROCESS OF PROGRAMMING

A program derivation in CIP-L does not need to be a linear graph (after all traces of backtracking in the development have been removed), but will rather be a tree or an acyclic directed graph: 'more structures emerge when alternative commitments are pursued and different implementations of the same specification (or multiple specifications for the same implementation) are obtained'. In fact, multiple redundant specifications can shed light on all facets of the specification that emerges from the informality of the requirement analysis.

Multiple derivations, however, and the knowledge of the branching points at which design decisions are possible and different commitments are made, increase the economical value of a derivation: duplication of labour can be avoided, and efficient variants of a program for special demands can be provided at low additional costs. Moreover, it is often possible to obtain derivations on the control structure side for many different data structures, or to use the same transformation of a type in many different control structures. Thus, generality comes often as a byproduct.

By using an inferential programming system, also the notion "reusability" of programs becomes practical: looking up the well-documented history of a derivation makes all relevant previous work useful for related problems.

2.3. THE SOCIAL PROCESS OF PROGRAMMING

Scherlis and Scott remark that the entire process of program development cannot be captured in the *text* of a single program. As an essential part of future programs we see their derivations and claim that the derivation structure provides a way of making the *rationale* for program structure explicit. Thus, programming in the CIP system is self-documenting: the system keeps the derivation history and allows to present it in an appropriate form together with the original specification and the derived program. This 'constitutes a much more useful proof than the usual sort of static program proof'. In this way the social process of understanding a program becomes transparent. "Reuse" of a program by a person different from the one that wrote it involves such a social process of programming; it should be much simpler in inferential programming than in the existing situation.

3. THE TECHNICAL PROCESS OF INFERENTIAL PROGRAMMING –
SURVEY OF THE PROGRAM TRANSFORMATION SYSTEM CIP-S

To free the human programmer from the error-prone burden of clerical work and to allow him to concentrate on the design ideas, an interactive system should support the development process.

However, there is a need to go a qualitative step beyond present-day programming tools:
- They are primarily syntax-oriented and do not help in reasoning about correctness.
- Tools for verification do not take into account program evolution.
- Most systems do not show well how to relate program versions to each other.

Large-scale programming needs the aid of semantically based mechanical tools. They help to do the *modifications* and *adaptions* which frequently arise in the software life cycle. Of course, they also perform *dull* modifications and adaptations. More important, they stimulate the user's creativity, notably by supporting experimentation. In the ideal case, they allow the *programmer's* role to be primarily *heuristic*. Programming *techniques* become manifest as *patterns* of derivation steps. The system can be constructed such that no transformation step goes by unquestioned and documentation is delivered as a byproduct. Complete control of the transformation process implies preservation of correctness; the total proof is broken down into the verification of the applicability of individual transformations.

The CIP system not only performs program transformations, it also makes whole program derivations manifest as data structures: It is able to
- construct
- store
- modify
- relate
derivations.

0.3 Survey of the transformation system CIP-S

Transformation steps of fundamental character are
- commitment, giving up freedom;
- simplification, using algebraic laws;
- change of style (change of operational semantics) based on definitional transformations;
- structuring, i.e. reducing a task to subtasks.

As to the last point, it introduces modularity and uses local specifications of the subtasks as *interfaces*.

In order to assist the user in monitoring a derivation, the system must have
- version control: bookkeeping, backtracking.

However, our intention is not to distill heuristic approaches for synthesizing programs fully automatically. Here we agree with /de Millo et al. 79/: 'There is a wealth of evidence that fully automated ... systems are out of the question.'

The system itself can be formulated in CIP-L. Although object language and meta-language have the same structure, they are clearly distinct, since the connection is established only after interpreting the basic algebraic types of the meta language as the syntactic and semantic entities of the object language. Thus, the user is, as with LCF (cf. /Gordon et al. 79/), permitted to handle programs on the one hand, and "programming programs" (a term used by Ershov), viz. frozen program transformations, on the other hand.

A prototype of the system is working since 1982 (cf. /Brass et al. 82/). The actual CIP system is at the moment being developed from a formal specification by algebraic types down to the level of PASCAL with the help of the prototype. This development of CIP-S will be documented in Volume II of this report.

PART I

INFORMAL SURVEY OF THE LANGUAGE

In this part, most examples are denoted both in the ALGOL-like ("ALGOL 84") and in the PASCAL-like ("PASCAL 84") external representation of the language (on the left- and right-hand side of the page); occasionally LISP-like, FP-like, or PROLOG-like representations are used. These representations try to stay as closely as possible with ALGOL 68 and PASCAL, resp. For instance, the ALGOL-like representation uses infix operators, whereas the PASCAL-like one employs keywords. Their use side by side is intended to exhibit their similarities rather than their differences; moreover it is hoped that the comparison also sheds some light on the commonalities in the concepts of ALGOL 68, PASCAL and other programming languages.

"At the present time I think we are on the verge of discovering at last what programming languages should really be like. I look forward to seeing many responsible experiments with language design during the next few years; and my dream is that by 1984 we will see a consensus developing for a really good programming language (or, more likely, a coherent family of languages). Furthermore, I'm guessing that people will become so disenchanted with the languages they are now using - even COBOL and FORTRAN - that this new language, UTOPIA 84, will have a chance to take over."

D. E. Knuth, 1974

1. THE EXPRESSION LANGUAGE FOR LOGIC AND FUNCTIONAL PROGRAMMING

1.1. EXPRESSIONS

An expression denotes objects of a certain kind. ("Kind" stands e.g. for a sort of an algebraic type or the functionality of a function; cf. the notions "mode" in ALGOL 68 or "type" in PASCAL.)

Fundamental expressions are the terms over basic object and operation symbols of an underlying algebraic type (see 6); the basic symbols have to be interpreted in some model of that type. Other examples of expressions are the application of an abstraction, guarded expressions, or descriptive expressions which denote objects implicitly.

Expressions with a boolean result are called <u>boolean expressions</u> (the algebraic type of boolean values (cf. II.1.4(a)) is generally presupposed). If all operations of the basic types are predicates, the corresponding kernel language allows nothing but logic programming.

Examples:
In a PROLOG-like external representation of CIP-L a predicative description of the sorting problem could be formulated as
issort(x, y) **if** issorted(y) **and** ispermutation(x, y) .

Another famous predicative description is given by
ismortal(x) **if** ishuman(x) .
If now the underlying algebraic type defines a constant socrates with the law
ishuman(socrates)
we may infer
ismortal(socrates) .

Although functions can always be rewritten in the form of predicates, this does usually not improve clarity.

1.1.1. GUARDED EXPRESSIONS

The guarded expression (of a kind ∎) is a modification of Dijkstra's "guarded commands" (cf. /Dijkstra 75/); it has the following general form:

$$
\begin{array}{l|l}
\textbf{if } B_1 \textbf{ then } E_1 & \textbf{if } B_1 \textbf{ then } E_1 \\
\Box \ B_2 \textbf{ then } E_2 & \Box \ B_2 \textbf{ then } E_2 \\
\ \ \vdots & \ \ \vdots \\
\Box \ B_n \textbf{ then } E_n \ \ \textbf{fi} & \Box \ B_n \textbf{ then } E_n \ \ \textbf{endif} \ .
\end{array}
$$

Here the guards B_i are boolean expressions and the E_i are expressions (conforming to the same non-functional kind ■). The object denoted by the guarded expression (its "value") is one of those objects E_i for which the corresponding B_i is true - which one is left open. Hence, the guarded expression is a "non-deterministic" construct associated with a *set* of possible values, called its breadth. If no B_i is true then the value of the guarded expression is not defined. Otherwise, if the breadth contains just one value, the expression is called determinate; if it contains more than one value, the expression is called non-determinate.

Example:

$$
\begin{array}{l|l}
\textbf{if } x \geq 0 \textbf{ then } \mathrm{succ}(0) & \textbf{if } x \geq 0 \textbf{ then } \mathrm{succ}(0) \\
\Box \ x \leq 0 \textbf{ then } \mathrm{pred}(0) \ \textbf{fi} & \Box \ x < 0 \textbf{ then } \mathrm{pred}(0) \ \textbf{endif}
\end{array}
$$

Here, the symbols .≤., .≥., 0, succ, pred can e.g. be interpreted in a model of the type INT characterizing integral numbers (cf. II.1.4(b)). If $x = 0$ holds, it is not determined whether the first or the second branch of the guarded expression will be evaluated, and, for this reason, the value is not uniquely determined.

If B is determinate, the guarded expression

$$
\begin{array}{l|l}
\textbf{if } B \textbf{ then } E_1 \ \Box \ \neg B \textbf{ then } E_2 \ \textbf{fi} & \textbf{if } B \textbf{ then } E_1 \ \Box \ \textbf{not } B \textbf{ then } E_2 \ \textbf{endif}
\end{array}
$$

coincides semantically with the usual (deterministic) conditional expression, i.e. the alternative with the condition B

$$
\begin{array}{l|l}
\textbf{if } B \textbf{ then } E_1 \textbf{ else } E_2 \ \textbf{fi} & \textbf{if } B \textbf{ then } E_1 \textbf{ else } E_2 \ \textbf{endif} \ .
\end{array}
$$

1.1.2. FUNCTION ABSTRACTION AND APPLICATION

An abstraction parameterizes an expression and thus makes it into a function. It is of the form

$$
\begin{array}{l|l}
(\mathbf{m}_1 \ x_1, \ ..., \ \mathbf{m}_n \ x_n) \ \mathbf{r} : E & (x_1 : m_1 \ ; \ ...; \ x_n : m_n) : r \ ; \ E
\end{array}
$$

$(n \geq 0)$ where $\mathbf{m}_1, \ ..., \ \mathbf{m}_n$ and r denote kinds and $x_1, \ ..., \ x_n$ parameter identifiers which may occur free in the expression E. If f stands for this abstraction and E_i are expressions of kinds $\mathbf{m}_i$, resp., then the application of f to $E_1, \ ..., \ E_n$ is expressed by

I.1.1 Expressions

$$f(E_1, \ldots, E_n) \qquad \qquad f(E_1, \ldots, E_n) \ .$$

It is an expression for an object of kind **r**, equivalent to the expression E with all free occurrences of x_i replaced by the same determinate denotation for some object in the breadth of E_i provided these objects are defined values ("call-by-value", "call-time choice", cf. /Hennessy, Ashcroft 76/).

$$\textbf{funct } (m_1, \ldots, m_n) \ \textbf{r} \qquad \qquad \textbf{function } (m_1 \ ; \ \ldots; \ m_n) : r$$

specifies the functionality (the kind) of f. Functions with $n = 0$ are called <u>parameterless functions</u>.

In PASCAL the application of a unary function f to an argument expression E may also be denoted by "E.f". Examples are n.succ or x.leftsum where x denotes an object of the mode E defined in 6.2 and leftsum is a corresponding selector.

A function with a boolean result is called a <u>predicate</u>, its application is a boolean expression.

The denotation of a function written in the above form with an expression E as its <u>body</u> uniquely determines a function. Nevertheless, this function may or may not be <u>determinate</u>[1] , depending on whether or not the expression E is determinate. We call the function <u>defined</u> if it yields defined values for all defined arguments.

Example:
  Let **int** (resp. int) be a sort symbol for integral numbers (cf. II.1.4(b)). Then

(int x) **int** :	(x : int) : int ;
if x $\geq$ 0 **then** x	**if** x $\geq$ 0 **then** x
$\Box$ x $\leq$ 0 **then** -x **fi**	$\Box$ x $\leq$ 0 **then** -x **endif**
denotes a determinate function, whereas	
(int x) **int** :	(x : int) : int ;
if x $\geq$ 0 **then** +1	**if** x $\geq$ 0 **then** +1
$\Box$ x $\leq$ 0 **then** -1 **fi**	$\Box$ x $\leq$ 0 **then** -1 **endif**

is non-determinate for $x = 0$.

In general, the kinds of the arguments indicated by the functionality of a function f do not specify the exact domain of f. For example the usual function for the subtraction of a natural number b from a natural number a is undefined for $a < b$. To express the restriction of the arguments, an appropriate boolean expression can follow the list of formal parameters as an

---

[1] Determinate functions are partially defined mappings in the mathematical sense; non-determinate functions are only correspondences (see also the notions of "ambiguous" and "non-ambiguous" functions in /McCarthy 63/). Note that in this report the term "function" generally stands for a non-determinate partial function.

explicit <u>assertion</u>; in our example

    (**nat** a, **nat** b : a ≥ b) **nat** :
      «...»

            (a : nat ; b : nat ‖ a ≥ b) : nat ;
              «...»

A restricted abstraction

    (**m** x : C) **r** : E

            (x : m ‖ C) : r

is equivalent to

    (**m** x) **r** : **if** C **then** E **fi**

            (x : m) : r ; **if** C **then** E **endif**

In a similar way, it is possible to restrict the results of a function.

Note that functions may occur as parameters and as results of functions.

1.1.3. FUNCTIONS DEFINED AS FIXPOINTS (RECURSION)

A function may not only be defined by an abstraction, but also as a fixpoint of a functional equation.

<u>Example</u>:

Consider the following functional equation in s (to be interpreted e.g. over an enrichment of NAT, cf. II.1.3.3):

           s = (**nat** a, **nat** b : a ≥ b) **nat** :
              if b = 0 **then** a
(*)   ⫿ a = b **then** 0
              ⫿ b > 0 **then** s(a-1, b-1)
              ⫿ a > b **then** s(a-1, b) + 1 **fi**

           s = (a : nat ; b : nat ‖ a ≥ b) : nat ;
              if b = 0 **then** a
           ⫿ a = b **then** 0
           ⫿ b > 0 **then** s(a-1, b-1)
           ⫿ a > b **then** s(a-1, b) + 1 **endif**

It has a minimal solution (with respect to the Egli-Milner ordering; see II.2.1.1), which equals the subtraction function; this solution is denoted by means of the fixpoint operator **Y** applied to a pair consisting of a function identifier and an abstraction with a free occurrence of this function identifier:

         (**Y** s : (**nat** a, nat b : a ≥ b) **nat** :
            if b = 0 **then** a
(**)   ⫿ a = b **then** 0

        (**Y** s : (a : nat ; b : nat ‖ a ≥ b) : nat ;
            if b = 0 **then** a
          ⫿ a = b **then** 0

I.1.1 Expressions

[] b > 0 **then** s(a-1, b-1)	[] b > 0 **then** s(a-1, b-1)
[] a > b **then** s(a-1, b) + 1 **fi**)	[] a > b **then** s(a-1, b) + 1 **endif**)

The binding of s is restricted to the abstraction, therefore s cannot be used outside the fixpoint expression as a name for the function. (For function declarations see 2.)

Note that (**Y** f : A) can be reduced to A itself if there is no free occurrence of f in A.

For symbolically evaluating the application of a fixpoint expression to some arguments, the associated functional equation has to be used repeatedly together with appropriate simplification steps (text replacement semantics of fixpoints, see e.g. /Bauer, Wössner 82/).

The fixpoint operator can, of course, also be used in recursive definitions of non-determinate functions. A famous example is McCarthy's function less which delivers some integer between 0 and m - 1, both included (cf. /McCarthy 63/):

(**Y** k : (**nat** m : m ≥ 1) **nat** :	(**Y** k : (m : nat ‖ m ≥ 1) : nat ;
if m ≥ 1 **then** m - 1	**if** m ≥ 1 **then** m - 1
[] m > 1 **then** k(m-1) **fi**)	[] m > 1 **then** k(m-1) **endif**)

In general, a system of functional equations can be used for defining several functions simultaneously. Let $f_1, ..., f_n$ be function identifiers and $A_1, ..., A_n$ be function abstractions; then

(**Y** $f_1, ..., f_n$: $A_1, ..., A_n$)	(**Y** $f_1, ..., f_n$: $A_1, ..., A_n$)

denotes the least fixpoint of the system.

As an example, we give a system of three predicates hasrestzero, hasrestone, hasresttwo that decide whether a natural number n, if divided by 3, leaves as rest 0, 1 or 2:

(**Y** hasrestzero, hasrestone, hasresttwo :	(**Y** hasrestzero, hasrestone, hasresttwo :
(**nat** n) **bool** :	(n : nat) : bool ;
if n = 0 **then** true	**if** n = 0 **then** true
[] n > 0 ∧ even(n)	[] n > 0 **and** even(n)
then hasrestzero(n ÷ 2)	**then** hasrestzero(n **div** 2)
[] n > 0 ∧ odd(n)	[] n > 0 **and** odd(n)
then hasrestone(n ÷ 2) **fi** ,	**then** hasrestone(n **div** 2) **endif** ,
(**nat** n) **bool** :	(n : nat) : bool ;
if n = 0 **then** false	**if** n = 0 **then** false
[] n > 0 ∧ even(n)	[] n > 0 **and** even(n)

> **then** hasresttwo(n ÷ 2)
> ▯ n > 0 ∧ odd(n)
> **then** hasrestzero(n ÷ 2) **fi** ,

> **then** hasresttwo(n **div** 2)
> ▯ n > 0 **and** odd(n)
> **then** hasrestzero(n **div** 2) **endif** ,

> (**nat** n) **bool** :
>   **if** n = 0 **then false**
>   ▯ n > 0 ∧ even(n)
>   **then** hasrestone(n ÷ 2)
>   ▯ n > 0 ∧ odd(n)
>   **then** hasresttwo(n ÷ 2) **fi**)

> (n : nat) : bool ;
>   **if** n = 0 **then** false
>   ▯ n > 0 **and** even(n)
>   **then** hasrestone(n **div** 2)
>   ▯ n > 0 **and** odd(n)
>   **then** hasresttwo(n **div** 2) **endif**)

The operator ÷ resp. **div** is to be interpreted as the usual integer division and the predicates even and odd decide whether a natural number is even or odd.

1.1.4. HIGHER-ORDER FUNCTIONS

Functions may also have functions as arguments and/or as results. Examples (over INT, cf. II.1.4(b)) are: a functional that applies a parameter function thrice to a parameter object,

> (**funct** (**int**) **int** f, **int** x) **int** :
>   f(f(f(x)))

> (f : **function** (int) : int ; x : int) : int ;
>   f(f(f(x)))

and a higher order function

> (**int** a, **int** b, **int** c, **int** d)
>   **funct** (**int**) **int** :
>   (**int** s) **int** : (a*s+b) ÷ (c*s+d)

> (a : int ; b : int ; c : int ; d : int) :
>   **function** (int) : int ;
>   (s : int) : int ; (a * s+b) **div** (c * s+d) .

Its result is a function

> (**int** s) **int** : (a*s+b) ÷ (c*s+d)

> (s : int) : int ; (a*s+b) **div** (c*s+d)

which denotes the linear substitution

$$s \mapsto (a * s + b) / (c * s + d) .$$

An application of this higher-order function is equivalent to the <u>partial application</u> f(a,b,c,d,·) of the following function f with five parameters:

I.1.1 Expressions

$$\begin{array}{ll}
(\textbf{int}\ a,\ \textbf{int}\ b,\ \textbf{int}\ c,\ \textbf{int}\ d,\ \textbf{int}\ s)\ \textbf{int:} & (a:\ int;\ b:\ int;\ c:\ int;\ d:\ int;\ s:\ int):\ int; \\
(a * s + b) + (c * s + d) & (a * s + b)\ \textbf{div}\ (c * s + d)\ .
\end{array}$$

An important class of higher-order functions are those which extend an operation defined on objects of a kind **n** to an operation on mappings **m** $\rightarrow$ **n** .

For example, the operation max (to be interpreted e.g. over INT, cf. II.1.4(b)) induces the higher-order function

$$\begin{array}{ll}
(\textbf{funct}(\textbf{int})\ \textbf{int}\ f,\ \textbf{funct}(\textbf{int})\ \textbf{int}\ g) & (f:\ \textbf{function}(int):int\ ;\ g:\ \textbf{function}(int):int)\ : \\
\quad \textbf{funct}\ (\textbf{int})\ \textbf{int}\ : & \quad \textbf{function}\ (int)\ :\ int\ ; \\
\quad (\textbf{int}\ x)\ \textbf{int}\ :\ max(f(x),\ g(x)) & \quad (x:\ int)\ :\ int\ ;\ max(f(x),\ g(x))
\end{array}$$

i.e. the maximum function MAX of two given functions from integers to integers.

There are two standard higher-order operations: function composition o and function tupling. For instance, the tuples

   (hasrestone, hasresttwo, hasrestzero) and

   (hasresttwo o succ, hasrestzero o succ, hasrestone o succ)

are equivalent. Since the argument sorts agree, we may also write the latter tuple in an FP-like style (cf. /Backus 78/) as

   [hasresttwo, hasrestzero, hasrestone] o succ .

1.1.5. FINITE CHOICE

A guarded expression with constantly true guards,

$$\begin{array}{ll}
\textbf{if true then}\ E_1 & \textbf{if true then}\ E_1 \\
\square\ \textbf{true then}\ E_2\ \textbf{fi} & \square\ \textbf{true then}\ E_2\ \textbf{endif}\ ,
\end{array}$$

describes the possibility to choose arbitrarily the first or the second branch when evaluating this expression. Hence, the set of possible values, i.e. the breadth, is the union of the breadth of E_1 and the breadth of E_2.

A guarded expression of the above form may be abbreviated by $(E_1\ \square\ E_2)$, a language construct called finite choice. With respect to the application of a function f, the finite choice shows the property that the expressions $f((E_1\ \square\ E_2))$ and $(f(E_1)\ \square\ f(E_2))$ have the same breadth since we employ call-by-value and call-time choice semantics (cf. /Hennessy, Ashcroft 76/). To avoid semantic difficulties, we rule out the non-deterministic choice between (higher-order) functions.

1.2. DESCRIPTIVE CONSTRUCTS FOR SPECIFICATION PURPOSES

Descriptive constructs allow the implicit specification of objects by their properties, i.e. by a certain predicate P. For simplicity, we suppose in Part I that P is a boolean-valued abstraction with one parameter x of sort **r**, and that P denotes a determinate and defined function.

1.2.1. DESCRIPTION

If P is a *characteristic* predicate, i.e. if there exists one and only one object x_0 satisfying $P(x_0)$, then the object specification

that r x : P(x) | **that** x : r $\parallel$ P(x)

denotes that unique object x_0 of kind **r** for which $P(x_0)$ is true. This construct is called a description. It obviously has the property

P(**that r** x : P(x)) | P(**that** x : r $\parallel$ P(x)) .

For example, the subtraction of natural numbers can now be specified by

(**nat** a, **nat** b : a $\geq$ b) **nat** : | (a : nat ; b : nat $\parallel$ a $\geq$ b) : nat ;
 that nat x : a = x + b | **that** x : nat $\parallel$ a = x + b

as the inverse of addition. It is easy to prove that this specification satisfies the functional equation (*) in 1.1.3 as well. If the descriptive specification is given first instead of the functional equation (*), the latter can be *derived("synthesized")* using the same arguments as the proof. This method was mentioned as *inferential programming* in Part 0.

As another example for the description consider the specification of the sorting problem:

(**sequ** s) **sequ** : | (s : sequ) : sequ ;
 that sequ t : | **that** t : sequ $\parallel$
    issorted(t) $\wedge$ ispermutation(s,t) | issorted(t) **and** ispermutation(s,t)

1.2.2. COMPREHENSIVE CHOICE

The comprehensive choice (or choice for short) denotes an object which is described - but in general not uniquely determined - by a predicate P. We use the keyword **some** for forming choices,

I.1.2 Descriptive constructs

some m x : P(x) $\qquad$ | $\qquad$ **some** x : m $\|$ P(x)

provided there exists at least one object x_0 satisfying $P(x_0)$, and P(y) is defined for all y.

Again it is obvious that the choice, if it is defined, has to satisfy the property

P(**some** m x : P(x)) $\qquad$ | $\qquad$ P(**some** x : m $\|$ P(x)) ,

and for this reason the predicate P characterizes the breadth of the choice, i.e. the set of possible values. An example for the comprehensive choice in the notation of logic programming (cf. /Kowalski 83/) is

$$\textbf{give } y : \text{sequ } \textbf{where } \text{issort}(x,y) \; .$$

Two choices are said to be equivalent if they have the same breadth; this is the case iff their predicates are logically equivalent.

Note, moreover, that the expressions

((**nat** x) **nat** : x + x)(**some nat** y : y < 5) $\quad$ | $\quad$ ((x : nat) : nat ; x + x)(**some** y : nat $\|$ y < 5)

and

(**some nat** y : y < 5) + (**some nat** y : y < 5) $\quad$ | $\quad$ (**some** y : nat $\|$ y < 5) + (**some** y : nat $\|$ y < 5)

are *not* equivalent. The breadth of the first expression is {0, 2, 4, 6, 8}, and for the second, one finds {0, 1, 2, 3, 4, 5, 6, 7, 8}.

The choice is a generalization of the finite choice, on the one hand, because $(E_1 \; [] \; E_2)$ and **some** m x : x = E1 $\bigvee$ x = E2 are equivalent provided E1 and E2 are defined and determinate. On the other hand, the choice generalizes the description in the sense that the description

that m x : P(x) $\qquad$ | $\qquad$ **that** x : m $\|$ P(x)

and the choice

some m x : $\qquad\qquad\qquad$ | $\qquad$ **some** x : m $\|$
$\quad$ (P(x) $\wedge$ $\forall$ m y : P(y) $\Rightarrow$ x=y) $\quad$ | $\quad$ (P(x) **and** $\forall$ y : m $\|$ P(y) **impl** x=y)

are equivalent for a determinate predicate P.

Using the comprehensive choice, McCarthy's function less (cf. 1.1.3) can also be specified by

(**nat** n : n ≥ 1) **nat** : **some nat** x : x < n	(n : nat ‖ n ≥ 1) : nat ; **some** x : nat ‖ x < n

The breadth of an application less(n) with a positive natural number n is the set of natural numbers less than n , including 0.

It is easily observed that under the assertion n ≥ 1 the comprehensive choice

some nat x : x < n	**some** x : nat ‖ x < n

is equivalent to

some nat x : (n ≥ 1 ∧ x = n - 1) ∨ (n > 1 ∧ x < n - 1)	**some** x : nat ‖ (n ≥ 1 **and** x = n - 1) **or** (n > 1 **and** x < n - 1) .

This leads immediately to the functional equation

less = (**nat** n : n ≥ 1) **nat** :
  if n ≥ 1 **then** n - 1
  [] n > 1 **then** less(n-1) **fi**
	less = (n : nat ‖ n ≥ 1) : nat ;
	  if n ≥ 1 **then** n - 1
	  [] n > 1 **then** less(n-1) **endif** .

The uniqueness property of the fixpoint, which can be demonstrated by induction methods leads to the equality

((**nat** n : n ≥ 1) **nat** :
  some nat x : x < n)
= (Y less : (**nat** n : n ≥ 1) **nat** :
  if n ≥ 1 **then** n - 1
  [] n > 1 **then** less(n-1) **fi**)
	((n : nat ‖ n ≥ 1) : nat ;
	  some x : nat ‖ x < n)
	= (Y less : (n : nat ‖ n ≥ 1) : nat ;
	  if n ≥ 1 **then** n - 1
	  [] n > 1 **then** less(n-1) **endif**)

(see 1.1.3).

1.2.3. DESCRIPTIVE SETS

Objects of a kind ■ may be assembled into a set forming a new object of the kind **set** ■ by a <u>set comprehension</u>: {■ x : P(x)} denotes the set of all objects of kind ■ for which P(x) is true. The enumeration

I.1.2 Descriptive constructs

$$\{E_1 , \ldots, E_n\} \qquad\qquad [E_1, \ldots, E_n]$$

is an abbreviation for the comprehension

$$\{\mathbf{m}\ x : x = E_1 \ \bigvee \ \ldots \ \bigvee \ x = E_n\} \qquad [x : m \ \| \ x = E_1 \ \bigvee \ \ldots \ \bigvee \ x = E_n]$$

(in case all E_i are determinate; see II.1.3(e) for the general case).

Related to McCarthy's function less one specifies

$$(\mathbf{nat}\ n)\ \mathbf{set\ nat} : \{\mathbf{nat}\ x : x < n\} \qquad (n : nat) : \mathbf{set\ of}\ nat\ ; \ [x : nat \ \| \ x < n]\ ,$$

i.e. a function yielding the (finite) set of all natural numbers less than n.

If the above function is called lesset, the functional equation

lesset = (**nat** n) **set nat** :	lesset = (n : nat) : **set of** nat ;
if n = 0 **then** {**nat** x : **false**}	**if** n = 0 **then** [x : nat ‖ false]
else {n-1} U lesset(n-1) **fi**	**else** [n-1] U lesset(n-1) **endif**

is satisfied.

$$\{\mathbf{nat}\ x : \mathbf{false}\} \qquad\qquad [x : nat \ \| \ false]$$

denotes the empty set, whereas

$$\{\mathbf{nat}\ x : \mathbf{true}\} \qquad\qquad [x : nat \ \| \ true]$$

denotes the entire object set **nat** (resp. nat) .

Descriptive sets are widely used because in many problem areas they support and guide the way of thinking in an excellent way. This may be illustrated by a small example which may be related to the area of geometric modelling (cf. /Requicha 77/).

Example:
A rigid solid S in a 3-dimensional euclidean space of kind E_3 can be described by a function $f : E_3 \rightarrow \mathbf{real}$ which is a polynomial function of the coordinates of a point p. S is then understood to be the set

$$\{E_3\ p : f(p) \geq 0\} \qquad\qquad [p : E_3 \parallel f(p) \geq 0]\ .$$

Then

$$
\begin{aligned}
\{E_3\ p : f_1(p) \geq 0\} \cup \{E_3\ p : f_2(p) \geq 0\} &\qquad [p : E_3 \parallel f_1(p) \geq 0] \cup [p : E_3 \parallel f_2(p) \geq 0]\\
= \{E_3\ p : f_1(p) \geq 0 \vee f_2(p) \geq 0\} &\qquad = [p : E_3 \parallel f_1(p) \geq 0 \text{ or } f_2(p) \geq 0]\\
= \{E_3\ p : \max(f_1(p),\ f_2(p)) \geq 0\} &\qquad = [p : E_3 \parallel \max(f_1(p),\ f_2(p)) \geq 0]\\
= \{E_3\ p : \mathrm{MAX}(f_1,\ f_2)(p) \geq 0\} &\qquad = [p : E_3 \parallel \mathrm{MAX}(f_1,\ f_2)(p) \geq 0]
\end{aligned}
$$

This example demonstrates that it may be much easier to understand manipulations of solids in the usual terms of union than in terms of the second order function MAX (cf. 1.1.4).

Descriptive sets give the kernel of CIP-L its full logical power. Note, however, that the power set of a countable set is no longer countable, and thus e.g. **set nat** can, without the restricition to finite sets, only be used in a descriptive way.

1.2.4. QUANTIFIERS

In CIP-L also expressions quantified with the help of the universal quantifier $\forall$ and the existential quantifier $\exists$ are available. Quantification is restricted to objects. The universal quantifier has been used already in 1.2.2 in order to establish the relationship between choice and description. In a similar way the unique existential quantifier $\exists_1$ can be introduced for a determinate predicate P if we define $\exists_1\ \mathbf{m}\ x : P(x)$ by

$$
\begin{aligned}
\exists\ \mathbf{m}\ x : P(x) \wedge &\qquad \exists\ x : m \parallel P(x)\ \mathbf{and}\\
\forall\ \mathbf{m}\ y : P(y) \Rightarrow (x=y) &\qquad\qquad \forall\ y : m \parallel P(y)\ \mathbf{impl}\ (x=y)\ .
\end{aligned}
$$

Note that the description **that m** $x : P(x)$ is defined iff $\exists_1\ \mathbf{m}\ x : P(x)$ holds.

In programming, the existential quantifier will often be found in a situation like

$$
\begin{aligned}
&\mathbf{if}\ \exists\ \mathbf{m}\ x : P(x)\ \mathbf{then}\ f(\mathbf{some}\ \mathbf{m}\ x : P(x)) &\qquad &\mathbf{if}\ \exists\ x : m \parallel P(x)\ \mathbf{then}\ f(\mathbf{some}\ x : m \parallel P(x))\\
&\qquad\qquad\qquad\qquad \mathbf{else}\ E \qquad\qquad\qquad \mathbf{fi} &\qquad &\qquad\qquad\qquad\qquad \mathbf{else}\ E \qquad\qquad\qquad \mathbf{endif}
\end{aligned}
$$

Assume f to be a defined and determinate function and let P and E be defined and determinate, too. Then this conditional expression may be transformed into

$$
\begin{aligned}
&\mathbf{some}\ \mathbf{n}\ y : (\exists\ \mathbf{m}\ x : P(x) \wedge y = f(x)) &\qquad &\mathbf{some}\ y : n \parallel (\exists\ x : m \parallel P(x)\ \mathbf{and}\ y = f(x))\\
&\qquad\qquad \vee (\forall\ \mathbf{m}\ x : \neg P(x) \wedge y = E) &\qquad &\qquad\qquad \mathbf{or}\ (\forall\ x : m \parallel \mathbf{not}\ P(x)\ \mathbf{and}\ y = E)\ .
\end{aligned}
$$

I.1.2 Descriptive constructs

For example, the expression

if $\exists$ **sequ** x : a & x = b   **if** $\exists$ x : sequ $\parallel$ a & x = b
  then f(**some sequ** x : a & x = b)   **then** f(**some** x : sequ $\parallel$ a & x = b)
  else empty   **fi**   **else** empty   **endif**

can be transformed into

some sequ y :   **some** y : sequ $\parallel$
  ($\exists$ **sequ** x : a & x = b $\wedge$ y = f(x)) $\vee$ ($\exists$ x : sequ $\parallel$ a & x = b **and** y = f(x)) **or**
  ($\forall$ **sequ** x : a & x $\neq$ b $\wedge$ y = empty)   ($\forall$ x : sequ $\parallel$ a & x $\neq$ b **and** y = empty)   .

2. THE FULL APPLICATIVE LANGUAGE

2.1. OBJECT DECLARATIONS

A collective object declaration

$$(m_1 \; x_1, \; ..., \; m_n \; x_n) \equiv (E_1, \; ..., \; E_n) \qquad\bigg| \qquad \textbf{const} \; (x_1 : m_1, \; ..., \; x_n : m_n) = (E_1, \; ..., \; E_n)$$

introduces the object identifiers $x_1, \; ..., \; x_n$ for objects denoted by $E_1, \; ..., \; E_n$. Note that the $x_1, \; ..., \; x_n$ must not occur free in the E_i; this avoids confusion with the recursive declaration of functions. Note also that the parentheses are omitted for $n = 1$; then we have

$$m \; x \equiv E \qquad\qquad\qquad x : m \; = \; E \; .$$

Object declarations usually occur in a segment

$$\ulcorner \; (m_1 \; x_1,...,m_n \; x_n) \equiv (E_1,...,E_n) \; ; \qquad \bigg| \qquad \textbf{begin const} \; (x_1:m_1,...,x_n:m_n) = (E_1,...,E_n) \; ;$$
$$E_0 \qquad\qquad\qquad\qquad \lrcorner \qquad\qquad E_0 \qquad\qquad\qquad\qquad\qquad\qquad\qquad \textbf{end}$$

This makes "intermediate results" available for "multiple use" within the expression E_0. The segment has by definition (cf. /Landin 65/) the same meaning as the function application

$$((m_1 \; x_1, \; ..., \; m_n \; x_n) \; r : E_0)(E_1, \; ..., \; E_n) \qquad \bigg| \qquad ((x_1 : m_1; \; ...; \; x_n : m_n): \; r \; ; \; E_0)(E_1, \; ..., \; E_n)$$

where r denotes the kind of the result of E_0.

2.2. FUNCTION DECLARATIONS

2.2.1. FUNCTION DECLARATIONS IN THE LAMBDA-CALCULUS STYLE

Object declarations are also admissible for function kinds m_i: Let A be an expression of functionality **funct** (m) n resp. **function** (m) : n, E an expression of kind m resp. m, and f an identifier which does not occur free in A and E. Then the segment

$$\ulcorner \; \textbf{funct} \; (m) \; n \; f \equiv A \; ; \; f(E) \; \lrcorner \qquad\qquad\bigg| \qquad \textbf{begin const} \; f : \textbf{function} \; (m) : n = A \; ; \; f(E)$$
$$\bigg| \qquad \textbf{end}$$

I.2.2 Function declarations

has the same meaning as

$$((\textbf{funct } (m) \text{ n f}) \text{ n : f(E))(A)} \qquad \Big| \qquad ((f : \textbf{function } (m) : n) : n ; f(E))(A) .$$

Due to the fact that E has no free occurrence of f, it is admissible to elaborate the function application simply by use of text replacement semantics. Thus, the above application has the same meaning as A(E).

As an example of a declaration we consider a specific instance of the function composition written in a LISP-like external representation of CIP-L:

```
(DEF COMP (LAMBDA (((FUNCT (N) R) G) ((FUNCT (M) N) F)) (FUNCT (M) R)
          (LAMBDA ((M X)) R
              (G (F X))            ) ) )
```

2.2.2. FUNCTION DECLARATIONS IN THE STYLE OF ALGOL-LIKE LANGUAGES

If A is simply an abstraction

$$(m \text{ x}) \text{ n : } E_0 \qquad \Big| \qquad (x : m) : n ; E_0 \ ,$$

it is only a matter of convenience to abbreviate within a function declaration the functionality **funct** (m) n f resp. **const** f : **function** (m) : n by **funct** f resp. by **function** f yielding

$$\textbf{funct } f \equiv (m \text{ x}) \text{ n : } E_0 \qquad \Big| \qquad \textbf{function } f \ (x : m) : n ; E_0$$

Similarly, a unary fixpoint operator **Y** may be suppressed by replacing

$$\textbf{funct } (m) \text{ n f} \equiv (\textbf{Y } f : (m \text{ x}) \text{ n : } E_0) \qquad \Big| \qquad \begin{array}{l} \textbf{const } f : \\ \textbf{function } (m) : n \equiv (\textbf{Y } f : (x : m) : n ; E_0) \end{array}$$

by

$$\textbf{funct } f \equiv (m \text{ x}) \text{ n : } E_0 \qquad \Big| \qquad \textbf{function } f(x : m) : n ; E_0$$

This leads to recursive declarations in a form well-known from ALGOL-like languages.

In case of a k-ary fixpoint operator an analogous transformation applies, leading to a system of (mutually recursive) function declarations, separated by commas.

Note that the Y-operator is a binding construct and, thus, **Y** f : (**m** x) **n** : E has no free occurrence of f whereas (**m** x) **n** : E may have such occurrences.

To give an example, we again take the subtraction (cf. 1.1.3): The declaration

funct (**nat** a, **nat** b : a ≥ b) **nat** sub ≡	**const** sub : **function** (a:nat ; b:nat ‖ a ≥ b) : nat
(**Y** s : (**nat** a, **nat** b : a ≥ b) **nat** :	= (**Y** s : (a : nat ; b : nat ‖ a ≥ b) : nat ;
if b = 0 **then** a	**if** b = 0 **then** a
◻ a = b **then** 0	◻ a = b **then** 0
◻ b > 0 **then** s(a-1, b-1)	◻ b > 0 **then** s(a-1, b-1)
◻ a > b **then** 0 **else** s(a-1, b) + 1 **fi**)	◻ a > b **then** s(a-1, b) + 1 **endif**)

introduces the name sub. After renaming s by sub the above abbreviation leads to

funct sub ≡ (**nat** a, **nat** b : a ≥ b) **nat** :	**function** sub (a : nat ; b : nat ‖ a ≥ b) : nat ;
if b = 0 **then** a	**if** b = 0 **then** a
◻ a = b **then** 0	◻ a = b **then** 0
◻ b > 0 **then** sub(a-1, b-1)	◻ b > 0 **then** sub(a-1, b-1)
◻ a > b **then** 0 **else** sub(a-1, b) + 1 **fi**	◻ a > b **then** sub(a-1, b) + 1 **endif**)

2.2.3. FUNCTION DECLARATIONS IN THE STYLE OF ALGEBRAIC TYPES

We sometimes prefer to separate the functionality of a function from the definition of its body. This leads to a notation similar to that of algebraic types (cf. 6). As examples consider the following function definitions in a PROLOG-like (left; cf. /Clocksin, Mellish 81/) and a HOPE-like (right; cf. /Burstall et al. 80/) external representation:

(1) **function** shouldtake	**dec** shouldtake :
(x : person ; y : drug) : Boolean ;	person # drug → truval
shouldtake(x, y) if	---shouldtake(x, y) ⇐
∃ z : illness ‖	∃ z **with**
hascomplained(x, z) ∧	hascomplained(x, z) ∧
suppresses(y, z) ∧	suppresses(y, z) ∧
agreeswith(x, y)	agreeswith(x, y)

with suitable primitives hascomplained, suppresses, agreeswith.

(2) **function** citizen	**dec** citizen :
(x : person ; y : country) : Boolean ;	person # country → truval
function born	**dec** born :
(x : person ; y : country) : Boolean ;	person # country → truval

I.2.2 Function declarations

```
function father                    dec father :
  (x,y : person) : Boolean ;         person # person → truval


citizen(x,y) if born(x,y) ;        ---citizen(x,y) ⇐
citizen(x,y) if                       born(x,y)  ∨
  ∃ z : person |                      ∃ z with
  father(x,z) ∧ born(z,y) ;             father(x,z) ∧ born(z,y)


born(x,y) if                       ---born(x,y) ⇐
  «person x born in country y» ;     «person x born in country y»


father(x,y) if                     ---father(x,y) ⇐
  «person x has person y as father»   «person x has person y as father»
```

2.3. OBJECT DECLARATIONS WITH ASSERTIONS

Restricting the arguments of functions by means of assertions leads to restricted object declarations: For the above example sub, the application

```
((nat a, nat b : a ≥ b) nat :      ((a : nat ; b : nat ‖ a ≥ b) : nat ;
  that nat x : a = x + b)(21, 4)      that x : nat ‖ a = x + b)(21, 4)
```

has the same meaning as the segment

```
⌈ (nat a, nat b : a ≥ b) ≡ (21, 4) ;   begin const (a:nat ; b:nat ‖ a ≥ b) = (21, 4) ;
  that nat x : a = x + b         ⌋       that x : nat ‖ a = x + b          end
```

2.4. CONSECUTIVE DECLARATIONS

Multiple function applications naturally induce consecutive declarations:

$$((m_1 \ x_1) \ n : ((m_2 \ x_2) \ n : E_0)(E_2))(E_1) \qquad ((x_1 : m_1) : n ; ((x_2 : m_2) : n ; E_0)(E_2))(E_1)$$

is, according to 2.1, equivalent to

```
⌈ m₁ x₁ ≡ E₁ ;                     begin const x₁ : m₁ = E₁ ;
⌈ m₂ x₂ ≡ E₂ ;                     begin const x₂ : m₂ = E₂ ;
  E₀         ⌋ ⌋                     E₀                      end end
```

If x_1 and x_2 are different, the inner brackets may be saved and thus the above segment may be abbreviated using association to the right:

```
┌ m₁ x1 ≡ E1 ;              begin const x1 : m1 = E1 ;
  m₂ x2 ≡ E2 ;               const x2 : m2 = E2 ;
  E0           ┘             E0                    end .
```

Function declarations are sequentialized in an analogous way.

With consecutive declarations one can decompose expressions: e.g. the expression 17-3*(2+4) becomes

```
┌ int h₁ ≡ 4 ;              begin const h1 : int = 4 ;
  int h₂ ≡ 2+h1 ;            const h2 : int = 2+h1 ;
  int h₃ ≡ 3 * h2 ;          const h3 : int = 3 * h2 ;
  int h₄ ≡ 17-h3 ;           const h4 : int = 17-h3 ;
  h4           ┘             h4                    end .
```

3. THE PROCEDURAL LANGUAGE

Of course CIP-L would not deserve to be called a wide spectrum language, if the usual state-transition-oriented concept of program variables together with assignments, conditional and guarded statements (Dijkstra's guarded commands), procedures, and their sequential composition were not incorporated as well. Program variables reflect the erasable storage of von Neumann type machines. Since most of the concepts and the related problems are standard in today's knowledge about programming languages, only some special aspects will be stressed here.

3.1. VARIABLES AND STATEMENTS

Similar to the object declaration, the formal introduction of variable declarations is based on the function application: Within a segment

$$\ulcorner \textbf{var m } x := E_1 \ ; \ E_2 \lrcorner \qquad\qquad | \qquad \textbf{begin var } x : m := E_1 \ ; \ E_2 \textbf{ end}$$

the identifier x denotes a (program) variable, which is initialized with the value of E_1. Assuming that $x_1, \ldots, x_n$ are the free program variables in E_2 distinct from x (the "global" variables), the meaning of the segment is by definition the same as that of

$$(+) \quad ((\textbf{m } x, \textbf{m}_1 \ x_1, \ldots, \textbf{m}_n \ x_n) \ \textbf{r} : E2) \qquad\qquad ((x : m \ ; \ x1 : m1 \ ; \ \ldots \ ; \ x_n : m_n) : r \ ; \ E2)$$
$$(E_1, x1, \ldots, x_n) \qquad\qquad\qquad\qquad\qquad (E_1, x1, \ldots, x_n) \ .$$

Note that the identifiers $x_1, \ldots, x_n$ in E2 change their nature since they are bound within the function abstraction. They are added as parameters to make the function independent of global variables.

The above definitional transformation is also correct if the variable declaration is preceded by an arbitrary sequence of declarations or statements. In the sequel each kind of statement followed by an expression is similarly reduced to an expression. Thus every segment using constructs of the procedural language can be transformed into the expression language by stepwise reduction from right to left. This "expression semantics" is dual to the state-transition-semantics.

The assignment to a variable x is introduced by defining

$$x := E_1 ; E_2$$

to have the same meaning as (+).

Consecutive declarations or assignments may again be associated to the right using ";" as a separator. This allows to decompose an expression, e.g. 17-3 * (2+4), in the following way:

```
┌ var int ac := 4 ;              begin var ac : int := 4 ;
  ac := 2 + ac ;                   ac := 2 + ac ;
  ac := 3 * ac ;                   ac := 3 * ac ;
  ac := 17 - ac ; ac ┘            ac := 17 - ac ; ac end
```

Thus, variables act as (from *left* to *right*) reusable object identifiers. This leads to the common state-transition semantics.

In analogy to a tuple of formal and actual parameters or to a collective declaration, a tuple of variables can and should be declared and initialized collectively, e.g.

$$(\text{var int } u, \text{var int } v) := (E_1, E_2) \qquad (\text{var } u : \text{int}, \text{var } v : \text{int}) := (E_1, E_2)$$

and their values may be changed by a collective assignment, e.g.

$$(u, v) := (u + v, u - v) .$$

There is no predefined order for the evaluation of the righthand side (the collection is collateral) and upon its completion the resulting objects are assigned collectively to u, v, resp. It should be mentioned that no formal parameter may occur more than once in a parameter list and thus no variable may occur more than once in the lefthand side of a collective assignment; this taboo would be violated e.g. by

$$(a, a) := (a + a, a - a) .$$

Just as applications induce variable declarations and assignments, segments lead to the notion of blocks by separating the expression at the end of a segment: Let $S_1, \ldots, S_n$ be statements and declarations. Then

I.3.2 Procedures

$$S_1 \; ; \; \ldots \; ; \; S_n \; ; \; E$$

can be transformed into a block followed by an expression

| $\lceil S_1 \; ; \; \ldots \; ; \; S_n \; \rfloor \; ; \; E$ | **begin** $S_1 \; ; \; \ldots \; ; \; S_n$ **end** ; E |

if the identifiers declared within the block have no free occurrence in E. (Note that the reverse transformation is only correct if the global variables assigned to in the block are re-declared at the beginning of the segment; cf. MAKESEGMENT in II.2.3.2.) In a similar way guarded expressions

if C_1 **then** $S_{1,1} \; ; \; \ldots \; ; \; S_{1,n_1} \; ; \; E$	**if** C_1 **then** $S_{1,1} \; ; \; \ldots \; ; \; S_{1,n_1} \; ; \; E$
...	...
$\Box$ C_k **then** $S_{k,1} \; ; \; \ldots \; ; \; S_{k,n_k} \; ; \; E$ **fi**	$\Box$ C_k **then** $S_{k,1} \; ; \; \ldots \; ; \; S_{k,n_k} \; ; \; E$ **endif**

with $n_i \geq 1$ for all $i = 1, \ldots, k$ lead to guarded statements in front of E:

if C_1 **then** $S_{1,1} \; ; \; \ldots \; ; \; S_{1,n_1}$	**if** C_1 **then** $S_{1,1} \; ; \; \ldots \; ; \; S_{1,n_1}$
...	...
$\Box$ C_k **then** $S_{k,1} \; ; \; \ldots \; ; \; S_{k,n_k}$ **fi** ; E	$\Box$ C_k **then** $S_{k,1} \; ; \; \ldots \; ; \; S_{k,n_k}$ **endif** ; E .

Using the **skip**-statement, which means "do nothing", one can always guarantee that $n_i \geq 1$ holds.

3.2. PROCEDURES

Expressions denote objects and thus only their values are relevant, whereas statements by their very nature cause side-effects which are relevant in a non-local context. The transition from applicative expressions to constructs with side-effects corresponds to the transition from functions to procedures. Procedures either explicitly change formal variable parameters or implicitly modify non-local variables (suppressed variable parameters).

In CIP-L, expressions are carefully separated from statements; no hybrid constructs are available in order to keep the collection of program transformations manageable. For this reason there are only pure procedures which, in contrast to functions, do not deliver any result.

Every procedure call is reduced to an assignment to the variable parameters, which makes use of a function yielding the final values of these parameters. (Note that for this reason a procedure must not contain any global jump; see below). Given, for example, the following declaration

```
proc incrdecr ≡ (var int va, var int vb) :        procedure incrdecr (var va:int ; var vb:int) ;
  ⌈ va := succ(va) ; vb := pred(vb) ⌋             begin va := succ(va) ; vb := pred(vb) end
```

where succ and pred denote the successor and the predecessor function within the domain of integers. A call of the procedure incrdecr is written in the form

$$\text{call incrdecr}(x, y) .$$

It is equivalent to $(x, y) := \text{inde}(x, y)$, where

```
funct inde ≡ (int a, int b)(int, int) :          function inde (a:int ; b:int):(int, int) ;
       (succ(a), pred(b))                                (succ(a), pred(b)) .
```

Another simple example with an iteration is related to the **mod**-function:

```
proc md ≡ (var nat a, nat b) :                    procedure md(var a : nat ; b : nat) ;
     if a ≥ b then a := a - b ;                         if a ≥ b then a := a - b ;
                 call md(a, b)                                       call md(a, b)
            else skip          fi                            else                endif .
```

Every call md(j, k) can be transformed into

$$j := \text{mod}(j, k)$$

where

```
funct mod ≡ (nat a', nat b) nat :                 function mod (a' : nat ; b : nat) : nat ;
     if a' ≥ b then mod(a'-b, b) else a' fi             if a' ≥ b then mod(a'-b, b) else a' endif .
```

Since procedures are allowed to have variables as parameters, an "actualization-taboo" is required here in connection with the above-mentioned restriction for collective assignments: No two (explicit or suppressed) variable parameters of a procedure may be associated with the same variable. This restriction becomes syntactically checkable by prohibiting that two variables with different identifiers may be identified ("alias-ban", cf. /Lampson et al. 77/).

4. THE CONTROL-ORIENTED LANGUAGE

The procedural language still works with recursion. For special types of recursion, however, there is an equivalent "control-flow semantics" comprising loops and jumps (and frequently associated with "flow diagrams"). The control-oriented language provides constructs for expressing these forms of flow control which correspond to the control mechanisms of von-Neumann-type machines.

4.1. ITERATION STATEMENTS

An iteration statement or loop may be defined to be a call of a specific kind of recursive procedures. The most simple one is the usual **while** loop

while C **do** S **od**	**while** C **loop** S **endloop**

where C is a boolean expression and S a sequence of declarations and statements. This loop is equivalent to

```
  proc iterate ≡:             begin procedure iterate ;
      if C then S ;               if C then S ;
              call iterate                call iterate
          else skip      fi ;      else         endif ;
      call iterate                 call iterate     end
```

provided that there is no recursive call of iterate within S.

The above procedure md may be transformed into the following form

```
  proc md ≡ (var nat a, nat b) :        procedure md (var a : nat ; b : nat) ;
      while a ≥ b do a := a - b od           while a ≥ b loop a := a - b endloop .
```

Another kind of iteration statement is Dijkstra's construct **do** S **od** where S is a non-empty sequence of statements and declarations. The iteration is terminated by the execution of a loop exit, viz. a **leave** (resp. **exit**) statement. This construct can easily be related to the call of a recursive procedure provided that it can be reduced to a form like:

```
  do if                         loop if
      ...                           ...
      [] Cᵢ then Sᵢ                 [] Cᵢ then Sᵢ
      ...                           ...
      [] Cⱼ then Sⱼ ; leave         [] Cⱼ then Sⱼ ; exit
      ...                           ...
  fi od                         endif endloop
```

where C_i, C_j are boolean expressions and where S_i, S_j are sequences of declarations or statements not containing a loop exit (or a non-local jump, see below). Then the above loop is equivalent to a call of the following parameterless procedure dood :

proc dood ≡ : **if**	**procedure** dood ; **if**
...	...
▯ C_i **then** S_i ; **call** dood	▯ C_i **then** S_i ; **call** dood
...	...
▯ C_j **then** S_j	▯ C_j **then** S_j
...	...
fi	**endif**

where the identifier dood does not occur in C_i, C_j, S_i or S_j.

Note that loop constructs may contain global jumps (see below). Due to the fact that procedures must not contain any global jumps, the general formal definition of loops and loop exits is given by means of jumps. Then jumps can be eliminated by means of procedures (cf. II.2.4). In general, however, the outcome will be a system which is mutually recursive and more complicated than the simple procedure dood.

4.2. LABELS AND JUMPS

A recursive procedure like dood can directly be transformed into a language style of labels and gotos:

proc dood ≡:	**procedure** dood ;
d : **if**	d : **if**
...	...
▯ C_i **then** S_i ; **goto** d	▯ C_i **then** S_i ; **goto** d
...	...
▯ C_j **then** S_j	▯ C_j **then** S_j
...	...
fi	**endif**

Now, expanding a call of dood leads to its removal. This kind of transformation may be generalized to systems of mutually recursive procedures in a straightforward way. By introducing labels and jumps, the system of procedures can be eliminated provided it is "repetitive" or "tail-recursive", i.e. every call of a procedure is the dynamically last action of the body in which it occurs (cf. /McCarthy 62/, /Knuth 74/). Then a jump is only a notational variant of a call of a parameterless procedure.

I.4.2 Labels and jumps

Jumps now enable us to give in an easy way a general description of the meaning of loop exits:

do ... **leave** ... **od**	**loop** ... **exit** ... **endloop**

may be transformed into

⌈ **do** ... **goto** l ... **od** ; l : **skip** ⌋	**begin loop** ... **goto** l ... **endloop** ; l : **end**

provided that the loop is the smallest loop enclosing the loop exit.

A construct which is very useful for terminating a procedure call is the **return** statement. It is, by definition, a jump to the static end of the procedure:

proc p ≡ (m x) : ⌈ ... **return** ... ⌋	**procedure** p(x : m) ; **begin** ... **return** ... **end**

may be reduced to

proc p ≡ (m x) : ⌈ ... **goto** fin ... ; fin : **skip** ⌋	**procedure** p(x :m) ; **begin** ... **goto** fin ... ; fin : **end**

5. PARALLEL CONSTRUCTS

The language allows a limited form of parallelism, viz. the parallel composition of blocks. Access to variables shared by such blocks must be protected using conditional critical regions of the form

$$\textbf{await } C \textbf{ then } PP \textbf{ endwait } .$$

As an example consider the producer-consumer problem (in the ALGOL-variant; see II.1.4(e) for the types QUEUE and SEQU):

```
funct procon ≡ (m startelem) sequ :

⌈ proc pro ≡ (var queue buffer, m x) :
     ⌈ n y ≡ produce(x) ;
       await ¬ isfull(buffer)
       then  buffer := buffer & y endwait ;
       if final(x) then skip
                    else call pro(buffer, next(x)) fi ⌋ ,

  proc con ≡ (var queue buffer, var sequ out) :
     ⌈ var m z ;
       await ¬ isempty(buffer)
       then (z, buffer) := (top(buffer), rest(buffer)) endwait ;
       out := out & consume(z) ;
       if lastprod(z) then skip
                       else call con(buffer, out) fi ⌋ ;

  (var queue buffer, var sequ out) := (emptyqueue, emptysequ) ;

  ⟦ call pro(buffer, startelem)  ‖  call con(buffer, out) ⟧      ⌋
```

where the predicates final and lastprod test whether their arguments are the last ones to be processed, next produces another element of m from a given one, and produce and consume are suitable basic operations.

I.6 Types, modes, computation structures

6. ALGEBRAIC TYPES, MODES, AND COMPUTATION STRUCTURES

In programs certain symbols (identifiers) are used for object sets (sorts), for elements of these sets (constants), and for functions operating on them (operations). Only after interpretation of these symbols a complete program results; before interpretation, we deal with program schemes ("scheme language").

There are two ways of explaining the meaning of the symbols:

- Within an algebraic type the meaning is specified algebraically by presenting the sorts, constants and operations with their functionality and by giving properties (laws, axioms) for them.
- A computation structure provides interpretations of such symbols by giving (descriptive or recursive) declarations of objects for the constant symbols and functions for the operation symbols such that they obey the given algebraic specification. Thus, computation structures allow to define models of algebraic types (they are also called "views" of such types).

An algebraic type may be based on other algebraic types, and a computation structure may be based both on types and on other computation structures. For certain frequently used types, which are called "modes" with reference to ALGOL 68, standard implementations are presupposed.

6.1. ALGEBRAIC TYPES

An algebraic type, briefly called type, consists of two main parts (cf. the type CHOICESET below):

- the signature, which is a list of symbols the meaning of which is specified within the type. Each symbol is associated with a specification of its kind: To symbols for carrier sets the key word **sort** is attributed, to symbols for constant elements their sort, and to operation symbols their functionality. A subset of these symbols is made available (visible) to the outside world by the list of constituents of the type. Symbols which are not made available are called hidden symbols. The signature determines a language of well-formed terms which may also contain free identifiers.

- the collection of laws, which specify the properties of the symbols. The laws are formulas built from equations and inequations with the help of the logical connectives $\land$, $\lor$, $\Rightarrow$, $\Leftrightarrow$, and of the quantifiers $\forall$, $\exists$ over sorts of the type i.e. they are from first order logic.

The meaning of a type T is defined to be the class of all term-generated models of T (cf. II.1.1.6).

Example:

type CHOICESET =	**abstracttype** CHOICESET =

list of parameters

(**sort m, m** nil, **funct** (m,m) **bool** eq :	(**sort** m ; nil : m ;
	eq : **function** (m;m) : bool ‖

parameter restriction

include EQUIVALENCE(m, eq))	**include** EQUIVALENCE(m, eq))

list of visible constituents

choiceset, empty, incorp, card,	choiceset , empty , incorp , card ,
certain, **n, z, c, g, p** :	certain, n, z, c, g, p :

primitive types

based on BOOL,	**based on** BOOL ,
include NAT **as** (n, z, c, g, p) ;	**include** NAT **as** (n, z, c, g, p) ;

specification of the constituents

sort choiceset ,	**sort** choiceset ,
choiceset empty ,	empty : choiceset ,
funct (**choiceset, m**)	**function** incorp (choiceset ; m)
choiceset incorp ,	: choiceset ,
funct (**choiceset, m**) **bool** contains ,	**function** contains (choiceset ; m) : bool ,
funct (**choiceset**) **m** certain ,	**function** certain (choiceset) : m ,

I.6.1 Algebraic types

funct (choiceset) **n** card ;	**function** card (choiceset) : **n** ;

laws

laws choiceset s, **m** x, **m** y :	**laws** s : choiceset ; x : m ; y : m ‖
contains(empty, x) ≡ **false** ,	contains(empty, x) = false ,
contains(s, nil) ≡ **false** ,	contains(s, nil) = false ,
eq(x, nil) ≡ **false** ⇒	eq(x, nil) = false **impl**
contains(incorp(s, x), y) ≡	contains(incorp(s, x), y) =
(eq(x, y) ∨ contains(s, y)) ,	(eq(x, y) **or** contains(s, y)) ,
incorp(s, nil) ≡ s,	incorp(s, nil) = s ,
incorp(incorp(s, x), y) ≡	incorp(incorp(s, x), y) =
incorp(incorp(s, y), x) ,	incorp(incorp(s, y), x) ,
incorp(incorp(s,x),x) ≡ incorp(s,x) ,	incorp(incorp(s,x),x) = incorp(s,x) ,
card(empty) ≡ z ,	card(empty) = z ,
contains(s, x) ≡ **true** ⇒	contains(s, x) = true **impl**
card(incorp(s, x)) ≡ card(s) ,	card(incorp(s, x)) = card(s) ,
(eq(nil, x) ∨	(eq(nil, x) ∨
contains(s, x)) ≡ **false** ⇒	contains(s, x)) = false **impl**
card(incorp(s, x)) ≡ c(card(s)) ,	card(incorp(s, x)) = c(card(s)) ,
eq(certain(empty), nil) ≡ **true** ,	eq(certain(empty), nil) = true ,
eq(nil, x) ≡ **false** ⇒	eq(nil, x) = false **impl**
contains(incorp(s, x),	contains(incorp(s, x),
certain(incorp(s, x))) ≡ **true**	certain(incorp(s, x))) = true
end of type	**endabstracttype**

From an intuitive point of view the type CHOICESET has the following "meaning", i.e. it abstracts the following data structure: choiceset is the set of all finite subsets of ■ which do not contain the object nil of ■; empty means the empty set; incorp incorporates into a subset an object which is different from nil; contains tests the membership; card yields the cardinality. Finally, certain selects a particular member from every non-empty subset (it is left open which one), or the object nil if the subset is empty. Note that CHOICESET is not sufficiently complete (cf. /Guttag 75/), since the behaviour of the function certain is not completely fixed by the axioms. In order to use certain for exhausting a finite set, a function must be added that yields a set minus its particular element.

A type T may depend on other types in three ways:

- The constituents of "primitive" types are made available, possibly with renaming, in a **based on** clause. In this case the primitive type is protected against modifications of the carrier sets of its models ("hierarchy-preservation", cf. /Wirsing et al. 83/); this guarantees independent implementability of the primitive type. The type BOOL (cf. II.1.4(a)) is universal and need not be mentioned.

- A type T can be made available by an "instantiation", possibly with renaming, in the form

    include T **as** $(m_1, x_1, x_2, ..., m_2, y_1, y_2, ...)$

    (if no renaming is desired, the part **as...** may be omitted). In contrast to the **based on** clause, an instantiation is equivalent to textual substitution of the body of T (with consistent renaming); there is no protection on the models of T in this case. Thus, instantiations are a mere shorthand notation for (large) type bodies; they have no independent semantics.

- Parameterization yields schemes of types ("generic types"). The list of type parameters may contain symbols for carrier sets, for constants, and for operations. The parameters are attributed in the same way as within a signature. (Thus, CHOICESET is an example of a type scheme.) Actualizations of such schemes may be used both in **based on** clauses and **include** clauses.

Example:
The functionality of contains in type CHOICESET is

funct (**choiceset**, **m**) **bool**	**function** (choiceset ; m) : bool

where **bool** is a constituent of the primitive type BOOL and **m** a sort parameter. Within the law

∀ **choiceset** s, **m** x :	∀ s : choiceset ; x : m ‖
(eq(nil, x) ∨ contains(s, x)) ≡ **false**	(eq(nil, x) **or** contains(s, x)) ≡ false
⇒ card(incorp(s, x)) ≡ c(card(s))	**impl** card(incorp(s, x)) ≡ c(card(s))

there are the constituents ∨ , **false** of BOOL, the constituent c of NAT, the type parameters **m**, eq, nil, the symbols **choiceset**, contains, card, incorp of the signature of CHOICESET and finally the bound identifiers s, x.

In an actualization the parameters of a type scheme T are textually replaced by appropriate constituents of other types. If the application of T occurs within a type S, then the signature and the laws are added to the signature and the laws of S respectively.

Example:
Let us assume that **object**, undef, and congruent are suitable constituents of a type; then CHOICESET(**object**, undef, congruent) is an application of the type scheme CHOICESET.

I.6.1 Algebraic types

An application of a type scheme may occur in three different situations:

- Within an instantiation like

include CHOICESET(**object,** undef, congruent) | **include** CHOICESET(object, undef, congruent)
    as (f, e, i, m, t, n, z, c, g, p)   **as** (f, e, i, m, t, n, z, c, g, p)

- As a parameter restriction, if the list of constituents of the type scheme is empty. The restriction occurs within the list of type parameters (cf. the restriction EQUIVALENCE(m, eq) in the type CHOICESET).

- As a shorthand for a collection of laws, if again the list of constituents is empty. Such an application is included within a collection of laws.

Example:
The type scheme EQUIVALENCE could be defined in the following way:

type EQUIVALENCE $\equiv$
    (**sort** m, **funct** (m, m) **bool** eq) :
    laws $\forall$ m x, m y, m z :
      eq(x, x) $\equiv$ **true** ,
      eq(x, y) $\equiv$ **true** $\Rightarrow$ eq(y, x) $\equiv$ **true**
      eq(x, z) $\equiv$ **true** $\wedge$ eq(y, z) $\equiv$ **true**
          $\Rightarrow$ eq(x, y) $\equiv$ **true**
end of type

abstracttype EQUIVALENCE =
    (**sort** m ; **function** eq(m ; m) : bool) :
    laws $\forall$ x : m ; y : m ; z : m $\parallel$
      eq(x, x) $\equiv$ **true** ,
      eq(x, y) $\equiv$ **true** **impl** eq(y, x) $\equiv$ **true** ,
      eq(x, z) $\equiv$ **true** **and** eq(y, z) $\equiv$ **true**
        impl eq(x, y) $\equiv$ **true**
endabstracttype

6.2. MODES

Modes are a shorthand notation for certain types and type schemes which are frequently used. Since standard implementations are presupposed for them, they can be used for the construction of implementations of other types (see 6.3). Modes are syntactically introduced by (possibly recursive) mode declarations. The semantics of mode declarations is explained by instantiation of the associated types (cf. II.1.3); thus recursive modes are explained in a straightforward way.

There are two basic kinds of mode declarations:

- A <u>product</u> is specified by (k $\geq$ 0)

mode m $\equiv$ c(m_1 s1, ..., m_k sk)   **type** m = c **record** s1 : m_1 ; ... ;
                                        s_k : m_k
                              endrecord

The carrier set m of the product contains objects which are composed from k other objects, called <u>components</u>. The components are elements of $m_1, ..., m_k$; c, having the functionality **funct** $(m_1, ..., m_k)$ m, is the <u>constructor</u> function. Thus, $c(x_1, ..., x_k)$ yields that object in m which is composed from $x_1 \in m_1, ..., x_k \in m_k$. The s_i (i = 1, ..., k) are the <u>selector</u> functions with functionality **funct** (m) m_i, and the laws $s_i(c(x_1, ..., x_i, ..., x_k)) \equiv x_i$ hold. In the case k=0, the product mode simply consists of a single constant c.

- The <u>sum</u> forms the disjoint union of a finite number of variants $m_1, ..., m_k$. The corresponding mode declaration is written in this way:

mode m = make$_1$(m$_1$ proj$_1$) | ... |
    make$_k$(m$_k$ proj$_k$)
	type m = make$_1$ **record** proj$_1$: m$_1$ **endrecord** | ... |
	    make$_k$ **record** proj$_k$: m$_k$ **endrecord**

The functions make$_i$ (i = 1, ..., k) have the functionality **funct** (m$_i$) m; they act as the constructor functions of the objects in m. In addition, the identifiers make$_i$ are used within a special boolean expression

$$x \text{ is make}_i$$

which tests for an object x in m whether it is constructed by means of make$_i$ or not, i.e. whether it is made from the variant m_i or not. If x is made from m_i, x can be converted back into an object in m_i using the <u>projection</u> proj$_i$. Then for all y in m_i

$$\text{proj}_i(\text{make}_i(y)) \equiv y .$$

The projections are partial functions on m, and their functionality is given by

funct (m x : x **is** make$_i$) m$_i$	**function** (x : m || x **is** make$_i$) : m$_i$.

As a special case, a number of constants may be introduced by

mode m $\equiv$ a$_1$ | ... | a$_n$	**type** m = a$_1$ | ... | a$_n$.

There is also a (quasi)ordered form of sums; as an example consider

mode sign $\equiv$ neg $\triangleleft$ zer $\triangleleft$ pos	**type** sign = neg $\triangleleft$ zer $\triangleleft$ pos

In addition to these basic principles the language provides convenient notational variations of the sum if a variant is a product or again a sum (cf. II.1.3.4).

I.6.2 Modes

As already mentioned, mode declarations may be recursive. Recursion is semantically meaningful if the right hand side has the form of a sum

mode m ≡ ME_1 | ... | ME_k | **type** m = ME_1 | ... | ME_k

where the ME_i (i = 1, ..., k, k ≥ 2) are mode expressions built from mode identifiers using products and sums, and where at least one of all mode expressions ME_i does not contain occurrences of **m**.

Example:

A very simple grammar for arithmetic expressions which are completely parenthesized may be given by

$$E ::= (E + E) | (E * E) | I$$

where I designates a set of identifiers that is defined elsewhere. Such a grammar leads immediately to a recursive mode declaration

mode E ≡	**type** E =
plus(E leftsum, E rightsum) |	plus **record** leftsum : E ;
	rightsum : E **endrecord** |
times(E leftfact, E rightfact) |	times **record** leftfact : E ;
	rightfact : E **endrecord** |
makeexpr(I identifier)	makeexpr **record** identifier : I **endrecord** .

An arithmetic expression like (x + ((y + x) * z)) can be represented as an object e in E:

$$e = plus(makeexpr(x), times(plus(makeexpr(y), makeexpr(x)), makeexpr(z))) \;.$$

By leftfact(rightsum(e)), that subexpression of e is selected which represents (y + x).

Just as a type may contain several type instantiations, (possibly mutually recursive) systems of mode declarations are allowed.

Example:

If I is again a set of identifiers, another grammar of arithmetic expressions may be given by

$$E ::= E + P | P \;,$$
$$P ::= P * F | F \;,$$
$$F ::= (E) | I \;.$$

This leads to a system of recursive mode declarations:

mode E ≡ plus(E leftsum, P rightsum)	**type** E = plus **record** leftsum : E ;
	rightsum : P **endrecord**
| me(P prod) ,	| me **record** prod : P **endrecord** ,
mode P ≡ times(P leftfact, F rightfact)	**type** P = times **record** leftfact : P ;
	rightfact : F **endrecord**
| mp(F fact) ,	| mp **record** fact : F **endrecord** ,
mode F ≡ parenth(E expr)	**type** F = parenth **record** expr : E **endrecord**
| mf(I identifier)	| mf **record** identifier : I **endrecord**

Note that modes should be distinguished carefully from the modes in ALGOL 68. The main differences are:
- In ALGOL 68, the constructors and selectors are not assumed to be functions.
- Recursive modes in ALGOL 68 may only occur in connection with referencing or proceduring, e.g.

$$\text{mode list} = \text{struct}(\text{m top, ref list rest}) \, .$$

6.3. COMPUTATION STRUCTURES

The main part of a computation structure is a collection of declarations (cf. CHOICEIMPLE below). Possible declarations are
- mode declarations
- declarations of the scheme language (cf. II.2.2), i.e. object and function declarations
- **based on** clauses which make available primitive types
- actualizations of type schemes like

    include XYZ **as** (**m, n,** e, f, g) | **include** XYZ **as** (m, n, e, f, g)

and of computation structures like

    structure (**m, n,** e, f, g) ≡ CSXYZ | **structure** (m, n, e, f, g) = CSXYZ .

These declarations give new identifiers to the constituents. Here also type and structure schemes are admissible.

The computation structure CHOICEIMPLE, for example, uses the primitive computation structure N (cf. II.3.1.1) and renames its constituents.

    structure CHOICEIMPLE = | **structure** CHOICEIMPLE =

structure parameters

    (**sort m, m** nil, | (**sort** m ; nil : m ;
     funct (**m, m**) **bool** eq, | **function** eq(m ; m) : bool ;
     funct (**m, m**) **bool** ord : | **function** ord(m ; m) : bool ‖

parameter restriction

    include LINORD(m, ord, eq)) | **include** LINORD(m, ord, eq))

list of visible constituents

    chset, mty, insert, length, max, | chset, mty, insert, length, max,
    n, z, c, g, p : | n, z, c, g, p :

I.6.3 Computation structures

declaration of constituents

```
structure (n, z, c, g, p) ≡ N ;          structure (n, z, c, g, p) = N ;
mode chset  ≡ mty |                       type chset = mty |
            inc(chset rest, m max) ;           inc record rest : chset ;
                                                          max : m
                                                      endrecord ;


funct insert ≡ (chset s, m x) chset :     function insert(s : chset ; x : m) : chset ;
   if eq(x,nil) then s                       if eq(x, nil) then s
               else inord(s,x) fi ,                    else inord(s, x) endif ,


funct inord ≡ (chset s, m x) chset :      function inord(s : chset ; x : m) : chset ;
   if s is inc                               if s is inc
   then if eq(max(s),x)                      then if eq(max(s), x)
      then s                                    then s
      else if ord(max(s),x)                     else if ord(max(s),x))
         then inc(s,x)                             then inc(s, x)
         else inc(inord(rest(s),x),                else inc(inord(rest(s), x),
                  max(s))                                  max(s))
         fi                                        endif
      fi                                        endif
   else inc(mty, x)                          else inc(mty, x)
   fi ,                                       endif ,


funct length ≡ (chset s) n :              function length(s : chset) : n ;
   if s is inc                               if s is inc
   then c(length(rest(s)))                   then c(length(rest(s)))
   else z                                    else z
   fi                                        endif


end of structure                          endstructure
```

In accordance with types, a computation structure has a list of constituents. It contains the identifiers which are declared inside the structure and which are made visible outside. The collection of declarations may include auxiliary declarations which are not made visible via the list of constituents (cf. inord of CHOICEIMPLE).

In a computation structure only the same kinds of constituents are permitted as in types; procedure identifiers or variable identifiers are ruled out.

Computation structures may depend on parameters in the same way as types ("generic structures"). Moreover, there can be a parameter restriction which is expressed by means of an application of a type without constituents. The parameter mechanism as well as the renaming of the constituents is defined by textual substitution, again in accordance with type schemes.

A computation structure is called a <u>syntactically correct</u> implementation of a type if after appropriate renaming the corresponding elements of the lists of constituents together with their functionalities are identical.

<u>Example:</u> CHOICEIMPLE is a <u>syntactically correct</u> implementation of CHOICESET with the following correspondence of the constituents:

choiceset	⇔	chset
empty	⇔	mty
incorp	⇔	insert
card	⇔	length
certain	⇔	max
n	⇔	n
z	⇔	z
c	⇔	c
g	⇔	g
p	⇔	p .

A computation structure is called a <u>semantically correct</u> implementation of a type (cf. II.3.1.2), if congruence relations can be defined on (subsets of) the carrier sets of the computation structure in such a way that the corresponding quotient structure (of the restriction to the subsets) is a model of the type. If in a carrier set ■ this congruence relation differs from the equality, it must explicitly be declared as an appropriate boolean operation.

<u>Example:</u> Consider again CHOICEIMPLE: Within the subset

$\{$**chset** s : isord(s) $\wedge \neg$ cont(s, nil)$\}$ │   [s : chset ‖ isord(s) **and not** cont(s, nil)]

the equality in **chset** is a congruence relation with respect to insert, length and max. The above functions isord and cont are defined in the following way:

```
funct isord ≡ (chset s) bool :          function isord(s : chset) : bool ;
  if s is inc then                         if s is inc then
    if rest(s) is inc then                   if rest(s) is inc then
      ord(max(rest(s)), max(s))                  ord(max(rest(s)), max(s))
    ∧ ¬ eq(max(rest(s)), max(s))            and not eq(max(rest(s)), max(s))
```

I.6.3 Computation structures

∧ isord(rest(s))
   else true fi
else true fi

      and isord(rest(s))
   else true **endif**
else true **endif**

and

funct cont ≡ (**chset** s, **m** x) **bool** :
   if ¬ s **is** inc **then** false **else**
      eq(max(s), x) ∨ cont(rest(s), x)
   fi

function cont(s : **chset** ; x : **m**) : **bool** ;
if not s **is** inc **then** false **else**
      eq(max(s), x) **or** cont(rest(s), x)
endif

Note that in order to demonstrate that a computation structure yields a model of a type, it is necessary to give also an interpretation for the hidden functions of the type. Thus the function contains of type CHOICESET corresponds to cont which (operatively) extends CHOICEIMPLE.

7. MODULES AND DEVICES, ARRAYS, POINTERS

As a further step in the process of implementing algebraic types one may want to pass to procedural variants of the operations. <u>Modules</u> are collections of functions and procedures; however, their routines must not use suppressed variable parameters. In this sense they are still fully referentially transparent. <u>Devices</u>, on the other hand, may possess an "inner state"; this is achieved by permitting their routines to depend on variables which, however, are hidden and can only be accessed via the device routines.

As an example we give a module and a device for stacks (again both are parameterized and thus "generic"):

    module MSTACK ≡ (**sort m**) **stack**, init, push, pop, top :
        based on (stack, empty, isempty, append, top, rest) ≡ STACK(**m**) ;

        proc init ≡ (**var stack** s) : s := empty ,
        proc push ≡ (**var stack** s, **m** x) : s := append(s, x) ,
        proc pop ≡ (**var stack** s : ¬ isempty(s)) : s := rest(s)
    end of module

    device DSTACK ≡ (**sort m**) dpush, dpop, dtop :
        based on (stack, empty, isempty, append, top, rest) ≡ STACK(**m**) ;
        var stack s := empty ;

        proc dpush ≡ (**m** x) : s := append(s, x) ,
        proc dpop ≡ : ⌈ **assert** ¬ isempty(s)) ;
                       s := rest(s)   ⌋ ,
        funct dtop ≡ () **m** : **if** ¬ isempty(s) **then** top(s) **fi**
    end of device

Note that DSTACK hides the sort **stack** as well as its variable s. Upon instantiation of the device the initializing assignment s := empty is performed; afterwards the hidden stack can only be changed using dpush and dpop. Several instances of a module or device can be obtained by using instantiation with renaming.

We should finally add the remark that there are no extra notations for working with arrays or pointers. Rather, in II.1.4 (d) and (g) we define algebraic types describing arrays and pointers and plexuses (pointer structures). Moreover, in II.3.4 a corresponding device for pointers is given; it models the pointer operations available e.g. in PASCAL.

PART II

DESCRIPTION OF THE LANGUAGE

Part II contains a "semi-formal" description of CIP-L . Therefore readability is considered more important than complete formality. In particular, context conditions are specified only verbally, and self-evident conditions (e.g. pairwise distinctness of identifiers in parameter-tuples) are not even mentioned explicitly.

The organization of Part II follows the conceptual structure of the language: Chapter 1 describes algebraic (data) types, which allow the algebraic definition of the basic objects and operations of a program. Chapter 2 introduces the scheme language which contains all constructs for building expressions, statements etc.; this scheme language comprises most of the classical programming language constructs. Chapter 3 defines programs as systems consisting of components, viz. of types, computation structures, modules, and devices. Computation structures give implementations for algebraic types in terms of the constructs of the scheme language based on certain "fundamental" algebraic types. They may use modules, i.e., collections of function and procedure declarations, and devices, which essentially are modules with an "inner state".

In Part II we use only the ALGOL-like external representation of the syntax; the reader should have no difficulty in translating into the PASCAL-like representation.

1. ALGEBRAIC TYPES

In this section we introduce the language constructs for specifying basic object sets together with operations on them. The concept of algebraic (data) types (briefly: types) provides the tools for specifying such basic objects and operations algebraically. Modes are abbreviations for certain frequently used types, for which standard implementations are presupposed.

For a discussion of types from a theoretical as well as from a methodological point of view we have to refer to the literature (e.g. /Wirsing et al. 83/). Here we can only present their syntactic and semantic integration into our language.

1.1. DEFINITION OF TYPES

1.1.1. INTRODUCTION

Types are used for specifying objects together with their characteristic operations in an abstract, representation-independent way, i.e., only by their properties. Type definitions have the form

list of visible constituents

type $T = ..., s_i, ..., c_j, ..., f_k, ...:$ } type heading

   $..., $ **based on** $P_1, ...;$ } designation of primitive types

   $..., $ **sort** $s_i, ...,$
   $..., s_j \ c_j, ...,$ } signature   } type body
   $..., $ **funct** $(s_1^k, ..., s_{n_k}^k) \ s^k \ f_k, ...;$

   $..., $ **laws** $L_m, ...$ } laws

   end of type

In the following sections we shall explain the various parts of such a type definition. The following type NATSET specifies finite sets of natural numbers in an extensional way; it will serve as an accompanying example (for the types BOOL and NAT cf. 1.4 (a) and 1.3.3):

   type NATSET $\equiv$ **bool, nat, natset,** emptyset, incorp, contains, sum :
      based on BOOL, **based on** NAT ;
      sort natset ,

> **natset** emptyset ,
> **funct** (**natset**, **nat**) **natset** incorp ,
> **funct** (**natset**, **nat**) **bool** contains ,
> **funct** (**natset**) **nat** sum ;
>
> **laws** $\forall$ **nat** x : contains(emptyset, x) $\equiv$ **false** ;
> **laws** $\forall$ **natset** s, **nat** x : contains(incorp(s, x), x) $\equiv$ **true** ;
> **laws** $\forall$ **natset** s, **nat** x, **nat** y : x $\not\equiv$ y $\Rightarrow$
>   contains(incorp(s, x), y) $\equiv$ contains(s, y) ;
> **laws** sum(emptyset) $\equiv$ zero ;
> **laws** $\forall$ **natset** s, **nat** x : contains(s, x) $\equiv$ **true** $\Rightarrow$
>   sum(incorp(s, x)) $\equiv$ sum(s) ;
> **laws** $\forall$ **natset** s, **nat** x : contains(s, x) $\equiv$ **false** $\Rightarrow$
>   sum(incorp(s, x)) $\equiv$ add(sum(s), x)
> **end of type**

A number of abbreviations for such a type definition are presented in 1.1.5.

1.1.2. THE CONSTITUENTS

The sequence of identifiers between $\equiv$ and : in the heading of a type designates those constituents, i.e. sorts, constants, and operations defined by the type, which are visible and thus made available to program components which use that type. To allow complete type-checking, the list must contain all sort symbols that occur in functionalities of visible constant or operation symbols (see below for the constituents of BOOL).

All constituents defined within the type but not listed as visible are hidden. Hidden sorts, constants, and operations therefore can only be used in the type body as auxiliaries for specification purposes.

Example:
    The type NATSET has as visible constituents the sorts **bool**, **nat**, **natset**, and, besides the boolean operations, the operations emptyset, incorp, contains, sum ; all other constituents of NAT, e.g. zero and add, are hidden.

1.1.3. PRIMITIVE TYPES

In general, a type T is hierarchical, i.e., it is based on other types P_1. Such a dependency is expressed using the keyword **based on** . All the visible sorts, constants, and operations of these P_1 can be used in the specification of the type T, too. However, in order to protect the P_1, their constituents are not visible for types based on T unless they are also listed as visible constituents of T.

We regard the type BOOL as universal; therefore it does not need to be mentioned in the **based on**-clause or in the list of constituents. This means that every type (except BOOL itself) has an implicit clause **based on** BOOL and, implicitly, the sort and operation symbols of BOOL as visible constituents.

Example:
   The type NATSET employs the sorts **bool** and **nat** as well as the constants **true, false,** zero and the operation add of its primitive types BOOL and NAT.

The types P_1 on which T is based are called <u>primitive</u> for T. Moreover, in contrast to the visibility-relation, the primitive-relation is transitive, i.e., if type T is based on type T', and T" is primitive for T', then T" is primitive for T as well. We require that a system of types forms a proper hierarchy, i.e., that the primitive-relation is irreflexive. This means that no type must be primitive for itself.

The semantics of the **based on**-clause is given in 1.1.6.

1.1.4. THE SIGNATURE OF A TYPE

The <u>signature</u> $\Sigma = \langle S, C, F \rangle$ of a type T is a triple of (possibly empty) finite sets of identifiers:

- the set S of <u>sort symbols</u> contains symbols for object sets;
- the set C of <u>constant symbols</u> contains symbols for objects; each constant symbol is associated with a sort;
- the set F contains <u>operation symbols</u>. Each operation symbol $f \in F$ is associated with a functionality **funct**$(s_1,\ldots,s_n)s$ $(n \geq 1)$ which indicates that f stands for a (partial) mapping with arguments of sorts $s_1, \ldots, s_n \in S$ and a result of sort $s \in S$.

The visible constituents of the primitive types P_1 of T are also part of the signature of T.

Example: For NATSET we have
   S = {**bool, nat, natset**} ,
   C = {**true, false,** zero, emptyset} ,
   F = {¬, ∧, ∨, succ, pred, iszero, .≤., incorp, contains, sum} .

The signature determines the well-formed terms of a type, which are defined as follows:
(i)   every constant symbol c of sort s and every identifier which is bound to the sort s by a
      quantification (see 1.1.5) is a well-formed term of sort s ;
(ii) if t_1, ..., t_n are well-formed terms of sorts s_1, ..., s_n and f is an operation symbol with
      functionality funct (s_1, ..., s_n) s , then f(t_1, ..., t_n) is a well-formed term of sort s;
(iii) these are all well-formed terms of sort s .

Example:

   For NATSET, we can build well-formed terms of sort **bool** like
   contains(incorp(emptyset, succ(zero)), zero) or
   contains(incorp(incorp(s, x), y), x).

1.1.5. THE LAWS OF A TYPE

The laws of a type are closed, well-formed first-order formulas over (in)equations between
terms. The principles of structured program design impose a number of constraints on the set of
laws of a type, above all certain criteria for completeness and consistency. For a discussion of
these issues we refer again to the literature (cf. e.g. /Wirsing et al. 83/).

Notational extensions

For reasons of brevity and easier readability we introduce a number of shorthand notations for
the laws:

(a) A quantification may extend over several formulas; thus

   laws s_1 x_1, ..., s_n x_n : F_1, ..., F_k

   (which is the same as

   laws $\forall$ s_1 x_1, ..., s_n x_n : $F_1 \wedge \cdots \wedge F_k$)

   is equivalent to

   laws $\forall$ s_1 x_1, ..., s_n x_n : F_1 ,

   $$\vdots$$

   laws $\forall$ s_1 x_1, ..., s_n x_n : F_k

   Note that in the abbreviated form the quantifier is omitted in order to disambiguate the
   syntax.

(b) An **if-then-else** notation may replace two alternative implications; thus

   $E_1 \equiv$ **if** F **then** E_2 **else** E_3 **fi**

   is equivalent to the laws

   $F \Rightarrow E_1 \equiv E_2$, $\neg F \Rightarrow E_1 \equiv E_3$.

II.1.1 Definition of types

Example: In the type NATSET the second and third laws could be replaced by
contains(incorp(s, x), y) ≡ **if** x ≡ y **then true**
else contains(s, y) **fi** .

(c) A formula **def** t where t is a term of sort s is an abbreviation for the formula ∃ s y : y ≡ t
which asserts that t is to be interpreted as a defined value (see (d) for an example).

(d) It is possible to express a restriction of the domain of an operation explicitly in its
functionality. Let C be a term of sort **bool** containing as a free identifier at most x of
sort s_1. The notation
funct (s_1 x : C) s_2 f
in the signature is then equivalent to the functionality
funct (s_1) s_2 f
together with the additional law
∀ s_1 x : **def** f(x) ⇒ C ≡ **true**
which states that f(x) can only be defined (i.e., have a value y), if the restriction C is
fulfilled. Note that even for x for which C ≡ **true**, f(x) may still be undefined.

Example:
If the type NATSET were to be enriched by an operation remove for deleting numbers from
sets, the domain of this operation could be restricted in the following way:
funct (**natset** s, **nat** x : contains(s, x)) **natset** remove .

Analogously, the domain of a quantification may be restricted by a term C of sort **bool**:
∀ (s x : C) : F   ∃ (s x : C) : F
are, resp., equivalent to
∀ s x : (C ≡ **true**) ⇒ F   ∃ s x : (C ≡ **true**) ∧ F

(e) To ease readability, we allow to write enabling conditions for the application of a partial
function after the law proper for such a function; the keyword **provided** serves as the
separator. Thus we define that
F **provided** G
is equivalent to
G ⇒ F .

(f) In analogy to boolean expressions, the suffix "≡ **true**" may be omitted in equations. Thus
terms of sort **bool** are admissible as formulas.

Example:
The last but one law of NATSET may be written as
sum(incorp(s, x)) ≡ sum(s) **provided** contains(s, x) .

Moreover, we define that $E_1 \equiv$ **if** t **then** E_2 **else** E_3 **fi** is equivalent to the laws
$t \equiv$ **true** $\Rightarrow E_1 \equiv E_2$, $t \equiv$ **false** $\Rightarrow E_1 \equiv E_3$, $\neg$ **def** t $\Rightarrow \neg$ **def** E_1 .

1.1.6. THE SEMANTICS OF A TYPE

Let T be a type with the signature $\Sigma = \langle S, C, F \rangle$, primitive types P_1, and a set E of laws.

Then a $\underline{\Sigma\text{-algebra}}$ A $= \langle (s^A)_{s\epsilon S}, (c^A)_{c\epsilon C}, (f^A)_{f\epsilon F} \rangle$ consists of
- a family $(s^A)_{s\epsilon S}$ of carrier sets (one for each sort);
- a family $(c^A)_{c\epsilon C}$ of objects such that c^A e s^A, if the symbol c has the sort s ;
- a family $(f^A)_{f\epsilon F}$ of determinate, partial functions f^A: s_1^A x ... x $s_n^A \rightarrow s^A$, if the symbol f has the functionality **funct** $(s_1, ..., s_n)$ s .

Note that every operation f^A of an algebra A is $\underline{\text{strict}}$, i.e., it is undefined whenever one of its arguments is undefined.

A Σ-algebra A is called $\underline{\text{term-generated}}$, if every element of any of the carrier sets s^A can be obtained from the objects c^A by finitely many applications of functions f^A; this means that every element is the interpretation t^A of some closed Σ-term t in A. (For a more precise characterization by means of the term-algebra and homomorphisms see e.g. /Wirsing et al. 83/). An equation $t_1 \equiv t_2$ between closed terms is $\underline{\text{valid}}$ in a Σ-algebra A iff t_1^A and t_2^A are both undefined or both defined and equal.

We adopt the $\underline{\text{Principle of Generation}}$: A Σ-algebra A is called a $\underline{\text{model}}$ of T if it is term-generated and all laws of T are valid in A (in the usual sense of first-order logic). A type is $\underline{\text{monomorphic}}$ if all its models are isomorphic. Note that since the c^A are defined values in all models of T, laws like **def** c always hold in T.

For a hierarchical type T we require moreover that a model A is $\underline{\text{hierarchy-preserving}}$, i.e., that for every primitive type P_1 of T the restriction of A to the signature of P_1 is a model of P_1, and thus, in particular, is generated by the operations of A that correspond to the operation symbols of P_1.

Another important property for a hierarchical type T is $\underline{\text{persistency}}$ which means that every model of the primitive types P_i can be extended to a model of T. This guarantees that types may be implemented independent of the components which are based on them. If the primitive types are monomorphic then the type T is either persistent or inconsistent.

The $\underline{\text{semantics}}$ of a persistent type T is the family of isomorphism classes of models of T. In Chapter 3 tools for the construction of models are provided by $\underline{\text{computation structures}}$.

II.1.1 Definition of types

Example:

The type NATSET has infinitely many (non-isomorphic) models. For a given model N of NAT, the set $\mathcal{P}_{fin}(N)$ of all finite subsets of N is the basis of one such model, but also sequences of elements of N may be chosen as well as tables, linked lists or characteristic functions.

Remark: Because of the restriction to term-generated algebras, proofs by structural induction (induction on the length or nesting-depth of terms) are possible. Note that this is the only second order principle available.

1.2. TYPE SCHEMES

The essential structure of a type is very often independent of the actual primitive constituents. For instance, sets of natural numbers, sets of integral numbers and even sets of sequences all look alike. This suggests the parameterization of types.

1.2.1. PARAMETERIZED TYPE SPECIFICATIONS

The specification of a type may be based on certain sorts, constants and operations which do not belong to a particular primitive type but act as parameters. We are then dealing with a type scheme (a "generic type"). Such type schemes are denoted in the form

    type T ≡ («type parameters») «constituents» :
        «type-body»
    end of type

The «constituents» and the «type-body» are just as in non-parameterized types. The «type parameters» are a collection of constituents
- **sort s**   for sorts,
- **s c**   for constants,
- **funct** (s_1, ..., s_k) **s** f for operations.

Example:

The type NATSET of section 1.1 can be generalized to the type of sets of objects of sort ■:

    type SET ≡ (**sort** ■, ■ e, **funct** (■, ■) ■ op) ■, **set**, emptyset, incorp, contains, total :
        sort set ,
        set emptyset ,
        funct (**set**, ■) **set** incorp ,
        funct (**set**, ■) **bool** contains ,

```
     funct (set) m total ;
     laws set s, m x, m y :
         contains(emptyset, x) ≡ false ,
         contains(incorp(s, x), x) ≡ true ,
         x ≠ y  ⇒  contains(incorp(s, x), y) ≡ contains(s, y) ,
         total(emptyset) ≡ e ,
         contains(s, x)    ⇒   total(incorp(s, x)) ≡ total(s) ,
         ¬ contains(s, x)  ⇒   total(incorp(s, x)) ≡ op(total(s), x)
 end of type
```

We do not associate an independent semantics with type schemes; only the semantics of types resulting from instantiations is specified.

1.2.2. INSTANTIATIONS OF TYPE SCHEMES

The parameter mechanism of type schemes allows us to specify several similar types in a very short and convenient way. Special types of this general form may then be obtained by instantiating the respective type scheme S , i.e., by supplying particular sort, constant, and operation symbols as actual parameters. The instantiation is denoted by

   include S(«type arguments») **as** («constituents») ;

it is explained by textual substitution ("unfolding") of the body of S with the «type parameters» replaced by the «type arguments» and the constituents of S renamed according to the «constituents». Thus all primitive types of the scheme S are also primitive in the type T containing the instantiation. Moreover, all hidden constituents of S remain hidden in T. The context condition for the instantiation is that the type which results by unfolding S must be context-correct. In particular, no cycles must be introduced into the primitive-relation.

Example:
   Given the type scheme SET we may define the type NATSET (cf. 1.1.1) as follows:

   type NATSET ≡ **nat**, natset, emptyset, incorp, contains, sum :
       based on NAT ,
       include SET(**nat**, zero, add) **as** (**natset**, emptyset, incorp, contains, sum)
   end of type

Several instantiations of type schemes may occur in the body of one type specification. It is understood that - after unfolding - duplicate parts of the signature are taken only once (duplication of laws does no harm anyhow). The order of occurrence of instantiations, as well as that of the other parts of a type, is arbitrary.

II.1.2 Type schemes

Example:
   The following type declaration is admissible:

   type NATSET1 ≡ **nat, natset1,** emptyset, incorp, contains, sum, prod :
      based on NAT ,
      include SET(**nat,** zero, add) **as** (**natset1,** emptyset, incorp, contains, sum) ,
      include SET(**nat,** one, mult) **as** (**natset1,** emptyset, incorp, contains, prod)
   end of type

We allow a restricted form of "recursive" instantiations: constituents from the «constituents»
may occur in the «type-arguments». Such instantiations are interesting mainly in connection with
recursive modes (cf. 1.3.3).

Since every type may be considered as a type scheme without parameters, the instantiation also
provides a convenient <u>renaming mechanism</u>. Constituents of S that are not needed in T may be
replaced by a dot; it is assumed that in unfolding S "new" auxiliary identifiers are substituted
for them.

Example:
   type NATSET2 ≡ **nat, natset2,** emptyset, incorp:
      based on NAT ,
      include SET(**nat,** zero, add) **as** (**natset2,** emptyset, incorp, <u>•</u>, <u>•</u>)
   end of type

In addition to the renaming facility, the instantiation also provides a convenient way of
specifying <u>extensions</u> where a given type or type scheme is enriched by additional sorts,
operations, or laws.

Example:
   To extend the type scheme SET to another type scheme MSET specifying sets with an operation
   for the extraction of the least element one may define

   type MSET ≡ (**sort m,** m e, **funct (m, m) m** op, **funct (m, m) bool** le)
                       set, emptyset, incorp, contains, total, min :
      include SET(**m,** e, op) **as** (set, emptyset, incorp, contains, total) ;
      funct (set) **bool** isempty ,
      funct (set s : ¬ isempty(s)) **m** min ;
      laws set s, **m** x :
         isempty(emptyset) ≡ **true** ,
         isempty(incorp(s, x)) ≡ **false** ,

$min(incorp(s, x)) \equiv$
    if isempty(s) **then** x
             else if $le(x, min(s))$ **then** x
                    else $min(s)$ **fi fi**

end of type

Note that the hidden function isempty is used for the specification of the desired function min.

Instantiations of type schemes may not only be used for obtaining new types but also for producing new type schemes.

Example:
    Using the type scheme SEQU (cf. 1.4 (e)) which specifies finite sequences of objects, we can define the type scheme SEQUSET of sets of sequences by instantiating the type scheme SET:

type SEQUSET $\equiv$ (**sort m**) sequset, emptyset, incorp, contains, concat :
    include SEQU(**m**) **as** (**sequ**, nullsequ, $\cdot$, $\cdot$, conc, $\cdot$, $\cdot$, $\cdot$, $\cdot$, $\cdot$, $\cdot$, $\cdot$, $\cdot$, $\cdot$),
    include SET(**sequ**, nullsequ, conc)
        as (**sequset**, emptyset, incorp, contains, concat)
end of type

Since conc is non-commutative in all models of SEQU(**m**) where **m** has at least two different elements, we have now for $x_1 \neq x_2$
    $concat(incorp(incorp(s, x_1), x_2)) \neq concat(incorp(incorp(s, x_2), x_1))$
and hence
    $incorp(incorp(s, x_1), x_2) \neq incorp(incorp(s, x_2), x_1)$
in all models of SEQUSET(**m**). This means that the extension to SEQUSET(**m**) has reduced the range of possible models for SEQU(**m**). Such situations can be avoided using parameter restrictions as defined in the next section.

The concept of instantiation (with renaming) of a scheme S may be coupled with the concept of primitive types, i.e., the type resulting from the instantiation may also be used as a primitive type of the surrounding type. This is denoted in the form
    based on («constituents») $\equiv$ S(«type arguments») .

Example:
    type NSET $\equiv$ **nat, nset,** nullset, put, member, sum :
        based on (nat, nset, nullset, put, member, sum) $\equiv$ NATSET
    end of type

II.1.2 Type schemes

Note that renaming is even inevitable for obtaining the desired effect if one type is instantiated twice with different parameter values; otherwise the set of generating operations would be doubled, and the reduct to either set of operations would not be generable by that set, i.e., the models of the resulting type would not be hierarchy-preserving.

1.2.3. RESTRICTIONS ON PARAMETERS OF TYPE SCHEMES

In analogy to restrictions on the domains of functions (cf. 1.1.5 (d)) it may also be necessary to restrict the sorts, constants and operations occurring as parameters of a type scheme. It is possible to express such requirements for parameters by adding formulas to the parameter-list.

Example:
     If we want to add to the type scheme SET the law
          laws $\forall$ **set** m, m x, m y :
               incorp(incorp(s, x), y) $\equiv$ incorp(incorp(s, y), x) ,
     then the operation op must also be commutative to give a consistent type. This is expressed
by
          type COMMSET $\equiv$ (**sort** m, m e, **funct** (m, m) m op :
                              laws $\forall$ m x, m y : op(x, y) $\equiv$ op(y, x))
                                        set, emptyset, incorp, contains, total :
               «type-body»
          end of type

For instantiations of restricted schemes we require that the restricting laws (with the formal parameters replaced by the actual ones) hold in all models of the type in which the instantiation occurs.

1.2.4. TYPE SCHEMES WITHOUT CONSTITUENTS

Instantiations of type schemes without constituents can be used to abbreviate collections of laws in parameter restrictions or in type bodies.

Examples:
     We want to express that a certain binary predicate q over m characterizes a quasiordering:

          type QUAORD $\equiv$ (**sort** m, **funct** (m, m) **bool** q) :
               laws m x, m y, m z :
                    def q(x, y) ,
                    q(x, x) ,
                    q(x, y) $\wedge$ q(y, z) $\Rightarrow$ q(x, z)
          end of type

Now we can use QUAORD for the characterization of equivalence relations:

    type EQUIV ≡ (**sort m**, **funct** (**m**, **m**) **bool** eq) :
        include QUAORD(**m**, eq) ;
        laws m x, **m** y : eq(x, y) ⇒ eq(y, x)
    end of type

Finally, we can define linear orderings:

    type LINORD ≡ (**sort m**, **funct** (**m**, **m**) **bool** le, **funct** (**m**, **m**) **bool** eq :
                   include EQUIV(**m**, eq)) :
        include QUAORD(**m**, le) ;
        laws m x, **m** y, **m** z :
            le(x, y) ∧ le(y, x) ⇔ eq(x, y) ,
            le(x, y) ∨ le(y, x)
    end of type

1.3. MODES

Types in full generality are not always easily handled. In this section we provide a shorthand notation for certain frequently occurring types with a rather obvious meaning. These special types, describing (cartesian) products and sums, are called <u>modes</u>. In order to provide a basis for constructing implementations of types, the modes are presupposed to be operational, i.e., to be associated with standard implementations.

In the sequel we define the various possibilities of mode construction by appropriate type schemes; mode declarations are then reduced by definitional transformations to special instantiations of these schemes. Recursive mode declarations are treated by the instantiation mechanism without additional effort.

In the definition of modes we use the notation

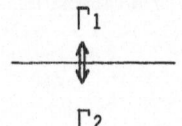

to express that the program part Γ_1 is by definition equivalent to Γ_2 .

II.1.3 Modes

1.3.1. PRODUCT

The product specifies objects composed from a finite number $k > 0$ of other objects, called components, together with operations for construction and selection. The product of k carrier sets is described by the following type scheme:

> **type** $PRODUCT_k \equiv$ (**sort** $m_1, ..., $ **sort** m_k) p, comp, sel$_1$, ..., sel$_k$:
>> **sort** p ,
>> **funct** $(m_1, ..., m_k)$ p comp ,
>> **funct** (p) m_1 sel$_1$, ..., **funct** (p) m_k sel$_k$;
>> **laws** m_1 x_1, ..., m_k x_k :
>>> sel$_1$(comp(x_1, ..., x_k)) $\equiv$ x_1 ,
>>>
>>> .
>>> .
>>> .
>>>
>>> sel$_k$(comp(x_1, ..., x_k)) $\equiv$ x_k
> **end of type**

This type scheme is monomorphic relative to the parameter sorts. Note that the constructor operation - like all operations defined by types - is strict in all arguments so that **p** is the smash product (cf. /de Roever 72/) of the m_j. Also, this product is non-associative in contrast to the product used in the description of the tuples of the scheme language (cf. 2.1.2 (c)).

The declaration of a product mode is then defined by

> **mode** $m \equiv c(m_1 \ s_1, ..., m_k \ s_k)$
> $$\Updownarrow$$
> **include** $PRODUCT_k(m_1, ..., m_k)$ **as** $(m, c, s_1, ..., s_k)$.

In 3.2 we give a possibility for defining restricted products, i.e., products in which certain relations between the components are required to hold.

1.3.2. SUM

The sum specifies the disjoint union of a finite number of carrier sets, which are called variants of the sum. In addition to the injection and projection operations, which are analogous to the constructor and selector operations of the product, one needs discriminating predicates as well. Thus the sum of $k > 0$ carrier sets is described by the following type scheme:

type $\text{SUM}_k \equiv$ (**sort** m_1, ..., **sort** m_k) s, make_1, ismake_1, pr_1, ..., make_k, ismake_k, pr_k :
    sort s ,
    funct (m_1) s make_1 ,
    funct (s) **bool** ismake_1 ,
    funct (s x : $\text{ismake}_1(x)$) m_1 pr_1 ,

         .
         .

    funct (m_k) s make_k ,
    funct (s) **bool** ismake_k ,
    funct (s x : $\text{ismake}_k(x)$) m_k pr_k ;
    laws m_1 x :
        $\text{ismake}_1(\text{make}_1(x)) \equiv$ **true** ,
        $\text{ismake}_2(\text{make}_1(x)) \equiv$ **false** , ..., $\text{ismake}_k(\text{make}_1(x)) \equiv$ **false** ,
        $\text{pr}_1(\text{make}_1(x)) \equiv x$;

         .
         .

    laws m_k x :
        $\text{ismake}_1(\text{make}_k(x)) \equiv$ **false** , ..., $\text{ismake}_{k-1}(\text{make}_k(x)) \equiv$ **false** ,
        $\text{ismake}_k(\text{make}_k(x)) \equiv$ **true** ,
        $\text{pr}_k(\text{make}_k(x)) \equiv x$
  end of type

The declaration of a sum mode is then defined by

$$\textbf{mode } m \equiv v_1(m_1\ p_1)\ |\ ...\ |\ v_k(m_k\ p_k)$$

$$\Updownarrow$$

  include $\text{SUM}_k(m_1, ..., m_k)$ **as** $(m, v_1, \text{isv}_1 , p_1, ..., v_k, \text{isv}_k , p_k)$.

The operations isv_1, ..., isv_k do not occur explicitly in a program text but are expressed with the help of a special keyword in the form
        x **is** v_i .
Note that the discriminating predicates make the sum type monomorphic relative to the parameter sorts; in particular, if laws are added that identify elements from different variants, the models of the resulting type will not be hierarchy-preserving wrt. BOOL. A representative of the class of models of SUM_k is the term algebra over the v_i and the elements of the parameter sorts.

Example:
  Let the following modes be given:
    mode pair $\equiv$ pair(**string** familyname, **string** christianname) ,
    mode triple $\equiv$ triple(**string** familyname, **string** christianname, **string** maidenname) .

II.1.3 Modes

Then we can define the new mode **name** by
> **mode name** ≡ male(**pair** p) | female(**triple** t) .

This allows us to write terms like
> female(triple('smith', 'susan', 'jones'))

and for a **name** n
> **if** n **is** female **then** maidenname(t(n))
> [] n **is** male   **then** familyname (p(n)) **fi**

(for a shorter notation see case (b) below).

Sums may also be quasiordered, i.e., all elements of one variant may be preceded in the quasiordering by all elements of another variant. For the case of two variants the corresponding type scheme reads

> **type** QUORDSUM$_2$ ≡ (**sort** m$_1$, **sort** m$_2$) s, make1, ismake1, pr1, make2, ismake2, pr2, le :
>   **include** SUM$_2$(m$_1$, m$_2$) ;
>   **funct** (s, s) **bool** le ;
>   **laws** ∀ s x, s y :
>   le(x, y) ≡ (ismake1(x) ∧ ismake1(y)) ∨
>   (ismake$_1$(x) ∧ ismake2(y)) ∨
>   (ismake2(x) ∧ ismake2(y))
> **end of type**

By these laws, le is indeed specified as the characteristic predicate of a quasiordering. The declaration of a quasiordered sum mode with two variants is then defined by

> **mode m** ≡ v1(m$_1$ p1) ⫽ v2(m$_2$ p2)

$$\Downarrow$$

> **include** QUORDSUM$_2$(m$_1$, m$_2$) **as** (m,v$_1$, isv$_1$, p$_1$, v$_2$, isv$_2$, p$_2$, .≤.)

Thus the quasiorder predicate is always denoted by the universal operator symbol ≤.

If the variants themselves are quasiordered, then the sum elements inherit the respective quasiorderings:

> **type** IQUORDSUM$_2$ ≡ (**sort** m$_1$, **sort** m2 ,
>   **funct** (m$_1$, m$_1$) **bool** le1 ,
>   **funct** (m$_2$, m$_2$) **bool** le2 :
>   **include** QUAORD(m$_1$, le1) ;
>   **include** QUAORD(m$_2$, le2))
>   s, make1, ismake1, pr1, make2, ismake2, pr2, le :
>   **include** SUM$_2$(m$_1$, m$_2$) ;

funct (s, s) bool le ;
laws $\forall$ **s** x, **s** y :
    le(x, y) $\equiv$
        if ismake$_1$(x) $\wedge$ ismake$_1$(y) **then** le$_1$(pr$_1$(x), pr$_1$(y))
      else if ismake$_2$(x) $\wedge$ ismake$_2$(y) **then** le$_2$(pr$_2$(x), pr$_2$(y))
                          else is$_1$(x) $\wedge$ is$_2$(y)   **fi fi**
  end of type

The schemes for the cases where only one variant is quasiordered are defined similarly.

We allow also nullary variants (without projections) of sum modes, i.e., variants which define new constant symbols.

Examples:
  (1) **mode sign** $\equiv$ plus | minus
  (2) **mode daytime** $\equiv$ morning ◁ noon ◁ afternoon ◁ evening ◁ night

To disambiguate mode expressions involving both quasiordered and non-ordered sums, we define that | binds stronger than ◁.

Example:
  The mode declaration
    mode ord $\equiv$ a ◁ b | c ◁ d ◁ e | f | g
  induces even an order relation .≤. with the order diagram

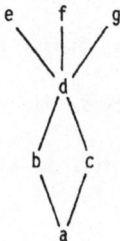

1.3.3. RECURSIVE MODES

The definitional transformation rules given in 1.3.1 and 1.3.2 suffice to explain even (systems of mutually) recursive mode declarations, i.e. declarations

II.1.3 Modes

> mode $m_1 \equiv ME_1$, ..., mode $m_k \equiv ME_k$,

where the mode expressions ME_i (mutually) contain occurrences of the m_j.

Example 1:

The natural numbers may be defined as a recursive quasiordered sum:

> type $NAT_0 \equiv$ **nat**, zero, succ, pred, iszero, .≤. :
>   **mode nat** $\equiv$ zero $\triangleleft$ succ(**nat** pred) ;
>   **funct** (**nat**) **bool** iszero ;
>   **laws** $\forall$ **nat** n : iszero(n) $\equiv$ (n **is** zero)
> **end of type**

According to the definitional transformation in 1.3.2, the declaration of the mode **nat** is equivalent to

> **include** $IQUORDSUM_2$(**nat**) **as** (**nat**, zero, iszero, succ, issucc, pred, .≤.) ,

and we obtain by textual substitution

> type $NAT_0 \equiv$ **nat**, zero, succ, iszero, pred, .≤. :
>   **sort nat** ,
>   **nat** zero ,
>   **funct** (**nat**) **bool** iszero ,
>   **funct** (**nat**) **nat** succ ,
>   **funct** (**nat**) **bool** issucc ,
>   **funct** (**nat** x : issucc(x)) **nat** pred ;
>
>   **laws nat** x :
>   iszero(zero) $\equiv$ **true** ,   issucc(zero) $\equiv$ **false** ,
>   iszero(succ(x)) $\equiv$ **false** ,   issucc(succ(x)) $\equiv$ **true** ,
>   pred(succ(x)) $\equiv$ x ;
>
>   **funct** (**nat**, **nat**) **bool** .≤. ;
>   **laws** $\forall$ **nat** x, **nat** y:
> $(x \leq y) \equiv$
>   **if** issucc(x) $\wedge$ issucc(y) **then** pred(x) $\leq$ pred(y)
>   **else if** iszero(x) $\wedge$ iszero(y) **then true**
>   **else** iszero(x) $\wedge$ issucc(y) **fi fi**
>   **end of type**

All models of NAT_0 are isomorphic. This basic type NAT_0 is enriched by the common arithmetic operations:

    type NAT ≡ **nat**, zero, succ, pred, iszero, .≤., one, add, sub, mult, div, mod:
        based on NAT_0 ;
        nat one ,
        funct (**nat, nat**) **nat** add ,
        funct (**nat** x, **nat** y : y ≤ x) **nat** sub ,
        funct (**nat, nat**) **nat** mult ,
        funct (**nat** x, **nat** y : ¬ iszero(y)) **nat** div ,
        funct (**nat** x, **nat** y : ¬ iszero(y)) **nat** mod ;

        laws nat x, **nat** y :
            one ≡ succ(zero) ,

            add(x, zero) ≡ x ,
            add(x, succ(y)) ≡ succ(add(x, y)) ,

            sub(x, zero) ≡ x ,
            sub(x, succ(y)) ≡ pred(sub(x, y)) **provided** (succ(y) ≤ x) ,

            mult(x, zero) ≡ zero ,
            mult(x, succ(y)) ≡ add(x, mult(x, y)) ,

            div(x, y) ≡ **if** y ≤ x **then** succ(div(sub(x, y), y))
                                else zero   **fi**
            provided ¬ iszero(y) ,

            mod(x, y) ≡ **if** y ≤ x **then** mod(sub(x, y), y)
                                else x   **fi**
            provided ¬ iszero(y)

    end of type

Example 2:

The S-expressions of LISP (cf. /McCarthy et al. 65/) together with some characteristic operations are defined by

    type SEXP ≡ (**sort atoms, funct** (**atoms, atoms**) **bool** eq : **include** EQUIV(**atoms**, eq))
        sexp, mks, atom, mkat, cons, car, cdr, equal :
        mode sexp ≡ mks(**atoms** mkat) | cons(**sexp** car, **sexp** cdr) ;

        funct (sexp) **bool** atom ,

        funct (sexp, sexp) **bool** equal ;

      laws $\forall$ **sexp** s : atom(s) $\equiv$ (s **is** mks) ;

      laws $\forall$ **sexp** s , **sexp** t :

          equal(s, t) $\equiv$

            if atom(s) $\wedge$ atom(t)

              then eq(mkat(s), mkat(t))

              else if (s **is** cons) $\wedge$ (t **is** cons)

                  then equal(car(s), car(t)) $\wedge$

                      equal(cdr(s), cdr(t))

                else false   **fi fi**

    end of type

Note that recursion over a product alone, such as

    mode strange $\equiv$ add(**bool** b, **strange** s) ,

is well defined by this mechanism; however, in all finitely generated models of a type in which this specification occurs, the carrier of sort **strange** will be empty.

The definitional transformation rules imply that modes which are isomorphic but have different names are not identified ("equivalence by name"). As an example assume two declarations

    mode dmark $\equiv$ dm(**nat** mval) ,

    mode dollar $\equiv$ dl(**nat** dval) .

They specify two distinct sorts **dmark** and **dollar**; in a context-correct program no term of sort **dmark** can be used in place of a term of sort **dollar** and vice versa.

1.3.4. NOTATIONAL EXTENSIONS

For greater notational flexibility one may not only write sorts $\blacksquare_i$ in the positions of product components, but also complete mode expressions ME_i, i.e., other products or sums. However, in order to associate sorts with the selector expressions $s_i(x)$, it is necessary to consider such a composed declaration as a system of single declarations. This is explained by the following transformation rule (where ME_i stands for some mode expression and $\blacksquare_i$ is a newly introduced "anonymous" mode identifier):

$$\textbf{mode } m \equiv c(\dots, ME_i \ s_i, \ \dots)$$

$$\Updownarrow$$

$$\textbf{mode } m_i \equiv ME_i \ ,$$
$$\textbf{mode } m \equiv c(\dots, m_i \ s_i, \ \dots)$$

Example:

    mode record $\equiv$ pair((a $\triangleleft$ b $\triangleleft$ c) mark, **data** inf)

is equivalent to the system

    mode aux $\equiv$ a $\triangleleft$ b $\triangleleft$ c ,

    mode record $\equiv$ pair(aux mark, **data** inf) .

The identifier **aux**, however, is anonymous and therefore cannot be used explicitly in the program. Nevertheless, the functionality of the corresponding quasiorder predicate .$\leq$. is internally well defined as

    funct (aux, aux) **bool** .

As in the case of the product, not only sorts m_i but also mode expressions ME_i may be variants of a sum. In many situations one can avoid the introduction of anonymous auxiliary mode identifiers for the ME_i and thus an extensive accumulation of injection and projection operations. It will suffice here to illustrate these extensions by short examples.

(a) Sum: For a construction like

    mode $m \equiv v_1(m_1 \ p_1) \mid v_2((v_3(m_3 \ p_3) \mid v_4(m_4 \ p_4)) \ p_2)$

the expression $p_2(x)$ for an object m x would not have an associated sort. Therefore, the above declaration is considered to be equivalent to

    mode $m_2 \equiv v_3(m_3 \ p_3) \mid v_4(m_4 \ p_4)$,

    mode $m \equiv v_1(m_1 \ p_1) \mid v_2(m_2 \ p_2)$

with a newly introduced anonymous sort m_2.

(b) Product: If a variant of a sum m is a product, then the injection and construction operations as well as the projection and selection operations may be combined. Hence we define

$$\textbf{mode } m \equiv v_1(m_1 \ p_1) \mid v_2(m_2 \ s_2, \ m_3 \ s_3)$$

$$\Updownarrow$$

$$\textbf{include } M(m_1, \ m_2, \ m_3) \textbf{ as } (m, \ v_1, \ is_1, \ p_1, \ v_2, \ is_2, \ s_2, \ s_3)$$

II.1.3 Modes

where M is the type scheme

> **type** $M \equiv$ (**sort** n_1, **sort** n_2, **sort** n_3) s, u, isu, p, v, isv, q, r :
>> **sort** s ,
>> **funct** (n_1) s u ,
>> **funct** (s) bool isu ,
>> **funct** (s x : isu(x)) n_1 p ,
>> **funct** (n_2, n_3) s v ,
>> **funct** (s) bool isv ,
>> **funct** (s x : isv(x)) n_2 q ,
>> **funct** (s x : isv(x)) n_3 r ;
>>
>> **laws** n_1 x :
>>> isu(u(x)) $\equiv$ **true** ,   isv(u(x)) $\equiv$ **false** ,
>>> p(u(x)) $\equiv$ x ;
>>
>> **laws** n_2 x, n_3 y :
>>> isu(v(x, y)) $\equiv$ **false** ,   isv(v(x, y)) $\equiv$ **true** ,
>>> q(v(x, y)) $\equiv$ x ,   r(v(x, y)) $\equiv$ y
>
> **end of type**

Here it is particularly convenient that the notation of the constructors of products and the discriminators of sums coincide.

Example:
> A function which either computes a certain date or returns an error code, may be specified with the help of the following result mode:
>> **mode rdate** $\equiv$ error(**code** message) | valid(**nat** year, **nat** month, **nat** day) .

1.4. STANDARD TYPES

For practical reasons the programming system for the language should already contain a collection of predefined types from which further programming activities can start. In this section a few such basic types are given.

(a) BOOLEAN VALUES

Because of its importance - especially in connection with conditionals - the type BOOL is universally available in all programs: its constants are denoted by the special keywords **true** and **false**. All models of this type are isomorphic ; their carrier sets consist of exactly two elements, and all operations are total.

type BOOL ≡ **bool, true, false,** ¬, ∧, ∨ :
    sort bool,
    bool true,
    bool false,
    funct (bool) bool ¬.,
    funct (bool, bool) bool . ∧ .,
    funct (bool, bool) bool . ∨ .;

    laws bool x, **bool** y:
      true ≢ **false,**
      (¬ **true**) ≡ **false,**
      (¬ **false**) ≡ **true,**
      (**true** ∧ x) ≡ x,
      (**false** ∧ x) ≡ **false,**
      (x ∨ y) ≡ ¬(¬x ∧ ¬y)
end of type

(b) <u>INTEGRAL NUMBERS</u>

The type of integral numbers is obtained from the type NAT (cf. 1.3.3) by omitting the parameter restriction in the operation pred and by employing a binary predicate ≤ (less than or equal to) instead of iszero:

type INT_0 ≡ **int,** 0, succ, pred, ≤ :
    sort int,
    int 0,
    funct (int) int succ,
    funct (int) int pred,
    funct (int, int) bool .≤.;

    laws int x, **int** y:
      pred(succ(x)) ≡ x,
      succ(pred(x)) ≡ x,
      (x ≤ x) ≡ **true,**
      (x ≤ y) ≡ **true** ⇒ (x ≤ succ(y)) ≡ **true,**
      (succ(x) ≤ x) ≡ **false,**
      (x ≤ y) ≡ **false** ⇒ (succ(x) ≤ y) ≡ **false**
end of type

Again, all models of INT_0 are isomorphic. The basic type INT_0 may be enriched by arithmetic operations, e.g.:

II.1.4 Standard types

type INT ≡ **int**, 0, succ, pred, ≤, ≥, =, -., +, .-., * :
  based on INT₀;
  funct (int, int) **bool** .≥.,
  funct (int, int) **bool** .=.,
  funct (int) **int** -.,
  funct (int, int) **int** .+.,
  funct (int, int) **int** .-.,
  funct (int, int) **int** .*.;

  laws int x, **int** y:
    $(x \geq y) \equiv (y \leq x)$,
    $(x = y) \equiv (x \leq y) \land (y \leq x)$,
    $- 0 \equiv 0$,
    $- succ(y) \equiv pred(- y)$,
    $- pred(y) \equiv succ(- y)$,
    $(x + 0) \equiv x$,
    $(x + succ(y)) \equiv succ(x + y)$,
    $(x + pred(y)) \equiv pred(x + y)$,
    $(x - y) \equiv (x + (- y))$,
    $(x * 0) \equiv 0$,
    $(x * succ(y)) \equiv (x * y + x)$,
    $(x * pred(y)) \equiv (x * y - x)$
end of type

(c) FINITE SETS AND MULTISETS

We want to characterize finite sets of elements of a given sort ▪ (i.e., finite subsets of the basic set ▪) by a type; note that term-generated algebras do not cover an extension to infinite sets.

  type FINSET = (**sort** m, **funct** (m, m) **bool** eq : **include** EQUIV(m, eq))
      fset, empty, incorp, contains, delete:
    sort fset,
    fset empty,
    funct (fset, m) **fset** incorp,
    funct (fset, m) **bool** contains,
    funct (fset, m) **fset** delete;

    laws fset s, ▪ x, ▪ y:
      $contains(empty,x) \equiv false$,
      $delete(empty,x) \equiv empty$,

```
        contains(incorp(s,x),y) ≡
          if eq(x,y) then true else contains(s,y) fi,
        delete(incorp(s,x),y) ≡
          if eq(x,y) then delete(s,y)
                        else incorp(delete(s,y),x) fi
  end of type
```

Since we are only considering models with determinate operations, there can be no operation yielding an arbitrary element of a given **fset**. One could only enrich FINSET by an operation

funct(fset) m elem

which yields, when applied to a non-empty set, an element according to a fixed hidden rule; the rule may vary from model to model (non-determinism over the models). A genuinely non-deterministic choice function can, however, be formulated in a program over the type FINSET using the constructs of the applicative part of the language, e.g.

funct select ≡ (fset s) **m** : **some m** x : contains(s,x)

(cf. 2.1.3 (c)).

Finite multisets (cf. /Dershowitz, Manna 79/) or bags are like finite sets except that they also record the number of times an element has been inserted. They are described by the following type:

```
  type BAG ≡ (sort m, funct (m, m) bool eq : include EQUIV(m, eq))
          m, nat, bag, null, insert, has, remove, number:
        based on NAT;
        sort bag,
        bag null,
        funct (bag, m) bag insert,
        funct (bag, m) bool has,
        funct (bag, m) bag remove,
        funct (bag, m) nat number;

        laws bag b, m x, m y:
          has(null,x) ≡ false,
          remove(null,x) ≡ null,
          number(null,x) ≡ 0,
          has(insert(b,x),y) ≡
            if eq(x,y) then true else has(b,y) fi,
          remove(insert(b,x),y) ≡
            if eq(x,y) then b
                        else insert(remove(b,y),x) fi,
```

II.1.4 Standard types

```
        number(insert(b,x),y) ≡
          if eq(x,y) then number(b,y)+1
                     else number(b,y)   fi
end of type
```

(d) <u>FINITE MAPPINGS</u>

The following type specifies partial mappings, which yield defined values of a sort **r** only at finitely many points of their domain **m**:

```
    type GREX ≡ (sort m, sort r, funct(m, m) bool eq : include EQUIV(m,eq))
            grex, vac, put, get, isaccessible:
        sort grex,
        grex vac,
        funct (grex, m, r) grex put,
        funct (grex g, m i: isaccessible(g,i)) r get,
        funct (grex, m) bool isaccessible;

        laws grex g, m i, m j, r x:
          isaccessible(vac,i) ≡ false,
          isaccessible(put(g,i,x),j) ≡
            if eq(i,j) then true else isaccessible(g,i) fi,
          isaccessible(g,j) ⇒
            get(put(g,i,x),j) ≡ if eq(i,j) then x else get(g,j) fi
    end of type
```

If we want to avoid partial mappings (and the predicate isaccessible), we can use a "default value" upon initialization and obtain mappings yielding a non-default value only at finitely many points:

```
    type TOTALGREX ≡ (sort m, sort r, funct(m, m) bool eq : include EQUIV(m,eq))
            grex, initialize, put, get:
        sort grex,
        funct (r) grex initialize,
        funct (grex, m, r) grex put,
        funct (grex, m) r get;

        laws grex g, m i, m j, r x:
          get(initialize(x),i) ≡ x,
          get(put(g,i,x),j) ≡ if eq(i,j) then x else get(g,j) fi
    end of type
```

If the sort **m** of these types is replaced by the integral numbers and the operation vac is supplemented by two integers indicating a lower and an upper bound for the domain of definition, then we get a characterization of arrays with fixed bounds:

> **type** ARRAY ≡ (**sort** r) **array**, vac, put, get, lob, hib, isaccessible:
> > **based on** INT;
> > **sort array**,
> > **funct** (**int**, **int**) **array** vac,
> > **funct** (**array** a, **int** k, r x: lob(a) ≤ k ∧ k < hib(a)) **array** put,
> > **funct** (**array** a, **int** l: isaccessible(a,l)) r get,
> > **funct** (**array**) **int** lob,
> > **funct** (**array**) **int** hib,
> > **funct** (**array**, **int**) **bool** isaccessible;
> > **laws** (**int** i, **int** m, **int** k, **int** l, **array** a, r x:
> > > lob(a) ≤ k ∧ k < hib(a)):
> > lob(vac(i,j)) ≡ i,
> > lob(put(a,k,x)) ≡ lob(a),
> > hib(vac(i,j)) ≡ j,
> > hib(put(a,k,x)) ≡ hib(a),
> > isaccessible(vac(i,j),l) ≡ **false**,
> > isaccessible(put(a,k,x),l) ≡
> > > **if** k ≡ l **then true else** isaccessible(a,l) **fi**,
> > isaccessible(put(a,k,x),l) ⇒
> > > get(put(a,k,x),l) ≡ **if** k ≡ l **then** x **else** get(a,l) **fi**
> **end of type**

In analogy to the type TOTALGREX the operation vac could be extended by a parameter of sort **r** specifying an "initial value" such that the operation get is always defined, provided that the index remains within the admissible interval.

(e) SEQUENCES

We shall first define a general kind of sequence with a rich set of operations:

> **type** SEQU ≡ (**sort** m) **sequ**, empty, isempty, make, &, top, rest, append,
> > > bottom, upper, stock, length, select, change:
> > **sort sequ**,
> > **sequ** empty,
> > **funct** (**sequ**) **bool** isempty,
> > **funct** (**m**) **sequ** make,
> > **funct** (**sequ**, **sequ**) **sequ** .&.,

II.1.4 Standard types

```
funct (sequ s : ¬isempty(s)) m top,
funct (sequ s : ¬isempty(s)) sequ rest,
funct (sequ, m) sequ append,
funct (sequ s : ¬isempty(s)) m bottom,
funct (sequ s : ¬isempty(s)) sequ upper,
funct (sequ, m) sequ stock,
funct (sequ) nat length,
funct (sequ s, nat i : 1 ≤ i ∧ i ≤ length(s)) m select,
funct (sequ s, nat i, m x : 1 ≤ i ∧ i ≤ length(s)) m change;


laws m x, sequ r, sequ s, sequ t:
  (r & (s & t)) ≡ ((r & s) & t),
  (s & empty) ≡ s, (empty & s) ≡ s,
  isempty(empty) ≡ true,
  isempty(make(x)) ≡ false,
  isempty(s & t) ≡ (isempty(s) ∧ isempty(t)),
  append(s,x) ≡ (make(x) & s),
  top(append(s,x)) ≡ x,
  rest(append(s,x)) ≡ s,
  stock(s,x) ≡ (s & make(x)),
  bottom(stock(s,x)) ≡ x,
  upper(stock(s,x)) ≡ s,
  length(empty) ≡ 0,
  length(make(x)) ≡ 1,
  length(s & t) ≡ length(s) + length(t),
  (1 ≤ length(s)) ⇒ select(s,1) ≡ top(s),
  (1 < i ∧ i ≤ length(s)) ⇒
      select(s,i) ≡ select(rest(s), i-1),
  (1 ≤ length(s)) ⇒ change(s,1,x) ≡ append(rest(s),x),
  (1 < i ∧ i ≤ length(s)) ⇒
      change(s,i,x) ≡ append(change(rest(s),i-1,x), top(s))
end of type
```

By "hiding" several of these operations, other sequence-like structures with restricted sets of access functions can be described; the hiding is indicated by omitting the respective operations from the list of visible constituents in the heading. For instance,

```
type STACK ≡ (sort m) stack, empty, isempty, append, top, rest:
    include SEQU(m) as (stack, empty, isempty, ·, ·, top, rest, append, ·, ·, ·, ·, ·,·)
end of type .
```

Because of the symmetry of SEQU we could also use the dual specification

> **type** STACK1 ≡ (**sort** m) **stack**, empty, isempty, append, top, rest:
>   **include** SEQU(m) **as** (**stack**, empty, isempty, ∙, ∙, ∙, ∙, ∙, top, rest, append, ∙, ∙, ∙)
> **end of type** .

Still another possibility is a direct definition of stacks using

> **mode stack** = empty | append(**stack** rest, m top) .

If we allow the adding of elements only at the "lower end" of a sequence and removal only at the "upper end", we obtain queues:

> **type** QUEUE ≡ (**sort** m) **queue**, empty, isempty, top, rest, stock:
>   **include** SEQU(m) **as** (**queue**, empty, isempty, ∙, ∙, top, rest, ∙, ∙, ∙, stock, ∙, ∙, ∙)
> **end of type** .

A re-symmetrisation of this structure leads to

> **type** DOUBLEENDEDQUEUE ≡ (**sort** m) **deque**, empty, isempty, top, rest, append,
>   bottom, upper, stock:
>   **include** SEQU(m) **as** (**deque**, empty, isempty, ∙, ∙, top, rest, append,
>   bottom, upper, stock, ∙, ∙, ∙)
> **end of type** .

(f) TREES

S-expressions (cf. 1.3.3) can be viewed as binary trees with atomic values in their leaves. In a more general kind of tree every node is marked with a value of a sort m, and an arbitrary number of immediate subtrees is allowed.

> **type** TREE ≡ (**sort** m)
>   **tree**, gentree, value, branches,
>   **branches**, empty, append, first, rest, isempty:
>   **mode tree** ≡ gentree(m value, **branches** branches),
>   **include** STACK(tree) **as** (**branches**, empty, isempty, append, first, rest)
> **end of type**

II.1.4 Standard types

(g) POINTERS AND PLEXUSES

Pointers essentially are used for identifying objects. However, in contrast to identifiers in a program text, they may be manipulated by the program; in particular, a comparison operation is defined for them.

We have adopted a view of pointers in which the association of pointers with objects may vary. This seems to capture adequately the situation on von Neumann type machines: The object referred to by an address may be changed (e.g. by selective updating). Moreover, uncoupling the generation from the binding of a pointer allows to stay within the framework of strict base functions. An applicative treatment of simultaneous generation and binding of pointers is only possible if mutual recursion between objects (infinite objects) and thus non-strict base functions are used (cf. /Möller 82/).

The association of pointers with objects is recorded in a "plexus" similar to the collection of pointers used in PASCAL and EUCLID. Pointers and plexuses are defined by the following type scheme:

> **type** PLEX ≡ (**sort m**) **pt, plex,** nil, .$\stackrel{.}{=}$., emptyplex, new, updatable,
> $\qquad\qquad\qquad\qquad$ pt, isdef, deref, update:
> $\quad$ **sort pt, sort plex,**
> $\quad$ **pt** nil,
> $\quad$ **funct (pt, pt) bool** .$\stackrel{.}{=}$.,
> $\quad$ **plex** emptyplex,
> $\quad$ **funct (plex) plex** new,
> $\quad$ **funct (pt, plex) bool** updatable,
> $\quad$ **funct (plex) pt** pt,
> $\quad$ **funct (pt, plex) bool** isdef,
> $\quad$ **funct (pt** p, **plex** q: isdef(p,q)) **m** deref,
> $\quad$ **funct (pt** p, **m** x, **plex** q: updatable(p,q)) **plex** update;
>
> $\quad$ **laws pt** p, **pt** p1, **plex** q, **plex** q1, **plex** q2, **m** x:
> $\qquad$ nil $\stackrel{.}{=}$ nil ≡ **true,**
> $\qquad$ nil $\stackrel{.}{=}$ pt(new(q)) ≡ **false,**
> $\qquad$ pt(new(q)) $\stackrel{.}{=}$ nil ≡ **false,**
> $\qquad$ pt(new(q1)) $\stackrel{.}{=}$ pt(new(q2)) ≡ pt(q1) $\stackrel{.}{=}$ pt(q2),
>
> $\qquad$ pt(emptyplex) ≡ nil,
> $\qquad$ updatable(p,q) $\Rightarrow$ pt(update(p,x,q)) ≡ pt(q),
> $\qquad$ isdef(p, emptyplex) ≡ **false,**
> $\qquad$ isdef(p, new(q)) ≡ isdef(p,q),
> $\qquad$ updatable(p1, q) $\Rightarrow$

$$\text{isdef}(p, \text{update}(p1,x,q)) \equiv (p \stackrel{\circ}{=} p1 \; \forall \; \text{isdef}(p,q)),$$

$$\text{updatable}(p, \text{emptyplex}) \equiv \textbf{false,}$$
$$\text{updatable}(\text{nil}, q) \equiv \textbf{false,}$$
$$\text{updatable}(p, \text{new}(q)) \equiv \text{updatable}(p,q) \; \bigvee \; p \stackrel{\circ}{=} \text{pt}(\text{new}(q)),$$
$$\text{updatable}(p1, q) \Rightarrow$$
$$\quad \text{updatable}(p, \text{update}(p1,x,q)) \equiv \text{updatable}(p,q),$$

$$\text{deref}(p, \text{new}(q)) \equiv \text{deref}(p,q),$$
$$\text{updatable}(p1, q) \Rightarrow$$
$$\quad \text{deref}(p, \text{update}(p1,x,q)) \equiv$$
$$\qquad \textbf{if } p \stackrel{\circ}{=} p1 \textbf{ then } x \textbf{ else } \text{deref}(p,q) \textbf{ fi}$$
end of type

The operations may be interpreted as follows:

.$\stackrel{\circ}{=}$. is the equality test for pointers. The application of new to a **plex** generates a new pointer which may be retrieved using the operation pt; updatable asks whether a pointer has already been generated and thus can be associated with an object. update is used for associating a pointer with an object. isdef allows asking whether an object is associated with a given pointer; if so, deref gives this object. Finally, emptyplex is a **plex** containing only the "pseudo-pointer" nil which may never be associated with an object.

Example:

    mode stackel $\equiv$ comp(**m** info, ptstackel next) ,
    include PLEX(**stackel**)
        as (ptstackel, stackplex,
            nil, .$\stackrel{\circ}{=}$., emptypl, new, updatable, pt, isdef, deref, update) ,

    mode stack $\equiv$ pair(**stackplex** list, **ptstackel** topelem)

Note that program variables could be introduced in a similar way by a type specifying them as re-usable object identifiers.

2. THE SCHEME LANGUAGE

In this section we introduce language constructs for writing specifications and algorithms using basic sort and operation symbols defined by an algebraic type. Since the meaning of the sentences of this language depends on the interpretation of the basic symbols, we speak of a scheme language. In Chapter 3, where scheme language and types are considered together, we shall introduce computation structures as a tool for providing such interpretations constructively.

The abstract syntax of the scheme language is given as a signature enriching the signatures of those types that specify the basic objects and operations. Transformation rules can then be viewed as rewriting rules for terms built over this signature. In order to modularize the description, we construct this signature as a hierarchy of several signatures corresponding to the language layers:

(a) The basic layer is formed by a (varying) collection of basic types $T_1, \ldots, T_n$, depending on the program under consideration.
(b) Over these types, an (applicative) kernel language is defined which introduces the sort **expr** of expressions for logic and functional programming.
(c) The applicative language is based on the kernel language and introduces an additional sort **decl** for declarations of objects and functions.
(d) The procedural language is based on the applicative language and introduces a new sort **stat** for statements comprising assignments and procedures.
(e) The parallel language is based on the procedural language and introduces an additional sort **pstat** for parallel statements containing conditional critical regions.
(f) Finally, the control-oriented language is based on the parallel language and introduces an additional sort **lstat** for labelled statements comprising gotos and labels.

Whereas the kernel language is defined by model-theoretic means, the latter five language layers are specified such that they are complete relative to the kernel language. This means that any expression containing declarations, statements, or jumps can be reduced in a finite number of steps to a pure expression of the kernel language using the transformation rules of the respective language layers ("transformational semantics"; see /Pepper 79/ for a more detailed description of this definition method). For easier readability we write the transformation rules in Part II in concrete syntax: If Γ_1 and Γ_2 are two program schemes of the same syntactic category (e.g. statements or labelled statements), a rule like

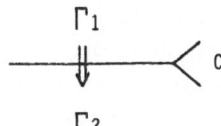

is equivalent to a conditional rewriting rule

$$|C| \Rightarrow |\Gamma_1| \mapsto |\Gamma_2|$$

on the abstract syntax representations $|C|$, $|\Gamma_i|$ of C, Γ_i over the corresponding signature. C is called the <u>enabling condition</u> of the rule. If we also have the rule

$$|C| \Rightarrow |\Gamma_2| \mapsto |\Gamma_1|$$

we combine these into one bidirectional rule using the notation

If C is always true it will be omitted.

The definitional transformation rules characterize the semantics of the additional language constructs in the following way: We call two program parts Γ_1 and Γ_2 <u>extensionally equivalent</u> (cf. /Broy, Wirsing 80/) under condition C if, for every fitting context $E[\![\,\cdot\,]\!]$ of sort **expr** the terms $E[\![\,\Gamma_1\,]\!]$ and $E[\![\,\Gamma_2\,]\!]$ can be reduced to expressions of the kernel language with the same possible values (i.e., with the same breadth, cf.2.1), provided that C holds. The classes of program parts modulo (unconditional) extensional equivalence can then be said to specify the semantics.

For each language layer we shall also provide certain <u>notational extensions</u>; they are defined by transformation rules without semantic enabling conditions.

Further Notations and Conventions

The enabling conditions of the transformation rules are usually formulated with the help of syntactic attributes and predicates (cf. /Knuth 68/):

- KIND $[\![E]\!]$ gives the kind of an expression E, e.g. the sort or functionality of the values it denotes. For identifiers x, KIND $[\![x]\!]$ serves also to distinguish identifiers for objects, functions, variables, procedures and labels.
- OCCURS $[\![x$ **in** $\Gamma]\!]$ is true iff the identifier x occurs free in the program part Γ.

OCCURS is a derived attribute whereas KIND is both inherited and derived. The other attributes and predicates should be self-explanatory; their precise definitions can be found in Part III.

To make the description of the semantics more concise we assume that, on the level of abstract syntax, each identifier is bound to a unique scope within the entire program. This property can be established by a consistent renaming; the transformation rules are given such that their

II.2 The scheme language

application maintains this property. On the level of concrete syntax, however, it may be convenient to allow nested use and overloading of identifiers, or omission of (infix) operators. Notational extensions of this kind will be used occasionally in examples and are briefly discussed in Appendix I.

It is often necessary to replace in a program part Γ the free occurrences of some identifiers x_i by other program parts Γ_i. This is denoted by

$$\Gamma \ [\![\Gamma_i \ \textbf{for} \ x_i]\!] \ .$$

We assume that during this substitution bound variables are renamed to resolve name clashes; for a formal definition of such a substitution operation see e.g. /Barendregt 84/.

2.1. THE KERNEL: AN EXPRESSION LANGUAGE FOR LOGIC AND FUNCTIONAL PROGRAMMING

The kernel language is characterized by the following properties: It is a pure expression language containing an explicit fixpoint operator Y for functions. The function application is based on a *call-by-value* evaluation mechanism, i.e., all functions are *strict*. This reflects the fact that CIP-L has been designed as a language in which to develop programs towards versions suitable for efficient execution on von Neumann type computers. Non-determinism is included by guarded expressions and the finite choice. In addition to this algorithmic part, non-operational ("pre-algorithmic") specification tools like infinite choice, quantification, and set comprehension are available.

This expressive power, in particular quantification over (infinite) sets, together with problems of non-termination makes a transformational specification of the kernel language unfeasible. Therefore we prefer to specify the kernel language in a model-theoretic way rather than by transformation rules.

2.1.1. SEMANTIC NOTIONS

OBJECT KINDS

We define the set OK of object kinds to be the smallest set satisfying:
(i) $s \in$ OK for all sort symbols s of the basic types.
(ii) If $m_i \in$ OK $(1 < i < n, n \geq 0)$ then $(m_1,...,m_n) \in$ OK. $(m_1,...,m_n)$ is called a tuple kind;
      for n = 0 it is the kind () of the empty tuple (which again is denoted by ()).
(iii) If $m \in$ OK then set $m \in$ OK. set m is a set kind, the kind of sets of objects of kind m.
OK contains the kinds of purely non-functional entities of the kernel language.

We distinguish these kinds from the kinds of functions, variables, etc. by the predicate
    OBJECTKIND $[\![m]\!] \iff m \in$ OK .

SEMANTIC FUNCTIONS AND DOMAINS

We associate with each object or function kind m a domain DOM $[\![m]\!]$ of proper semantic values of kind m. Each of these domains carries a partial order reflecting the "information contents" of its elements (cf. /Scott 70/). Given such a domain D with ordering $\leq$, we enrich it by an error element $\perp$ to
    $D^+ = D \cup \{\perp\}$
with the ordering
    $x \sqsubseteq y \iff x = \perp \lor x \leq y$.

II.2.1 The kernel: an expression language

In this way, $\perp$ becomes the least element of D^+; this reflects the view that $\perp$ is the (improper) value of an erroneous or non-terminating evaluation which gives "no information".

An expression is called <u>closed</u> if it does not contain <u>free identifiers</u>, i.e., identifiers that are not bound by one of the basic algebraic types or by one of the binding constructs of the language (see below). $EXPR_m$ denotes the set of closed expressions of kind m. To avoid the use of environments (cf. /Scott, Strachey 71/) we only specify the semantics of closed expressions. For this purpose, we consider the semantic values in $DOM[\![m]\!]^+$ as expressions in $EXPR_m$ as well; this gives rise to "mixed expressions" containing syntactic and semantic elements (cf. /Broy et al. 79/). The semantics is specified in such a way that the meaning function is only applied to expressions whose free identifiers have been replaced by suitable semantic values.

We associate with every closed expression E of kind m a set $B_m[\![E]\!] \subseteq DOM[\![m]\!]^+$ of "possible values"; $B_m[\![E]\!]$ is called the <u>breadth</u> of E (cf. /Broy et al. 79/). We may exclude the empty set of values, since, in the case of an erroneous or non-terminating evaluation, we have at least the improper value $\perp$. Thus the breadth is a family of mappings (one for each kind m)

$$B_m: EXPR_m \rightarrow \mathcal{P}(DOM[\![m]\!]^+)\backslash\{\emptyset\}$$

(in the sequel we will always omit the indices m). For semantic values u we set $B[\![u]\!] = \{u\}$. In the specification of the constructs of the kernel language we will use the abbreviation

$$B^-[\![E]\!] = B[\![E]\!]\backslash\{\perp\}$$

to denote the set of defined values of an expression E.

We call an expression <u>determinate</u> if its breadth is a singleton set; thus a semantic value is a determinate expression. The semantic predicate DETERMINATE characterizes the determinate expressions. An expression E is <u>defined</u> if it cannot lead to undefined evaluations, i.e., if we have $\perp \notin B[\![E]\!]$; these expressions are characterized by the semantic predicate DEFINED.

To keep the semantic complexity manageable we have decided to exclude non-determinism at the level of (higher-order) functions from the language. Therefore, expressions of a function kind **funct(m)n** will always be determinate.

Let us now define the domains belonging to the kinds[1] . Since we specify the semantics of the kernel language relative to a fixed collection $A_1,...,A_n$ of models of the basic types $T_1,...,T_n$, we associate with a sort s of some T_i the domain

$$DOM[\![s]\!] = s^{A_i} ,$$

i.e., the carrier set of sort s in A_i. As order relation on $DOM[\![s]\!]$ we take the identity relation; then every element is only comparable to itself, i.e., all proper semantic values of kind s contain an equal amount of information. In this way, $DOM[\![s]\!]^+$ becomes a <u>flat domain</u> with the ordering (cf. /Manna 74/)

---

[1] Here, we have tried to define the domains in as straightforward a way as possible to keep the description halfways readable. The formal definition in Part III actually uses more refined versions of these domains which are (isomorphic to) subdomains of those considered here.

$$x \sqsubseteq y \iff x = \bot \; \lor \; x = y .$$

Besides the basic objects we distinguish three other kinds of semantic values:
- tuples $(u_1,...,u_n)$ of values u_i $(n \geq 0)$
- sets of non-functional values (e.g. of basic objects or of other sets)
- possibly non-determinate functions (i.e., correspondence relations) over semantic values (with the restriction that functions having functions as results must be determinate).

The corresponding semantic domains are the following:

- For a tuple kind $(m_1,..,m_n)$ we set
   $$DOM[\![(m_1,...,m_n)]\!] = DOM[\![m_1]\!] \; x \; \cdots \; x \; DOM[\![m_n]\!]$$
   where x denotes the associative cartesian product. By this associativity, "nested" tuples like $((x_1, x_2), (x_3, (x_4, x_5)))$ are equivalent to "linear" ones like $(x_1, x_2, x_3, x_4, x_5)$. Therefore, tuples are different from the elements of direct products as defined in 1.3.3. We have chosen the associative product to enable easy composition of functions with tuples as arguments and results. For n=0, $DOM[\![()]\!] = \{()\}$.

   The order between tuples is defined componentwise, i.e.,
   $$(x_1,...,x_n) < (y_1,...,y_n) \iff x_1 < y_1 \land \; ... \; \land \; x_n < y_n .$$

   Note that there are no $\bot$-components in tuples; $DOM[\![(m_1,...,m_n)]\!]^+$ is the smash product of the $DOM[\![m_i]\!]^+$. This reflects the call-by-value semantics of the language: if in evaluating a function application the evaluation of one expression in a tuple of arguments does not terminate, then the whole tuple is considered as undefined (evaluation of all arguments *before* evaluation of the function body).

- For an object kind m,
   $$DOM[\![\textbf{set } m]\!] = \mathcal{P}(DOM[\![m]\!]) ,$$
   i.e., each element of $DOM[\![\textbf{set } m]\!]$ is a set $s \subseteq DOM[\![m]\!]$. The order on $DOM[\![\textbf{set } m]\!]$ is the identity relation; thus $DOM[\![\textbf{set } m]\!]^+$ is again a flat domain.

- $DOM[\![\textbf{funct}(m)r]\!] =$
   $$\{f \subseteq DOM[\![m]\!] \; x \; DOM[\![r]\!]^+ : \forall \; x \in DOM[\![m]\!] : \exists \; y \in DOM[\![r]\!]^+ : (x,y) \in f\} .$$
   The domain of these correspondences does not contain $\bot$, since the case of undefined arguments will be treated separately in the specification of the function application. For $f \in DOM[\![\textbf{funct}(m)r]\!]$ and $u \in DOM[\![m]\!]$ we denote by $f(u)$ the set $\{v \in DOM[\![r]\!]^+ : (u, v) \in f\}$.

   Note that we allow also nullary functions, i.e., functions without parameters. As a special case which is needed for the semantics of certain procedures and jumps, we also include
   $$DOM[\![\textbf{funct}()()]\!] = \{ \{((),\bot)\} , \{((),())\} , \{((),\bot) , ((),())\} \} .$$

II.2.1 The kernel: an expression language

To define an order on $DOM[\![\,\textbf{funct(m)r}\,]\!]$ we introduce the Egli-Milner relation (cf. /Plotkin 76/) on sets of values:

For $S_1,S_2 \subseteq DOM[\![\,\textbf{m}\,]\!]^+$ we set
$$S_1 \sqsubseteq_{EM} S_2 \iff (\forall\ x\epsilon S_1\ \exists\ y\epsilon S_2 : x\sqsubseteq y)\ \wedge$$
$$(\forall\ y\epsilon S_2\ \exists\ x\epsilon S_1 : x\sqsubseteq y)\ .$$

If $DOM[\![\,\textbf{m}\,]\!]^+$ is a flat domain this is equivalent to
$$S_1 \sqsubseteq_{EM} S_2 \iff (\perp\notin S_1\ \wedge\ S_1 = S_2)\ \vee$$
$$(\perp\epsilon S_1\ \wedge\ S_1\backslash\{\perp\} \subseteq S_2\backslash\{\perp\})$$
Thus, S_2 is "more defined" than S_1 if it has "at least as many" proper values.

In the case of a flat domain $DOM[\![\,\textbf{m}\,]\!]^+$, the relation $\sqsubseteq_{EM}$ is even an order. Note that in any case we have for singleton sets
$$\{x\} \sqsubseteq_{EM} \{y\} \iff x\sqsubseteq y\ .$$
This will be of particular importance for the breadth of functional expressions.

For $f_1,f_2 \epsilon DOM[\![\,\textbf{funct(m)r}\,]\!]$ we now set
$$f_1 \leqslant f_2 \iff \forall\ x\epsilon DOM[\![\,\textbf{m}\,]\!] : f_1(x) \sqsubseteq_{EM} f_2(x)\ .$$

There is another important relation on $DOM[\![\,\textbf{funct(m)r}\,]\!]$: We say that f_1 is a descendant of f_2 (cf. /McCarthy 63/) if for all $x \epsilon DOM[\![\,\textbf{m}\,]\!]$ we have $f_1(x) \subseteq f_2(x)$, or, equivalently, if $f_1 \subseteq f_2$ as correspondences. In this case we also write $f_1 \sqsubseteq_D f_2$; it means that f_1 is "more determinate" ("less ambiguous") than f_2 .

The two semantic relations on functions are also important for arbitrary expressions. Let $E_1,E_2 \epsilon EXPR_{\textbf{m}}$ for an object kind $\textbf{m}$.

- We say that E_1 and E_2 are in the Egli-Milner relation if we have $B[\![E_1]\!] \sqsubseteq_{EM} B[\![E_2]\!]$. In this case we write also $E_1 \sqsubseteq_{EM} E_2$. This relation is used in the least-fixpoint semantics of recursive functions: monotonicity wrt. the Egli-Milner relation guarantees the existence of least fixpoints (cf. /Markowsky 76/). Therefore, all language constructs are defined in such a way that they are monotonic wrt. this relation.

However, monotonicity does not guarantee that the least fixpoint can also be obtained as the limit of a computation sequence; this is only ensured by the stronger requirement of continuity. Whereas all "algorithmic" constructs are continuous, the "pre-algorithmic" ones, such as set comprehension, infinite choice, or quantification, in general are not (cf. /Broy et al. 79/).

- E_1 is a <u>descendant</u> of E_2 if $B[\![E_1]\!] \subseteq B[\![E_2]\!]$ (cf. /McCarthy 63/); then E_1 is "more determinate" than E_2. In this case we write also $E_1 \sqsubseteq_D E_2$. For a program development by local transformations it is essential that all language constructs be monotonic wrt. this ordering: A local reduction of the breadth of a program part then also causes a breadth reduction of the whole program.

For functional expressions $\sqsubseteq_{EM}$ and $\sqsubseteq_D$ have already been defined; for tuples containing both functions and values of object kinds the relations are again defined componentwise. For non-closed expressions E_1, E_2 with free identifiers $x_1,\ldots,x_n$ of kinds $m_1,\ldots,m_n$ the notation $E_1 \sqsubseteq_{EM} E_2$ means that $E_1[\![u_1,\ldots,u_n \text{ for } x_1,\ldots,x_n]\!] \sqsubseteq_{EM} E_2[\![u_1,\ldots,u_n \text{ for } x_1,\ldots,x_n]\!]$ holds for all $u_i \in DOM[\![m_i]\!]$; the notation $E_1 \sqsubseteq_D E_2$ is explained analogously.

We write

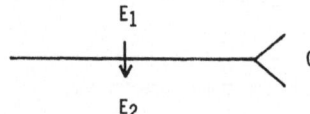

for C $\Rightarrow$ $E_2 \sqsubseteq_D E_1$, and

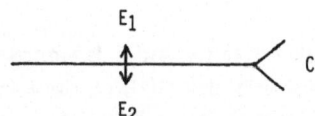

for C $\Rightarrow$ $E_2 \sqsubseteq_D E_1 \wedge E_1 \sqsubseteq_D E_2$. If in these relations C is always true it may be omitted. We call E_1 and E_2 <u>mathematically equivalent</u> if we have

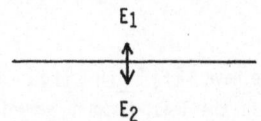

i.e., if E_1 and E_2 have the same breadth.

The single-line arrow $\downarrow$ therefore denotes relations which hold only in the special semantic model constructed by means of the breadth function B whereas the double-line arrow $\Downarrow$ is a rewriting-arrow and thus induces equivalences which are independent of the special semantic model of the kernel. Since the layers extending the kernel language are specified using exclusively the latter type of equivalence, the connections between the language layers are independent of the semantics of the kernel language.

II.2.1 The kernel: an expression language

2.1.2. ALGORITHMIC CONSTRUCTS

The following constructs are called algorithmic, since not only a mathematical semantics but also an operational semantics may be defined for them in full generality. All these constructs are both monotonic and continuous in the Egli-Milner ordering.

As a general basis we use the type BOOL as defined in 1.4.

(a) BASIC IDENTIFIER

The only identifiers whose values are not defined in one of the following constructs are those of basic objects and operations. Their values depend on the particular model of the basic type(s): For basic identifiers c for constants and f for operations we set

$$B[\![c]\!] = \{c^A\} ,$$
$$B[\![f]\!] = \{\bar{f}^A\}$$

where $\bar{f}^A$ is the natural extension (cf. /Manna 74/) of f^A defined by

$$\bar{f}^A(u) = \begin{cases} f^A(u) & \text{if this is defined} \\ \bot & \text{otherwise} . \end{cases}$$

Example:

For pred of the type NAT (cf. 1.3.3) we have

$$B[\![pred]\!] = \{ \{ (zero^A, \bot) \} \cup \{ (succ^{n+1}(zero)^A, succ^n(zero)^A) : n \in \mathbb{N} \} \}$$

where A is the underlying model of NAT.

(b) CONDITIONAL EXPRESSION

The conditional expression is used to choose between two given expressions E_1, E_2 (of the same kind) depending on the value of a boolean expression C: It is denoted by

$$\text{if } C \text{ then } E_1 \text{ else } E_2 \text{ fi} .$$

If C yields **true** then E_1 is chosen, if C yields **false** then E_2 is chosen. If C does not yield a defined value, then the value of the conditional expression is undefined, too.

More formally, $B[\![\text{if } C \text{ then } E_1 \text{ else } E_2 \text{ fi}]\!]$ is the smallest set $V \subseteq DOM[\![m]\!]^+$ such that

$$\text{true} \in B[\![C]\!] \implies B[\![E_1]\!] \subseteq V ,$$
$$\text{false} \in B[\![C]\!] \implies B[\![E_2]\!] \subseteq V ,$$
$$\bot \in B[\![C]\!] \implies \bot \in V .$$

Note that

$$\text{if } C \text{ then } E \text{ else } E \text{ fi}$$

is equivalent to E only if C is defined; otherwise it yields $\bot$. Thus we have the rule

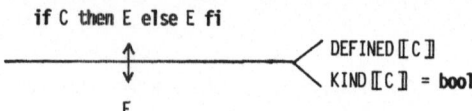

if C then E else E fi

$\Big\langle$ DEFINED $[\![\,C\,]\!]$
KIND $[\![\,C\,]\!]$ = **bool**

E

Obviously, also the following transformation rules are valid:

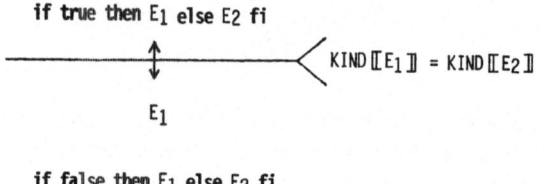

if **true** then E_1 else E_2 fi

$\Big\langle$ KIND $[\![\,E_1\,]\!]$ = KIND $[\![\,E_2\,]\!]$

E_1

if **false** then E_1 else E_2 fi

$\Big\langle$ KIND $[\![\,E_1\,]\!]$ = KIND $[\![\,E_2\,]\!]$

E_2

The usual boolean operations are the strict extensions of the respective operations of the type BOOL. Hence, for boolean expressions E_1, E_2 we have

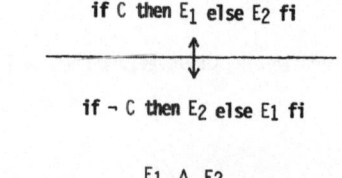

if C then E_1 else E_2 fi

if $\neg$ C then E_2 else E_1 fi

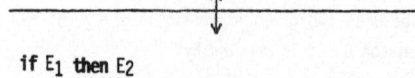

$E_1 \wedge E_2$

if E_1 then E_2
    else if E_2 then false else false fi fi

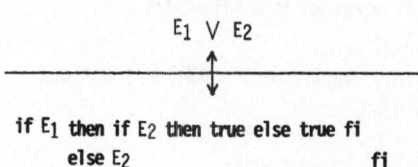

$E_1 \vee E_2$

if E_1 then if E_2 then true else true fi
    else E_2 fi

The complicated form of these rules is due to the fact that a strict operation must evaluate all its arguments. McCarthy's "conditional and" (denoted by $\wedge$) and "conditional or" (denoted by $\vee$) are no operations in the strict sense but notational variants of simpler expressions:

II.2.1 The kernel: an expression language

$$E_1 \wedge E_2$$

$$\updownarrow$$

if E_1 then E_2 else false fi

$$E_1 \vee E_2$$

$$\updownarrow$$

if E_1 then true else E_2 fi

$$E_1 \Rightarrow E_2$$

$$\updownarrow$$

if E_1 then E_2 else true fi

Note, however, that these "conditional" or "sequential" forms of the logical connectives are not commutative.

Examples:

(1) Absolute value of an integer x:

   if $x \geq 0$ then x else -x fi

(2) Characterization of sequences s (cf. 1.4 (e)) with
   - at most one element:

      isempty(s) $\vee$ isempty(rest(s))

   - more than one element:

      ¬ isempty(s) $\wedge$ ¬ isempty(rest(s))

(3) Characterization of dates d (cf. 1.3.4 (b)) of a certain year:

      d is valid $\Rightarrow$ year(d) = 1984

(c) TUPLE

Tuples serve for collecting values, e.g. arguments or results of a function. They are specified by

$$B^{\sim} [\![(E_1,\ldots,E_n)]\!] = B^{\sim}[\![E_1]\!] \times \cdots \times B^{\sim}[\![E_n]\!]$$

and

$$\bot \in B [\![(E_1,\ldots,E_n)]\!] \iff \bigvee_{i=1}^{n} \bot \in B[\![E_i]\!] .$$

Thus, a tuple is defined iff all its components are. Moreover, if $(E_1,...,E_n)$ is defined, it is determinate iff all the E_i are.

Tuples of values are well-distinguished from the elements of a product mode (cf. 1.3.1); they avoid construction and selection operations. Moreover, there are no "nested" tuples; they are "flattened" by the use of the associative smash product. This is very convenient for function applications (cf. (f)).

Example:
(1) Polar coordinates   (sqrt(5), $\pi/4$)
(2) Splitting a non-empty sequence s   (top(s), rest(s))

(d) FINITE CHOICE

The arbitrary choice between expressions E_1, E_2 of an object kind ■ is denoted by
$$(E_1 \ □ \ E_2) .$$
Its meaning is simply described by
$$B [\![(E_1 \ □ \ E_2)]\!] = B [\![E_1]\!] \ U \ B [\![E_2]\!] .$$
It is immediate from this definition that the finite choice is associative, commutative, and idempotent. Because of the associativity we may also write $(E_1 \ □ \ ... \ □ \ E_n)$ instead of $(E_1 \ □ \ (E_2 \ □ \ ...(E_{n-1} \ □ \ E_n)...))$.

We stress again that non-deterministic choice between functions is ruled out.

Examples:
(1) An arbitrary solution of $y^2 = 16$ (4 □ -4)
(2) An arbitrary non-working-day   (saturday □ sunday)
(3) An arbitrary prime number less than 10 (2 □ 3 □ 5 □ 7)
(4) Splitting a non-empty sequence   ((top(s), rest(s)) □
                                          (bottom(s), upper(s)))

The finite choice introduces non-determinacy into the language. The relation

$$E [\![(E_1 \ □ \ E_2) \ \text{for} \ x]\!]$$
$$\Big\downarrow \qquad\qquad\qquad i \in \{1,2\}$$
$$E [\![E_i \ \text{for} \ x]\!]$$

expresses that all constructs of the language are monotonic wrt. the descendant ordering.

II.2.1 The kernel: an expression language

(e) FUNCTION ABSTRACTION

A function abstraction parameterizes an expression and thus makes it into a function. Let E be an expression of kind **r** and y a free identifier of kind **m**. Then the abstraction

$$(\mathbf{m}\ y)\mathbf{r} : E$$

denotes a correspondence; its breadth is given by

$$B[\![(\mathbf{m}\ y)\mathbf{r} : E]\!] = \{f\} \quad \text{where}$$
$$f = \{ (u,v) \in DOM[\![\mathbf{m}]\!] \times DOM[\![\mathbf{r}]\!]^+ : v \in B[\![E[\![u\ \text{for}\ y]\!]]\!] \} .$$

x is the formal parameter of the abstraction.

Note that there are no pairs $(\perp, v)$ in the correspondence, i.e., an abstraction can only be applied to defined values. Also, $\perp$ is not contained in the breadth of the abstraction itself, since an abstraction denotes a correspondence and therefore yields a defined object. (The pointwise undefined correspondence Ω consisting only of pairs $(u, \perp)$ is a defined value and thus well-distinguished from the undefined value $\perp$.) Therefore, an abstraction is a determinate and defined expression. **m** is called the parameter kind and **r** the result kind of the abstraction. The generalization to abstractions with several parameters and results is obvious. Note also that E need not depend on y at all.

Example:
$$B[\![(\mathbf{nat}\ n)\mathbf{nat} : (4 \div n \ [] \ 5)]\!] =$$
$$\{ \{ (0, \perp), (1,4), (2, 2), (3, 1), (4, 1) \} \ \mathbf{U}$$
$$\{ (u, 0) : u \geq 5 \} \ \mathbf{U}$$
$$\{ (u, 5) : u \geq 0 \} \qquad\qquad\qquad \}$$
where u ranges over the semantic objects in the carrier set **nat**[A] of a model A of the basic type NAT.

An abstraction binds its parameter identifiers and associates with them kinds that define their domains. It also constitutes a scope for these identifiers. Consistent renaming within the scope (α-conversion in the terminology of the lambda-calculus) is possible:

$$(\mathbf{m}\ x)\ \mathbf{r} : E$$
$$\underset{(\mathbf{m}\ y)\ \mathbf{r} : E[\![y\ \text{for}\ x]\!]}{\longleftrightarrow} \prec \neg\ OCCURS[\![y\ \text{in}\ E]\!]$$

Example:
Consider the (higher-order) abstraction
$$(\mathbf{nat}\ x)\ \mathbf{funct(nat)nat} : (\mathbf{nat}\ y)\ \mathbf{nat} : x+y .$$
It can be transformed (by α-conversion of its body) into
$$(\mathbf{nat}\ x)\ \mathbf{funct(nat)nat} : (\mathbf{nat}\ z)\ \mathbf{nat} : x+z .$$

Afterwards, since now no parasitic binding of y in the inner abstraction will be introduced, x can be renamed into y yielding

(**nat** y) **funct**(**nat**)**nat** : (**nat** z) **nat** : y+z .

Also in analogy to the lambda-calculus, the language follows the rule of static binding of parameter identifiers.

(f) FUNCTION APPLICATION

The central concept of the kernel language is the application of a function to arguments. The application is typed, i.e., the parameter kind of the function must agree with the kind of the argument tuple.

For an expression F of kind **funct**(**m**)**r** with value $B[\![F]\!] = \{f\}$ and a determinate <u>actual parameter expression</u> E of kind **m** with value $B[\![E]\!] = \{u\}$ the application F(E) is defined by

$$B[\![F(E)]\!] = \begin{cases} f(u) & \text{if } u \neq \bot \ \wedge \ f \neq \bot \\ \{\bot\} & \text{otherwise} \end{cases}$$

(see 2.1.1 for the definition of f(u)). Note that **m** and **r** may stand for tuples $(m_1,...,m_k)$ and $(r_1,...,r_n)$ of parameter and result kinds.

This definition is generalized to non-determinate expressions E by

$$B[\![F(E)]\!] = \bigcup_{e \in B[\![E]\!]} B[\![F(e)]\!] .$$

According to this definition, every argument is fixed once and for all for the whole application even if the actual parameter expression is non-determinate (call-time choice, cf. /Hennessy, Ashcroft 76/). Moreover, the function application obeys a call-by-value semantics and thus is strict in its function expression F as well as in its actual parameter expression E.

Examples:
    (1) Absolute value

        $B[\![$ ((**int** x)**int** : **if** x ≥ 0 **then** x **else** -x **fi**)(-3) $]\!]$ = {3}

    (2) Splitting a character sequence at the top or bottom:

        Let F be the abstraction

        (**charsequ** s)(**char, charsequ**) :

            ((top(s), rest(s)) ☐ (bottom(s), upper(s))) .

        Then $B[\![F('' \ ☐ \ 'END')]\!]$ = { ⊥, ('E','ND'), ('D','EN') } .

II.2.1 The kernel: an expression language

Fundamental for the application of a function is the rule of *unfolding*:

$$
\frac{((\mathbf{m}\ x)\ \mathbf{r} : E_1)(E_2)}{E_1\ [\![\ E_2\ \text{for}\ x\ ]\!]}
\Bigg\langle
\begin{array}{l}
\text{DEFINED}\ [\![\ E_2\ ]\!] \\
\text{DETERMINATE}\ [\![\ E_2\ ]\!]
\end{array}
$$

Both conditions are mandatory: the expression E_2 must be determinate since x may occur several times within E_1 and has to be replaced by the same value at every point (call-time choice!). If E_1 is not strict wrt. x it may happen that non-termination of E_2 does not lead to non-termination of the bottom scheme whereas it will always cause non-termination in the top scheme; therefore E_2 must be defined as well.

The converse of this rule, called *folding*, reads

$$
\frac{E_1\ [\![\ E_2\ \text{for}\ x\ ]\!]}{((\mathbf{m}\ x)\ \mathbf{r} : E_1)(E_2)}
\Bigg\langle
\begin{array}{l}
\text{KIND}\ [\![\ E_1\ ]\!] = \mathbf{r} \\
\text{KIND}\ [\![\ E_2\ ]\!] = \mathbf{m} \\
\text{DEFINED}\ [\![\ E_2\ ]\!]
\end{array}
$$

Folding and unfolding correspond to β-conversion in the lambda-calculus.

The arguments of a function with several parameters may also be provided by tuple-valued functions; in this case the "nested" argument tuple is "flattened" into a linear one.

Example:
Consider the three abstractions
$$A \triangleq (\mathbf{nat}\ a, \mathbf{nat}\ b, \mathbf{nat}\ c, \mathbf{nat}\ d, \mathbf{nat}\ e, \mathbf{nat}\ f)\ (\mathbf{nat}, \mathbf{nat}, \mathbf{nat}) :$$
$$(a + b - c,\ d + 2,\ e * f)\ ,$$
$$B \triangleq (\mathbf{nat}\ x, \mathbf{nat}\ y)\ (\mathbf{nat}, \mathbf{nat}, \mathbf{nat}) :$$
$$(x + y,\ x - y,\ 0)\ ,$$
$$C \triangleq (\mathbf{nat}\ u, \mathbf{nat}\ v, \mathbf{nat}\ w)\ (\mathbf{nat}, \mathbf{nat}) :$$
$$(u + w,\ w - v)\ .$$
Then the expression
$$A(B(9, 7), 3, C(1, 5, 6))$$
is equivalent to
$$A((16, 2, 0), 3, (7, 1))$$
which is linearized to
$$A(16, 2, 0, 3, 7, 1)$$
and thus has the value $(18, 5, 7)$.

(g) FIXPOINT

In the kernel language, functions (correspondences) can be specified recursively using a fixpoint operator Y. The semantics is given by the least solutions of functional equations.

Let $f_1,...,f_n$ be pairwise different identifiers, and let $A_1,...,A_n$ be abstractions of the kinds **funct(m_j)r_j** containing, besides constituent identifiers of the basic types, at most the free identifiers $f_1,...,f_n$. Then the semantics of a system of recursive functions is defined by

$$B[\![(Y\ f_1,...,f_n : A_1,...,A_n)]\!] = \{\ (g_1,...,g_n)\ \}$$

where $(g_1,...,g_n) \in DOM[\![(\textbf{funct}(m_1)r_1,...,\textbf{funct}(m_n)r_n)]\!]$ is the least tuple of functions such that

$$B[\![A_j[\![g_i\ \textbf{for}\ f_i]\!]]\!] = \{g_j\} \ .$$

Since all constructs used are monotonic wrt. the Egli-Milner ordering, the existence of this element is guaranteed (cf. /Markowsky 76/).

Note that the identifiers f_i are bound by the fixpoint operator; their scope is the fixpoint expression.

If all constructs used in the abstractions A_j are even continuous wrt. the Egli-Milner ordering, then the least fixpoint coincides with the least upper bound of a functional iteration, viz. with

$$\bigsqcup_{k \in \mathbb{N}} (g_1^{(k)},...,g_n^{(k)}) \qquad \text{where} \quad \begin{array}{l} g_j^{(0)} = \Omega \ \text{and} \\ \{\ g_j^{(k+1)}\ \} = B[\![A_j[\![g_i^{(k)}\ \textbf{for}\ f_i]\!]]\!] \ . \end{array}$$

Examples:

(1) Integral dual logarithm:
    (Y logd: (**nat** n)**nat** : if n=1 **then** 0
                            else logd(n÷2) + 1 **fi**)

(2) Arbitrary prefix of a sequence:
    (Y prefix : (**charsequ** s)**charsequ** :
                if isempty(s) **then** empty
                        else (s ▯ prefix(upper(s))) **fi**)

(3) Factorial (repetitive version):
    (Y fac, fc : (**int** n)**int** : fc(n, 1) ,
                (**int** n, **int** m)**int** : if n=0 **then** m
                             else fc(n-1, n ∗ m) **fi**)

(4) A variant of Backus' while-combinator (cf. /Backus 78/):
    (Y cwhile : (**funct**(m)**bool** p, **funct**(m)m f, m x) m :
                if p(x) **then** cwhile(p, f, f(x))
                      else x   **fi**)

II.2.1 The kernel: an expression language

The characteristic property of the fixpoint is that it is preserved under unfolding:

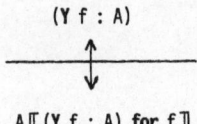

$$(Y\ f : A)$$

$$\uparrow$$

$$\downarrow$$

$$A\llbracket (Y\ f : A)\ \textbf{for}\ f\rrbracket$$

In particular, for a non-recursive function we have

$$(Y\ f : A)$$

$$\uparrow \qquad\qquad \longleftarrow \neg\ OCCURS\llbracket f\ \textbf{in}\ A\rrbracket$$

$$\downarrow$$

$$A$$

i.e., the least fixpoint agrees with the value of the abstraction itself.

In the sequel we shall need expressions with the breadth $\{\bot\}$. Let $\blacksquare$ be a kind. Then the expression

$$ERROR_{\blacksquare} = (Y\ f : ()\blacksquare : f()\ )\ ()$$

has the property that $B\llbracket ERROR_{\blacksquare}\rrbracket = \{\bot\}$ and $KIND\llbracket ERROR_{\blacksquare}\rrbracket = \blacksquare$.

NOTATIONAL EXTENSION: FUNCTION COMPOSITION

The composition of two expressions F, G of functional kind is denoted by

$$F \circ G .$$

The function composition is typed, that is, the parameter kind of F and the result kind of G have to agree. We define

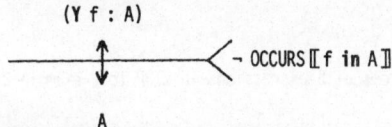

$$F \circ G$$

$$\Uparrow \qquad\qquad\qquad\qquad KIND\llbracket G\rrbracket = \textbf{funct}(\textbf{m})\textbf{n}$$

$$\Downarrow \qquad\qquad\qquad\qquad KIND\llbracket F\rrbracket = \textbf{funct}(\textbf{n})\textbf{r}$$

$$((\textbf{funct}(\textbf{n})\textbf{r}\ f,\ \textbf{funct}(\textbf{m})\textbf{n}\ g)\ \textbf{funct}(\textbf{m})\textbf{r} :$$

$$(\blacksquare\ x)\ \textbf{r} : f(g(x))\ )\ (F,\ G)$$

Like function application, composition is strict in both arguments and follows a call-by-value semantics.

By unfolding we obtain the rule

$$\frac{\text{F o G}}{(\mathbf{m}\ x)\mathbf{r} : F(G(x))} \quad\Bigg\backslash \quad \begin{array}{l}\text{DEFINED}[\![F,\ G]\!]\\ \neg\ \text{OCCURS}[\![x\ \mathbf{in}\ F,G]\!]\end{array}$$

Note that the definedness condition is mandatory: an abstraction is a defined expression whereas the function composition is undefined if F or G is.

Examples:

(1) Selector functions for subtrees of S-expressions in LISP (cf. example 2 in 1.3.3):

   CAAR ≙ car o car
   CADR ≙ car o cdr
   CDAR ≙ cdr o car
   CDDR ≙ cdr o cdr

   and so on.

(2) A (partial) function deleting the first n elements of a sequence:

   (**Y** cut : (**nat** n)**funct**(**sequ**)**sequ** :
                   if n=0 **then** id
                           else cut(n-1) o rest **fi**)

(3) Function composition iterated n times:

   (**Y** it : (**funct**(**m**)**m** f, **nat** n)**funct**(**m**)**m** :
                   if n=0 **then** id
                           else it(f, n-1) o f **fi**)

   Obviously we have cut(n) = it(rest, n) .

The function composition is associative:

$$\frac{\text{F o (G o H)}}{\text{(F o G) o H}}$$

Therefore, the parentheses may be omitted in the concrete syntax.

II.2.1 The kernel: an expression language

2.1.3. PREALGORITHMIC CONSTRUCTS

Besides the algorithmic constructs, the wide spectrum language also comprises constructs for the descriptive specification of problems. For these constructs we define a mathematical semantics; in general, however, it is not possible to define for them an operational semantics yielding all values specified by the mathematical semantics. We therefore speak of prealgorithmic constructs. They are of particular importance for logic programming (see e.g. /Kowalski 83/).

Nevertheless there exist transformation rules which under certain circumstances allow the transformation of prealgorithmic constructs into constructs for which an operational semantics can be given, i.e., rules that convert suitable specifications into algorithms (cf. /Bauer, Gnatz 79/).

Notational conventions

For some of the descriptive language constructs the semantics is defined using the semantics of their determinate descendants. Let E be an expression of kind r containing a free identifier x of kind m. We associate with E the set $D[\![E]\!]$ of all determinate descendants of the value f of the abstraction $(m\ x)r : E$, i.e.,

$$D[\![E]\!] = \{ v \in DOM[\![\mathbf{funct(m)}r]\!] : v \sqsubseteq_D f \ \wedge \ DETERMINATE[\![v]\!] \cdot\}$$

where $\{f\} = B[\![(m\ x)r : E]\!]$.

Furthermore, for an element $u \in DOM[\![m]\!]$ we write E<u> for the expression $E[\![u\ \mathbf{for}\ x]\!]$.

(a) UNIVERSAL EQUALITY TEST

For expressions E_1, E_2 of the same object kind the equality test
$$E_1 = E_2$$
may yield
- $\perp$ if any of E_1, E_2 may yield $\perp$
- **true** if E_1 and E_2 may yield equal (defined) values
- **false** if E_1 and E_2 may yield different (defined) values .

More formally,

$$\mathbf{true} \in B[\![E_1 = E_2]\!] \quad \Leftrightarrow \quad \exists\ u_1 \in B^-[\![E_1]\!],\ u_2 \in B^-[\![E_2]\!] : u_1 = u_2 ,$$
$$\mathbf{false} \in B[\![E_1 = E_2]\!] \quad \Leftrightarrow \quad \exists\ u_1 \in B^-[\![E_1]\!],\ u_2 \in B^-[\![E_2]\!] : u_1 \neq u_2 ,$$
$$\perp \in B[\![E_1 = E_2]\!] \quad \Leftrightarrow \quad \perp \in B[\![E_1]\!] \ \vee \ \perp \in B[\![E_2]\!] .$$

For functions the equality test would not be monotonic in the Egli-Milner ordering; it is therefore excluded from the language.

Note that $B[\![E = E]\!]$ may be any non-empty subset of $\{\bot, \text{true}, \text{false}\}$ except $\{\text{false}\}$ or $\{\bot, \text{false}\}$, depending on the definedness and determinacy of E.

The universal equality test has the following properties related to the usual notions of reflexivity, symmetry, and transitivity:

(1) $B[\![E=E]\!] = \{\text{true}\}$ $\Leftrightarrow$ $\text{DETERMINATE}[\![E]\!] \;\wedge\; \text{DEFINED}[\![E]\!]$

(2) $B[\![E_1=E_2]\!] = B[\![E_2=E_1]\!]$

(3) $\text{true} \in B[\![E_1=E_2]\!] \;\wedge\; \text{true} \in B[\![E_2=E_3]\!] \;\Rightarrow\; \text{true} \in B[\![E_1=E_3]\!]$

In contrast to the "strong", two-valued equality which has been used in the description of types, the universal equality test is "weak" in that it yields undefined whenever one of its operands does. In particular,

$$B[\![\bot=\bot]\!] = \{\bot\} .$$

Examples:

(1) $B[\![(0 \;\Box\; 1) = (0 \;\Box\; 1)]\!] = \{\text{true}, \text{false}\}$

(2) $B[\![(0 \;\Box\; 1{\div}0) = (0 \;\Box\; 1{\div}0)]\!] = \{\bot, \text{true}\}$

(3) Differences to laws of algebraic types:
Let $s \in \text{DOM}[\![\text{sequ}]\!]$. Then

$$B[\![\neg \text{isempty}(s) \Rightarrow \text{append}(\text{top}(s),\text{rest}(s)) = s]\!] = \begin{cases} \{\text{true}\} & \text{if } \neg \text{isempty}(s) \\[2mm] \{\bot\} & \text{if isempty}(s) \end{cases}$$

However, the axiom

$\text{isempty}(s) \equiv \text{false} \;\Rightarrow\; \text{append}(\text{top}(s),\text{rest}(s)) \equiv s$

is valid in the type SEQU, since the invalid equation on the right-hand-side in the case of an empty s is protected by the implication. The same effect can be achieved in boolean expressions by using the conditional variants of the boolean operators:

$B[\![\neg \text{isempty}(s) \stackrel{\Rightarrow}{\Rightarrow} \text{append}(\text{top}(s),\text{rest}(s)) = s]\!] = \{\text{true}\}$.

In general the value of the equality test depends on the particular models of the basic types under consideration. By providing such a universal equality test, the strict modularization (and the corresponding protection mechanism) of the algebraic types of Chapter 1 is violated: by asking for the equality of certain terms it may be possible to find out which model of the basic type(s) (e.g. the initial or terminal one) is used. Thus the abstraction principle is violated when the equality test is used; therefore the program may no longer be independent of the actual implementation of the basic type(s). Moreover, since sets are also admissible as arguments of the universal equality, this test will in general be undecidable. For these reasons the universal equality test has to be viewed as a non-algorithmic construct, i.e., a program containing this universal equality is not executable (of course, it becomes operative as soon as the universal equality is replaced by an explicitly specified algorithm for the equality test (see 3.1.2)).

II.2.1 The kernel: an expression language

The inequality test is introduced by the obvious definitional transformation

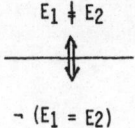

$$E_1 \neq E_2$$
$$\Updownarrow$$
$$\neg \ (E_1 = E_2)$$

(b) QUANTIFICATION

For a determinate boolean expression C containing at most one free identifier x of object kind **m** the universal quantification

$$\forall \ \textbf{m} \ x : C$$

yields

> **true**   iff C<u> yields **true** for all u ∈ DOM⟦**m**⟧ ,
>
> ⊥   iff C<u> yields ⊥ for at least one u ∈ DOM⟦**m**⟧ ,
>
> **false** iff C<u> is defined for all u ∈ DOM⟦**m**⟧ and yields
>   **false** for at least one u ∈ DOM⟦**m**⟧ .

According to this definition, the universal quantification can be implemented by an exhaustive search if DOM⟦**m**⟧ is finite. Note that quantification over functions is excluded; in the only semantics that would agree with the basic call-by-value structure of the language it would always yield ⊥ anyway.

Examples:

> $\forall$ **nat** x : x ≥ 0   yields **true** ,
>
> $\forall$ **nat** x : x < 10   yields **false** ,
>
> $\forall$ **nat** x : 100÷x = 20   yields ⊥ since 100÷0 is not defined.

For a convenient way of appropriately restricting the domain of quantification see 2.1.4.4(b).

We extend the definition to possibly non-determinate predicates C:

> B⟦ $\forall$ **m** x : C ⟧ contains
>
> **true**   iff $\forall$u∈DOM⟦**m**⟧ : **true** ∈ B⟦C<u>⟧,
>
> **false** iff $\exists$u∈DOM⟦**m**⟧ : **false** ∈ B⟦C<u>⟧ $\wedge$ $\forall$u∈DOM⟦**m**⟧ : B⟦C<u>⟧ ≠ {⊥} ,
>
> ⊥   iff $\exists$u∈DOM⟦**m**⟧ : ⊥ ∈ B⟦C<u>⟧.

Examples:

> B⟦ $\forall$ **nat** x : (x ≥ 0 ▯ x < 10) ⟧ = {**true, false**}
>
> B⟦ $\forall$ **nat** x : (x < 10 ▯ 100÷x = 20) ⟧ = {⊥, **false**}
>
> B⟦ $\forall$ **nat** x : (x ≥ 0 ▯ 100÷x = 20) ⟧ = {⊥, **true, false**}

The existential quantification is introduced as a derived construct by the definitional transformation rule

$$\exists \, m \, x : C$$

$$\neg \, (\forall \, m \, x : \neg \, C)$$

In this way the fundamental duality between universal and existential quantification holds also for non-determinate and for partial predicates.

Explicitly,
$B[\![\exists \, m \, x : C]\!]$ contains

false	iff	$\forall u \epsilon DOM[\![m]\!] : \textbf{false} \, \epsilon \, B[\![C\langle u\rangle]\!]$,
true	iff	$\exists u \epsilon DOM[\![m]\!] : \textbf{true} \, \epsilon \, B[\![C\langle u\rangle]\!] \, \wedge \, \forall u \epsilon DOM[\![m]\!] : B[\![C\langle u\rangle]\!] \neq \{\bot\}$,
$\bot$	iff	$\exists u \epsilon DOM[\![m]\!] : \bot \, \epsilon \, B[\![C\langle u\rangle]\!]$.

Examples:

$B[\![\exists \, \textbf{nat} \, x : x \geq 10]\!] = \{\textbf{true}\}$

$B[\![\exists \, \textbf{nat} \, x : x < 0]\!] = \{\textbf{false}\}$

$B[\![\exists \, \textbf{nat} \, x : 100 \div x = 20]\!] = \{\bot\}$

$B[\![\exists \, \textbf{nat} \, x : (x \geq 10 \; [] \; 100 \div x = 20)]\!] = \{\bot, \textbf{true}\}$

$B[\![\exists \, \textbf{nat} \, x : (x < 10 \; [] \; 100 \div x = 20)]\!] = \{\bot, \textbf{false}\}$

Note that both universal and existential quantification constitute scopes and bind the identifiers being quantified over; the same holds for the comprehensive choice, the description, and the set comprehension to be defined below.

(c) COMPREHENSIVE CHOICE

The comprehensive choice is a quantifier ("choice operator") which allows to choose an element characterized by a boolean expression C. For an object kind **m** the expression

some $m \, x : C$

(with determinate C) yields some value $u \, \epsilon \, DOM[\![m]\!]$ such that $C\langle u\rangle$ yields **true**, provided such a value exists. If such a value does not exist, or if $C\langle u\rangle$ is not defined for some u, then the expression does not yield a defined value. Of course, the comprehensive choice is non-determinate in general, therefore we restrict its use to non-functional kinds.

II.2.1 The kernel: an expression language

More formally, with $V = \{ u \in DOM[\![m]\!] : B[\![C<u>]\!] = \{true\} \}$,

$$B[\![some \ m \ x : C]\!] = \begin{cases} V & if \ V \neq \emptyset \ and \ \forall \ u \in DOM[\![m]\!] : \bot \notin B[\![C<u>]\!] \\ \{\bot\} & otherwise \end{cases}$$

Examples:

$B[\![some \ nat \ x : x < 10]\!] = \{0, 1, 2, \ldots, 9\}$

$B[\![some \ nat \ x : 100 \div x = 20]\!] = \{\bot\}$

$B[\![some \ nat \ x : x * x = 2]\!] = \{\bot\}$

Arbitrary splitting of a character sequence into two parts:

$B[\![some \ charsequ \ a, \ charsequ \ b : a \ \& \ b = 'END']\!] =$
  $\{ ('', 'END'), ('E', 'ND'), ('EN', 'D'), ('END', '') \}$

For non-determinate C the meaning of the comprehensive choice is defined by

$$B[\![some \ m \ x : C]\!] = \bigcup_{c \in D[\![C]\!]} B[\![some \ m \ x : c(x)]\!] .$$

There is a close connection between the comprehensive choice and the existential quantifier, which may be indicated by the following semantical implications:

$true \in B[\![\exists \ m \ x : C]\!] \quad \Leftrightarrow \quad true \in B[\![C[\![(some \ m \ x : C) \ for \ x]\!]]\!]$

$false \in B[\![\exists \ m \ x : C]\!] \quad \Rightarrow \quad \bot \in B[\![C[\![(some \ m \ x : C) \ for \ x]\!]]\!]$

There exists also a connection with the finite choice:

$$\text{some } m \ x : x = E_1 \ \bigvee \ x = E_2$$

$$\Updownarrow \qquad \Big\langle \begin{array}{l} \text{DETERMINATE}[\![E_i]\!] \\ \text{DEFINED}[\![E_i]\!] \end{array}$$

$$(E_1 \ [] \ E_2)$$

(d) <u>DESCRIPTION</u>

The description is a special case of the comprehensive choice ("description operator"). It is introduced as a notational extension by the transformation rule

$$\text{that } m \ x : C$$

$$\Updownarrow$$

$$\text{some } m \ x : (C \ \bigwedge \ \forall \ m \ y : C[\![y \ for \ x]\!] \Rightarrow x = y)$$

The description is determinate iff C is determinate. Then it denotes that element u ∈ DOM⟦m⟧ for which C⟨u⟩ yields **true**, if there exists exactly one such element, and ⊥ otherwise.

Examples:

(1) integral dual logarithm of a natural number n:

that nat x : n+2 < 2↑x ∧ 2↑x ≤ n   or

that nat x : 2↑x ≤ n ∧ n < 2↑(x+1)

(2) rest of a non-empty sequence s:

that sequ r : ∃ m t : make(t) & r = s

(3) rest of the integral division a÷b:

that nat r : (∃ **nat** q : a = r+q*b ∧ 0 ≤ r ∧ r < b)

There is again a close connection between the description and the quantification "there exists exactly one element x such that C holds".

(e) DESCRIPTIVE SET CONSTRUCTS

To denote a subset of a domain DOM⟦m⟧ by a characteristic boolean expression C we introduce the set comprehension

$$\{m \; x : C\} \; .$$

We restrict the comprehension to object kinds **m** (and thus to flat domains); otherwise, as in the case of the universal equality, non-monotonic operations would arise.

For determinate C, the set {m x : C} consists of all elements u ∈ DOM⟦m⟧ for which C⟨u⟩ yields **true**. If for some u ∈ DOM⟦m⟧ the value of C⟨u⟩ is not defined then the value of the set comprehension is not defined as well.

Note that these *descriptive* sets are quite different from the elements of the carrier of sort **choiceset** in a model of CHOICESET (cf. I.6.1) or of sort **fset** in a model of FINSET (cf. 1.4 (c)). In particular, sets of kind **set m** may be infinite, whereas all **choicesets** and **fsets** represent finite sets.

Examples:

{**nat** x : x < 10}   denotes the set {0, 1, 2, 3, 4, 5, 6, 7, 8, 9}

{**nat** x : (x÷2)*2 = x}   denotes the set of even numbers

{**nat** x : x*x = 2}   denotes the empty set

{**nat** x : 100÷x = 20}   is not defined since 100÷0 is not defined .

If C is a non-determinate expression then

$$B⟦\{m \; x : C\}⟧ \quad = \quad \bigcup_{c \in D⟦C⟧} \quad B⟦\{m \; x : c(x)\}⟧ \; .$$

II.2.1 The kernel: an expression language

Examples:

(1) $B[\![\{\text{nat } x : (x < 2 \; [] \; x*x = 9)\}]\!] = \mathcal{P}(\{0, 1, 3\})$

(2) $B[\![\{\text{nat } x : (x < 2 \; [] \; 9 \div x = 3)\}]\!] = \mathcal{P}(\{0, 1, 3\}) \cup \{\bot\}$

(3) $B[\![\{\text{nat } x : (\text{true } [] \text{ false})\}]\!] = \mathcal{P}(\text{DOM}[\![\text{nat}]\!])$

A basic operation on descriptive sets is the element-relation e. Consider semantic values $e \in \text{DOM}[\![\mathbf{m}]\!]$ and $s \in \text{DOM}[\![\text{set } \mathbf{m}]\!]$. Then we have

$$B[\![e \; e \; s]\!] = \begin{cases} \{\text{true}\} & \text{if } e \neq \bot \text{ and } s \neq \bot \text{ and } e \; e \; s \\ \{\text{false}\} & \text{if } e \neq \bot \text{ and } s \neq \bot \text{ and } e \notin s \\ \{\bot\} & \text{if } e = \bot \text{ or } s = \bot \end{cases}$$

For $E \in \text{EXPR}_\mathbf{m}$ and $S \in \text{EXPR}_{\text{set } \mathbf{m}}$ we define

$$B[\![E \; e \; S]\!] = \underset{e e B[\![E]\!]}{U} \quad \underset{s e B[\![S]\!]}{U} \quad B[\![e \; e \; s]\!] \; .$$

Thus, $\bot \; e \; B[\![E \; e \; S]\!] \iff \bot \; e \; B[\![E]\!] \lor \bot \; e \; B[\![S]\!]$.

Obviously the following transformation rule is valid:

Common operations on descriptive sets such as union, intersection, and complement are introduced as notational extensions by definitional transformation rules:

SET INCLUSION

PROPER SET INCLUSION

SET UNION

$S_1 \cup S_2$

$KIND[\![S_1]\!] = KIND[\![S_2]\!] = set\ \blacksquare$

$((set\ \blacksquare\ s_1, set\ \blacksquare\ s_2)\ set\ \blacksquare :$
$\{\blacksquare\ x : x\ \epsilon\ s_1\ \vee\ x\ \epsilon\ s_2\})\ (S_1, S_2)$

SET INTERSECTION

$S_1 \cap S_2$

$KIND[\![S_1]\!] = KIND[\![S_2]\!] = set\ \blacksquare$

$((set\ \blacksquare\ s_1, set\ \blacksquare\ s_2)\ set\ \blacksquare :$
$\{\blacksquare\ x : x\ \epsilon\ s_1\ \wedge\ x\ \epsilon\ s_2\})\ (S_1, S_2)$

SET DIFFERENCE

$S_1 \setminus S_2$

$KIND[\![S_1]\!] = KIND[\![S_2]\!] = set\ \blacksquare$

$((set\ \blacksquare\ s_1, set\ \blacksquare\ s_2)\ set\ \blacksquare :$
$\{\blacksquare\ x : x\ \epsilon\ s_1\ \wedge\ \neg\ (x\ \epsilon\ s_2)\})\ (S_1, S_2)$

SET COMPLEMENT

$C\ S$

$KIND[\![S]\!] = set\ \blacksquare$

$\{\blacksquare\ x : \mathbf{true}\} \setminus S$

For determinate set expressions the transformations above can of course be simplified to the usual mathematical definitions, e.g.

$S_1 \subseteq S_2$

$KIND[\![S_1]\!] = KIND[\![S_2]\!] = set\ \blacksquare$
$DETERMINATE[\![S_1]\!]\ \wedge\ DETERMINATE[\![S_2]\!]$

$\forall\ \blacksquare\ x : x\ \epsilon\ S_1\ \Rightarrow\ x\ \epsilon\ S_2$

II.2.1 The kernel: an expression language

Finally, we introduce the possibility of explicitly enumerating the elements of a finite set:

$$\{E_1, \ldots, E_n\}$$

$$\Updownarrow \qquad\qquad\qquad \text{KIND} [\![E_i]\!] = \blacksquare$$

$$((\blacksquare\ x_1,\ldots,\blacksquare\ x_n)\ \textbf{set}\ \blacksquare : $$
$$\{\blacksquare\ x\ :\ x{=}x_1\ \bigvee\ \cdots\ \bigvee\ x{=}x_n\})\ (E_1,\ldots,E_n)$$

Examples:

(1) $\{\textbf{nat}\ x\ :\ (x < 2\ \square\ x{*}x = 9)\}\ \subseteq\ \{\textbf{nat}\ x\ :\ x < 4\}$ yields **true**

(2) $B [\![(\{0\}\ \square\ \{1\})\ \wedge\ (\{0\}\ \square\ \{1\})]\!] = \{\emptyset, \{0\}, \{1\}\}$

(3) $B [\![\{\textbf{nat}\ x\ :\ x < 4\} \setminus \{\textbf{nat}\ x\ :\ (x < 2\ \square\ 9{\div}x = 3)\}]\!] =$
   $\{\ \bot,\ \{1,2,3\},\ \{2,3\},\ \{1,2\},\ \{2\}\ \}$

(4) $B [\![\{(0\ \square\ 1),\ (2\ \square\ 3)\}]\!] = \{\ \{0,2\},\ \{0,3\},\ \{1,2\},\ \{1,3\}\ \}$

2.1.4. FURTHER NOTATIONAL EXTENSIONS

2.1.4.1. GUARDED EXPRESSION

By combining the concepts of finite choice and conditional expression we introduce guarded expressions as a notational extension. It is an important practical tool in programming, since it shows the conditions for each branch explicitly.

Let $E_1,\ldots,E_n$ be expressions of an object kind $\blacksquare$. The following transformation rules define the meaning of the guarded expression:

if C_1 **then** E_1 $\square$ ...
$\square$ C_n **then** E_n **else** E_{n+1} **fi**

$$\Updownarrow \qquad\qquad\qquad n \geq 2$$

(**if** C_1 **then** E_1 **else** G_1 **fi** $\square$ ...
$\square$ **if** C_n **then** E_n **else** G_n **fi**   )

where

$G_i \hat{=}$ **if** C_1 **then** E_1 $\square$ ... $\square$ C_{i-1} **then** E_{i-1}
        $\square$ C_{i+1} **then** E_{i+1} $\square$ ... $\square$ C_n **then** E_n **else** E_{n+1} **fi**

The **else**-part of the guarded expression may be omitted. In this case the guarded expression does not yield a defined value if all guards yield **false**:

$$
\begin{array}{l}
\text{if } C_1 \text{ then } E_1 \;[]\; \dots \\
[]\; C_n \text{ then } E_n \qquad\qquad \text{fi} \\
\Updownarrow \\
\text{if } C_1 \text{ then } E_1 \;[]\; \dots \\
[]\; C_n \text{ then } E_n \\
\qquad \text{else ERROR}_m \text{ fi}
\end{array}
\qquad
\left\langle
\begin{array}{l}
n > 0 \\
\text{KIND}[\![E_i]\!] = \blacksquare
\end{array}
\right.
$$

(In 2.1.2 (g), ERROR$_m$ was defined as an expression of kind $\blacksquare$ with the only value $\bot$.)

A guarded expression of functional kind is not admissible since it would lead to a non-deterministic choice between functions.

Examples:

(1) Absolute value:

      if $x \geq 0$ **then** x

      $[]$ $x \leq 0$ **then** -x **fi**

By the definitional transformations this can be reduced to

    (**if** $x \geq 0$ **then** x **else if** $x < 0$ **then** -x **else** ERROR$_{int}$ **fi fi**

    $[]$ **if** $x \leq 0$ **then** -x **else if** $x \geq 0$ **then** x **else** ERROR$_{int}$ **fi fi**) .

(2) "Inverse" of the absolute value:

      if $y \geq 0$ **then** (y $[]$ -y) **fi**

This is equivalent to

      if $y \geq 0$ **then** (y $[]$ -y) **else** ERROR$_{int}$ **fi** .

From the definitional transformation rules above, we can derive the following two rules:

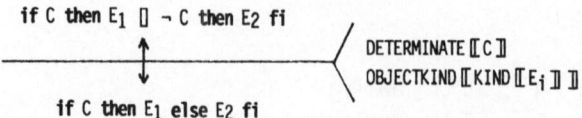

$$
\begin{array}{c}
\text{if } C \text{ then } E_1 \;[]\; \neg\, C \text{ then } E_2 \text{ fi} \\
\Updownarrow \\
\text{if } C \text{ then } E_1 \text{ else } E_2 \text{ fi}
\end{array}
\qquad
\left\langle
\begin{array}{l}
\text{DETERMINATE}[\![C]\!] \\
\text{OBJECTKIND}[\![\text{KIND}[\![E_i]\!]]\!]
\end{array}
\right.
$$

II.2.1 The kernel: an expression language

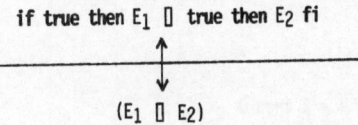

Note that these two rules also could be used to introduce the conditional expression and the finite choice on the basis of the guarded expression. However, we prefer to keep the concepts of finite choice and conditional expression clearly separated from each other.

2.1.4.2. PARTIAL APPLICATION

When an expression F denoting an n-ary function (n≥1) of kind **funct**(m_1,...,m_n)r is applied to an n-tuple (E_1,...,E_n) of argument expressions E_i, an arbitrary number k (1≤k≤n) of arguments E_{p_1},...,E_{p_k} ({p_1,...,p_k} ⊆ {1,...,n}) are allowed to be missing. This partial application is by definition equivalent to forming a k-ary function which has the missing arguments as parameters (generalized "Currying"). For example, in the case n = 3, k = 2, and (p_1, p_2) = (1, 3) we have for determinate and defined expressions F and E_2:

$$F(\underline{\cdot}, E_2, \underline{\cdot})$$
$$\Updownarrow$$
$$(m_1\ x_1,\ m_3\ x_3)\ r : F(x_1, E_2, x_3)$$

KIND⟦E_2⟧ = m_2, KIND⟦F⟧ = **funct**(m_1,m_2,m_3)r
¬ OCCURS⟦x_1,x_3 **in** F,E_2⟧
DEFINED⟦F⟧
DEFINED⟦E_2⟧ ∧ DETERMINATE⟦E_2⟧

In the general case of possibly undefined E_2 or F or non-determinate E_2 the bottom scheme is embedded into an application of a functional:

$$F(\underline{\cdot}, E_2, \underline{\cdot})$$
$$\Updownarrow$$

KIND⟦F⟧ = **funct** (m_1, m_2, m_3) r,
KIND⟦E_2⟧ = m_2,

((**funct** (m_1, m_2, m_3) r f, m_2 x2) **funct** (m_1, m_3) r:
   ((m_1 x1, m_3 x3) r : f(x1, x2, x3)))(F, E2)

The generalization of this definitional transformation to arbitrary n, k is straightforward.

Partial application has been studied in /Ershov 78/; it allows a number of interesting and powerful applications.

Examples:
(1) A variant of Ackermann's function
   (**Y** ackermann:

(**nat** i, **nat** x, **nat** y) **nat**:
if i = 0 **then** succ(y)
      else if y = 0 **then if** i = 1 **then** x
              else if i = 2 **then** 0
                 else 1 **fi fi**
      else ackermann(pred(i), x, ackermann(i, x, pred(y))) **fi fi**)

By partial application one obtains

successor:	ackermann(0, **some nat** x : **true**, $\cdot$)
addition:	ackermann(1, $\cdot$, $\cdot$)
multiplication:	ackermann(2, $\cdot$, $\cdot$)
power:	ackermann(3, $\cdot$, $\cdot$)
Ackermann-Peter-Function:	ackermann($\cdot$, 2, $\cdot$)

(2) A selector function on sequences
    (**Y** sel:
      (**nat** n, **charsequ** s : $1 \le n \wedge n \le \text{length}(s)$) **charsequ** :
      if n = 1 **then** top(s)
           else sel(n-1, rest(s)) **fi**)

The partial application sel(n, $\cdot$) then yields a selector function for the n-th element of a sequence; it is equivalent to
      top o rest o ... o rest

$$\underbrace{\phantom{\text{top o rest o ... o rest}}}_{n-1}$$

(3) Backus' while-combinator (cf. /Backus 78/) is obtained by partial application of the function cwhile (cf. 2.1.2 (g), Example (4)):
    (**Y** while, cwhile:
      (**funct** (m) **bool** p, **funct** (m) m f) **funct** (m) m :
          cwhile(p, f, $\cdot$),
      (**funct** (m) **bool** p, **funct** (m) m f, m x) m :
         if p(x) **then** cwhile(p, f, f(x))
             else x   **fi**   )

II.2.1 The kernel: an expression language

For the partial application various transformation rules can be proved, e.g.

$$F(E_1, \underline{\cdot}, \underline{\cdot})(\underline{\cdot}, E_3) \quad \Big/ \quad \begin{array}{l} KIND[\![F]\!] = \textbf{funct } (m_1, m_2, m_3) \ r \\ KIND[\![E_1]\!] = m_1 \\ KIND[\![E_3]\!] = m_3 \end{array}$$

$$\Updownarrow$$

$$F(E_1, \underline{\cdot}, E_3)$$

If all arguments are (stepwise) supplied, of course partial application and function application coincide:

$$F(E_1, \underline{\cdot}, \underline{\cdot})(E_2, E_3) \quad \Big/ \quad \begin{array}{l} KIND[\![F]\!] = \textbf{funct } (m_1, m_2, m_3) \ r \\ KIND[\![E_i]\!] = m_i \quad (i=1, 2, 3) \end{array}$$

$$\Updownarrow$$

$$F(E_1, E_2, E_3)$$

If all arguments are missing then the partial application and the function expression are equivalent:

$$F(\underline{\cdot}, \underline{\cdot}, \underline{\cdot}) \quad \Big< \quad KIND[\![F]\!] = \textbf{funct } (m_1, m_2, m_3) \ r$$

$$\Updownarrow$$

$$F$$

2.1.4.3. FUNCTION TUPLING AND FUNCTION CONSTRUCTION

We allow also that a tuple $(f_1,...,f_n)$ of functions of the kinds $\textbf{funct}(m_i)r_i$ be applied to a tuple $(u_1,...,u_n)$ of kind $(m_1,...,m_n)$ to yield the tuple $(f_1(u_1),...,f_n(u_n))$ of kind $(r_1,...,r_n)$. The definitional transformation reads as follows:

$$F(E) \quad \Big/ \quad \begin{array}{l} KIND[\![F]\!] = (\textbf{funct}(m_1)r_1,...,\textbf{funct}(m_n)r_n) \\ KIND[\![E]\!] = (m_1,...,m_n) \end{array}$$

$$\Updownarrow$$

$$((\textbf{funct}(m_1)r_1 \ f_1,...,\textbf{funct}(m_n)r_n \ f_n, \ m_1 \ x_1,...,m_n \ x_n) \ (r_1,...r_n) :$$
$$\quad (f_1(x_1),...,f_n(x_n)) \qquad\qquad) \ (F, E)$$

Function construction is a special case of function tupling. For expressions F_i of kind $\textbf{funct}(m)r_i$ $(1 \leq i \leq n)$ the expression $[F_1,...,F_n]$ is of kind $\textbf{funct}(m)(r_1,...,r_n)$. Its meaning is specified by

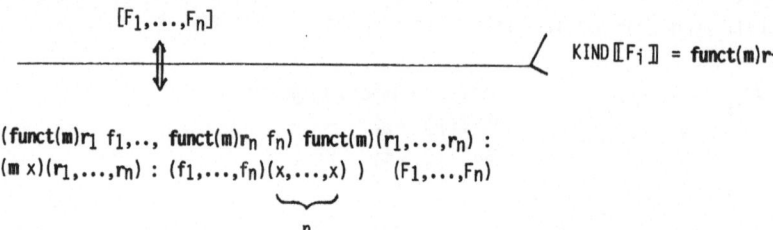

$$((\textbf{funct(m)}r_1 \ f_1,.., \ \textbf{funct(m)}r_n \ f_n) \ \textbf{funct(m)}(r_1,...,r_n) :$$
$$(\textbf{m} \ x)(r_1,...,r_n) : (f_1,...,f_n)(x,...,x) \ ) \quad (F_1,...,F_n)$$

n

This construct is also used in Backus' functional language FP (cf. /Backus 78/).

Example:
  (1) Negative of a rational number represented as a pair of integers:
      $B [\![(\ (\textbf{int} \ i)\textbf{int: } -i \ , \ (\textbf{int} \ i)\textbf{int: } i \ )(3,5)]\!]$ = { (-3,5) }
  (2) Application of a function to all elements of a sequence:
      (Y applytoall:
          (funct(char)char f, charsequ s) charsequ:
          if isempty(s)
            then s
            else append o [f o top, applytoall(f, ·) o rest] (s) fi)

2.1.4.4. ASSERTIONS

Assertions or restrictions are boolean expressions that state certain properties at particular
"places" in a program. Essentially there are two ways of viewing assertions: Either they are
treated as "formal comments" which do not influence the semantics of a program; then we can
talk about "the correctness of a program with respect to its assertions". Or we consider the
assertions to be relevant for the semantics of a program, i.e., every assertion is evaluated, and
if it is false, then the result of the program is undefined. We follow the second alternative,
since then transformation rules containing assertions are guaranteed to be meaning-preserving
also with respect to assertions. Note that in this view a program containing non-algorithmic
assertions is non-algorithmic itself.

II.2.1 The kernel: an expression language

(a) <u>PARAMETER AND RESULT RESTRICTIONS</u>

The restriction of the domain of a function is expressed by a predicate in the parameter list.
We define

$$(m\ x\ :\ C)\ \mathbf{r}\ :\ E$$
$$\Updownarrow$$
$$(m\ x)\ \mathbf{r}\ :\ \mathbf{if}\ C\ \mathbf{then}\ E\ \mathbf{fi}\ .$$

KIND$[\![\,C\,]\!]$ = **bool**
KIND$[\![\,E\,]\!]$ = **r**

According to this rule, the application of this function to an element u ∈ DOM$[\![\,m\,]\!]$ that does
not satisfy C<u> yields ⊥ .

<u>Example:</u>
 (Y mod : (**nat** a, **nat** b : b > 0) **nat** :
  if a < b **then** a
    else mod(a - b, b) **fi**) .

Analogously, the restriction of the range of a function is defined by

$$(m\ x)(\mathbf{r}\ y\ :\ C)\ :\ E$$
$$\Updownarrow$$
$$(m\ x)\ \mathbf{r}\ :\ ((\mathbf{r}\ y)\ \mathbf{r}\ :\ \mathbf{if}\ C\ \mathbf{then}\ y\ \mathbf{fi})(E)\ .$$

KIND$[\![\,C\,]\!]$ = **bool**
KIND$[\![\,E\,]\!]$ = **r**

Dually to the parameter restriction which acts as a precondition, the result restriction C
asserts a postcondition.

<u>Example:</u>
 (Y square : (**real** x)(**real** y : y ≥ 0) : x * x)

(b) <u>QUANTIFICATION OVER RESTRICTED DOMAINS</u>

The restriction of the domain of a quantifier can be expressed locally; it is defined by the
following transformations:

Universal quantification:

$$\forall \ (\text{m} \ x : C_1) : C_2$$

$$\forall \ \blacksquare \ x : C_1 \ \dot{\Rightarrow} \ C_2$$

Existential quantification, comprehensive choice, description:
Let Q stand for any of the quantifiers $\exists$, **some**, **that**. Then

$$Q \ (\text{m} \ x : C_1) : C_2$$

$$Q \ \blacksquare \ x : C_1 \ \wedge \ C_2$$

Set Comprehension:

$$\{(\text{m} \ x \ : C_1) : C_2\}$$

$$\{\blacksquare \ x : C_1 \ \wedge \ C_2\}$$

Examples:

$\exists$ (**nat** $x : x > 0$) : $100 \div x = x$	yields	**true**
some (**nat** $x : x > 0$) : $100 \div x = x$	yields	10
$\forall$ (**nat** $x : x * x = 2$) : $100 \div x = x$	yields	**true**
some (**nat** $x : x * x = 2$) : $100 \div x = x$	does not yield a defined value.	

(c) RESTRICTION OF SETS AND FUNCTIONALITIES

The restriction of the base kind of a set kind is simply extended to a restriction of the set kind:

$$\text{set} \ (\text{m} \ x : C)$$

$$(\text{set} \ \blacksquare \ s : \forall \ \blacksquare \ x : x \in s \ \Rightarrow \ C)$$

This technique does not apply to function kinds with restricted parameter and result kinds since an analogous specification of the restricted functionality would lead to a non-strict predicate. Instead, the restriction of a function parameter f is propagated to all occurrences of f

II.2.1 The kernel: an expression language

according to the rule

$$(n\ a,\ \textbf{funct}(m\ y : C_1)(r\ z : C_2)\ f)p : E$$

⇕

$$(n\ a,\ \textbf{funct}(m)r\ f)p : E[\![((m\ y : C_1)(r\ z : C_2) : f(y))\ \textbf{for}\ f]\!]\ .$$

Note that according to this rule the restriction is only checked if the parameter f is actually applied within E.

If a restricted functionality occurs as the range of an abstraction, the restriction is moved into the body by the transformation

$$(n\ z)\textbf{funct}(m\ x : C_1)(r\ y : C_2) : E$$

⇕

$$(n\ z)\textbf{funct}(m)r : ((m\ x : C_1)(r\ y : C_2) : E(x))\ .$$

Example:
  If sqrt gives the square root of a positive real number, a functional constructing the root of a function is defined by

$$(\ \textbf{funct}\ (\textbf{real}\ x)(\textbf{real}\ y : y \geq 0)\ f\ )\ \textbf{funct}\ (\textbf{real}\ x)(\textbf{real}\ y : y \geq 0) :$$
$$\text{sqrt} \circ f$$

2.2. THE FULL APPLICATIVE LANGUAGE: DECLARATIONS

2.2.1. SURVEY

Following general mathematical conventions we introduce declarations of objects and functions. Such declarations in general improve the readability of programs considerably, but, of course, they do not increase their computational power. Their semantics can therefore be defined by axiomatic transformation rules (similar to those in /Landin 64, 66/). The extended applicative language obtained in this way still satisfies the requirement of "referential transparency" (cf. /Quine 60/).

In order to provide a syntactic frame for expressions together with declarations, we introduce a new syntactic entity, called section. The scope of a declared identifier ranges from its declaration to the end of the smallest surrounding section. In the case of collective function declarations which introduce identifiers for a system of (mutually recursive) functions, the declarations themselves are included in the scope; in the case of object declarations they are not, which means that objects must not be defined recursively (infinite objects are ruled out).

2.2.2. SEMANTICS OF THE FULL APPLICATIVE LANGUAGE

(a) OBJECT DECLARATION

The meaning of an object declaration is defined by the transformation rule

$$
\begin{array}{c}
\ulcorner \mathbf{m}\ x \equiv E_1 \ ; \ E_2 \lrcorner \\
\Updownarrow \\
((\mathbf{m}\ x)\ \mathbf{r} : E_2)(E_1)
\end{array}
\left\{
\begin{array}{l}
\neg\ \text{OCCURS}\llbracket x \text{ in } E_1 \rrbracket \\
\mathbf{r} = \text{KIND}\llbracket E_2 \rrbracket
\end{array}
\right.
$$

The symbol ";" can be read as "within". Note that $\mathbf{m}$ x and $\mathbf{r}$ in general stand for tuples $(\mathbf{m}_1\ x_1, \ \ldots, \ \mathbf{m}_n\ x_n)$ and $(\mathbf{r}_1, \ \ldots, \ \mathbf{r}_k)$.

Examples:
    (1) Square roots of an integer y:
        $\ulcorner$ int r $\equiv$ some int x : y = x$\uparrow$2 ; (r, -r) $\lrcorner$
    (2) Square of the area of a triangle:
        $\ulcorner$ real s $\equiv$ (a + b + c)/2 ; s $*$ (s - a) $*$ (s - b) $*$ (s - c)/2 $\lrcorner$

(b) FUNCTION DECLARATION

The explanation of the function declaration in general requires the application of the fixpoint operator Y in order to cope with recursion:

$$
\begin{array}{c}
\textbf{funct}\ f \equiv (\mathbf{m}\ x)\ \mathbf{r} : E \\
\Updownarrow \\
\textbf{funct}\ (\mathbf{m})\ \mathbf{r}\ f \equiv (Y\ f : (\mathbf{m}\ x)\ \mathbf{r} : E)
\end{array}
$$

Thus, the declaration is reduced to an object declaration (specifying an object of functionality **funct** (**m**) **r**). In this rule the fixpoint operator is applied even if the identifier f does not occur in E. In this latter case the following rule (cf. 2.1.2 (g)) can be applied and leads to a simplification:

II.2.2 The applicative language

$$\mathbf{Y}\ f : (\mathbf{m}\ x)\ \mathbf{r} : E$$

$\neg$ OCCURS $[\![\, f$ in $E\,]\!]$

$$(\mathbf{m}\ x)\ \mathbf{r} : E$$

The generalization to a system

      funct $f_1 \equiv A_1, \ldots,$ **funct** $f_n \equiv A_n$

of mutually recursive functions is straightforward. Note that each f_i may occur in any of the abstractions A_j.

Example:

  ⌈ **funct** isprefix ≡ (**charsequ** s, **charsequ** t) **bool** :

        if isempty(s)

          then true

          else if isempty(t) **then false**

                   else top(s) = top(t) $\wedge$ isprefix(rest(s), rest(t)) **fi fi** ;

    isprefix('HOT', 'HOTEL')   ⌋

(c) <u>SECTION</u>

To simplify the notation, we avoid accumulations of section brackets by using association to the right. The definitional transformation rule reads

$$\lceil D_1\ ;\ \ldots\ ;\ D_k\ ;\ \lceil D_{k+1}\ ;\ E_2\ \rfloor\ \rfloor$$

$k \geq 1$

$$\lceil D_1\ ;\ \ldots\ ;\ D_k\ ;\ D_{k+1}\ ;\ E_2\ \rfloor$$

where the D_i are function declarations or object declarations.

2.2.3. NOTATIONAL EXTENSIONS

(a) POSTPONED DECLARATION

Sometimes the readability of a program is increased if the declarations follow the applications. This is enabled by a notational extension defined by

$$\ulcorner \text{E } \textbf{where } D \urcorner$$

$$\Updownarrow$$

$$\ulcorner D \text{ ; } E \urcorner$$

Example:

$\ulcorner$ twice(square) (3) < 100 **where**

    funct twice ≡ (**funct** (**nat**) **nat** f) **funct** (**nat**) **nat** :

        (**nat** n) **nat** : f(f(n)) ,

    funct square ≡ (**nat** n) **nat** : n * n $\urcorner$

(b) ASSERTION FOR AN OBJECT DECLARATION

Corresponding to the restriction of the parameters in a function abstraction we can give an assertion for a declared object:

$$(\textbf{m } x : C) \equiv E$$

$$\Updownarrow$$

$$\textbf{m } x \equiv ((\textbf{m } x : C) \textbf{ m} : x)(E)$$

Thus applications of functions with parameter restrictions can be transformed into object declarations with restrictions:

$$((\textbf{m } x : C) \textbf{ r} : E_2)(E_1)$$

$$\Updownarrow \qquad \begin{cases} \neg \text{ OCCURS} \llbracket x \textbf{ in } E_1 \rrbracket \\ \text{KIND} \llbracket E_2 \rrbracket = r \end{cases}$$

$$\ulcorner (\textbf{m } x : C) \equiv E_1 \text{ ; } E_2 \urcorner$$

Examples:

$\ulcorner$ (**nat** n : n < b) ≡ mod(a, b) ; b - n $\urcorner$

$\ulcorner$ (**real** y : y ≥ 0) ≡ x * x; y $\urcorner$

II.2.2 The applicative language

(c) FUNCTION DECLARATION IN THE STYLE OF ALGEBRAIC TYPES

Especially in connection with program transformations it may be advantageous to separate the functionality of a function from its body. The corresponding notation resembles that used in the signature and the laws of an algebraic type. It is introduced by

> **funct** (m y : C) **r** f,
>   f(x) ≡ E

$$\Updownarrow$$

funct f ≡ (m x : C⟦x for y⟧) **r** : E

The generalization to systems of functions is obvious.

Example:
    The functions hasrestzero, hasrestone, hasresttwo of I.1.1.3 may also be defined as follows:

```
funct (nat) bool hasrestzero,
funct (nat) bool hasrestone,
funct (nat) bool hasresttwo,

hasrestzero(n) ≡
    if n=0              then true
    [] n>0 ∧ even(n) then hasrestzero(n ÷ 2)
    [] n>0 ∧ odd(n)  then hasrestone(n ÷ 2)  fi ,

hasrestone(n)  ≡
    if n=0              then false
    [] n>0 ∧ even(n) then hasresttwo(n ÷ 2)
    [] n>0 ∧ odd(n)  then hasrestzero(n ÷ 2) fi ,

hasresttwo(n)  ≡
    if n=0              then false
    [] n>0 ∧ even(n) then hasrestone(n ÷ 2)
    [] n>0 ∧ odd(n)  then hasresttwo(n ÷ 2)  fi
```

2.3. THE PROCEDURAL LANGUAGE: PROGRAM VARIABLES AND PROCEDURES

2.3.1. SURVEY

In contrast to the applicative language, the constructs of the procedural language are more oriented towards the common type of machine (often called "von Neumann type machine"). Usually, one central notion in the treatment of such machines is that of a *(machine) state* (cf. /McCarthy 60/, /Floyd 67/, /Hoare 69/, /Scott, Strachey 71/, /Dijkstra 76/), or of *erasable store*. In the case of *program variables*, the state reflects the association of values with identifiers at a given moment. A statement then denotes a state transition.

In CIP-L, statements may only occur within a segment which forms a new expression out of a sequence of declarations and statements followed by an expression. The value of such a segment is the value of its final expression after execution of its statements.

Rather than explicitly specifying the state transition that corresponds to each statement, we shall again use the definition method of transformational semantics: The semantics of statements is specified by giving rules that allow to reduce every segment to an expression of the kernel language.

Variables are allowed for all objects of the kernel language, i.e., also for sets and functions. In order to retain the property of referential transparency for expressions, we rule out segments with side-effects, i.e., statements that would change the state. Furthermore, all program variables must be initialized upon declaration. We shall show in 2.3.3 how to obtain the effects of non-initialized variables as well.

2.3.2. SEMANTICS OF THE PROCEDURAL LANGUAGE

CONTEXT CONDITIONS AND ATTRIBUTES

The scope of identifiers of program variables is defined in the same way as for object and function identifiers. In collective assignments, no identifier may occur twice on the left hand side ("actualization taboo").

The definitional transformations will use the following (context-dependent) attributes (PP stands for a sequence of phrases, i.e., of declarations and statements):

USED $[\![$ PP $]\!]$ gives the set of all free identifiers of PP.

USEDVARS $[\![$ PP $]\!]$ gives the set of all free variable identifiers occurring in PP.

ASSIGNEDVARS $[\![$ PP $]\!]$ gives the set of all free variable identifiers to which an assignment occurs within PP.

II.2.3 The procedural language

KIND$[\![x]\!]$ will now either be an applicative kind $\blacksquare$, or **var** $\blacksquare$ where $\blacksquare$ is an applicative kind, or **proc**$(k_1,...,k_n)$ where the k_j are applicative or variable kinds.

ABUSED$[\![E]\!]$ is the set of free identifiers occurring within abstractions in the expression E.

DECLARATION$[\![x]\!]$ gives the routine declaration corresponding to x.

KNOWNPROCS$[\![p]\!]$ gives the set of procedures known to p from surrounding scopes.

VARIABLES AND STATEMENTS

We give all defining transformations in such a way that we do not introduce non-local variables into function bodies. First, we give a modified definition for object declarations (cf. 2.2.2 (a)): The non-local variables are converted into explicit parameters when this expression is transformed into the body of a function.

$$\blacksquare\ x \equiv E_1\ ;\ E_2$$

$$\Updownarrow$$

$$\text{KIND}[\![E_2]\!] = r\ ,$$
$$\text{USEDVARS}[\![E_2]\!] = \{x_1,\ ...,\ x_k\}$$
$$\text{KIND}[\![x_j]\!] = \blacksquare_j$$

$$((\blacksquare\ x,\ \blacksquare_1\ x_1,\ ...,\ \blacksquare_k\ x_k)\ r\ :\ E_2)(E_1,\ x_1,\ ...,\ x_k)$$

The definition of function declarations is modified analogously. Below, however, we will allow, as a notational extension, functions that *read* global variables.

(a) SEGMENT AND PHRASE

A phrase is either a declaration or a statement. A segment is a bracketed (non-empty) sequence of phrases followed by an expression.

When phrases are combined with an expression into a segment we must introduce auxiliary variables for all variables assigned in those phrases, since the direct juxtaposition might lead to a segment with a side-effect. Since such a segment construction occurs in several of the following rules, we abbreviate it by defining

$$\text{MAKESEGMENT}[\![PP,\ E]\!] =$$
$$\lceil\ (\textbf{var}\ \blacksquare_1\ y_1,\ ...,\ \textbf{var}\ \blacksquare_n\ y_n) := (x_1,\ ...,\ x_n)\ ;$$
$$PP[\![y_j\ \textbf{for}\ x_j]\!]\ ;\ E[\![y_j\ \textbf{for}\ x_j]\!]\ \rfloor$$

where $\{x_1, \ldots, x_n\}$ = ASSIGNEDVARS $[\![$ PP $]\!]$,   KIND $[\![x_j]\!]$ = **var** m_j

and $\neg$ OCCURS $[\![y_1, \ldots, y_n$ **in** PP, E $]\!]$

hold.

Example:

     MAKESEGMENT $[\![$ **var int** $x := x + y;\ y := x * y$, $2 - y]\!]$

        $\cong \lceil$ **var int** $z := y;$ **var int** $x := x + z;\ z := z * x;\ 2 - z \rfloor$

     is a correct expression, whereas the "direct" combination

        $\lceil$ **var int** $x := x + y;\ y := x * y;\ 2 - y \rfloor$

     would be an expression with a side effect on the global variable y.

In the sequel we will give transformation rules for reducing segments to expressions of the extended applicative language.

(b) DECLARATION OF VARIABLES

Since expressions must not have side-effects, a variable-declaration followed immediately by an expression is equivalent to an object declaration:

     var m $x := E_1$; E_2

          $\Updownarrow$

     m $x \equiv E_1$; E_2

Example:

     Horner evaluation of a polynomial of degree two

        $\lceil$ **var real** $s := a_0 * x + a_1$; $s * x + a_2 \rfloor$

(c) ASSIGNMENT

Quite analogously, the last assignment to a variable before an expression can be replaced by an object declaration:

     $x := E_1$; E_2

          $\Updownarrow$ KIND $[\![x]\!]$ = **var** m, KIND $[\![E_1]\!]$ = m

                     $\neg$ OCCURS $[\![y$ **in** $E_1, E_2]\!]$

                     $x \notin$ ABUSED $[\![E_2]\!]$

     m $y \equiv E_1$; $E_2 [\![y$ **for** $x]\!]$

II.2.3 The procedural language

Since E_1 may depend on x, renaming is necessary to avoid a context error in this object declaration. It is obvious how this rule generalizes to the collective assignment. The condition $x \notin \text{ABUSED} [\![E_2]\!]$ guarantees that the bottom-up direction of this rule does not produce an abstraction with non-local variable identifiers.

Example:
Evaluation of a polynomial of degree four

$$\ulcorner \textbf{var real } s := a_0 * x + a_1 ;$$
$$s := s * x + a_2 ;$$
$$s := s * x + a_3 ;$$
$$s * x + a_4 \qquad \lrcorner$$

(d) EMPTY STATEMENT

skip means "do nothing". Therefore

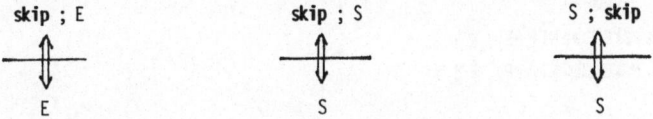

(e) ABORT STATEMENT

The statement **abort** is characterized by

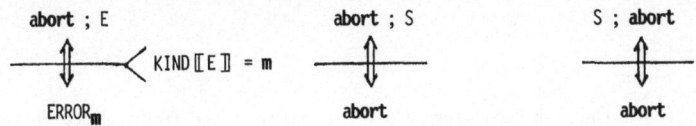

(for ERROR$_m$ cf. 2.1.2(g)).

(f) <u>BLOCK</u>

A <u>block</u> parenthesizes a (non-empty) sequence of phrases to yield a new statement. It is defined by

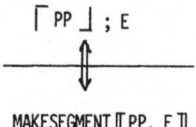

$$\ulcorner PP \urcorner \; ; \; E$$
$$\Updownarrow$$
$$\text{MAKESEGMENT} \llbracket PP, \; E \rrbracket$$

(g) <u>CONDITIONAL STATEMENT</u>

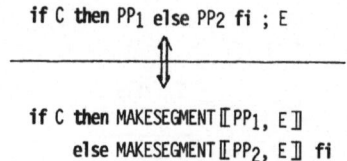

if C **then** PP$_1$ **else** PP$_2$ **fi** ; E
$$\Updownarrow$$
if C **then** MAKESEGMENT $\llbracket$ PP$_1$, E $\rrbracket$
        else MAKESEGMENT $\llbracket$ PP$_2$, E $\rrbracket$ **fi**

<u>Examples</u>:
  (1) **if** x < 0 **then** x := -x **else skip fi**
  (2) **if** y ≥ 0 **then** y := (y ▯ -y) **else abort fi** .

(h) <u>FINITE CHOICE</u>

Analogous to the finite choice between expressions, we introduce the finite choice between phrases:

$$\ulcorner PP_1 \; ▯ \; ... \; ▯ \; PP_n \urcorner \; ; \; E$$
$$\Updownarrow$$
$$(\; \text{MAKESEGMENT} \llbracket PP_1, E \rrbracket \; ▯ \; ... \; ▯ \; \text{MAKESEGMENT} \llbracket PP_n, E \rrbracket \;)$$

<u>Example</u>:
  Square of an arbitrary prime number less than 10
    $\ulcorner$ x := 2 ▯ x := 3 ▯ x := 5 ▯ x := 7 $\urcorner$; x * x

II.2.3 The procedural language

EXTENSION: FUNCTIONS THAT READ GLOBAL VARIABLES

During the transition from applicative to procedural programs frequently variables are suppressed as explicit parameters. Therefore we allow as an extension that functions depend on global variables; however, they must not produce side-effects. Such functions must not be passed as parameters or yielded as results, and the corresponding abstractions must not be used as expressions.

The semantics of such functions is specified using functions that have the global variables as additional parameters:

funct $f \equiv$ (**m** x) **r** : E

$$\Updownarrow \qquad \begin{array}{l} \text{USEDVARS}\,[\![\,E\,]\!] = \{y\} \\ \text{KIND}\,[\![\,y\,]\!] = \textbf{var n} \\ \neg\ \text{OCCURS}\,[\![\,z \textbf{ in } E,\, x,\, y\,]\!] \end{array}$$

funct $f \equiv$ (**m** x) **r** : g(x, y),
funct $g \equiv$ (**m** x, **n** z) **r** :
$\quad$ E$[\![\,g(E'\,[\![\,z \textbf{ for } y\,]\!],\, z)\textbf{ for } f(E')\,]\!]$

The definitional transformation for the application of such a function presupposes that the above transformation already has been applied:

$\qquad$ f(E)

$$\Updownarrow \qquad \begin{array}{l} \text{DECLARATION}\,[\![\,f\,]\!] = \textbf{funct } f \equiv (\textbf{m } x)\ \textbf{r} : g(x,\, y) \\ \text{USEDVARS}\,[\![\,g\,]\!] = \emptyset \\ \text{KIND}\,[\![\,g\,]\!] = \textbf{funct } (m,\, n)\ \textbf{r},\ \text{KIND}\,[\![\,y\,]\!] = \textbf{var n} \end{array}$$

$\qquad$ g(E, y)

The generalization to several parameters and to systems of (mutually recursive) functions is obvious.

Example:
$\quad$ **var char** x := 'a' ;
$\quad$ **funct** isin $\equiv$ (**charsequ** s) **bool** :
$\qquad$ **if** isempty(s) **then false**
$\qquad\qquad\qquad$ **else** x = top(s) $\forall$ isin(rest(s)) **fi**

PROCEDURES

Procedure declarations and procedure calls abbreviate and generalize statements in a similar way as function declarations and function applications abbreviate and generalize expressions (by means of parameters). Their syntactic form therefore closely resembles that of functions, and also their semantics is explained with the help of "associated functions". The essential differences are that procedures do not yield results and that they may use program variables as parameters.

The context conditions for procedures are analogous to those for functions, including overloading (cf. Appendix I). As actual parameters of kind **var m** only identifiers of variables of this kind are allowed.

In order to guarantee the absence of aliasing of variables, an "actualization-taboo" is imposed on the procedure call: two (local or global) variable parameters must not be actualized by the same variable. In order to prevent unexpected side-effects, we require that procedure calls within function bodies or other expressions must not assign to variables global to the functions.

(i) PROCEDURE DECLARATION

The essential rule for the semantics of procedures is given by the following rule dealing with a single procedure with one variable parameter and one local variable:

proc $p \equiv$ (**var m** x) : S

$$\Updownarrow \quad \left\{ \begin{array}{l} \text{KNOWNPROCS} [\![\, p \,]\!] = \emptyset \\ \text{ASSIGNEDVARS} [\![\, S \,]\!] = \{x\} \\ \neg \text{ OCCURS} [\![\, y \text{ in } S, x \,]\!] \end{array} \right.$$

proc $p \equiv$ (**var m** x) : $x := f(x)$,
funct $f \equiv$ (**m** y) **m** : $\lceil$ **var m** $x := y$; S ; $x \rfloor$

Here the function f is intended to capture the state transition effected by p. If p is recursive then rule (j) below allows the elimination of the calls of p within S in the body of f thus making f recursive.

II.2.3 The procedural language

To be able to deal with the use of global variables as implicit variable parameters as well as with additional constant parameters we have the following variant of the first rule:

proc p ≡ (**var** m x, **r** c) : S

$$\Updownarrow$$

ASSIGNEDVARS⟦S⟧ = {x, y}
KIND⟦y⟧ = **var** n
¬ OCCURS⟦x', y' **in** S, x, c⟧

proc p ≡ (**var** m x, **r** c) : (x, y) := f(x, y, c) ,
funct f ≡ (m x', n y', **r** c)(m, n) :
⌈ (**var** m x, **var** n y) := (x', y') ; S'; (x, y) ⌋

where x', y' are new identifiers and S' results from S by unfolding all calls of p (see (j)). (Since p has the implicit variable parameter y its use within f would violate the context conditions).

The generalization to several parameters and to systems of (mutually recursive) procedures is obvious.

Examples:
(1) Computing the 8th power
      proc pow8 ≡ (**var real** x, **real** a) :
        ⌈ x := a * a ;
           x := x * x ;
           x := x * x ⌋
(2) Exchanging the values of two variables
      proc exchange ≡ (**var** m x, **var** m y) : (x, y) := (y, x)

For procedures without used or assigned variables the associated function will be of kind **funct**()(). E. g. the procedure

    proc p ≡ : ⌈ **skip** ▯ **call** p ⌋

is equivalent to

    proc p ≡ : () := f() ,
    funct f ≡ : ()() : (() ▯ f()) ,

i.e., to a procedure that "modifies" only the empty tuple of variables by the effect of a function which only chooses between termination and non-termination.

(j) PROCEDURE CALL

The call of a procedure is executed by first evaluating its object parameters and then executing its body (with the actual parameters substituted for the formal ones); this is expressed by the rule (called "unfolding"):

call p(v, E)

$$\Downarrow \qquad \text{DECLARATION}[\![\,p\,]\!] = \textbf{proc } p \equiv (\textbf{var m } x, \textbf{n } c) : S$$

$\lceil\ \textbf{n } c \equiv E\ ;\ S[\![\,v\ \textbf{for } x\,]\!]\ \rfloor$

Note that in general only this unfolding direction of the rule is valid, since folding within the declaration of a procedure might lead to non-termination.

Example:
   Checking whether a sequence of signs totals to "positive" or "negative" (we assume a
   declaration **mode sign** = plus | minus) :
   funct ispos ≡ (**signsequ** s) **bool** :
   $\lceil$ (**var signsequ** a, **var bool** r) := (s, **true**) ;
       proc isp ≡ :
           if isempty(a) **then skip**
           else if top(a) **is** plus **then** a := rest(a) ; **call** isp
                                   else a := rest(a) ; **call** isn **fi fi** ,
       proc isn ≡ :
           if isempty(a) **then** r := **false**
           else if top(a) **is** minus **then** a := rest(a) ; **call** isp
                                   else a := rest(a) ; **call** isn **fi fi** ;
       call isp ;
       r $\rfloor$

II.2.3 The procedural language

2.3.3. NOTATIONAL EXTENSIONS

(a) GUARDED STATEMENT

In analogy to the applicative language, guarded statements can be defined in terms of finite choice and conditional (PP stands for a sequence of phrases):

$$\textbf{if } C_1 \textbf{ then } PP_1$$
$$\square \; ...$$
$$\square \; C_n \textbf{ then } PP_n \textbf{ else } PP_{n+1} \textbf{ fi}$$

$$\Updownarrow \qquad\qquad n \geq 2$$

$$(\;\; \textbf{if } C_1 \textbf{ then } PP_1 \textbf{ else } G_1 \textbf{ fi}$$
$$\square \; ...$$
$$\square \;\; \textbf{if } C_n \textbf{ then } PP_n \textbf{ else } G_n \textbf{ fi} \;)$$

where $G_i \triangleq \textbf{if } C_1 \quad \textbf{then } PP_1 \quad \square \; ... \; \square \; C_{i-1} \textbf{ then } PP_{i-1}$
$$\square \; C_{i+1} \textbf{ then } PP_{i+1} \; \square \; ... \; \square \; C_n \quad \textbf{then } PP_n \textbf{ else } PP_{n+1} \textbf{ fi}$$

We define

$$\textbf{if } C_1 \textbf{ then } PP_1 \; \square \; ... \; \square \; C_n \textbf{ then } PP_n \textbf{ fi}$$

$$\Updownarrow$$

$$\textbf{if } C_1 \textbf{ then } PP_1 \; \square \; ... \; \square \; C_n \textbf{ then } PP_n \textbf{ else abort fi}$$

Note that, according to this definition, **if false then** S **fi** is extensionally equivalent to **abort**. This contrasts with most other languages where that statement would be equivalent to **skip**; however, it corresponds to the behaviour of the conditional expression **if false then** E **fi** .

Example:
  Merging two sorted sequences
  proc merge = (**var charsequ** r, **var charsequ** s, **var charsequ** t) :
      if isempty(s) **then** r := r & t
      $\square$ isempty(t) **then** r := r & s
                      else if top(t) $\leq$ top(s)
                          then (r, s) := (stock(r, top(s)), rest(s))
                      $\square$ top(s) $\leq$ top(t)
                          then (r, t) := (stock(r, top(t)), rest(t)) **fi** ;
                      merge(r, s, t)   **fi**

(b) LOCAL ASSERTION

A local assertion is a statement of the form

        assert C

which is equivalent to

        if C **then skip fi** ,

i.e., to

        if C **then skip else abort fi** .

If an object declaration (m x : C) ≡ E with an assertion is converted into an assignment to a program variable (cf. 2.3.2), then we get

        x := E ; **assert** C .

Examples:
- (1) **var nat** n := mod(a, b) ; **assert** n < b
- (2) **var real** y := x * x ; **assert** y ≥ 0

As a notational variant we allow local assertions in variable declarations,

      (**var m** v : C) := E

      ⇕

      var m v := E ; **assert** C ,

and in procedure headings,

      proc p ≡ (**var m** x, n y : C) : S

      ⇕

      proc p ≡ (**var m** x, n y) : ⌈ **assert** C ; S ⌋ ,

where the bottom scheme is equivalent to

      proc p ≡ (**var m** x, n y) : **if** C **then** S **fi**

(cf. the analogous rule for functions).

Example:
    proc pop ≡ (**var stack** s : ¬ isempty(s)) : s := rest(s)

II.2.3 The procedural language

(c) NON-INITIALIZED PROGRAM VARIABLE

Up to now only initialized declarations of variables have been considered. Especially if we want to deliver results of procedures by means of result parameters, non-initialized variables occur in the program development. For this purpose we define a segment or block with a sequence PP of phrases (and an expression E)

$\lceil$ **var** m v ; PP {; E} $\rfloor$

(where {; E} means that the part "; E" may be missing) to be equivalent to

mode mm $\equiv$ nonvalue$_m$ $|$ cons$_m$(m val$_m$) ;

...

$\lceil$ **var** mm v := nonvalue$_m$; $\overline{PP}$ {; $\overline{E}$} $\rfloor$

$\overline{E}$ results from E by substituting val$_m$(v) for v. $\overline{PP}$ is derived from PP by replacing
- v by val$_m$(v) in all expressions contained in PP,
- every assignment v := E' by v := cons$_m$(E') ,
- every call **call** p(..., v, ...) of a procedure **proc** p $\equiv$ (..., **var** m w, ...) : S by
  call $\overline{p}$(..., v, ...) , where **proc** $\overline{p}$ $\equiv$ (..., **var** mm w, ...) : $\overline{S}$ and $\overline{S}$ results from S like
  $\overline{PP}$ from PP. Note that the declaration of p can only be deleted if p is never called with an
  initialized variable for the parameter w.

The mode declaration which defines an auxiliary object "missing value" is inserted into the surrounding structure body at most once for every m.

For non-initialized variables, restricted declarations are considered as ordinary declarations, since there is no value for which to test the condition:

(**var** m x : C) ; PP

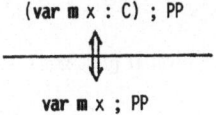

var m x ; PP

2.4. CONSTRUCTS FOR PARALLEL PROGRAMMING WITH SHARED VARIABLES

2.4.1. SURVEY

There exist numerous proposals for languages and language constructs for concurrent programming. So it is even more difficult than in sequential programming to select an appropriate subset. The wide spectrum language CIP-L has been designed as a language for the specification, design and development of programs for the classical sequential stored-program machine. Thus the extension of CIP-L by language constructs for concurrent programming takes this also as the main design objective: The communication mechanism is completely based on the concept of shared memory and protected access to it.

2.4.2. CONTEXT CONDITIONS AND ATTRIBUTES

For the formulation of the context conditions for the parallel constructs we introduce two syntactic predicates:

CONFLICT $[\![$ S1, S2 $]\!]$ holds iff there occurs a program variable v in S1 (or in S2 resp.) on the left hand side of an assignment and v occurs in S2 (or in S1 resp.) outside of an **await**-statement (or inside an **await**-statement that itself occurs inside a parallel block).

WAIT $[\![$ S $]\!]$ holds iff an **await**-statement occurs in S outside of a parallel block.

A parallel composition $[\![$ p_1 $\|$ ... $\|$ p_n $]\!]$ of statements p_i is properly protected if

$\quad \forall$ i, j: $1 \le i < j \le n$: $\neg$ CONFLICT $[\![$ p_i, p_j $]\!]$.

For simplicity we restrict our language by context conditions to those parallel programs that are properly protected.

Of course, an **await**-statement makes sense only within a parallel block. So, if an **await**-statement that is not contained in a parallel block occurs within an expression, the program is not context correct. Moreover we do not allow nested **await**-statements.

A further restriction concerns the use of recursion in parallel programs: In the body of a recursively defined procedure, a recursive call must not occur within a parallel composition. Thus we can only write parallel programs with a statically determined structure of parallel compositions.

II.2.4 The parallel language

2.4.3. DEFINITIONAL TRANSFORMATIONS

As shown in /Broy 80/ the concurrent constructs do not increase the expressive power of the language in an extensional sense. They just assume another <u>operational semantics</u>. Parallel execution of statements with protected access to shared memory can always be reduced to sequential execution of non-deterministic statements.

If we adopt the principle of <u>transformational induction</u> as given in /Broy 80/ we can always reduce syntactically (i.e. without execution) every concurrent program to a sequential one, as long as all accesses to shared memory are properly protected, i.e., as long as the context conditions are satisfied.

The reduction of parallel programs to sequential ones and, vice versa, the development of parallel programs from sequential ones can be performed according to the following transformation rules.

(a) The parallel composition is commutative:

$$\llbracket\ S_1\ \|\ldots\|\ S_n\ \rrbracket$$

$$\Updownarrow$$

$$\llbracket\ S_i\ \|\ S_2\ \|\ldots\|\ S_{i-1}\ \|\ S_1\ \|\ S_{i+1}\ \|\ldots\|\ S_n\ \rrbracket$$

(b) For purely sequential programs the parallel composition defines the identity:

$$\llbracket\ S\ \rrbracket$$

$$\Updownarrow \quad\longleftarrow\ \neg\ \text{WAIT}\llbracket\,S\,\rrbracket$$

$$S$$

(c) An empty statement does not contribute anything to the parallel composition; it can be trivially added/deleted:

$$\llbracket\ \textbf{skip}\ \|\ S_1\ \|\ldots\|\ S_n\ \rrbracket$$

$$\Updownarrow$$

$$\llbracket\ S_1\ \|\ldots\|\ S_n\ \rrbracket$$

(d) Let now for $1 \le i \le n$ P_i stand for

$$\textbf{if } G_1^i \textbf{ then } S_1^i; T_1^i \; \square \; ... \; \square \; G_{k_i}^i \textbf{ then } S_{k_i}^i \; ; \; T_{k_i}^i \textbf{ fi}$$

and for $n < j \le m$ P_j stand for

$$\textbf{await } C^j \textbf{ then } K^j \textbf{ endwait} \; ; \; T^j \; .$$

For the parallel composition $PC = \llbracket P_1 \parallel ... \parallel P_m \rrbracket$ we denote by $PC\llbracket T/i \rrbracket$ the parallel composition that results from replacing the i-th branch of PC by T, viz. the parallel composition $\llbracket P_1 \parallel ... \parallel P_{i-1} \parallel T \parallel P_{i+1} \parallel ... \parallel P_m \rrbracket$. The following main transformation rule allows replacing the leading await-statements in the branches of a parallel composition by branches of a guarded statement and thus reducing parallelism to non-deterministic choice:

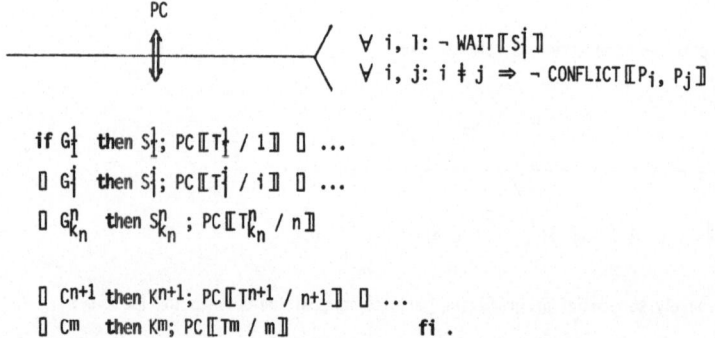

PC

$\forall \; i, 1: \neg \; \text{WAIT}\llbracket S_1^i \rrbracket$

$\forall \; i, j: i \ne j \Rightarrow \neg \text{CONFLICT}\llbracket P_i, P_j \rrbracket$

$$\textbf{if } G_1^1 \quad \textbf{then } S_1^1; PC\llbracket T_1^1 \; / \; 1 \rrbracket \; \square \; ...$$
$$\square \; G_1^i \quad \textbf{then } S_1^i; PC\llbracket T_1^i \; / \; i \rrbracket \; \square \; ...$$
$$\square \; G_{k_n}^n \quad \textbf{then } S_{k_n}^n \; ; \; PC\llbracket T_{k_n}^n \; / \; n \rrbracket$$

$$\square \; C^{n+1} \quad \textbf{then } K^{n+1}; PC\llbracket T^{n+1} \; / \; n+1 \rrbracket \; \square \; ...$$
$$\square \; C^m \quad \textbf{then } K^m; PC\llbracket T^m \; / \; m \rrbracket \qquad \qquad \textbf{fi} \; .$$

By this transformation, the phrases K guarded by an await-statement **await** C **then** K **endwait** are treated as an indivisible unit. Note that one can think of more sophisticated systems considering also programs that are not <u>syntactically</u> protected, but just <u>semantically</u> (such as e.g. by semaphors).

As shown in /Broy 80/, every parallel program written only with parameter-free procedures in tail-recursive form can be reduced to a purely sequential program. Since every program can be brought into this particular form with the help of transformation rules, our definitional transformation rules for the parallel constructs suffice for reducing every context-correct parallel program to a purely sequential program.

For an example of the use of these constructs see 3.4.

II.2.5 The control-oriented language

2.5. THE CONTROL-ORIENTED LANGUAGE: LABELS AND JUMPS

2.5.1. SURVEY

Labels and jumps have to be included into a wide spectrum language in order to provide a smooth transition to the "low" levels of machine programming: The state of a von Neumann type machine includes control of the flow of actions. The basic situation where **goto**s are valuable is the (with respect to the common type of machines) efficient representation of "tail recursion" in procedures. For example,

$$\textbf{proc } p \equiv : \lceil \textbf{ if } C \textbf{ then } S_1 \text{ ; } \textbf{call } p \textbf{ else } S_2 \textbf{ fi } \rfloor$$

is (by definition) equivalent to

$$\textbf{proc } p \equiv : \lceil 1 : \textbf{if } C \textbf{ then } S_1 \text{ ; } \textbf{goto } 1 \textbf{ else } S_2 \textbf{ fi } \rfloor$$

However, the coexistence with "higher-level" constructs like procedures imposes certain restrictions: Jumps into procedures and blocks (and thus into conditionals) and over declarations in the same block as well as jumps out of procedures are ruled out. The reasons for these restrictions are of technical as well as of methodological nature: not only does the "wild" **goto** make compilers complex and semantic descriptions clumsy, it also makes programs extremely hard to read and understand, especially if used in recursive procedures. Exceptions or external events should not be handled using non-local jumps but by suitable routines called on the spot. Note that by a proper use of transformations from procedural to control-oriented programs no "wild" **goto**s are introduced.

2.5.2. SEMANTICS OF THE CONTROL-ORIENTED LANGUAGE

CONTEXT CONDITIONS AND ATTRIBUTES

As in most languages, a label declaration takes the form $1 : S$ where S is a statement. The scope of 1 is the statement sequence containing this declaration: Let the phrases PP be the body of a block or a segment, or a branch of a conditional, or of a finite choice. If PP contains a labelled statement then PP must be of the form

$$D \text{ ; } s_1 \text{ ; } \dots \text{ ; } 1 : s_k \text{ ; } \dots \text{ ; } s_n$$

where "D ;" is either empty or a sequence of declarations and statements not containing jumps and labels, and the s_j are statements. Then the scope of 1 is $s_1; \dots; 1 : s_k; \dots; s_n$. This excludes jumps into blocks, conditional statements or procedures, and over declarations in the same block.

As further context conditions, we rule out jumps to non-local labels in functions and procedures, and jumps out of segments.

The attribute LABELS $[\![\, \Gamma \,]\!]$ yields all free labels of the program part Γ, i.e., all labels which occur in jumps in Γ but are not declared in Γ.

DEFINITIONAL TRANSFORMATIONS

At first there are a few rules expressing basic properties of jumps and labels:

(a) New labels can be introduced or superfluous labels can be eliminated:

$$PP_1 \; ; \; S \; ; \; PP_2$$

$\Updownarrow$ $\quad \neg$ OCCURS$[\![\, 1 \text{ in } PP_1, PP_2, S \,]\!]$

$$PP_1 \; ; \; 1 \; : \; S; \; PP_2$$

(b) Superfluous jumps "on the spot" may be created or eliminated:

goto 1 ; 1 : S

$\Updownarrow$

1 : S

(c) Branching instructions may be expressed by means of conditional jumps and labels:

if C **then** PP_1 **else** PP_2 **fi**

$\Updownarrow$ $\quad \neg$ OCCURS$[\![\, 1_1, 1_2, m \text{ in } PP_1, PP_2 \,]\!]$

$\lceil$ **if** C **then goto** 1_1 **else goto** 1_2 **fi** ;
$1_1 : \lceil PP_1 \rceil$; **goto** m ;
$1_2 : \lceil PP_2 \rceil$; m : **skip** $\qquad \rfloor$

II.2.4 The control-oriented language

(d) A finite choice between statements is transformed into an "arbitrary branching":

$$\lceil PP_1 \; \square \; PP_2 \rfloor$$

$\Updownarrow$ $\neg$ OCCURS $[\![l_1, l_2, m \text{ in } PP_1, PP_2]\!]$

$$\lceil \lceil \textbf{goto } l_1 \; \square \; \textbf{goto } l_2 \rfloor \; ;$$
$$l_1 : \lceil PP_1 \rfloor \; ; \textbf{goto } m \; ;$$
$$l_2 : \lceil PP_2 \rfloor \; ; m : \textbf{skip} \rfloor$$

A sequence S of statements is <u>jump-normal</u> if jumps occur in S only in statements of the form GOTO where GOTO is an abbreviation for either

    goto l   or

    if C **then goto** l_1 **else goto** l_2 **fi**   or

    $\lceil$ **goto** l_1 $\square$ **goto** l_2 $\rfloor$

(e) Again for normalization purposes we need the following rule:

$$\lceil PP \rfloor \; ; \text{GOTO}$$

$\Updownarrow$ LABELS $[\![\text{GOTO}]\!]$ $\cap$ DECLARED $[\![PP]\!]$ = $\emptyset$

$$\lceil PP \; ; \text{GOTO} \rfloor$$

Given a set L of labels, we say that a statement S <u>cleanly separates</u> the jumps according to L if it is jump-normal, LABELS $[\![S]\!]$ $\subseteq$ L , and for all statements of the form GOTO in S either LABELS $[\![\text{GOTO}]\!]$ $\subseteq$ L or LABELS $[\![\text{GOTO}]\!]$ $\cap$ L = $\emptyset$. Finally, S is in <u>tail normal form</u> wrt. L if it, first, cleanly separates the jumps according to L and, second, has either the form S'; GOTO such that LABELS $[\![\text{GOTO}]\!]$ $\subseteq$ L and LABELS $[\![S']\!]$ = $\emptyset$, or the form $\lceil PP; \text{GOTO} \rfloor$ such that LABELS $[\![\text{GOTO}]\!]$ $\subseteq$ L.

(f) Finally we establish a correspondence between a system of local jumps and a system of procedures in tail recursion. We use the fact that program pieces P_i of the form

    $l_i : S_i \; ; \textbf{goto } m_i$

(where S_i is a statement sequence), that are activated only by jumps but not by the "normal" flow of control, commute wrt. the ';'-operation, i.e., P_i; P_j and P_j; P_i are equivalent. Therefore, every such P_i can be made into a procedure named l_i and the jumps can be replaced by calls of the l_i .

Let PP be a sequence of phrases which is empty or ends with a declaration, and S_i be sequences of statements. Then

$\lceil$ PP; l_1 : S_1;...;
$\qquad l_n$: S_n; l_{n+1} : **skip** $\rfloor$

$\Updownarrow$ ⟩ LABELS$[\![S_i]\!] \subseteq \{l_1,...,l_{n+1}\}$
S_i is in tail normal form
wrt. $\{l_1,...,l_{n+1}\}$

$\lceil$ PP;
$\quad$ **proc** $l_1 \equiv : \overline{S}_1$,...,
$\quad$ **proc** $l_n \equiv : \overline{S}_n$, **proc** $l_{n+1} \equiv :$ **skip** ;
$\quad$ **call** l_1 $\qquad\qquad\qquad\qquad$ $\rfloor$

where for $S_i = S'_i$; $GOTO_i$
$\quad \overline{S}_i = \lceil S'_i; GOTO_i [\![$ **call** l_j **for goto** $l_j]\!] \rfloor$
and for $S_i = \lceil PP_i; GOTO_i \rfloor$
$\quad \overline{S}_i = \lceil PP_i [\![\overline{GO}$ **for** GO $]\!]; \overline{GOTO}_i; \overline{l} :$ **skip** $\rfloor$
with a new label $\overline{l}$. Here, GO ranges over all maximal statements in PP_i of the form GOTO, and

$$\overline{GO} = \begin{cases} GO [\![\textbf{call } l_j \textbf{ for goto } l_j]\!]; \textbf{goto } \overline{l} & \text{if LABELS}[\![GO]\!] \subseteq \{l_1,..., l_{n+1}\} \\ GO & \text{otherwise} \end{cases}$$

By means of the above transformation rules each piece of program text containing jumps and labels can be reduced to an equivalent one consisting of a system of mutually recursive procedures. Since many of these procedures do not call themselves directly, simple unfolding of such procedures can be used to re-establish as much of the original appearance of the program as possible - at least at those points where only technical reasons caused changes of the program structure.

To illustrate these transformations we consider the following piece of program:
$\lceil$ **var int** x := y ;
$\quad$ 1 : $\lceil$ x := b(x);
$\qquad$ **if** C **then goto** k **else goto** r **fi** ;
$\qquad$ r : **goto** 1 ; k : **skip** $\qquad$ $\rfloor$;
$\quad$ x := e(x) $\qquad\qquad\qquad\qquad$ $\rfloor$

By the rules (a), (b), (e) and 2.3.2 (d) this program can be transformed into
$\lceil$ **var int** x := y;
$\quad$ 1 : $\lceil$ x := b(x);
$\qquad$ **if** C **then goto** k **else goto** r **fi** ;
$\qquad$ r : **goto** 1 ; k : **goto** m $\qquad$ $\rfloor$;

II.2.5 The control-oriented language

⌈ m : x := e(x) ; **goto** n ;

n : **skip**   ⌋

Now application of rule (f) yields

⌈ **var int** x := y ;

proc l ≡ : ⌈ x := b(x);

if C **then goto** k **else goto** r **fi** ;

r : **call** l ; **goto** l' ;

k : **call** m ; **goto** l' ; l' : **skip** ⌋ ,

proc m ≡ : ⌈ x := e(x) ; **call** n ⌋ ,

proc n ≡ : **skip** ;

call l   ⌋

Unfolding of the procedure n and simplification according to rule (b) and 2.3.2 (d) yield

⌈ **var int** x := y ;

proc l ≡ : ⌈ x := b(x) ;

if C **then goto** k **else goto** r **fi** ;

r : **call** l ; **goto** l' ;

k : **call** m ; **goto** l' ; l' : **skip** ⌋ ,

proc m ≡ : x := e(x) ;

call l   ⌋

Now the body of l is treated analogously, leading to

proc l ≡ : ⌈ **proc** u ≡ : ⌈ x := b(x) ;

if C **then call** k

else call r **fi** ⌋ ,

proc r ≡ : ⌈ **call** l ; **call** l' ⌋ ,

proc k ≡ : ⌈ **call** m ; **call** l' ⌋ ,

proc l'≡ : **skip** ;

call u   ⌋

Then again a number of unfoldings finally simplify the program to

⌈ **var int** x := y ;

proc l ≡ : ⌈ x := b(x) ;

if C **then** x := e(x)

else call l **fi** ⌋ ;

call l   ⌋

2.5.3. EXTENSIONS

(a) RETURN JUMP

A special form of exit jump is the return jump in procedures and functions:

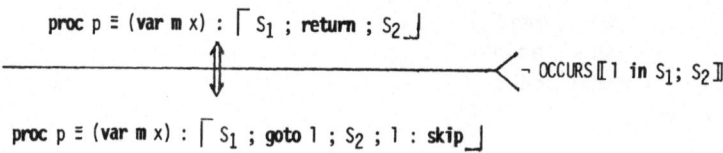

proc $p \equiv$ (**var m** x) : $\lceil$ S_1 ; **return** ; S_2 $\rfloor$

$\neg$ OCCURS $\llbracket 1$ **in** S_1; $S_2 \rrbracket$

proc $p \equiv$ (**var m** x) : $\lceil$ S_1 ; **goto** 1 ; S_2 ; 1 : **skip** $\rfloor$

Example:
Computing the n-th power:

```
proc pow ≡ (real a, nat n, var real res) :
    ⌈ (var real x, var nat i) := (a, n) :
     res := 1 ;
     loop : if i = 0 then return
                 else if odd(i) then (i, res) := (i - 1, res ⋆ x)
                             else skip                          fi ;
                 (i, x) := (i ÷ 2, x ⋆ x) ;
                 goto loop                                   fi ⌋
```

(b) LOOPS

Loops are considered as a more controlled and "more structured" way of using **gotos** . Loops with "exit"-jumps denoted by **leave** are defined by

do PP **od**

$\neg$ OCCURS $\llbracket 1_1, 1_2$ **in** PP $\rrbracket$

$\lceil$ 1_1 : PP $\llbracket$ **goto** 1_2 **for leave** $\rrbracket$;
   goto 1_1; 1_2 : **skip** $\rfloor$

where only the occurrences of **leave** outside of other **do–od** constructions are free.

II.2.4 The control-oriented language

The **while**-loop provides a specific form of a loop:

while C **do** S **od**

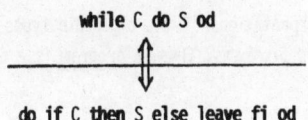

do if C **then** S **else leave fi od**

Examples:
  Computing the n-th power:
  (1) **proc** pow ≡ (**real** a, **nat** n, **var real** res) :
      ⌈ (**var real** x, **var nat** i) := (a, n) ;
        res := 1 ;
        do if i = 0
              then leave
              else if odd(i) **then** (i, res) := (i - 1, res * x)
                              else skip   **fi** ;
                  (i, x) := (i ÷ 2, x * x)   **fi**
      od   ⌋
  (2) **proc** pow ≡ (**real** a, **nat** n, **var real** res) :
      ⌈ (**var real** x, **var nat** i) := (a, n) ;
        res:= 1 ;
        while i ‡ 0
              do if odd(i) **then** (i, res) := (i - 1, res * x)
                              else skip   **fi** ;
                  (i, x) := (i ÷ 2, x * x)
                  od   ⌋

3. PROGRAMS

Computation structures, modules, and devices provide interpretations of the algebraic types that underly the scheme language. They are grouped together as programs. Thus, a program is a finite set of components which may be
- types (cf. 1)
- computation structures (cf. 3.1)
- modules (cf. 3.3)
- devices (cf. 3.4).

The program is operated by invoking (operative) visible constituents of its computation structures. Note that by the whole structure of the language a program cannot have a "state" (there is no independent semantics for variables); hence the essential components of the program are the computation structures, whereas modules and devices are used as auxiliaries in the construction of computation structures.

3.1. COMPUTATION STRUCTURES

A computation structure is a collection of declarations for sorts, objects, and functions that are made available to the outside. Internally, auxiliary procedures may be explicitly defined or imported by module instantiations (cf. 3.3). Computation structures provide a means for supplying models for types; they also define components whose input/output behaviour is described by the relations between parameters and results of the functions.

3.1.1. DECLARATION OF COMPUTATION STRUCTURES

The declaration of a computation structure has the form

$$\textbf{structure } CS \equiv \text{«constituents»} :$$
$$D_1; \ldots; D_r$$
$$\textbf{end of } \text{structure}$$

The list of constituents corresponds to that of a type: It consists of symbols for sorts, constants, and functions, which are "visible" to the outside. Since computation structures are intended as implementations for types (cf. 3.1.2) we do not allow procedure identifiers in the list of constituents.

The body $D_1; \ldots; D_r$ of the structure CS provides definitions at least for these symbols; in addition "hidden" entities may be defined for internal use. If a definition applies a type (schema) T, CS is considered as parameterized by the constituents of T (restricted by the laws of T). The following kinds of definitions are admissible in structures:

II.3.1 Computation structures

- Instantiations of (primitive) types and type schemes (cf. 1.2.2). Again, unfolding of the instantiations must not lead to cycles in the primitive-relation. If the parameters of the type scheme are restricted (cf. 1.2.3 and 1.2.4) the restrictions must be satisfied by the arguments of the instantiation.
- Instantiations of (parameterized) structures (cf. 3.1.3)
- Mode declarations (cf. 1.3)
- Function declarations (cf. 2.2.2 (b))
- (Collective) object declarations (cf. 2.2.2 (a))
- Declarations of procedures (without global variables) (cf. 2.3.2 (i))
- Instantiations of modules (cf. 3.3).

Example:
A computation structure for the natural numbers can be given in terms of sequences of "bits" without leading zeros (the type STACK is defined in 1.4 (e)):

```
structure N ≡ nat, zero, succ, iszero, pred :
    mode bit ≡ O | L ,
    based on (nat, empty, isempty, append, top, rest) ≡ STACK(bit) ,
    nat zero ≡ empty ,
    funct iszero ≡ (nat n) bool : isempty(n) ,
    funct succ ≡ (nat n) nat :
        if isempty(n)
            then append (empty, L)
            else if top(n) is O then append(rest(n), L)
              [] top(n) is L then append(succ(rest(n)), O) fi fi ,
    funct pred ≡ (nat n : ¬ iszero(n)) nat :
        if top(n) is O then append(pred(rest(n)), L)
        [] top(n) is L then if isempty(rest(n))
                                then empty
                                else append(rest(n)), O) fi fi
end of structure
```

3.1.2. COMPUTATION STRUCTURES AS IMPLEMENTATIONS OF TYPES

One way of implementing a given type T is to formulate another type T' (usually by enriching some type T" by suitable operations) such that a quotient of every model of T' is also a model of T. In this case, T' is called an implementation of T over T" (cf. /Broy et al. 85/). As an example consider an implementation of sets over sequences; the quotient is formed by identifying sequences that differ only in the order and in the number of occurrences of their elements.

A special case of this process is to use as laws for all newly added operations f only explicit equations, i.e., equations of the form

$$f(x_1,\ldots,x_n) \equiv t$$

with variables x_i and a suitable term t which contains at most these variables. Such a type may be immediately rewritten into a purely applicative computation structure; viewed the other way round, the computation structure obtained in this way is an explicitly defined model of that type. Since giving an explicit model is the second way of implementing a type, computation structures are special implementations of types.

However, they also provide the link to the procedural language: By transforming the function definitions towards the procedural level one finally reaches modules and devices (cf. 3.3 and 3.4), i.e., procedural implementations of algebraic types (cf. /Laut 80/).

Let us now consider the implementation relation in more detail. A computation structure CS is called a <u>syntactically correct</u> implementation of a type T if the elements of the respective constituent lists together with their sorts and functionalities coincide after consistent renaming. (This renaming also involves primitive types or structures that directly define constituents of T or CS.) The sort or functionality of an identifier defined by an object or function declaration is determined in an obvious way. Note that in this way only "first order" objects and functions can be treated, i.e., objects that are not of set or function kind and functions that have no sets or functions as parameters or results (cf. 1.1.6). Thus computation structures defining visible higher order functions cannot be viewed as implementations of algebraic types. The same holds for functions with more than one result since the operation symbols of types have only one result sort.

A syntactically correct implementation CS of a type T is called <u>semantically correct</u>, if a congruence can be specified on (subsets of) the carrier sets of CS such that the corresponding quotient structure is a model of T (see below). For the types and type schemes applied by CS, arbitrary models are presupposed; the semantic correctness must not depend on the choice of these models.

In order to prove the semantic correctness of the implementation, <u>all</u> sorts, constants, and operations of T must be associated with a counterpart in CS (cf. 1.1.6), whereas for syntactic correctness only the constituents are matched. This also concerns all primitive types of T and is in general a complex task. If, however, T and CS are analogously constructed, i.e., if every primitive type T' of T corresponds to a primitive structure CS' of CS, the proof can be modularized by showing that every CS' is a semantically correct implementation of the corresponding type T'.

II.3.1 Computation structures

Since a model of a type associates an unambiguous object with every constant symbol and a mapping in the mathematical sense with every operation symbol, only computation structures with determinate object and function declarations can be semantically correct implementations. Thus non-determinacy is excluded from algebraic specification just as higher order functions and functions with tuples as results.

However, a computation structure with non-determinate operations arises naturally from a type in which the behaviour of certain operations is not completely specified; in this case one has to make sure that all values in the breadth of the application of such an operation f satisfy the laws given for f. One way of achieving this is to use in the respective computation structure comprehensive choice with the conjunction of the laws for f as the quantified expression. Then all determinate descendants of this structure are models of the type.

If the congruence relation establishing semantic correctness differs from the equality (cf. 2.1.3 (a)) on a carrier set of CS, then it must explicitly be defined by means of a predicate.

Example:
The structure N from 3.1.1 is a syntactically correct implementation of the type NAT from 1.3.3: The constituents coincide even without renaming. Moreover it is a semantically correct implementation: Whereas the carrier set of the sort **nat** comprises arbitrary sequences, the constants and functions generate only sequences without leading zeros. Hence, we consider the algebra based on this restricted set. As the congruence relation for the verification of the laws we can use the usual equality on sequences. The hidden operation symbol issucc of NAT is easily associated with a function:
$$\textbf{funct } \text{issucc} \equiv (\textbf{nat } s) \textbf{ bool} : \neg \text{ isempty}(s) \ .$$

3.1.3. PARAMETERIZED STRUCTURES

"Implementation schemes" are analogous to type schemes. They are denoted as parameterized structures (generic structures) of the form (cf. 1.2.1):

$$\textbf{structure } \text{CS} \equiv (\ll\text{parameters}\gg) \ll\text{constituents}\gg :$$
$$D_1, \ ..., \ D_r$$
end of structure

Again arbitrary collections of sort, constant, and operation symbols are admissible as parameters. Furthermore, the parameters may be restricted by laws (which are possibly abbreviated by type schemes without constituents, cf. 1.2.3 and 1.2.4).

In analogy to types (cf. 1.2.2) a (parameterized) structure CS can be instantiated by the construct

structure («constituents'») ≡ CS(«arguments»)

which is explained by replacing this construct by the body of CS (after respective renaming). If the parameters of CS are restricted by laws, the instantiation is admissible only if the arguments satisfy these laws. Again, this construct also serves for renaming.

A parameterized structure CS can also be used to implement a type scheme T; all parameters of T must also be defined as parameters of CS. Just as the signature of a type scheme comprises the parameters (cf. 1.2.1), the definitions of syntactically and semantically correct implementations (cf. 3.1.2) must be extended to include the parameters: Syntactic correctness matches not only the constituents but also the parameters of T and CS and requires coinciding sorts and functionalities. Semantic correctness extends this matching for the hidden symbols of T and requires that (a quotient structure of a subalgebra of) CS is a model of T, no matter which carrier sets, domains, and objects are associated with the parameters of CS (only the restrictions on these parameters may be presupposed, if any).

Example:
The following structure S implements the type scheme SET from 1.2.1:

```
structure S = (sort m, m e, funct (m, m) m op)
                  set, emptyset, incorp, contains, total :
      mode set ≡ emptyset | incorp(set s, m m) ,
      funct contains ≡ (set x, m y) bool :
          x ≠ emptyset ∧ (m(x) = y ∀ contains(s(x), y)) ,
      funct total ≡ (set x) m :
          if x is emptyset
            then e
            else if contains(s(x), m(x))
                    then total(s(x))
                    else op(total(s(x)), m(x)) fi fi
      end of structure
```

S defines an initial model of the polymorphic type SET. If SET would contain laws like

incorp(incorp(s, x), x) ≡ incorp(s, x)

then S would have to define a coarser congruence relation than the equality introduced by the mode delaration for set.

3.2. EXTENSION: SUBMODES

Submodes are used as a convenient shorthand notation for expressing restrictions on objects. Let **m** denote a sort and C a boolean expression. Then one can declare a submode **sm** of **m** by

> **mode sm** ≡ **m** x : C .

The meaning of this submode is explained by textual substitution (see below). **m** is called the base mode of **sm**. If **m** itself denotes a submode, this definition must be applied repeatedly. We require that this process always terminates (i.e., a submode must not be a submode of itself).

Submodes are explained by the following rules:

(1) In a parameter position, the submode **sm** leads to a restriction of this parameter (see 2.1.4.4 (a) and 2.3.3 (b)):

> (**sm** x) **r** : E

is equivalent to

> (**m** x : C) **r** : E

and thus to

> (**m** x) **r** : **if** C **then** E **fi** .

Submodes in result positions, quantifications, set comprehensions, and set and function kinds are treated analogously (cf. 2.1.4.4).

Example:

Given the submode declaration

> **mode weekday** ≡ **nat** x : $1 \leq x \wedge x \leq 7$,

the function

> **funct** nextweekday ≡ (**weekday** x) **weekday**: mod(x, 7) + 1

is equivalent to

> **funct** nextweekday ≡
> (**nat** x : $1 \leq x \wedge x \leq 7$)(**nat** y : $1 \leq y \wedge y \leq 7$) : mod(x, 7) + 1

(2) The use of submodes in object declarations leads to restricted declarations (see 2.2.3 (b)):

> **sm** x ≡ E

is equivalent to

> (**m** x : C) ≡ E ,

i.e. to

> **m** x ≡ **if** C **then** E **fi** .

(3) In connection with program variables we get invariant assertions for these variables (see 2.3.3 (b)): A declaration

    var sm x := E

is equivalent to

    (**var ■** x : C) := E .

An assignment

    x := E

is then equivalent to

    ⌈ x := E; **assert** C ⌋ ,

and similarly

    call p(x)

means

    ⌈ **call** p(x); **assert** C ⌋ .

Procedures with global variables and submodes in variable parameters are treated analogously.

(4) A type or structure instantiation (cf. 1.2.2 and 3.1.3) using the submode **sm** is equivalent to an instantiation using the base mode together with a re-declaration of the **sm**-constants and of the operations that have **sm** as a parameter or result kind. Given the type scheme

    type T ≡ (**sort s,** ...) c, f, ... :

        s c, **funct** (s) s f, ...

    end of type ,

the instantiation

    include T(**sm**) **as** (d, g, ...)

is equivalent to

    include T(**■**) **as** (d', g', ...),

    sm d ≡ d' ,

    funct g ≡ (**sm** x) **sm** : g'(x) .

An analogous rule applies to the **based on** clause.

Example (cf. 1.4(e)):

    mode pnat ≡ **nat** n : n > 0 ,

    based on (**stack**, empty, isempty, append, top, rest) ≡ STACK(**pnat**)

  is equivalent to

    mode pnat ≡ **nat** n : n > 0 ,

    based on (**stack**, empty, isempty, append', top', rest) ≡ STACK(**nat**) ,

    funct append ≡ (**stack** s, **pnat** n) **stack** : append'(s, n) ,

    funct top ≡ (**stack** s) **pnat** : top'(s)

II.3.2 Submodes

(5) It can also be tested whether an object belongs to a submode:

$$\frac{E \text{ is } sm}{((m\ x)\ \textbf{bool}\ :\ C)\ (E)} \quad \Bigg\langle \quad \text{DECLARATION}[\![sm]\!] = \textbf{mode } sm \equiv m\ x\ :\ C$$

If m itself is a submode of a mode n the bottom scheme of this transformation has to read
$((n\ x)\ \textbf{bool}\ :\ x \text{ is } m\ \wedge\ C)\ (E)$.

Note that if m is again a submode, say
$$\textbf{mode } m \equiv m_0\ x\ :\ C_0$$
then repeated application of the rules (1) to (5) on the one hand, and "unfolding" m in the declaration of sm,
$$\textbf{mode } sm \equiv m_0\ x\ :\ C_0 \wedge C\ ,$$
on the other hand, lead to equivalent programs.

The above transformations are also applicable to mode declarations, which are special type instantiations (cf. 1.3). In particular, for restricted product modes we obtain

$$\textbf{mode } sm \equiv cons(m_1\ s_1,\ ...,\ m_n\ s_n\ :\ C)$$
$$\Big\Updownarrow$$
$$\textbf{mode } m \equiv cons'(m_1\ s_1,\ ...,\ m_n\ s_n);$$
$$\textbf{funct } cons \equiv (m_1\ s_1,\ ...,\ m_n\ s_n\ :\ C)\ sm:$$
$$cons'(s_1,\ ...,\ s_n)$$

where m and $cons'$ are new identifiers. In the case of the direct sum we have

$$\textbf{mode } sm \equiv cons_1\ (m_1\ s_1\ :\ C_1)\ |\ ...\ |\ cons_k(m\ s_k\ :\ C_k)\ |$$
$$cons_{k+1}(m_{k+1}\ s_{k+1})\ |\ ...\ |\ cons_n(m_n\ s_n)$$
$$\Big\Updownarrow$$
$$\textbf{mode } m \equiv cons_1'(m_1\ s_1)\ |\ ...\ |\ cons_k'(m_k\ s_k)\ |$$
$$cons_{k+1}(m_{k+1}\ s_{k+1})\ |\ ...\ |\ cons_n(m_n\ s_n)\ ;$$
$$\textbf{funct } cons_1 \equiv (m_1\ s_1\ :\ C_1)\ sm:\ cons_1'(s_1),\ ...,$$
$$\textbf{funct } cons_k \equiv (m_k\ s_k\ :\ C_k)\ sm:\ cons_k'(s_k)$$

3.3. MODULES

Modules are similar to computation structures except that they may also export procedures, whereas the visible constituents of computation structures must be purely applicative. Thus, modules provide a step on the way from applicative to procedural formulations (cf. /Laut 80/).

The declaration of a module takes the form

    module M ≡ «constituents» :
        $D_1, \ldots, D_k$
    end of module

Like structures, modules may be parameterized; instantiation and constituent renaming of a (parameterized) module MS are written in the form

    module («constituents») ≡ MS(«arguments») .

Example:
  A module for message switching (cf. 1.4 (e) for the type QUEUE)

    module MMESSAGE ≡ (**sort data**) **queue**, emptyqueue, msend, mreceive :
        based on (**queue**, emptyqueue, isempty, top, rest, .&.) ≡ QUEUE(**data**) ,
        proc msend ≡ (**var queue** q, **data** d) :
            q := q & d ,
        proc mreceive ≡ (**var queue** q, **var data** m : ¬ isempty(q)) :
            (q, m) := [top, rest](q)
    end of module

Like procedures, modules do not have an independent semantics. Rather, a module instantiation is equivalent to unfolding the body with appropriate parameter substitution and renaming. Then the definitional transformation rules of the scheme language take over.

LOCAL INSTANTIATIONS

We allow local instantiations of components also within constructs of the scheme language. This will be important for the semantics of devices (cf. 3.4). These instantiations may occur everywhere declarations may occur. The context condition is that the actual parameters of the instantiation (if any) must not be local entities other than constituents provided by other local instantiations of *types*. This prohibits mutual recursion between types and functions which would lead into considerable semantic difficulties.

II.3.3 Modules

The semantics is explained by moving all local instantiations inside a scheme language construct to the declarations of the component in which the construct occurs (possibly with renaming to avoid name clashes).

3.4. DEVICES

Devices couple the concepts of modules and variables. Besides the constituents of a module they may additionally contain variable definitions as well as statements. However, the variables must not occur in the list of constituents, i.e. they are hidden. In this way they can only be accessed using the routines of the module and cannot be manipulated wildly. The statement part (if any) provides an initialization for the hidden variables.

Devices may contain instantiations of types, structures, modules, and other devices; however, they must not be based on each other cyclically. The instantiation of a (parameterized) device DS may occur everywhere a statement may occur. It is denoted by

device (≪constituents≫) ≡ DS(≪arguments≫)

and is again explained by textual substitution of the body of DS (after appropriate renaming) for the instantiation. In particular, the statement part is executed upon instantiation. The context condition for the instantiation is that the phrases which result from the unfolding are context-correct again (for instance, the instantiation must not introduce recursive object declarations).

Examples:

(a) A device for pointers and plexes (cf. 1.4(g) for the type PLEX):

> **device** PT ≡ (**sort m**) **pt**, nil, $\hat{=}$, pnew, pisdef, pderef, pupdatable, pupdate;
>   **based on** PLEX(**m**);
>   **var plex** q := emptyplex;
>   **proc** pnew ≡ (**var pt** p) : $\lceil$ q := new(q); p := pt(q) $\rfloor$,
>   **funct** pisdef ≡ (**pt** p) **bool** : isdef(p, q) ,
>   **funct** pderef ≡ (**pt** p: pisdef (p)) **m** : deref(p, q),
>   **funct** pupdatable ≡ (**pt** p) **bool** : updatable(p, q),
>   **proc** pupdate ≡ (**pt** p, **m** x: pupdatable (p)) : q := update(p, x, q)
> **end of device**

Note that the sort **plex** is not visible outside the module. This corresponds to the fact that in most programming languages the store is treated as an implicit global parameter.

(b) A device for loosely coupled message switching (cf. 1.4 (e) for the type QUEUE):

```
device MESSAGE ≡ (sort data) send, receive:
      based on QUEUE(data);
      var queue q := empty;
      proc send ≡ (data d);
           await true then q := stock(q, d) endwait,
      proc receive ≡ (var data v):
           await ¬ isempty(q)
           then (v, q) := [top, rest](q) endwait
end of device
```

The procedures send and receive are convenient tools for expressing communication between concurrent processes via channels.

PART III

FORMAL DEFINITION OF THE LANGUAGE

This Part contains the formal specification of the language. Conceptually, it is organized like Part II: The basis is formed by systems of algebraic types; the scheme language comprises expressions over the sorts, constants, and operation symbols of the basic types; the computation structures, modules and devices are built using declarations of the scheme language.

Formally, the language is regarded as a hierarchy of signatures corresponding to the abstract syntax. Its semantics is defined partly by mathematical models (viz. the algebraic types, the kernel of the scheme language, and the computation structures) and partly by definitional transformation rules (viz. the full applicative, procedural, parallel and machine-oriented languages as well as modules and devices).

III.0 Fundamentals

0. FUNDAMENTALS OF THE DESCRIPTION

This section briefly sketches the theoretical background and the organization of the language definition. For more details, especially on the theory of algebraic types and on fixpoint theory, we have to refer to the literature (cf. e.g. /Wirsing et al. 83/, /Markowsky 76/).

0.1. LANGUAGE LEVELS AS A HIERARCHY OF SIGNATURES

The whole language is built up as a hierarchy of signatures. The basic layer is formed by the signature of a system of user-defined algebraic types. Since the semantics of the following layers depends on the models associated with these types, we speak of a "scheme language".

The first language level over these basic data types is a pure expression language introducing the new sort **expr**. The next level defines a new sort **decl** for explicit declarations; three more levels introduce the sorts **stat** for statements, **pstat** for parallel statements, and **lstat** for labels and gotos. Finally the sort **program** comprises systems of algebraic types, computation structures, modules, and devices.

0.2. ABSTRACT SYNTAX OF THE LANGUAGE

The transition from the usual BNF description of a language to a description by a signature is technically done as follows (cf. /ADJ 78/ and /Laut 78, 82/): For each production

$$s_0 ::= t_0 \; s_1 \; t_1 \; \ldots \; t_n \; s_n \; t_{n+1}$$

with nonterminals s_i and terminal strings t_i one defines an operation symbol

$$f : s_1 \; x \; \ldots \; x \; s_n \rightarrow s_0 \; .$$

Hence, each nonterminal leads to a sort and each production to an operation. The transition from the concrete syntax to the abstract syntax as described by this signature is given by a mapping

$$A : \; \ll\text{concrete syntax}\gg \; \rightarrow \; \ll\text{abstract syntax}\gg \; .$$

The function A is not injective but maps several concrete terms onto the same abstract term over the signature. This establishes a congruence relation on the concrete terms and thus allows to minimize the description. The mapping A is given only for one representative of a congruence class (together with the semantical specification of the corresponding abstract term), which establishes a "skeleton" for the language. The other constructs of the class are viewed as notational variants, i.e. as "language extensions" as defined in Part II. Thus the abstract syntax is kept comparatively small.

In the main, the definition of the mapping A can be given depending on the context-free concrete syntax only. However, in order to make all identifiers occurring in the abstract terms distinct, more information is required. This is done by inserting the auxiliary symbol $\text{BIND}\llbracket x \rrbracket$ at the declaration of an identifier x and the symbol $\text{UNIQUE}\llbracket x \rrbracket$ at all applied occurrences of x. These auxiliary symbols are then eliminated from the inside outward as follows: Consider a term t and a subterm u of t such that for some concrete identifier x_j, u has an occurrence of UNIQUE $[\![x_j]\!]$ and some occurrences of BIND $[\![x_j]\!]$, but no proper subterm of u does. We associate a unique abstract identifier y_j with the concrete identifier x_j and replace all occurrences of BIND $[\![x_j]\!]$ and of UNIQUE $[\![x_j]\!]$ within u by y_j. Note that identical concrete identifiers x_j are associated with the same abstract identifier y_j, and thus context errors due to duplicate declarations etc. are still recognizable. Having in this way eliminated all occurrences of BIND in u, we can pass to another subterm of t of the same form. We proceed in this way until all occurrences of BIND have disappeared. For all remaining terms of the form UNIQUE $[\![x]\!]$, the identifier x must be defined by one of the basic types.

For this process we need a signature describing the set **id** of abstract identifiers. We may think of this signature as providing an unbounded set of constant symbols. By NEW we denote the subset of those abstract identifiers which are not used in the abstract term under consideration. Formally, NEW is just another attribute (cf. 0.3); however, we do not want to inflate the description by defining it precisely.

As in Part II, $c_1 [\![c_2 \text{ for } c_3]\!]$ denotes the consistent replacement of a term c_3 in c_1 by c_2 with appropriate renaming of bound identifiers.

We write $s_1 \uplus s_2$ for the direct sum (disjoint union) of two sorts s_1, s_2 to avoid excessively many new auxiliary sorts and injection and projection operations. Also, it is often necessary to describe sequences (e.g. of parameters, statements, etc.) or finite sets. The sort of sequences resp. finite sets of elements of sort **s** is denoted by $\langle s \rangle$ resp. **finset s** . We use the shorthand notations

$$\langle x_1, \ldots, x_n \rangle \text{ or equivalently } \langle x_i \rangle , \text{ and}$$
$$\{x_1, \ldots, x_n\} \text{ or equivalently } \{x_i\}$$

with the following conventions:

(i) & denotes concatenation of sequences; $\langle \rangle$ denotes the empty sequence.

(ii) Sequences of pairs, triples etc. will be written as $\langle (a_1, b_1), \ldots, (a_n, b_n) \rangle$ or, abbreviated, as $\langle a_i, b_i \rangle$.

(iii) The function length gives the number of components of a sequence.

(iv) For a sequence $\langle x_i \rangle$ we denote by $\{x_i\}$ the corresponding set

$$\{x_i \mid 1 \leq i \leq length(\langle x_i \rangle)\} .$$

(v) Given a function $F : \mathbf{s} \to \mathbf{r}$ where $(\mathbf{r}, o, 1)$ is a monoid, for a sequence $\langle x_i \rangle$ or a set $\{x_i\}$ of n elements of sort **s**, we write briefly $o\, F[\![x_i]\!]$ instead of $\overset{n}{\underset{i=1}{o}}\, F[\![x_i]\!]$, where we set $o\, F[\![x_i]\!] = 1$ if $n = 0$.

E.g. for $\mathbf{r} = \mathbf{bool}$, $o = \wedge$, and $1 = \mathbf{true}$ we obtain $\wedge\, F[\![x_i]\!]$ instead of $\overset{n}{\underset{i=1}{\wedge}}\, F[\![x_i]\!]$.

III.0.3 Context conditions

0.3. CONTEXT CONDITIONS

The mapping A turns every concrete program into an abstract program. A meaning will, however, be defined for context-correct programs only. These programs are characterized by context-conditions on the abstract syntax which are specified with the help of attributes (cf. /Knuth 68/). A program is context-correct iff all its parts are; therefore the context-conditions are formulated separately for all language constructs. Since the context-correctness of a piece of a program depends on the position of that piece within the whole program, we shall always consider pairs consisting of a program piece p and a "surrounding program" s, i.e. a program with a "hole" such that insertion of the piece into this hole yields a complete program. Pairs (p,s) are called program parts.

Program parts can be formalized using terms over the signatures specifying the abstract syntax. A context is a term K in which exactly one identifier x occurs and in which x occurs only once. For a term t of the sort of x, K$[\![t]\!]$ denotes the term that results from K by replacing x by t. A program part is a pair (K,p) where K is a context and p is a term of the sort of the identifier of K; then K$[\![p]\!]$ is the program from which the part is taken.

The attributes we use will be defined in terms of these program parts. In order to ease reading, the context K will remain implicit in the sequel.

For a set-valued attribute F : s $\rightarrow$ **finset r**, the extension F^* : <s> $\rightarrow$ **finset r** is defined by $F^*[\![<x_i>]\!]$ = $\mathbf{U}$ F$[\![x_i]\!]$. We will denote F^* again by F.

0.4. SEMANTIC SPECIFICATION

For the algebraic types a mathematical semantics is given using partial heterogeneous algebras. They form the basic level of the language. Each signature for a certain level of the scheme language has the signature of the previous level as its primitive part. The specification of the new level is given in the form of conditional rewriting rules which allow to reduce every term t of a primitive sort to a primitive term p (this means that p only contains function symbols of the primitive signature that corresponds to the previous level). These rules are denoted in the form P $\Rightarrow$ t_1 $\mapsto$ t_2 ; if, in addition, we have the converse rule P $\Rightarrow$ t_2 $\mapsto$ t_2 , both rules are combined by writing P $\Rightarrow$ t_1 $\leftarrow\!\!\mid\!\!\mapsto$ t_2 .

An exception from this specification scheme occurs in the kernel, since the expression language differs in two repects from the other levels. First, the possibility of non-termination of programs may lead to infinite reduction sequences. (The non-termination problem of the subsequent language levels can be reduced to the non-termination problem of this expression language.) Second, one also has to deal with non-operational constructs like set comprehension, which are not even continuous and therefore lead to further complications in rewriting. For these reasons, we have decided to specify the kernel language using the techniques of denotational semantics.

0.5. TABLE OF IDENTIFIERS

In the following Chapters we use identifiers in lower case letters to denote variables for terms. The correspondence is given by the following table:

Identifier(s)	Sort in the abstract syntax
m, n, r, s, w	kind
m, r, s	sort
a, c, f, l, p, q, t, u, v, x, y, z	id
co, p	constituent
la	law
r	law ө inst
b	facet
f, fb, ff, fr, g, gb, gg, gr, ufb, ufr	\<facet\>
y, z	term
u	univ
c, e, f, g	expr
a	abstraction
s	stat
ps	pstat
psq	\<pstat\>
p, dp	phrase
pp, dsq	\<phrase\>
ls	lstat

Of course, these identifiers are indexed or modified by primes, bars, hats, or tildes as the need arises. The sort of an overloaded identifier can always be inferred from the context.

III.1 Algebraic types

1. ALGEBRAIC TYPES

This section defines <u>algebraic types,</u> i.e. the language constructs for the algebraic specification of basic object sets together with operations on them. Mode declarations are not considered here, since they are mere notational extensions (cf. II.1.3). Also, we assume that overloading of identifiers has already been resolved (see Appendix I).

For every type the meaning is defined as a set of partial heterogeneous algebras. This semantic specification is given in section 1.3. The paragraphs before introduce attributes which provide the signature of the algebras aimed at and the laws they must fulfil.

Parameterized types and type systems are considered together with structures, modules, and devices in Chapter 3.

1.1. ABSTRACT SYNTAX OF TYPES

> sort: **id** $\rightarrow$ **constituent**
> funct: **<id>** x **id** x **id** $\rightarrow$ **constituent**
> const: **id** x **id** $\rightarrow$ **constituent**
>
> tvalue: **id** $\rightarrow$ **term**
> tapply: **id** x **<term>** $\rightarrow$ **term**
>
> tequ: **term** x **term** $\rightarrow$ **law**
> tnot: **law** $\rightarrow$ **law**
> tconj: **law** x **law** $\rightarrow$ **law**
> tall: **<id** x **id>** x **law** $\rightarrow$ **law**
>
> constit: **constituent** $\rightarrow$ **facet**
> law: **law** $\rightarrow$ **facet**
> prim: **facet** $\rightarrow$ **facet**
>
> type: **id** x **<constituent>** x **<law ⊕ inst>** x **<id>** x **<facet>** $\rightarrow$ **component**

Constituents and laws are called **facets** of a type. Facets may be primitive (in a nested fashion) or non-primitive (cf. Chapter 3 for mechanisms of distinguishing facets as primitive). We use an auxiliary syntactic mapping Å that translates the concrete syntax into the "non-lifted" versions of facets (**constituent, law**).

Furthermore we define the abstract syntax of kinds:
Every identifier may denote a sort. So we have an operation
> simple: **id** $\rightarrow$ **kind** .

Moreover, we have the operations
> tuplekind: **<kind>** $\rightarrow$ **kind**
> functkind: **kind** x **kind** $\rightarrow$ **kind**

sortkind: → **kind**
typekind: → **kind** .

This context-free syntax defines more kinds than actually are in the language proper. Therefore we use three restricting predicates

PROPERKIND, EXPRKIND, OBJECTKIND : **kind** → **bool** .

OBJECTKIND characterizes the purely non-functional kinds, whereas PROPERKIND characterizes the set of admissible kinds for our language. EXPRKIND, finally, characterizes the kinds of terms and expressions (cf. 2). These predicates are defined as follows:

$\forall$ **kind** m : OBJECTKIND $[\![$ m $]\!]$ $\Rightarrow$ EXPRKIND $[\![$ m $]\!]$

$\forall$ **kind** m : EXPRKIND $[\![$ m $]\!]$ $\Rightarrow$ PROPERKIND $[\![$ m $]\!]$

PROPERKIND $[\![$ simple(y) $]\!]$

OBJECTKIND $[\![$ simple(y) $]\!]$

PROPERKIND $[\![$ tuplekind($<m_i>$) $]\!]$ = $\bigwedge$ OBJECTKIND $[\![$ m_i $]\!]$

OBJECTKIND $[\![$ tuplekind($<m_i>$) $]\!]$ = $\bigwedge$ OBJECTKIND $[\![$ m_i $]\!]$

EXPRKIND $[\![$ tuplekind($<m_i>$) $]\!]$ = $\bigwedge$ EXPRKIND $[\![$ m_i $]\!]$

PROPERKIND $[\![$ functkind(m,r) $]\!]$ = OBJECTKIND $[\![$ m $]\!]$ $\wedge$ OBJECTKIND $[\![$ r $]\!]$ $\wedge$

$r \neq$ tuplekind($<m_i>$) for all m_i ,

   i.e. higher-order operations and tuple-valued operations are not permitted in types

PROPERKIND $[\![$ functkind(m,r) $]\!]$ $\Rightarrow$ EXPRKIND $[\![$ functkind(m,r) $]\!]$

$\neg$ OBJECTKIND $[\![$ functkind(m,r) $]\!]$

PROPERKIND $[\![$ sortkind $]\!]$ $\wedge$ $\neg$ EXPRKIND $[\![$ sortkind $]\!]$

PROPERKIND $[\![$ typekind $]\!]$ $\wedge$ $\neg$ EXPRKIND $[\![$ typekind $]\!]$

Moreover, since nested tuples are equivalent to "flattened" ones (cf. II.2.1.1(c),(f)), we add a corresponding "flattening" rule for kinds:

ksq_1 & $<$tuplekind($<m_i>$)$>$ & ksq_2 $\longleftrightarrow$ ksq_1 & $<m_i>$ & ksq_2 .

1.2. ATTRIBUTES AND CONTEXT CONDITIONS

The attribute KNOWN is inherited, which implies that it does not need to be defined for the "atomic" constructs. KIND is both inherited and derived, whereas all other attributes are derived.

KIND : **id** $\circ$ **term** → **kind**

For an identifier c, KIND $[\![$ c $]\!]$ may be

- sortkind (i.e. c is a sort identifier)
- the sort s of a constant
- functkind(tuplekind($<s_i>$), r) (i.e. c is an operation symbol with the indicated functionality)
- typekind (i.e. c is a type identifier).

For a term e, KIND $[\![$ e $]\!]$ gives the result sort of the outermost operator in the term.

III.1.2 Attributes and context conditions

USED : **id ꝺ facet ꝺ constituent ꝺ term ꝺ law → finset id**
USED gives all sort, constant, operation and free identifiers used in its argument.

DECLARED : **id ꝺ facet → finset constituent**
DECLARED gives the sorts, constants, and operations that are defined immediately, i. e. not via instantiations (cf. 3), by its argument.

LAWS : **id ꝺ facet → finset law**
LAWS gives the set of laws that are defined immediately (not via instantiations, cf. Chapter 3) in its argument.

CONSTITUENTS : **id → finset id**
CONSTITUENTS⟦x⟧ gives the set of identifiers that are declared in the body of the type x and are made visible via the list of constituents of x.

HIDDEN : **id → finset id**
HIDDEN⟦x⟧ = {ID⟦c⟧ : c ꝺ DECLARED⟦x⟧} \ CONSTITUENTS⟦x⟧ .

ID : **component ꝺ constituent → id**
ID gives the identifier of a type or constituent.

KNOWN : **facet → finset id**
KNOWN⟦b⟧ gives the set of all identifiers that may be used within b; see Chapter 3 for its definition.

For convenience we will filter out subsets of identifiers of a certain kind by writing e.g. DECLAREDSORTS, USEDTYPES, etc.

We now give the rules for propagating the attributes; with the help of these attributes the context conditions are specified.

1.2.1. CONSTITUENTS

(a) <u>Sort</u>

Syntactic mapping:
$\hat{A}⟦\textbf{sort s}⟧ = sort(\hat{A}⟦s⟧)$

Let so = sort(s) .

Context conditions: none

Attributes:
   KIND $[\![$ s $]\!]$ = sortkind
   USED $[\![$ so $]\!]$ = $\emptyset$
   ID $[\![$ so $]\!]$ = s

(b) Operation

Syntactic mapping:
   $\hat{A} [\![\textbf{funct}(\textbf{s}_1, ..., \textbf{s}_n)\textbf{r } f]\!]$ = funct($\langle \hat{A} [\![\textbf{s}_i]\!] \rangle$, $\hat{A} [\![\textbf{r}]\!]$, $\hat{A} [\![f]\!]$)

Let fu = funct($\langle s_i \rangle$, r, f) .

Context conditions:
   Since we treat nullary operations separately as constants, an operation must have at least
   one argument:
      length($\langle s_i \rangle$) $\geq$ 1
   $\forall$ i : KIND $[\![s_i]\!]$ = sortkind
   KIND $[\![r]\!]$ = sortkind

Attributes:
   KIND $[\![f]\!]$ = functkind(tuplekind($\langle s_i \rangle$), r)
   USED $[\![fu]\!]$ = $\{s_i\} \cup \{r\}$
   ID $[\![fu]\!]$ = f

(c) Constant

Syntactic mapping:
   $\hat{A} [\![s \ c]\!]$ = const($\hat{A} [\![s]\!]$, $\hat{A} [\![c]\!]$)

Let co = const(s, c) .

Context conditions: none

Attributes:
   KIND $[\![c]\!]$ = simple(s)
   USED $[\![co]\!]$ = $\{s\}$
   ID $[\![co]\!]$ = c

III.1.2 Attributes and context conditions

1.2.2. TERMS

Terms are used in the axioms of a type, which are formulas over equations between well-formed terms over the constant and operation symbols of the type as well as over quantified identifiers.

(d) Free identifier and constant

Syntactic mapping:
$Â[\![x]\!]$ = tvalue(UNIQUE$[\![x]\!]$)

Let v = tvalue(x) .

Context condition:
OBJECTKIND$[\![$KIND$[\![x]\!]]\!]$

Attributes:
KIND$[\![v]\!]$ = KIND$[\![x]\!]$
USED$[\![v]\!]$ = BASESORTS$[\![$KIND$[\![x]\!]]\!]$ **U** {x}

(e) Application

Syntactic mapping:
$Â[\![f(E_1, ..., E_n)]\!]$ = tapply($Â[\![f]\!]$, $\langle Â[\![E_i]\!]\rangle$)

Let a = tapply(f, $\langle e_i\rangle$) .

Context condition:
KIND$[\![f]\!]$ = functkind(tuplekind($\langle\!\langle$KIND$[\![e_i]\!]\rangle$), r) for some sort r

Attributes:
KIND$[\![a]\!]$ = r
USED$[\![a]\!]$ = {r, f} **U** (**U** USED$[\![e_i]\!]$)

1.2.3. LAWS

Laws are first-order formulas over equations between terms.

(f) <u>Equation</u>

 Syntactic mapping:
  $\hat{A}[\![E_1 = E_2]\!] = tequ(\hat{A}[\![E_1]\!], \hat{A}[\![E_2]\!])$

 Let $g = tequ(e_1, e_2)$.

 Context condition:
  $KIND[\![e_1]\!] = KIND[\![e_2]\!]$

 Attributes:
  $USED[\![g]\!] = USED[\![e_1]\!] \ \mathbf{U} \ USED[\![e_2]\!]$

(g) <u>Logical connective</u>

 Syntactic mapping:
  $\hat{A}[\![\neg F]\!] = tnot(\hat{A}[\![F]\!])$
  $\hat{A}[\![F \wedge G]\!] = tconj(\hat{A}[\![F]\!], \hat{A}[\![G]\!])$

 Context conditions: none

 Attributes:
  $USED[\![tnot(g)]\!] = USED[\![g]\!]$,
  $USED[\![tconj(g_1,g_2)]\!] = USED[\![g_1]\!] \ \mathbf{U} \ USED[\![g_2]\!]$

(h) <u>Quantification</u>

 Syntactic mapping:
  $\hat{A}[\![\forall \ s_1 \ x_1, \ ..., \ s_n \ x_n : G]\!] = tall(\langle\hat{A}[\![s_i]\!], BIND[\![x_i]\!]\rangle, \hat{A}[\![G]\!])$

 Let $a = tall(\langle s_i, x_i\rangle, g)$.

 Context conditions:
  $n \geq 1$
  $\forall \ i, j : 1 \leq i < j \leq n \Rightarrow x_i \neq x_j$

III.1.2 Attributes and context conditions

Attributes:
$$\forall i : 1 \leq i < n \Rightarrow KIND[\![x_i]\!] = free(s_i)$$
$$USED[\![a]\!] = (USED[\![g]\!] \cup \{s_i\}) \setminus \{x_i\}$$

1.2.4. FACETS OF A TYPE

(i) Constituent

Syntactic mapping: For a constituent C,
$$A[\![C]\!] = constit(\hat{A}[\![C]\!])$$

Let $c = constit(co)$.

Context conditions:
$$EXPRKIND[\![KIND[\![co]\!]]\!] \vee KIND[\![co]\!] = sortkind$$
$$USED[\![c]\!] \subseteq KNOWN[\![c]\!]$$

Attributes:
$$DECLARED[\![c]\!] = \{ID[\![co]\!]\}$$
$$USED[\![c]\!] = USED[\![co]\!]$$
$$LAWS[\![c]\!] = \emptyset$$

(j) Law

Syntactic mapping: For a law L,
$$A[\![L]\!] = law(\hat{A}[\![L]\!])$$

Let $l = law(la)$.

Context condition:
$$USED[\![l]\!] \subseteq KNOWN[\![l]\!]$$
This implies that la is a closed formula over the constituents of the respective type (cf. 1.3).

Attributes:
$$DECLARED[\![l]\!] = \emptyset$$
$$USED[\![l]\!] = USED[\![la]\!]$$
$$LAWS[\![l]\!] = \{la\}$$

(k) Primitive facet

Let pr = prim(b) .

Context condition: none

Attributes:
    DECLARED $[\![$ pr $]\!]$ = DECLARED $[\![$ b $]\!]$
    USED $[\![$ pr $]\!]$ = USED $[\![$ b $]\!]$
    LAWS $[\![$ pr $]\!]$ = LAWS $[\![$ b $]\!]$
    KNOWN $[\![$ b $]\!]$ = KNOWN $[\![$ pr $]\!]$

1.3. SEMANTICS OF NON-PARAMETERIZED TYPES

Syntactic mapping:
    A $[\![$ **type** X $\equiv$ <res_k> : <$facet_1$> **end of type** $]\!]$ =
    type(A $[\![$ X $]\!]$, <>, <>, <A $[\![$ res_k $]\!]$ >, <A $[\![$ $facet_1$ $]\!]$ >)

Let t = type(x, <>, <>, <y_k>, <b_1>) .

For the context conditions and attributes see 3.2.2.

Semantic specification:
    Let S = DECLAREDSORTS $[\![$ x $]\!]$, F = DECLAREDFUNCTS $[\![$ x $]\!]$, C = DECLAREDCONSTS $[\![$ x $]\!]$; then
    Σ = (S, F, C) is the <u>signature corresponding to x</u>, where the functionality of f $\in$ F is
    $s_1 x...x s_n \rightarrow r$ if KIND $[\![$ f $]\!]$ = functkind(tuplekind(<$s_1,...,s_n$>), r) .

Consider a term-generated Σ-algebra (cf.II.1.1.6)
    A = ({s^A : s $\in$ S}, {f^A : f $\in$ F}, {c^A : c $\in$ C}) .

Call a formula or a term q <u>closed</u> wrt. the type x if USED $[\![$ q $]\!]$ $\subseteq$ DECLARED $[\![$ x $]\!]$. We define
when a closed formula g $\in$ **law** is <u>valid</u> in A, in signs A $\models$ g : First enrich the sort **term** by
all elements of the carrier sets of A as new constants. The <u>interpretation</u> q_A of a closed
term q $\in$ **term** in A is defined by
    q_A = q if q $\in$ s^A for some s $\in$ S
    tvalue(c)$_A$ = c^A if KIND $[\![$ c $]\!]$ = s

$$\text{tapply}(f, <e_1, ..., e_n>)_A = \begin{cases} f^A(e_{1A}, ..., e_{nA}) \text{ if this is defined} \\ \bot \text{ otherwise} \end{cases}$$

III.1.3 Semantics

Let y be an identifier with $KIND[\![y]\!]$ = simple(s) and a ϵ s^A. The <u>substitution</u> $q[\![a \text{ for } y]\!]$ is defined by

$q[\![a \text{ for } y]\!]$ = q if q ϵ A or q = tvalue(z) with z $\neq$ y

$tvalue(y)[\![a \text{ for } y]\!]$ = tvalue(a)

$tapply(f, <e_1, ..., e_n>)[\![a \text{ for } y]\!]$ = $tapply(f, <e_1[\![a \text{ for } y]\!], ..., e_n[\![a \text{ for } y]\!]>)$.

Now,

$A \models tall(<s_i, y_i>, g)$ iff for all a_i ϵ s_i^A we have $A \models g[\![a_i \text{ for } y_i]\!]$

$A \models tnot(g)$ iff $A \models g$ does not hold

$A \models tand(g_1, g_2)$ iff $A \models g_1$ and $A \models g_2$

$A \models tequ(e_1, e_2)$ iff $e_{1A} = e_{2A}$

Consider a type x all of whose laws are closed wrt. x. We say that a term-generated Σ-algebra A is a <u>model</u> of x if $A \models g$ for all g ϵ $LAWS[\![x]\!]$.

For a signature $\overline{\Sigma} = (\overline{S}, \overline{F}, \overline{C})$ such that $\overline{S} \subseteq S$, $\overline{F} \subseteq F$, $\overline{C} \subseteq C$, and a Σ-algebra A, the $\overline{\Sigma}$-reduct $A|\overline{\Sigma}$ is defined by $sA|\overline{\Sigma} = sA$ for s ϵ $\overline{S}$, $fA|\overline{\Sigma} = fA$ for f ϵ $\overline{F}$, $cA|\overline{\Sigma} = cA$ for c ϵ $\overline{C}$.

The <u>primitive type</u> of x is found by collecting all primitive facets: Let p be a new identifier, let $\overline{t}$ be the type definition

$type(p, <>, <>, <>, \& \overline{b}_j)$

where $\overline{b}_j = <\hat{b}_j>$ if $b_j = prim(\hat{b}_j)$ and $\overline{b}_j = <>$ otherwise.

Let $\overline{\Sigma} = (\overline{S}, \overline{F}, \overline{C})$ be the signature corresponding to p. A is called <u>hierarchy-preserving</u> if its $\overline{\Sigma}$-reduct is a model of p. x is <u>persistent</u> if for every model $\overline{A}$ of p there is a model A of x with $A|\overline{\Sigma} \cong \overline{A}$.

Now the semantics of the type x can be defined as the class of reducts of models of x to the visible signature:

Let $S' = \{s \epsilon S : s \epsilon <y_i>\}$, $F' = \{f \epsilon F : f \epsilon <y_i>\}$, $C' = \{c \epsilon C : c \epsilon <y_i>\}$, and $\Sigma' = (S', F', C')$. The <u>semantics</u> of the type x is given by all Σ'-algebras that are Σ'-reducts of hierarchy-preserving models of x, provided that x is persistent.

2. THE SCHEME LANGUAGE

This Chapter specifies those elements of the language which (in an operational view) determine the "flow of control". The basic concepts here are expressions, declarations, simple statements, and statements with parallel constructs and with jumps.

Let **construct = expr ⊕ decl ⊕ stat ⊕ pstat ⊕ lstat ⊕ abstraction ⊕ routine** .

The attributes KNOWN, BODY, and DECLARATION are inherited, whereas KIND and ADMISSIBLE are both inherited and derived. All other attributes are derived. The overloading of the identifiers KIND, DECLARED, and USED should not cause any confusion.

KIND : **id ⊕ expr → kind**

KIND⟦c⟧ may be
- a kind m, i.e. a sort of a basic type, a set kind, or a function kind (see 2.1.1), or a sequence of such kinds
- a variable-kind of the form varkind($<m_i>$)
- a procedure-kind of the form prockind($<m_i>$, $<m_j>$)
- labelkind (i.e. c is a label identifier)

DECLARED : **decl ⊕ stat ⊕ pstat ⊕ lstat → finset id**

DECLARED⟦c⟧ gives those identifiers which are declared in c and are not local to an inner scope of c.

USED : **id ⊕ construct → finset id**

USED⟦c⟧ gives all (non-local) identifiers which are used in c, i.e. which occur free in c. If c is an identifier for a function or a procedure, the set USED⟦c⟧ always is the transitive closure over all calls of functions and procedures in the body of c.

OCCURS : **id × (id ⊕ construct) → bool**

OCCURS⟦x in c⟧ = x e USED⟦c⟧

ASSIGNED : **id ⊕ stat ⊕ pstat ⊕ lstat → finset id**

ASSIGNED⟦c⟧ gives all identifiers which occur within c on the left-hand side of assignments. Again, for a procedure call not only the actual variable-parameters but also the non-local variables assigned in the body are included.

KNOWN : **construct → finset id**

KNOWN⟦c⟧ gives the set of all identifiers that may be used within c (i.e. c is contained in the scope of these identifiers).

III.2 The scheme language

DECLARATION : **id** → **routine**
BODY : **id** → **stat ⊕ pstat**
    DECLARATION⟦x⟧ gives the routine named by x, while BODY⟦x⟧ gives the body of that routine.

ADMISSIBLE : **kind** x **construct** → **bool**
    ADMISSIBLE⟦m at q⟧ ⟺ PROPERKIND⟦m⟧ ∧ BASESORTS⟦m⟧ ⊆ KNOWN⟦q⟧ .

For convenience, we will filter out subsets of identifiers of a certain kind by writing e.g. USEDVARS, DECLAREDLABS, KNOWNKINDS, etc.

2.1. THE KERNEL : AN EXPRESSION LANGUAGE

A program of the kernel language consists of a collection of "basic" algebraic data types and an expression. The connection between the two parts is established as follows: The algebraic data types provide an environment for the expression, i.e. their sorts, constants, and operation symbols form the set of identifiers available for the expression (attribute KNOWN). Hence, the signature for the kernel language is syntactically based on the signature IDENTIFIER only (note that in the abstract syntax identifiers for sorts, objects, operations etc. are not distinguished). Semantically, every identifier is associated with a carrier set, an object, or a partial operation of a model of the basic types. Presupposing a model A of the basic types, we construct semantic domains for all applicative kinds. We start from flat domains M^+ consisting of the carrier sets M of the model A extended by the "undefined" value ⊥ as the least element. From these flat domains the further domains are constructed using product, powerset and function spaces.

In this Part, we use refinements of the domains given in II.2.1.1 by associating with each kind m two sets of semantic values:
    D⟦m⟧ characterizes values that occur as function arguments of kind m ;
    R⟦m⟧ characterizes (sets of) result values of kind m .
The domains are chosen in such a way that we have always R⟦m⟧ ⊆ ℙ⟦D⟦m⟧$^+$⟧ where the power domain operator ℙ⟦·⟧ is defined below.

The semantics of an expression E of kind **m** is then given by its <u>breadth</u> B⟦E⟧ ∈ R⟦**m**⟧, i.e. by its set of possible values. The breadth will be defined inductively on the structure of the abstract syntax: The (sub)terms of sort **expr** will be successively replaced by their corresponding semantic values. Thus we get intermediate terms where syntactic and semantic constructs are mixed (cf. /Schütte 67/).

2.1.1. SEMANTIC DOMAINS

We first define the abstract syntax of kinds:

For every sort identifier s of the basic types we have, as before, a nullary operation

$\hat{s} : \rightarrow \textbf{kind}$.

Moreover, we have the operations

setkind: **kind** $\rightarrow$ **kind**

tuplekind: **‹kind›** $\rightarrow$ **kind**

functkind: **kind** x **kind** $\rightarrow$ **kind** .

The rules for the restricting predicates PROPER, EXPRKIND, OBJECTKIND and an additional predicate VALKIND are modified as follows:

PROPER $[\![$ setkind(m) $]\!]$ = OBJECTKIND $[\![$ m $]\!]$

PROPER $[\![$ setkind(m) $]\!]$ $\Rightarrow$ OBJECTKIND $[\![$ setkind(m) $]\!]$

$\forall$ **kind** m : EXPRKIND $[\![$ m $]\!]$ $\Rightarrow$ VALKIND $[\![$ m $]\!]$ $\land$ BASEKIND $[\![$ m $]\!]$ = m

$\neg$ VALKIND $[\![$ sortkind $]\!]$

$\neg$ VALKIND $[\![$ typekind $]\!]$

The rules for tuplekind and functkind are replaced by the following ones:

PROPER $[\![$ tuplekind($\langle m_i \rangle$) $]\!]$ = $\land$ EXPRKIND $[\![$ m_i $]\!]$

PROPER $[\![$ tuplekind($\langle m_i \rangle$) $]\!]$ $\Rightarrow$ EXPRKIND $[\![$ tuplekind($\langle m_i \rangle$) $]\!]$

OBJECTKIND $[\![$ tuplekind($\langle m_i \rangle$) $]\!]$ = $\land$ OBJECTKIND $[\![$ m_i $]\!]$

PROPER $[\![$ functkind(m,r) $]\!]$ = EXPRKIND $[\![$ m $]\!]$ $\land$ EXPRKIND $[\![$ r $]\!]$

PROPER $[\![$ functkind(m,r) $]\!]$ $\Rightarrow$ EXPRKIND $[\![$ functkind(m,r) $]\!]$

$\neg$ OBJECTKIND $[\![$ functkind(m,r) $]\!]$

Now we are going to associate domains with the kinds for which PROPER and EXPRKIND are true. By a _predomain_ we mean a partially ordered set $(M, \leq)$ in which every countable ascending chain $x_1 \leq x_2 \leq ...$ ($x_i \in M$) has a least upper bound $(\bigsqcup_{x_i}) \in M$. A _domain_ is a predomain with a least element $\bot$. Given a predomain $(M, \leq)$ and an element $\bot \notin M$, we denote by M^+ the domain $(M \cup \{\bot\}, \sqsubseteq)$ ordered by

$x \sqsubseteq y :\Leftrightarrow x = \bot \lor x \leq y$.

If $(M, \leq)$ is trivially ordered by the identity relation, M^+ is called a _flat domain_.

For the predomains D_1 and D_2 we denote by $D_1 \rightarrow D_2$ the predomain of all monotonic functions from D_1 to D_2 ordered by

$f \leq g :\Leftrightarrow \forall x \in D_1 : f(x) \leq g(x)$.

For predomains D_i ($1 \leq i \leq k$) the _product_ $\prod_{i=1}^{k} D_i$ is the usual cartesian product with the componentwise ordering.

III.2.1 The kernel: an expression language

Given a domain D, its power domain $\mathbb{P}[\![D]\!]$ is given by

$\quad \mathbb{P}[\![D]\!] := \{X \subseteq D \mid X \neq \emptyset\}$

quasi-ordered by the Egli-Milner-relation (cf. /Plotkin 76/)

$\quad X \sqsubseteq_{EM} Y :\Leftrightarrow (\forall x \in X: \exists y \in Y: x \leq y) \wedge (\forall y \in Y: \exists x \in X: x \leq y).$

If D is a flat domain, $\mathbb{P}[\![D]\!]$ is again a domain.

For a set X in $\mathbb{P}[\![D]\!]$, we denote by X- the set $X\backslash\{\bot\}$ of "defined" values of X. For elements X_i of the powerdomains $\mathbb{P}[\![D_i]\!]$ we define their s-product ("smash" product) by

$$\overset{n}{\underset{i=1}{\text{\Large\bf a}}}\, X_i := \prod_{i=1}^{n} X_i^- \cup \begin{cases} \emptyset & \text{if} \quad \forall i : \bot \notin X_i \\ \{\bot\} & \text{otherwise} \end{cases}$$

As an example consider

$\quad \{\bot,1\} \text{ \bf a } \{a,b\} = \{(1,a), (1,b), \bot\}.$

We associate now with every proper kind m a predomain $D[\![m]\!]$ and a domain $R[\![m]\!]$ as follows:
- For a basic sort s we set

  $D[\![\text{simple}(s)]\!] := s^A$, ordered trivially,

    where s^A is the carrier set of sort s in the presupposed model A of the basic types.

  $R[\![\text{simple}(s)]\!] := \mathbb{P}[\![D[\![\text{simple}(s)]\!]^+]\!]$
- For a set kind m = setkind(n) we set

  $D[\![m]\!] := \tilde{P}(D[\![n]\!])$ (power set), ordered trivially,

  $R[\![m]\!] := \mathbb{P}[\![D[\![m]\!]^+]\!]$
- For a tuple kind m = tuplekind($<m_1, ..., m_k>$) we set

  $$D[\![m]\!] := \prod_{i=1}^{k} D[\![m_i]\!]$$

  $$R[\![m]\!] := \{\,\overset{k}{\underset{i=1}{\text{\bf a}}}\, X_i \mid X_1 \in R[\![m_1]\!], ..., X_k \in R[\![m_k]\!]\,\}$$
- For a function kind m = functkind(n,r) we set

  $D[\![m]\!] := D[\![n]\!] \to R[\![r]\!]$

  $R[\![m]\!] := \{\,\{f\} \mid f \in D[\![m]\!]^+\,\}$

This reflects the restriction that functional expressions must always be determinate.

In /Berghammer, Hangel 84/ it is shown that this defines indeed domains and that for all kinds $\blacksquare$ we have $R[\![\blacksquare]\!] \subseteq \mathbb{P}[\![D[\![\blacksquare]\!]^+]\!]$.

2.1.2. ABSTRACT SYNTAX

Since we include semantic objects into our expressions, we need an extra constructor semval for them in the abstract syntax. Let

univ = { u : $\exists$ **kind** m : PROPER $[\![m]\!]$ $\bigwedge$ u $\in$ D $[\![m]\!]^+$ } .

Then we have the following operations:

semval:	**univ** $\rightarrow$ **expr**
value:	**id** $\rightarrow$ **expr**
cond:	**expr** x **expr** x **expr** $\rightarrow$ **expr**
tuple:	**⟨expr⟩** $\rightarrow$ **expr**
finchoice:	**⟨expr⟩** $\rightarrow$ **expr**
abstract:	**abstraction** $\rightarrow$ **expr**
apply:	**expr** x **expr** $\rightarrow$ **expr**
fixpoint:	**⟨id⟩** x **⟨abstraction⟩** $\rightarrow$ **expr**
equal:	**expr** x **expr** $\rightarrow$ **expr**
all:	**⟨kind x id⟩** x **expr** $\rightarrow$ **expr**
some:	**⟨kind x id⟩** x **expr** $\rightarrow$ **expr**
comprehend:	**⟨kind x id⟩** x **expr** $\rightarrow$ **expr**
element:	**expr** x **expr** $\rightarrow$ **expr**
abs :	**⟨kind x id⟩** x **kind** x **expr** $\rightarrow$ **abstraction**

Here, **abstraction** is an auxiliary sort that serves to simplify the definition of the context conditions.

Note that the above signature completely specifies the functionalities of the operations and thus also fixes the ranges of free identifiers in the formulas below. For instance, in the term some($\langle m_i, x_i \rangle$, e) each m_i and x_i stands for a kind or, resp., an identifier, and e stands for an expression.

2.1.3. SPECIFICATION OF THE ALGORITHMIC CONSTRUCTS

We now give the attributes, context conditions, and the breadth for every expression of the kernel language. By B$^-[\![E]\!]$ we denote the set B$[\![E]\!]\setminus\{\perp\}$ of "defined" values of an expression E. For a semantic value u $\in$ D$[\![m]\!]^+$ we set

KIND$[\![semval(u)]\!]$ = m
USED$[\![semval(u)]\!]$ = $\emptyset$
B$[\![semval(u)]\!]$ = {u} .

III.2.1 The kernel: an expression language

(a) Identifier

Syntactic mapping:
$A[\![x]\!]$ = value(UNIQUE$[\![x]\!]$)

Let e = value(x).

Context conditions:
x e KNOWN$[\![e]\!]$
ADMISSIBLE$[\![KIND[\![x]\!]$ at e$]\!]$
VALKIND$[\![KIND[\![x]\!]$ $]\!]$

Attributes:
KIND$[\![e]\!]$ = BASEKIND$[\![KIND[\![x]\!]$ $]\!]$
USED$[\![e]\!]$ = {x}

Semantic specification:
In context-correct programs, the semantic function B is only applied to value(x) if x denotes a constant or operation of a basic type. In this case let A be the presupposed model of the basic types. Then

$B[\![c]\!]$ = {c^A} for constant identifiers c
$B[\![f]\!]$ = {$\bar{f}^A$} for constant identifiers f,

where $\bar{f}^A$ is the natural extension (cf. /Manna 74/) of f^A defined by

$$\bar{f}^A(u_1,\ldots,u_n) = \begin{cases} f^A(u_1,\ldots,u_n) & \text{if this is defined} \\ \perp & \text{otherwise .} \end{cases}$$

(b) Conditional Expression

Syntactic mapping:
$A[\![\text{if } C \text{ then } E_1 \text{ else } E_2 \text{ fi}]\!]$ = cond($A[\![C]\!]$, $A[\![E_1]\!]$, $A[\![E_2]\!]$)

Let e = cond(c, e_1, e_2).

Context conditions:
KIND$[\![c]\!]$ = bool
KIND$[\![e_1]\!]$ = KIND$[\![e_2]\!]$

Attributes:
$$KIND[\![e]\!] = KIND[\![e_1]\!]$$
$$USED[\![e]\!] = USED[\![c]\!] \ \cup \ USED[\![e_1]\!] \ \cup \ USED[\![e_2]\!]$$
$$KNOWN[\![c]\!] = KNOWN[\![e_1]\!] = KNOWN[\![e_2]\!] = KNOWN[\![e]\!]$$

Semantic specification:
$$B[\![e]\!] = S_1 \cup S_2 \cup \begin{cases} \{\bot\} & \text{if } \bot \in B[\![c]\!] \\ \emptyset & \text{otherwise} \end{cases}$$

$$\text{where } S_1 = \begin{cases} B[\![e_1]\!] & \text{if true} \in B[\![c]\!] \\ \emptyset & \text{otherwise} \end{cases}$$

$$S_2 = \begin{cases} B[\![e_2]\!] & \text{if false} \in B[\![c]\!] \\ \emptyset & \text{otherwise} \end{cases}$$

(c) Tuple

Syntactic mapping:
$$A[\![(E_1, ..., E_k)]\!] = tuple(\langle A[\![E_i]\!]\rangle)$$

Let $e = tuple(\langle e_i \rangle)$.

Context conditions: none.

Attributes:
$$KIND[\![e]\!] = tuplekind(\langle KIND[\![e_i]\!]\rangle)$$
$$USED[\![e]\!] = \cup \ USED[\![e_i]\!]$$
$$\forall i : KNOWN[\![e_i]\!] = KNOWN[\![e]\!]$$

Semantic specification:
$$B[\![e]\!] = \{\langle u_i \rangle \mid u_i \in B{-}[\![e_i]\!]\} \cup \begin{cases} \{\bot\} & \text{if } \exists i: \bot \in B[\![e_i]\!] \\ \emptyset & \text{otherwise} \end{cases}$$

Note: If some of the u_i are tuples themselves, then the "nested tuple" as well as the corresponding kind are "flattened" into single sequences.

III.2.1 The kernel: an expression language

(d) Finite Choice

Syntactic mapping:
$$A[\![(E_1 \;[]\; ... \;[]\; E_k)]\!] = finchoice(\langle A[\![E_i]\!]\rangle)$$

Let $e = finchoice(\langle e_i\rangle)$.

Context conditions:
$$length(\langle e_i\rangle) \geq 2$$
$$\forall\, i, j : KIND[\![e_i]\!] = KIND[\![e_j]\!]$$
$$OBJECTKIND[\![KIND[\![e_1]\!]]\!]$$

Attributes:
$$KIND[\![e]\!] = KIND[\![e_1]\!]$$
$$USED[\![e]\!] = \mathbf{U}\; USED[\![e_i]\!]$$
$$\forall\, i : KNOWN[\![e_i]\!] = KNOWN[\![e]\!]$$

Semantic specification:
$$B[\![e]\!] = \mathbf{U}\; B[\![e_i]\!]$$

(e) Function Abstraction

Syntactic mapping:
$$A[\![(m_1x_1, ..., m_kx_k)\;(r_1, ..., r_n) : E]\!] =$$
$$\quad abstract(\overline{A}[\![(m_1x_1, ..., m_kx_k)\;(r_1, ..., r_n) : E]\!])$$
$$\overline{A}[\![(m_1x_1, ..., m_kx_k)\;(r_1, ..., r_n) : E]\!] =$$
$$\quad abs(\langle A[\![m_i]\!], BIND[\![x_i]\!]\rangle, tuplekind(\langle A[\![r_j]\!]\rangle), A[\![E]\!])$$

Let $ab = abs(\langle m_i, x_i\rangle, r, e)$, $a = abstract(ab)$, and $m = tuplekind(\langle m_i\rangle)$.

Context conditions:
$$\forall\, i, j : i \neq j \Rightarrow x_i \neq x_j$$
$$\forall\, i : ADMISSIBLE[\![m_i \text{ at } a]\!]$$
$$KIND[\![e]\!] = tuplekind(\langle r_j\rangle)$$

Attributes:
$$\forall\, i : KIND[\![x_i]\!] = m_i$$
$$KIND[\![ab]\!] = KIND[\![a]\!] = functkind(m, r)$$
$$USED[\![ab]\!] = USED[\![a]\!] = USED[\![e]\!] \setminus \{x_i\}$$
$$KNOWN[\![e]\!] = KNOWN[\![a]\!] \;\mathbf{U}\; \{x_i\}$$

Semantic specification:
$$B[\![a]\!] = \{ \{ ((u_1,...,u_n), y) \mid u_i \in D[\![m_i]\!], y \in B[\![e[\![u_i \text{ for value}(x_i)]\!]]\!] \} \}$$

(f) Function Application

Syntactic mapping:
$$A[\![F(E_1, ..., E_k)]\!] = \text{apply}(A[\![F]\!], A[\![(E_1, ..., E_k)]\!])$$

Let $a = \text{apply}(f, e)$.

Context conditions:
$$KIND[\![f]\!] = \text{functkind}(KIND[\![e]\!], r) \quad \text{for some kind } r$$

Attributes:
$$KIND[\![a]\!] = r \quad \text{with } r \text{ as above}$$
$$USED[\![a]\!] = USED[\![f]\!] \ U \ USED[\![e]\!]$$
$$KNOWN[\![f]\!] = KNOWN[\![e]\!] = KNOWN[\![a]\!]$$

Semantic specification:
Let $B[\![f]\!] = \{g\}$. Then

$$B[\![a]\!] = S \ U \begin{cases} \{\bot\} & \text{if } g = \bot \text{ or } \bot \in B[\![e]\!] \\ \emptyset & \text{otherwise} \end{cases}$$

where $S = \{y \mid (x, y) \in g \land x \in B^-[\![e]\!]\}$

(g) Fixpoint

Syntactic mapping:
$$A[\![(Y \ f_1, ..., f_k : A_1, ..., A_n)]\!] = \text{fixpoint}(\triangleleft BIND[\![f_i]\!]>, \triangleleft A[\![A_j]\!]>)$$

Let $f = \text{fixpoint}(<f_1, ..., f_k>, <a_1, ..., a_n>)$.

Context conditions:
$$k = n \geq 1$$
$$\forall i, j : i \neq j \Rightarrow f_i \neq f_j$$

III.2.1 The kernel: an expression language

Attributes:
$\forall$ i : KIND $[\![f_i]\!]$ = KIND $[\![a_i]\!]$
KIND $[\![f]\!]$ = tuplekind($\ll$KIND $[\![a_i]\!]\gg$)
USED $[\![f]\!]$ = (U USED $[\![a_i]\!]$) \ $\{f_i\}$
$\forall$ j : KNOWN $[\![a_j]\!]$ = KNOWN $[\![f]\!]$ U $\{f_i\}$

Semantic specification:
B $[\![f]\!]$ = { $\langle u_1, ..., u_k\rangle$ }
where the relations u_i are defined to be the least fixpoints of the system of equations

$\{u_1\}$ = B $[\![a_1']\!]$

$\vdots$ where a_i' = $a_i[\![u_j$ for value$(f_j)]\!]$

$\{u_m\}$ = B $[\![a_m']\!]$

In /Berghammer, Hangel 84/ it is shown that for all expressions e of the kernel language the mappings

$\langle u_i\rangle \mapsto B[\![e[\![u_i$ for value$(x_i)]\!]\,]\!]$

(x_i arbitrary identifiers, u_i e D $[\![$KIND $[\![x_i]\!]\,]\!]$) are monotonic; for an expression of the algorithmic sublanguage they are even continuous. Hence the semantics above is well-defined by the fixpoint theorem (cf. e.g. /Markowsky 76/).

2.1.4. SPECIFICATION OF THE PREALGORITHMIC CONSTRUCTS

(a) Universal Equality Test

Syntactic mapping:
A $[\![E_1 = E_2]\!]$ = equal(A $[\![E_1]\!]$, A $[\![E_2]\!]$)

Let e = equal(e_1, e_2) .

Context conditions:
KIND $[\![e_1]\!]$ = KIND $[\![e_2]\!]$
OBJECTKIND $[\![$KIND $[\![e_1]\!]\,]\!]$

Attributes:
KIND $[\![e]\!]$ = bool
USED $[\![e]\!]$ = USED $[\![e_1]\!]$ U USED $[\![e_2]\!]$
KNOWN $[\![e_1]\!]$ = KNOWN $[\![e_2]\!]$ = KNOWN $[\![e]\!]$

Semantic specification:

$$B[\![e]\!] = S \cup \begin{cases} \{\bot\} & \text{if } \bot \in B[\![e_1]\!] \text{ or } \bot \in B[\![e_2]\!] \\ \\ \emptyset & \text{otherwise} \end{cases}$$

where true $\in S \Leftrightarrow \exists\ u_1 \in B^-[\![e_1]\!],\ u_2 \in B^-[\![e_2]\!] : u_1 = u_2$

false $\in S \Leftrightarrow \exists\ u_1 \in B^-[\![e_1]\!],\ u_2 \in B^-[\![e_2]\!] : u_1 \neq u_2$

(b) Quantification

Syntactic mapping:

$A[\![\ \forall m_1 x_1, \ldots, m_k x_k : C\ ]\!] = \text{all}(\langle A[\![m_i]\!], \text{BIND}[\![x_i]\!]\rangle, A[\![C]\!])$

Let $e = \text{all}(\langle m_i, x_i\rangle, c)$ and $m = \text{tuplekind}(\langle m_i\rangle)$.

Context conditions:

$\text{length}(\langle m_i, x_i\rangle) \geq 1$

$\forall i,j : i \neq j \Rightarrow x_i \neq x_j$

$\text{KIND}[\![c]\!] = \text{bool}$

$\forall i : \text{ADMISSIBLE}[\![m_i \text{ at } e]\!]$

$\forall i : \text{OBJECTKIND}[\![m_i]\!]$

Attributes:

$\forall i : \text{KIND}[\![x_i]\!] = m_i$

$\text{KIND}[\![e]\!] = \text{bool}$

$\text{USED}[\![e]\!] = \text{USED}[\![c]\!] \setminus \{x_i\}$

$\text{KNOWN}[\![c]\!] = \text{KNOWN}[\![e]\!] \cup \{x_i\}$

Semantic specification:

Let $c(u)$ with $u = \langle u_i\rangle$ stand for $c[\![u_i \text{ for value}(x_i)]\!]$. Then

$B[\![e]\!] = S$ where

true $\in S \Leftrightarrow \forall u \in D[\![m]\!] : \text{true} \in B[\![c(u)]\!]$

false $\in S \Leftrightarrow \exists u \in D[\![m]\!] : \text{false} \in B[\![c(u)]\!] \wedge$
$\qquad\qquad\qquad \forall u \in D[\![m]\!] : B[\![c(u)]\!] \neq \{\bot\}$

$\bot \quad \in S \Leftrightarrow \exists u \in D[\![m]\!] : \bot \in B[\![c(u)]\!]$

III.2.1 The kernel: an expression language

(c) Comprehensive Choice

Syntactic mapping:
$A[\![\textbf{some}\ \textbf{m}_1\ x_1, \ldots, \textbf{m}_k\ x_k : C]\!] = \text{choice}(\langle A[\![\textbf{m}_i]\!], \text{BIND}[\![x_i]\!]\rangle, A[\![C]\!])$

Let $e = \text{choice}(\langle m_i, x_i\rangle, c)$ and $m = \text{tuplekind}(\langle m_i\rangle)$.

Context conditions: as for all$(\langle m_i, x_i\rangle, c)$.

Attributes:
$\forall\ i : \text{KIND}[\![x_i]\!] = m_i$
$\text{KIND}[\![e]\!] = m$
$\text{USED}[\![e]\!] = \text{USED}[\![c]\!] \setminus \{x_i\}$
$\text{KNOWN}[\![c]\!] = \text{KNOWN}[\![e]\!]\ \textbf{U}\ \{x_i\}$

Semantic specification:
Let $S = B[\![\text{comprehend}(\langle m_i, x_i\rangle, c)]\!]$ (see(d)).

Then $B[\![e]\!] = \{y \mid y\ e\ s\ \text{for some}\ s\ e\ S^-\}\ \textbf{U}\ \begin{cases} \{\perp\} & \text{if}\ \perp\ e\ S\ \text{or}\ \emptyset\ e\ S \\ \emptyset & \text{otherwise} \end{cases}$

(d) Set Comprehension

Syntactic mapping:
$A[\![\{\textbf{m}\ x_1, \ldots, \textbf{m}_k\ x_k : C\}]\!] = \text{comprehend}(\langle A[\![\textbf{m}_i]\!], \text{BIND}[\![x_i]\!]\rangle, A[\![C]\!])$.

Let $e = \text{comprehend}(\langle m_i, x_i\rangle, c)$ and $m = \text{tuplekind}(\langle m_i\rangle)$.

Context conditions: as for all$(\langle m_i, x_i\rangle, c)$

Attributes:
$\forall\ i : \text{KIND}[\![x_i]\!] = m_i$
$\text{KIND}[\![e]\!] = \text{setkind}(m)$
$\text{USED}[\![e]\!] = \text{USED}[\![c]\!] \setminus \{x_i\}$
$\text{KNOWN}[\![c]\!] = \text{KNOWN}[\![e]\!]\ \textbf{U}\ \{x_i\}$

Semantic specification:
Let $c(u)$ with $u = \langle u_i\rangle$ stand for $c[\![u_i\ \textbf{for}\ \text{value}(x_i)]\!]$. Then

$$B[\![e]\!] = S \cup \begin{cases} \{\bot\}, \text{ if } \exists u \in D[\![m]\!] : \bot \in B[\![c(u)]\!] \\ \emptyset, \text{ otherwise} \end{cases}$$

where $S = \{s \subseteq D[\![m]\!] \mid \forall u \in D[\![m]\!] : u \in s \Rightarrow \text{true} \in B[\![c(u)]\!] \; \wedge$
$\qquad\qquad\qquad\qquad\qquad\qquad u \notin s \Rightarrow \text{false} \in B[\![c(u)]\!] \qquad \}$

(e) Element Relation

Syntactic mapping:
$A[\![E_1 \; \epsilon \; E_2]\!] = \text{element}(A[\![E_1]\!], A[\![E_2]\!])$

Let $e = \text{element}(e_1, e_2)$.

Context conditions:
$KIND[\![e_2]\!] = \text{setkind}(KIND[\![e_1]\!])$
$ADMISSIBLE[\![KIND[\![e_2]\!] \text{ at } e]\!]$

Attributes:
$KIND[\![e]\!] = \text{bool}$
$USED[\![e]\!] = USED[\![e_1]\!] \cup USED[\![e_2]\!]$
$KNOWN[\![e_1]\!] = KNOWN[\![e_2]\!] = KNOWN[\![e]\!]$

Semantic specification:
$$B[\![e]\!] = S \cup \begin{cases} \{\bot\} \text{ if } \bot \in B[\![e_1]\!] \text{ or } \bot \in B[\![e_2]\!] \\ \emptyset \text{ otherwise} \end{cases}$$

where $\text{true} \in S \Leftrightarrow \exists u \in B^-[\![e_1]\!], z \in B^-[\![e_2]\!] : u \in z$
$\qquad\quad \text{false} \in S \Leftrightarrow \exists u \in B^-[\![e_1]\!], z \in B^-[\![e_2]\!] : u \notin z$

III.2.2 The applicative language

2.2. THE FULL APPLICATIVE LANGUAGE: DECLARATIONS

Explicit function and object declarations avoid multiple nestings of abstractions and applications as well as the need for the fixpoint operator. These new language constructs lead to the introduction of a new sort **decl** and an auxiliary sort **routine** which will comprise declarations of functions and (in the next section) of procedures. We employ an abstract syntax mapping A_r for routines. Routines are incorporated into the expression language by means of segments, which consist of a sequence of declarations followed by an expression using (possibly) the declared identifiers. Since function and object declarations will also be admissible in segments of the procedural language. Generally, segments containing declarations and statements are considered and reduced from right to left into the kernel language by the rules of this and the following section.

2.2.1. ABSTRACT SYNTAX

Let **phrase** = **decl** φ **stat** .

segment:	**<phrase>** $\times$ **expr** $\to$ **expr**
objects:	**<kind** $\times$ **id>** $\times$ **expr** $\to$ **decl**
function:	**id** $\times$ **abstraction** $\to$ **routine**
system:	**<routine>** $\to$ **decl**

In this section only segments without statements are considered. The auxiliary sort **routine** serves to simplify the context conditions.

For all declarations d we set ASSIGNED$[\![d]\!]$ = $\emptyset$.

2.2.2. SPECIFICATION

(a) Object Declaration

Syntactic mapping:
$$A[\![(m_1x_1, ..., m_kx_k) \equiv E]\!] = objects(<A[\![m_i]\!], BIND[\![x_i]\!]>, A[\![E]\!])$$

Let obj = objects($<m_i, x_i>$, e) .

Context conditions:
$$\forall\, i, j : i \neq j \Rightarrow x_i \neq x_j$$
$$\forall\, i : x_i \notin USED[\![e]\!]$$

$$KIND \llbracket e \rrbracket = \langle m_i \rangle$$
$$\forall i : ADMISSIBLE \llbracket m_i \text{ at } obj \rrbracket$$

Attributes:

$$\forall i : KIND \llbracket x_i \rrbracket = m_i$$
$$DECLARED \llbracket obj \rrbracket = \{x_i\}$$
$$USED \llbracket obj \rrbracket = USED \llbracket e \rrbracket$$
$$KNOWN \llbracket e \rrbracket = KNOWN \llbracket obj \rrbracket$$

Semantic specification:

An object declaration followed by an expression is reduced to an application of an abstraction. To keep referential transparency, all used global variables are passed as parameters (cf. II. 2.3.2):

(2.1) rule:

$$segment(dsq \ \& \ \langle objects(\langle m_i, x_i \rangle, e_1) \rangle, \ e_2) \leftrightarrow\mapsto segment(dsq, \ e')$$

$$\text{where } e' = apply(abstract(abs(\langle m_i, x_i \rangle \ \& \ \langle w_j, z_j' \rangle, \ r, \ e_2 \llbracket z_j' \text{ for } z_j \rrbracket)),$$
$$tuple(\langle e_1 \rangle \ \& \ \langle value(z_j) \rangle) \qquad\qquad),$$
$$\{z_j\} = USEDVARS \llbracket e_2 \rrbracket,$$
$$\{z_j'\} \equiv NEW,$$
$$KIND \llbracket z_j \rrbracket = varkind(w_j),$$
$$r = KIND \llbracket e_2 \rrbracket$$

(b) <u>Function Declaration</u>

Syntactic mapping:

$$A_r \llbracket \textbf{funct } f \equiv A \rrbracket = function(BIND \llbracket f \rrbracket, \overline{A} \llbracket A \rrbracket)$$
$$A \llbracket R_1, \ldots, R_k \rrbracket = system(\langle A_r \llbracket R_1 \rrbracket, \ldots, A_r \llbracket R_k \rrbracket \rangle)$$
$$\text{for routines } R_i = \textbf{funct } f_i \equiv A_i .$$

Let sys = $system(\langle d_i \rangle)$ where $d_i = function(f_i, a_i)$.

Context condition:

$$\forall i, j : i \neq j \Rightarrow f_i \neq f_j$$

Attributes:

$$\forall i : KIND \llbracket f_i \rrbracket = KIND \llbracket a_i \rrbracket$$
$$DECLARED \llbracket sys \rrbracket = \{f_i\}$$
$$USED \llbracket sys \rrbracket = (U \ USED \llbracket d_i \rrbracket) \setminus \{f_i\}$$
$$\forall_i : KNOWN \llbracket a_i \rrbracket = KNOWN \llbracket sys \rrbracket \ U \ \{f_i\}$$

III.2.2 The applicative language

$$\forall\, i\, :\, DECLARATION[\![\, f_i\,]\!] \;=\; d_i$$

Semantic specification:

(2.2) rule:

$$system(<function(f_i,\ abs(<m_{ij},\ x_{ij}>,\ r_i,\ e_i))>)$$

$$\longleftrightarrow objects(<functkind(<m_{ij}>,\ r_i),\ f_i,\ fixpoint(<f_i'>,\ <a_i'>))$$

where $\{f_i'\} \subseteq NEW$,

$$\forall\, i\, :\, a_i' \;=\; a_i[\![\, f_j'\ \text{for}\ f_j\,]\!].$$

(c) <u>Segment:</u>

Syntactic mapping:

$$A[\![\ \overline{DS}_1;\ \ldots\ ;\ DS_k\ ;\ E\,\rfloor\ ]\!] \;=\; segment(<A[\![\, DS_i\,]\!]>,\ A[\![\, E\,]\!])$$

Let $seg = segment(<ds_i>,\ e)$.

Context conditions:

$$\forall\, i,j\, :\, i \neq j \Rightarrow DECLARED[\![\, ds_i\,]\!]\ \cap\ DECLARED[\![\, ds_j\,]\!] \;=\; \emptyset$$

$$(\textbf{U}\ ASSIGNED[\![\, ds_i\,]\!])\ \backslash\ (\textbf{U}\ DECLARED[\![\, ds_i\,]\!]) \;=\; \emptyset \qquad (\text{i.e. no side effects})$$

Attributes:

$$KIND[\![\, seg\,]\!] \;=\; KIND[\![\, e\,]\!]$$

$$USED[\![\, seg\,]\!] \;=\; (\textbf{U}\ USED[\![\, ds_i\,]\!]\ \textbf{U}\ USED[\![\, e\,]\!])\ \backslash\ (\textbf{U}\ DECLARED[\![\, ds_j\,]\!])$$

$$\forall\, i\, :\, KNOWN[\![\, ds_i\,]\!] \;=\; KNOWN[\![\, seg\,]\!]\ \textbf{U}\ (\underset{j<i}{\textbf{U}}\ DECLARED[\![\, ds_j\,]\!])$$

$$KNOWN[\![\, e\,]\!] \;=\; KNOWN[\![\, seg\,]\!]\ \textbf{U}\ (\textbf{U}\ DECLARED[\![\, ds_i\,]\!])$$

Semantic specification:

Since the declarations in segments are successively eliminated by the rules 2.1 and 2.2, we only need to reduce segments with empty declaration sequence:

(2.3) rule: $segment(<>,\ e) \longleftrightarrow e$

2.3 THE PROCEDURAL LANGUAGE: VARIABLES AND PROCEDURES

The introduction of program variables, assignments, procedures etc. leads to a new sort **stat** for statements. Again a number of rules will allow to reduce every term of sort **expr** containing subterms of the sort **stat** to a term of the applicative language.

2.3.1. ABSTRACT SYNTAX

variables:	$\langle$kind x id$\rangle$ x **expr** $\rightarrow$ **decl**
assign:	$\langle$id$\rangle$ x **expr** $\rightarrow$ **stat**
skip:	$\rightarrow$ **stat**
abort:	$\rightarrow$ **stat**
block:	$\langle$phrase$\rangle$ $\rightarrow$ **stat**
condstat:	**expr** x **stat** x **stat** $\rightarrow$ **stat**
choicestat:	$\langle$stat$\rangle$ $\rightarrow$ **stat**
procedure:	**id** x $\langle$kind x id$\rangle$ x $\langle$kind x id$\rangle$ x **stat** $\rightarrow$ **routine**
call:	**id** x $\langle$expr$\rangle$ x $\langle$id$\rangle$ $\rightarrow$ **stat**
varkind:	**kind** $\rightarrow$ **kind**
prockind:	**kind** x **kind** $\rightarrow$ **kind**

We have the following new rules for the predicates PROPER, EXPRKIND, and OBJECTKIND:

PROPER $[\![$ varkind(m) $]\!]$ = PROPER $[\![$ m $]\!]$ $\wedge$ EXPRKIND $[\![$ m $]\!]$

PROPER $[\![$ prockind(m,n) $]\!]$ = PROPER $[\![$ m $]\!]$ $\wedge$ PROPER $[\![$ n $]\!]$ $\wedge$
$\qquad\qquad\qquad\qquad$ EXPRKIND $[\![$ m $]\!]$ $\wedge$ EXPRKIND $[\![$ n $]\!]$

$\neg$ EXPRKIND $[\![$ varkind(m) $]\!]$

$\neg$ EXPRKIND $[\![$ prockind(m,n) $]\!]$.

VALKIND $[\![$ varkind(m) $]\!]$

$\neg$ VALKIND $[\![$ prockind(m,n) $]\!]$

BASEKIND $[\![$ varkind(m) $]\!]$ = m

BASESORTS $[\![$ varkind(m) $]\!]$ = BASESORTS $[\![$ m $]\!]$

BASESORTS $[\![$ prockind(m,n) $]\!]$ = BASESORTS $[\![$ m $]\!]$ **U** BASESORTS $[\![$ n $]\!]$

For all statements s we set DECLARED $[\![$ s $]\!]$ = $\emptyset$.

2.3.2. SPECIFICATION

The rules are given in such a way that any sequence of declarations and statements which is followed by an expression is reduced from the right until it is completely converted into an expression. This way of proceeding sometimes makes it necessary to convert global variables into

III.2.3 The procedural language

local ones in order to keep all expressions free of side effects. This conversion is denoted by

$$\text{MAKESEGMENT}[\![\,\text{dsq, e}\,]\!] =$$
$$\text{segment}(<\text{variables}(<m_j, y_j>, \text{tuple}(<\text{value}(x_i)>)> \,\&\, \text{dsq'},\ \text{e'})$$

$$\text{where}\ \{x_i\} = \text{ASSIGNED}[\![\,\text{block(dsq)}\,]\!]\quad(\text{cf.(f)})$$
$$\text{varkind}(m_j) = \text{KIND}[\![\,x_j\,]\!]$$
$$\{y_j\} \in \text{NEW}$$
$$\text{dsq'} = \text{dsq}[\![\,y_i\ \textbf{for}\ x_i\,]\!]$$
$$\text{e'} = \text{e}[\![\,y_i\ \textbf{for}\ x_i\,]\!]$$

The resulting segment contains for each global variable x_i a local variable y_i of the same kind, which is initialized with the value of x_i and replaces x_i in all statements and in the final expression.

(a) Segment

Segments have already been introduced in the applicative language. They are reduced by the rules of the sections 2.2.2 and 2.3.2.

(b) Declaration of Variables

Syntactic mapping:
$$A[\![\,(\textbf{var}\ m_1x_1, \ldots, \textbf{var}\ m_kx_k) := E\,]\!] = \text{variables}(<A[\![\,m_i\,]\!], \text{BIND}[\![\,x_i\,]\!]>, A[\![\,E\,]\!])$$

Let vars = variables($<m_i, x_i>, e$) .

Context conditions:
$$\forall\ i, j : i \neq j \Rightarrow x_i \neq x_j$$
$$\forall\ i : x_i \notin \text{USED}[\![\,e\,]\!]$$
$$\text{KIND}[\![\,e\,]\!] = \text{tuplekind}(<m_i>)$$
$$\forall\ i : \text{ADMISSIBLE}[\![\,m_i\ \textbf{at}\ \text{vars}\,]\!]$$

Attributes:
$$\forall\ i : \text{KIND}[\![\,x_i\,]\!] = \text{varkind}(m_i)$$
$$\text{DECLARED}[\![\,\text{vars}\,]\!] = \{x_i\}$$
$$\text{USED}[\![\,\text{vars}\,]\!] = \text{USED}[\![\,e\,]\!]$$
$$\text{KNOWN}[\![\,e\,]\!] = \text{KNOWN}[\![\,\text{vars}\,]\!]$$

Semantic specification:

    (3. 1) rule :

$$\text{segment}(dsq \ \& \ <\text{variables}(<m_i, x_i>, e_1)>, \ e_2)$$

$$\longleftrightarrow \text{segment}(dsq \ \& \ <\text{objects}(<m_i, x_i>, e_1)>, \ e_2)$$

(c) Assignment

Syntactic mapping:

$$A[\![(x_1, \ ..., \ x_k) := E]\!] \ = \ \text{assign}(<\text{UNIQUE}[\![x_i]\!]>, \ A[\![E]\!])$$

Let as = $\text{assign}(<x_i>, e)$.

Context conditions:

$$\forall \ i, j : i \neq j \Rightarrow x_i \neq x_j$$

$$\forall \ i : x_i \ \epsilon \ \text{KNOWN}[\![as]\!] \ \land \ \text{KIND}[\![x_i]\!] = \text{varkind}(m_i)$$

$$\text{KIND}[\![e]\!] = \text{tuplekind}(<m_i>)$$

Attributes:

$$\text{USED}[\![as]\!] \ = \ \text{USED}[\![e]\!]$$

$$\text{ASSIGNED}[\![as]\!] \ = \ \{x_i\}$$

$$\text{KNOWN}[\![e]\!] \ = \ \text{KNOWN}[\![as]\!]$$

Semantic specification:

    (3.2) rule:

$$\text{segment}(dsq \ \& \ <\text{assign}(<x_i>, e_1)>, \ e_2)$$

$$\longleftrightarrow \text{segment}(dsq \ \& \ <\text{objects}(<m_i, y_i>, e_1)>, \ e_2')$$

$$\text{where varkind}(m_i) = \text{KIND}[\![x_i]\!] \ ,$$

$$\{y_i\} \ \epsilon \ \text{NEW} \ ,$$

$$e_2' \ = \ e_2 [\![y_i \ \textbf{for} \ x_i]\!]$$

(d) Empty statement

Syntactic mapping:

$$A[\![\textbf{skip}]\!] = \text{skip}$$

III.2.3 The procedural language

Context conditions: none

Attributes:
USED$[\![$ skip $]\!]$ = $\emptyset$
ASSIGNED$[\![$ skip $]\!]$ = $\emptyset$

Semantic specification:
(3.3) rule:
segment(dsq & <skip>, e) $\longleftrightarrow$ segment(dsq, e)

(e) <u>Abort statement</u>

Syntactic mapping:
A$[\![$ **abort** $]\!]$ = abort

Context conditions: none

Attributes:
USED$[\![$ abort $]\!]$ = $\emptyset$
ASSIGNED$[\![$ abort $]\!]$ = $\emptyset$

Semantic specification:
(3.4) rule:
segment(dsq & <abort>, e) $\longleftrightarrow$ error
where error stands for an expression with breadth $\{\perp\}$ (cf. II.2.1.2(g)).

(f) <u>Block</u>

Syntactic mapping:
A$[\![$ $\lceil DS_1 ; \ldots ; DS_k \rfloor$ $]\!]$ = block($<A[\![DS_i]\!]>$)

Let bl = block($<ds_i>$) .

Context conditions:
$\forall$ i, j : i $\neq$ j $\Rightarrow$ DECLARED$[\![ds_i]\!]$ $\cap$ DECLARED$[\![ds_j]\!]$ = $\emptyset$
k $\geq$ 1

Attributes:
USED$[\![$ bl $]\!]$ = ($\cup$ USED$[\![ds_i]\!]$) \ ($\cup$ DECLARED$[\![ds_i]\!]$)
ASSIGNED$[\![$ bl $]\!]$ = ($\cup$ ASSIGNED$[\![ds_i]\!]$) \ ($\cup$ DECLARED$[\![ds_i]\!]$)
$\forall$ i : KNOWN$[\![ds_i]\!]$ = KNOWN$[\![$ bl $]\!]$ $\cup$ ($\underset{j<i}{\cup}$ DECLARED$[\![ds_j]\!]$)

Semantic Specification:
    (3. 5) rule:
        $USED [\![e]\!] \wedge DECLARED [\![dsq_2]\!] = \emptyset \Rightarrow$
        $segment(dsq_1 \ \& \ \langle block(dsq_2) \rangle, \ e)$
            $\longleftrightarrow segment(dsq_1, \ MAKESEGMENT [\![dsq_2, \ e]\!])$

(g) Conditional statement

Syntactic mapping:
    $A [\![\ \text{if } C \text{ then } PP_1 \text{ else } PP_2 \text{ fi}]\!] = condstat(a [\![C]\!], block(A [\![PP_1]\!]), block(A [\![PP_2]\!]))$

Let $co = condstat(c, s_1, s_2)$.

Context conditions:
    $KIND [\![c]\!] = bool$

Attributes:
    $USED [\![co]\!] = USED [\![c]\!] \ \cup \ USED [\![s_1]\!] \ \cup \ USED [\![s_2]\!]$
    $ASSIGNED [\![co]\!] = ASSIGNED [\![s_1]\!] \ \cup \ ASSIGNED [\![s_2]\!]$
    $KNOWN [\![c]\!] = KNOWN [\![s_1]\!] = KNOWN [\![s_2]\!] = KNOWN [\![co]\!]$

Semantic specification:
    (3.6) rule :
        $segment(dsq \ \& \ \langle co \rangle, \ e) \longleftrightarrow segment(dsq, \ e')$
        $where \ e' = cond(c, MAKESEGMENT [\![\langle s_1 \rangle, \ e]\!], MAKESEGMENT [\![\langle s_2 \rangle, \ e]\!])$

(h) Finite choice

Syntactic mapping:
    $A [\![\ \lceil PP_1 \ [] \ ... \ [] \ PP_n \rfloor \ ]\!] = choicestat(\langle block(A [\![PP_i]\!]) \rangle)$

Let $ch = choicestat(\langle s_i \rangle)$.

Context condition:
    $length(\langle s_i \rangle) \geq 2$

Attributes:
    $USED [\![ch]\!] = \cup \ USED [\![s_i]\!]$
    $ASSIGNED [\![ch]\!] = \cup \ ASSIGNED [\![s_i]\!]$
    $\forall \ i : KNOWN [\![s_i]\!] = KNOWN [\![ch]\!]$

III.2.3 The procedural language

Semantic specification:

(3.7) rule :

segment(dsq & ⟨choicestat(⟨s_i⟩), e) ⟷ segment(dsq, e')

where e' = finchoice(⟨MAKESEGMENT $⟦⟨s_i⟩, e⟧$⟩)

(i) Procedure declaration

Syntactic mapping:

A_r $⟦$**proc** p ≡ (m_1 z_1, ..., m_k z_k, **var** w_1 x_1, ..., **var** w_n x_n) : S$⟧$

= procedure(BIND$⟦$p$⟧$, ⟨A$⟦$$m_i$$⟧$, BIND$⟦$$z_i$$⟧$⟩, ⟨A$⟦$$w_j$$⟧$, BIND$⟦$$x_j$$⟧$⟩, A$⟦S⟧$)

Note: Without loss of generality we can assume the parameters of a procedure to be arranged according to their kinds: First the object parameters, then the variable parameters are listed.

Let proc = procedure(p, ⟨m_i, z_i⟩, ⟨w_j, x_j⟩, s) .

Context conditions:

The z_i and x_j are pairwise distinct.

USEDLABS$⟦$p$⟧$ = ∅   (cf. 2.5)

∀ i : ADMISSIBLE$⟦$$m_i$ at proc$⟧$

∀ j : ADMISSIBLE$⟦$$w_j$ at proc$⟧$

Attributes:

∀ i : KIND$⟦$$z_i$$⟧$ = m_i

∀ j : KIND$⟦$$x_j$$⟧$ = varkind(w_j)

KIND$⟦$p$⟧$ = prockind(tuplekind(⟨m_i⟩), tuplekind(⟨w_j⟩))

BODY$⟦$p$⟧$ = s

USED$⟦$proc$⟧$ = USED$⟦$s$⟧$ \ ({z_i} U {x_j} U {p}) = USED$⟦$p$⟧$

DECLARED$⟦$proc$⟧$ = {p}

KNOWN$⟦$s$⟧$ = KNOWN$⟦$proc$⟧$ U {p} U {z_i} U {x_j}

ASSIGNED$⟦$p$⟧$ = ASSIGNED$⟦$s$⟧$ \ {x_j}

DECLARATION$⟦$p$⟧$ = proc

Semantic specification:

Every procedure is associated with a function that makes all assignments to the variable parameters and to global variables explicit ("call-by-value/result"). Moreover, to keep the abstraction involved independent of side effects, we convert not only those global variables which are assigned to but all occurring variables into object parameters. Thus we have to consider

- the object parameters z_i of the procedure

- the used variables u_1 of the body s (which in general comprise the variable parameters x_j).

Without loss of generality we can assume that in a system of routines the functions precede the procedures.

Let psys = system(<function(f_i, a_i)> & <procedure(p_j, <m_{jk}, z_{jk}>, <w_{j1}, x_{j1}>, s_j)>) ,
    {u_{j1}} = USEDVARS$[\![s_j]\!]$,
    n = length(<p_j>),
    varkind(r_{j1}) = KIND$[\![u_{j1}]\!]$,
    {g_j} $\cup$ {z'_{jk}} $\cup$ {u'_{j1}} $\cup$ {u''_{j1}} $\subseteq$ NEW

(3.8) rule:
    KNOWNPROCS$[\![psys]\!]$ = $\emptyset$ $\Rightarrow$
    psys $\longleftrightarrow$ system(<function(f_i, a_i)> &
                    <function(g_j, <m_{jk}, z'_{jk}> & <r_{j1}, u'_{j1}>, <r_{j1}>, e'_j)> &
                      <procedure(p_j, <m_{jk}, z_{jk}>, <w_{j1}, x_{j1}>, s'_j)>)
    where s'_j = assign(<u_{j1}>,
                      apply(value(g_j), tuple(<value(z_{jk})> & <value(u_{j1})>))),
        e'_j = segment(<variables(<r_{j1}, u''_{j1}>, tuple(<value(u'_{j1})>)), s''_j>,
                  tuple(<value(u''_{j1})>)   )
    and s''_j = unfold(s_j)$[\![z'_{jk}$ for z_{jk}, u''_{j1} for $u_{j1}]\!]$
        where unfold(s_j) results from replacing all subterms of s_j of the form
             call(p_r, <l_k>, <v_k>) (1 $\leq$ r $\leq$ n) by $s'_r[\![e_k$ for value(z_{rk}), v_k for $x_{rk}]\!]$.

(j) <u>Procedure call</u>

Syntactic mapping:
    A$[\![$**call** $p(E_1, ..., E_k, v_1, ..., v_n)]\!]$ = call(UNIQUE$[\![p]\!]$, <A$[\![E_1]\!]$>, <UNIQUE$[\![v_j]\!]$>)

Let ca = call(p, <e_1>, <v_j>) .

Context conditions:
    p, v_1, ..., v_n $\in$ KNOWN$[\![ca]\!]$
    KIND$[\![p]\!]$ = prockind(tuplekind(<m_i>), tuplekind(<w_j>)) for some m_i, w_j
    KIND$[\![$tuple(<e_1>)$]\!]$ = tuplekind(<m_i>)
    $\forall$ j : KIND$[\![v_j]\!]$ = varkind(w_j)

III.2.3 The procedural language

Let $\{v_{n+1}, \ldots, v_q\}$ = ASSIGNED$[\![\,p\,]\!]$.
Then $\forall\ i, j\ \epsilon\ \{1,\ldots,q\} : i \neq j \Rightarrow v_i \neq v_j$

Attributes:

USED$[\![\,ca\,]\!]$ = $\{p\}\ \mathbf{U}$ USED$[\![\,\langle e_1 \rangle\,]\!]\ \mathbf{U}\ \{v_j\}\ \mathbf{U}$ USED$[\![\,p\,]\!]$

(Note that USED$[\![\,p\,]\!]$ gives the set of identifiers used in the body of p)

ASSIGNED$[\![\,ca\,]\!]$ = $\{v_j\}\ \mathbf{U}$ ASSIGNED$[\![\,p\,]\!]$

$\forall\ i$: KNOWN$[\![\,e_i\,]\!]$ = KNOWN$[\![\,ca\,]\!]$

Semantic specification:

(3.9) rule :

call(p, $\langle e_1 \rangle$, $\langle v_j \rangle$) $\longmapsto$ block($\langle$objects($\langle m_i, y_i \rangle$, tuple($\langle e_1 \rangle$)), s'$\rangle$)

where DECLARATION$[\![\,p\,]\!]$ = procedure(p, $\langle m_i, z_i \rangle$, $\langle w_j, x_j \rangle$, s)

s' = s$[\![\,y_i$ for z_i, v_j for $x_j\,]\!]$,

$\{y_i\} \subseteq$ NEW

Note that, since folding within a routine body may introduce non-termination, only this "unfolding" direction of the rule is generally sound.

By induction on the length of the declaration and statement sequences and on the nesting depths of blocks, conditionals, and choices it can be proved that every program of the procedural language can be reduced to one of the applicative language using the rules given (see /Nickl 83/ for details):

- Segments with empty declaration and statement sequence are reduced by the rule (2.3).
- If the end of the sequence is an object declaration, rule (2.1) shortens the sequence.
- A function or variable declaration or an assignment is transformed into an object declaration by the rule (2.2), (3.1), (3.2) and further reduced by (2.1)).
- The reduction for skip and abort is obvious.
- The rules (3.5), (3.6), (3.7) for blocks, conditionals, and choices again shorten the declaration and statement sequence. But the operation MAKESEGMENT introduces new segments. However, as there are only finitely many blocks, conditionals, and choices, the maximal number of sequences to be considered is bounded.
- Procedure declarations are made non-recursive by rule (3.8). The unfolding achieved by rule (3.9) therefore allows to successively eliminate all calls of the procedure in favour of applications of the associated function. When there are no more calls of the procedure left, its declaration may be deleted. We have not given an extra rule for this, since the same effect can be obtained using the rules of the parallel language, notably rule (4.10).

2.4. CONSTRUCTS FOR PARALLEL PROGRAMMING WITH SHARED VARIABLES

For a clear separation of language levels, the presence of parallel constructs must lead to a new class of statements. Hence the sort **pstat** is introduced.

2.4.1. ABSTRACT SYNTAX

 pblock: <decl **o** pstat> → **pstat**
 guards: <expr x pstat> x **pstat** → **pstat**
 par: <pstat> → **pstat**
 wait: **expr** x **pstat** → **pstat**
 pprocedure: **id** x <**kind** x **id**> x <**kind** x **id**> x **pstat** → **routine**
 pcall: **id** x <expr> x <**id**> → **pstat**

There are two more functions that provide the transitions between the statements of the previous section and the parallel statements:

 pmake: **stat** → **pstat**
 elpstat: **pstat** → **stat**

We extend the abstract syntax mapping A to a mapping A' on parallel statements.

2.4.2. SPECIFICATION

We first introduce a number of additional attributes; INSIDEPAR is inherited, whereas all other attributes are derived.

WAIT : **pstat** → **bool**
 WAIT $[\![$ ps $]\!]$ holds iff in ps there is an **await**-statement that occurs outside of a parallel composition.

PROTECTED : **id** x (**pstat o stat**) → **bool**
 PROTECTED $[\![$ x **in** ps $]\!]$ holds iff x occurs in ps only inside **await**-statements.

NOCONFLICT : **pstat** x **pstat** → **bool**
 NOCONFLICT $[\![$ ps$_1$, ps$_2$ $]\!]$ =
  $\forall$x e ASSIGNED $[\![$ ps$_1$ $]\!]$: OCCURS $[\![$ x **in** ps$_2$ $]\!]$ $\Rightarrow$
   PROTECTED $[\![$ x **in** ps$_1$ $]\!]$ $\wedge$ PROTECTED $[\![$ x **in** ps$_2$ $]\!]$ $\wedge$
  $\forall$x e ASSIGNED $[\![$ ps$_2$ $]\!]$: OCCURS $[\![$ x **in** ps$_1$ $]\!]$ $\Rightarrow$
   PROTECTED $[\![$ x **in** ps$_1$ $]\!]$ $\wedge$ PROTECTED $[\![$ x **in** ps$_2$ $]\!]$

III.2.4 The parallel language

PARCALLED : construct → finset id

PARCALLED $[\![s]\!]$ is the set of identifiers of procedures that are called in parallel compositions within s. Its formal definition reads as follows:

PARCALLED $[\![$ declare($\langle m_i, x_i \rangle$, e) $]\!]$ = PARCALLED $[\![e]\!]$

PARCALLED $[\![$ variables($\langle m_i, x_i \rangle$, e) $]\!]$ = PARCALLED $[\![e]\!]$

PARCALLED $[\![$ assign($\langle x_i \rangle$, e) $]\!]$ = PARCALLED $[\![e]\!]$

PARCALLED $[\![$ skip $]\!]$ = PARCALLED $[\![$ abort $]\!]$ = $\emptyset$

PARCALLED $[\![$ block($\langle ds_i \rangle$) $]\!]$ = U PARCALLED $[\![ds_i]\!]$

PARCALLED $[\![$ condstat(c, s_1, s_2) $]\!]$ =

　　PARCALLED $[\![c]\!]$ U PARCALLED $[\![s_1]\!]$ U PARCALLED $[\![s_2]\!]$

PARCALLED $[\![$ choicestat($\langle s_i \rangle$) $]\!]$ = U PARCALLED $[\![s_i]\!]$

PARCALLED $[\![$ procedure(q, $\langle n_j, z_j \rangle$, $\langle r_k, u_k \rangle$, s) $]\!]$ = PARCALLED $[\![s]\!]$

PARCALLED $[\![$ call(q, $\langle e_j \rangle$, $\langle v_k \rangle$) $]\!]$ = (U PARCALLED $[\![e_j]\!]$) U PARCALLED $[\![$ BODY $[\![q]\!]$ $]\!]$

PARCALLED $[\![$ elpstat(ps) $]\!]$ = PARCALLED $[\![ps]\!]$

PARCALLED $[\![$ pblock($\langle dp_i \rangle$) $]\!]$ = U PARCALLED $[\![dp_i]\!]$

PARCALLED $[\![$ guards($\langle c_i, ps_i \rangle$, ps) $]\!]$ =

　　(U PARCALLED $[\![c_i]\!]$) U (U PARCALLED $[\![ps_i]\!]$) U PARCALLED $[\![ps]\!]$

PARCALLED $[\![$ par($\langle ps_i \rangle$) $]\!]$ = U USEDPROCS $[\![ps_i]\!]$

PARCALLED $[\![$ wait(e, ps) $]\!]$ = PARCALLED $[\![e]\!]$ U PARCALLED $[\![ps]\!]$

PARCALLED $[\![$ pprocedure(q, $\langle n_j, z_j \rangle$, $\langle r_k, u_k \rangle$, ps) $]\!]$ = PARCALLED $[\![ps]\!]$

PARCALLED $[\![$ pcall(q, $\langle e_j \rangle$, $\langle v_k \rangle$) $]\!]$ = (U PARCALLED $[\![e_j]\!]$) U PARCALLED $[\![$ BODY $[\![q]\!]$ $]\!]$

PARCALLED $[\![$ pmake(s) $]\!]$ = PARCALLED $[\![s]\!]$

TAILRECURSIVE : id → bool

TAILRECURSIVE tests whether a procedure is tail-recursive. It is specified as

TAILRECURSIVE $[\![p]\!]$ = TAILOCC $[\![p$ in BODY $[\![p]\!]$ $]\!]$

where the auxiliary predicate TAILOCC : id x construct → bool is defined as follows:

TAILOCC $[\![p$ in declare($\langle m_i, x_i \rangle$, e) $]\!]$ = ¬ OCCURS $[\![p$ in e $]\!]$

TAILOCC $[\![p$ in variables($\langle m_i, x_i \rangle$, e) $]\!]$ = ¬ OCCURS $[\![p$ in e $]\!]$

TAILOCC $[\![p$ in assign($\langle x_i \rangle$, e) $]\!]$ = ¬ OCCURS $[\![p$ in e $]\!]$

TAILOCC $[\![p$ in skip $]\!]$

TAILOCC $[\![p$ in abort $]\!]$

TAILOCC $[\![p$ in block($\langle ds_1, ..., ds_n \rangle$) $]\!]$ =

　　$(\bigwedge\limits_{i=1}^{n-1}$ ¬ OCCURS $[\![p$ in $ds_i]\!]$) $\wedge$ TAILOCC $[\![p$ in $ds_n]\!]$

TAILOCC $[\![p$ in condstat(c, s_1, s_2) $]\!]$ =

　　¬ OCCURS $[\![p$ in c $]\!]$ $\wedge$ ($\bigwedge$ TAILOCC $[\![p$ in $s_i]\!]$)

TAILOCC $[\![p$ in choicestat($\langle s_i \rangle$) $]\!]$ = $\bigwedge$ TAILOCC $[\![p$ in $s_i]\!]$

TAILOCC $[\![p$ in procedure(q, $\langle n_j, z_j \rangle$, $\langle r_k, u_k \rangle$, s) $]\!]$

TAILOCC $[\![p$ in call(q, $\langle e_j \rangle$, $\langle v_k \rangle$) $]\!]$ =

　　($\bigwedge$ ¬ OCCURS $[\![p$ in $e_j]\!]$) $\wedge$ TAILOCC $[\![p$ in BODY $[\![q]\!]$ $]\!]$

TAILOCC $[\![$ p **in** elpstat(ps) $]\!]$ = TAILOCC $[\![$ p **in** ps $]\!]$

TAILOCC $[\![$ p **in** pblock($<ds_1,...,ds_n>$) $]\!]$ =

$$(\bigwedge_{i=1}^{n-1} \neg \text{OCCURS} [\![\text{p in } ds_i]\!]) \wedge \text{TAILOCC} [\![\text{p in } ds_n]\!]$$

TAILOCC $[\![$ p **in** guards($<c_i, ps_i>$, ps) $]\!]$ =

$(\wedge \neg \text{OCCURS} [\![\text{p in } c_i]\!]) \wedge (\wedge \text{TAILOCC} [\![\text{p in } ps_i]\!]) \wedge \text{TAILOCC} [\![\text{p in ps}]\!]$

TAILOCC $[\![$ p **in** par($<ps_i>$) $]\!]$ = $\wedge$ TAILOCC $[\![$ p **in** ps_i $]\!]$

TAILOCC $[\![$ p **in** wait(e, ps) $]\!]$ = $\neg$ OCCURS $[\![$ p **in** e $]\!]$ $\wedge$ TAILOCC $[\![$ p **in** ps $]\!]$

TAILOCC $[\![$ p **in** pprocedure(q, $<n_j, z_j>$, $<r_k, u_k>$, ps) $]\!]$

TAILOCC $[\![$ p **in** pcall(q, $<e_j>$, $<v_k>$) $]\!]$ =

$(\wedge \neg \text{OCCURS} [\![\text{p in } e_j]\!]) \wedge \text{TAILOCC} [\![\text{p in BODY} [\![q]\!]]\!]$

TAILOCC $[\![$ p **in** pmake(s) $]\!]$ = TAILOCC $[\![$ p **in** s $]\!]$

INSIDEPAR : **construct** $\rightarrow$ **bool**

INSIDEPAR $[\![$ q $]\!]$ holds iff q lies inside a parallel composition.

INSIDEPAR $[\![$ e $]\!]$ = INSIDEPAR $[\![$ declare($<m_i, x_i>$, e) $]\!]$

INSIDEPAR $[\![$ e $]\!]$ = INSIDEPAR $[\![$ variables($<m_i, x_i>$, e) $]\!]$

INSIDEPAR $[\![$ e $]\!]$ = INSIDEPAR $[\![$ assign($<x_i>$, e) $]\!]$

$\forall$ i : INSIDEPAR $[\![$ ds_i $]\!]$ = INSIDEPAR $[\![$ block($<ds_i>$) $]\!]$

INSIDEPAR $[\![$ c $]\!]$ = INSIDEPAR $[\![$ s_1 $]\!]$ = INSIDEPAR $[\![$ s_2 $]\!]$

= INSIDEPAR $[\![$ condstat(c, s_1, s_2) $]\!]$

$\forall$ i : INSIDEPAR $[\![$ s_i $]\!]$ = INSIDEPAR $[\![$ choicestat($<s_i>$) $]\!]$

INSIDEPAR $[\![$ s $]\!]$ = INSIDEPAR $[\![$ procedure(q, $<n_j, z_j>$, $<r_k, u_k>$, s) $]\!]$

$\forall$ i : INSIDEPAR $[\![$ e_j $]\!]$ = INSIDEPAR $[\![$ call(q, $<e_j>$, $<v_k>$) $]\!]$

INSIDEPAR $[\![$ BODY $[\![$ q $]\!]$ $]\!]$ = INSIDEPAR $[\![$ call(q, $<e_j>$, $<v_k>$) $]\!]$

INSIDEPAR $[\![$ ps $]\!]$ = INSIDEPAR $[\![$ elpstat(ps) $]\!]$

$\forall$ i : INSIDEPAR $[\![$ dp_i $]\!]$ = INSIDEPAR $[\![$ pblock($<dp_i>$) $]\!]$

$\forall$ i : INSIDEPAR $[\![$ c_i $]\!]$ = INSIDEPAR $[\![$ ps_i $]\!]$ = INSIDEPAR $[\![$ guards($<c_i, ps_i>$, ps) $]\!]$

INSIDEPAR $[\![$ ps $]\!]$ = INSIDEPAR $[\![$ guards($<c_i, ps_i>$, ps) $]\!]$

INSIDEPAR $[\![$ ps_i $]\!]$ for all constituents ps_i of a parallel composition par($<ps_i>$)

INSIDEPAR $[\![$ e $]\!]$ = INSIDEPAR $[\![$ ps $]\!]$ = INSIDEPAR $[\![$ wait(e, ps) $]\!]$

INSIDEPAR $[\![$ ps $]\!]$ = INSIDEPAR $[\![$ pprocedure(q, $<n_j, z_j>$, $<r_k, u_k>$, ps) $]\!]$

$\forall$ i : INSIDEPAR $[\![$ e_j $]\!]$ = INSIDEPAR $[\![$ pcall(q, $<e_j>$, $<v_k>$) $]\!]$

INSIDEPAR $[\![$ BODY $[\![$ q $]\!]$ $]\!]$ = INSIDEPAR $[\![$ pcall(q, $<e_j>$, $<v_k>$) $]\!]$

INSIDEPAR $[\![$ s $]\!]$ = INSIDEPAR $[\![$ pmake(s) $]\!]$

We have the following global context-conditions on programs with parallel constructs:

(i) For all statements s:

$\forall$ **id** p : p $\in$ PARCALLED $[\![$ s $]\!]$ $\Rightarrow$ TAILRECURSIVE $[\![$ p $]\!]$

(ii) $\forall$ **id** p : p $\notin$ PARCALLED $[\![$ BODY $[\![$ p $]\!]$ $]\!]$

III.2.4 The parallel language

(a) Elementary Statement

(i) If the concrete statement S is a statement of the procedural language then
$$A'[\![S]\!] = pmake(A[\![S]\!])$$

Let ps = pmake(s) .

Context conditions: none

Attributes:
DECLARED$[\![ps]\!]$ = $\emptyset$
USED$[\![ps]\!]$ = USED$[\![s]\!]$
KNOWN$[\![s]\!]$ = KNOWN$[\![ps]\!]$
ASSIGNED$[\![ps]\!]$ = ASSIGNED$[\![s]\!]$
$\neg$ WAIT$[\![ps]\!]$
PROTECTED$[\![x$ in $s]\!]$ = $\neg$ OCCURS$[\![x$ in $s]\!]$

(ii) If the concrete statement PS does not contain **await**-statements outside of parallel compositions, it can be converted into a statement of the procedural language:
$$A[\![PS]\!] = elpstat(A'[\![PS]\!])$$

Let el = elpstat(ps) .

Context conditions:
$\neg$ WAIT$[\![ps]\!]$

Attributes:
USED$[\![el]\!]$ = USED$[\![ps]\!]$
KNOWN$[\![ps]\!]$ = KNOWN$[\![el]\!]$
ASSIGNED$[\![el]\!]$ = ASSIGNED$[\![ps]\!]$
PROTECTED$[\![x$ in el$]\!]$ = PROTECTED$[\![x$ in ps$]\!]$

Semantic specification:
The semantics for elementary statements is given by the following cancellation rule:
(4.1) rule :
elpstat(pmake(s)) $\longleftrightarrow$ s.

(b) Parallel block

Syntactic mapping:
$$A'[\![\ \lceil\ DP_1\ ;\ \dots\ ;\ DP_n\ \rfloor\!\!\rfloor\ ]\!] = pblock(\langle A'[\![DP_i]\!]\rangle)$$

Let pb = pblock(<dp_i>) .

Context conditions:
$\forall$ i,j : i $\neq$ j $\Rightarrow$ DECLARED $[\![$ dp_i $]\!]$ $\cap$ DECLARED $[\![$ dp_j $]\!]$ = $\emptyset$
k $\geq$ 1

Attributes:
DECLARED $[\![$ pb $]\!]$ = $\emptyset$
USED $[\![$ pb $]\!]$ = (U USED $[\![$ dp_i $]\!]$) \ (U DECLARED $[\![$ dp_i $]\!]$)
$\forall$ i : KNOWN $[\![$ dp_i $]\!]$ = KNOWN $[\![$ pb $]\!]$ U ($\underset{j<i}{U}$ DECLARED $[\![$ dp_j $]\!]$
ASSIGNED $[\![$ pb $]\!]$ = (U ASSIGNED $[\![$ dp_i $]\!]$) \ (U DECLARED $[\![$ dp_i $]\!]$)
$\neg$ WAIT $[\![$ pb $]\!]$
PROTECTED $[\![$ x **in** pb $]\!]$

(c) Guarded statement

Syntactic mapping:
A' $[\![$ **if** C_1 **then** PP_1 $[]$ ... $[]$ C_n **then** PP_n **else** PP_{n+1} **fi** $]\!]$ =
guards(<A' $[\![$ C_i $]\!]$, pblock(A' $[\![$ PP_i $]\!]$)>, pblock(A' $[\![$ PP_{n+1} $]\!]$))

Let gu = guards(<c_i, ps_i>, ps) .

Context condition:
$\forall$ i : KIND $[\![$ c_i $]\!]$ = bool

Attributes:
DECLARED $[\![$ gu $]\!]$ = $\emptyset$
USED $[\![$ gu $]\!]$ = (U USED $[\![$ c_i $]\!]$) U (U USED $[\![$ ps_i $]\!]$) U USED $[\![$ ps $]\!]$
KNOWN $[\![$ c_i $]\!]$ = KNOWN $[\![$ ps_i $]\!]$ = KNOWN $[\![$ ps $]\!]$ = KNOWN $[\![$ gu $]\!]$
ASSIGNED $[\![$ gu $]\!]$ = (U ASSIGNED $[\![$ ps_i $]\!]$) U ASSIGNED $[\![$ ps $]\!]$
WAIT $[\![$ gu $]\!]$ = ($\vee$ WAIT $[\![$ c_i $]\!]$) $\vee$ ($\vee$ WAIT $[\![$ ps_i $]\!]$) $\vee$ WAIT $[\![$ ps $]\!]$
PROTECTED $[\![$ x **in** gu $]\!]$ = ($\wedge$ PROTECTED $[\![$ x **in** c_i $]\!]$) $\wedge$
($\wedge$ PROTECTED $[\![$ x **in** ps_i $]\!]$) $\wedge$ PROTECTED $[\![$ x **in** ps $]\!]$

Semantic specification:
Every statement can be made into a guarded statement:
(4.2) rule :
ps $\longleftrightarrow$ guards(<semval(true), ps>, pmake(abort))

A guarded statement containing only sequential statements is equivalent to a choice
between nested conditional statements:

III.2.4 The parallel language

(4.3) rule :
$\neg$ WAIT$[\![$gu$]\!]$ $\Rightarrow$
gu $\leftarrow\!\!\shortmid\!\!\mapsto$ choicestat($\langle$condstat(c_i, elpstat(ps_i), g_i)$\rangle$)
where g_i = elpstat(guards($\langle c_1, ps_1\rangle$ & ... & $\langle c_{i-1}, ps_{i-1}\rangle$ &
$\langle c_{i+1}, ps_{i+1}\rangle$ & ... & $\langle c_n, ps_n\rangle$, ps))

(d) Await-Statement

Syntactic mapping:
A'$[\![$**await** C **then** PP **endwait**$]\!]$ = wait(A'$[\![$C$]\!]$, pblock(A'$[\![$PP$]\!]$))

Let aw = wait(c, ps) .

Context conditions:
KIND$[\![$c$]\!]$ = bool
$\neg$ WAIT$[\![$ps$]\!]$

Attributes:
DECLARED$[\![$aw$]\!]$ = $\emptyset$
USED$[\![$aw$]\!]$ = USED$[\![$c$]\!]$ U USED$[\![$ps$]\!]$
KNOWN$[\![$c$]\!]$ = KNOWN$[\![$ps$]\!]$ = KNOWN$[\![$aw$]\!]$
ASSIGNED$[\![$aw$]\!]$ = ASSIGNED$[\![$ps$]\!]$
WAIT$[\![$aw$]\!]$
PROTECTED$[\![$x **in** aw$]\!]$

Semantic specification:
An await statement which is not (directly or indirectly) surrounded by a parallel composition
is equivalent to a guarded statement. Let aw = wait(c, pq) .
(4.4) rule:
$\neg$ INSIDEPAR$[\![$aw$]\!]$ $\Rightarrow$
aw $\leftarrow\!\!\shortmid\!\!\mapsto$ guards($\langle c, pq\rangle$, pmake(abort))

(e) Parallel composition

Syntactic mapping:
A'$[\![$ $\ulcorner$PP$_1$ $\|$ ... $\|$ PP$_n$ $\lrcorner$ $]\!]$ = par($\langle$pblock(A'$[\![$PP$_i$$]\!]$)$\rangle$)

Let pc = par($\langle ps_i \rangle$) .

Context conditions:
   $i \neq j \Rightarrow$ NOCONFLICT $[\![ps_i, ps_j]\!]$

Attributes:
   DECLARED $[\![pc]\!]$ = $\emptyset$
   USED $[\![pc]\!]$ = **U** USED $[\![ps_i]\!]$
   $\forall i$: KNOWN $[\![ps_i]\!]$ = KNOWN $[\![pc]\!]$
   ASSIGNED $[\![pc]\!]$ = **U** ASSIGNED $[\![ps_i]\!]$
   $\neg$ WAIT $[\![pc]\!]$
   PROTECTED $[\![x \text{ in } pc]\!]$ = $\neg$ OCCURS $[\![x \text{ in } pc]\!]$

Semantic specification:
   (4.5) rule :
      $\neg$ WAIT $[\![ps]\!]$ $\Rightarrow$ par($\langle ps \rangle$) $\longleftrightarrow$ ps

   (4.6) rule :
      par(psq_1 & psq_2) $\longleftrightarrow$ par(psq_2 & psq_1)

   (4.7) rule :
      par($\langle$pmake(skip)$\rangle$ & psq) $\longleftrightarrow$ par(psq)

   (4.8) rule :
      Let for $1 \leq i \leq n$ p_i = guards($\langle q_{il} \rangle$, pmake(abort))   ($l=1,\ldots,n_i$)
      where q_{il} = $\langle g_{il}$, pblock($\langle s_{il} \rangle$ & dp_{il})$\rangle$,
      and for $n < j \leq m$ p_j = pblock($\langle$wait(c_j, ps_j)$\rangle$ & dp_j) .

      Then we have for p = par($\langle p_u \rangle$) (u=1,...,m)
        p $\longleftrightarrow$ guards($\overline{q}_{11},\ldots,\overline{q}_{1n_1},\ldots,\overline{q}_{n1},\ldots,\overline{q}_{nn_n}$,
                       $\overline{p}_{n+1},\ldots,\overline{p}_m$ >,
                       pmake(abort)   )
      where $\overline{q}_{il}$ = $\langle g_{il}$, pblock($\langle s_{il}$, p$[\![$pblock(dp_{il})/i$]\!] \rangle$)$\rangle$
      and $\overline{p}_j$ = $\langle c_j$, pblock($\langle ps_j$, p$[\![$pblock(dp_j)/j$]\!] \rangle$)$\rangle$.
      Here p$[\![ps/u]\!]$ = par($\langle p_1,\ldots,p_{u-1}$, ps, $p_{u+1},\ldots,p_m \rangle$) .

(f) Procedure with parallel statements

Syntactic mapping:
   A'$[\![$**proc** p $\equiv$ (m_1 z_1, ..., m_m z_m, **var** w_1 x_1, ..., **var** w_n x_n) : S$]\!]$
      = pprocedure(BIND $[\![p]\!]$, $\langle$A$[\![m_j]\!]$, BIND $[\![z_j]\!] \rangle$, $\langle$A$[\![w_k]\!]$, BIND $[\![x_k]\!] \rangle$, A'$[\![S]\!]$)

III.2.4 The parallel language

Note: Without loss of generality we can assume the parameters of a procedure to be arranged according to their kinds: First the object parameters, then the variable parameters are listed.

Let pproc = pprocedure(p, $\langle n_j, z_j \rangle$, $\langle r_k, u_k \rangle$, ps) .

Context conditions:
   The z_j and u_k are pairwise distinct.
   USEDLABS$[\![p]\!]$ = $\emptyset$
   $\forall$ j : ADMISSIBLE$[\![n_j$ at pproc$]\!]$
   $\forall$ k : ADMISSIBLE$[\![r_k$ at pproc$]\!]$

Attributes:
   $\forall$ j : KIND$[\![z_j]\!]$ = n_j
   $\forall$ k : KIND$[\![x_j]\!]$ = varkind(w_j)
   KIND$[\![p]\!]$ = prockind(tuplekind($\langle n_j \rangle$), tuplekind($\langle r_k \rangle$))
   BODY$[\![p]\!]$ = ps
   USED$[\![pproc]\!]$ = USED$[\![s]\!]$ \ ($\{z_j\}$ U $\{u_k\}$ U $\{p\}$) = USED$[\![p]\!]$
   DECLARED$[\![pproc]\!]$ = $\{p\}$
   KNOWN$[\![s]\!]$ = KNOWN$[\![pproc]\!]$ U $\{p\}$ U $\{z_j\}$ U $\{u_k\}$
   ASSIGNED$[\![p]\!]$ = ASSIGNED$[\![s]\!]$ \ $\{u_k\}$
   DECLARATION$[\![p]\!]$ = pproc

Semantic specification:
   If the body of a procedure does not contain await-statements outside of parallel compositions, the procedure is equivalent to a procedure of the previous section:
   (4.9) rule:
       $\neg$ WAIT$[\![ps]\!]$ $\Rightarrow$
       psq $\longleftrightarrow$ $\langle$system($\langle d \rangle$)$\rangle$ & $\overline{psq}$
       where DECLARATION$[\![q]\!]$ = pprocedure(q, $\langle n_j, z_j \rangle$, $\langle r_k, u_k \rangle$, ps)
               d = procedure($\overline{q}$, $\langle n_j, \overline{z_j} \rangle$, $\langle r_k, \overline{u_k} \rangle$, s)
               $\{\overline{q}\}$ U $\{\overline{z_j}\}$ U $\{\overline{u_k}\}$ $\subseteq$ NEW
               s = elpstat($\overline{ps}$)
               $\overline{ps}$ = ps$[\![$pmake(call($\overline{q}$, $\langle e_j \rangle$, $\langle v_k \rangle$)) for pcall(q, $\langle e_j \rangle$, $\langle v_k \rangle$)$]\!]$
                       $[\![\overline{z_j}$ for z_j, $\overline{u_k}$ for $u_k]\!]$
               $\overline{psq}$ = psq$[\![$pmake(call($\overline{q}$, $\langle e_j \rangle$, $\langle v_k \rangle$)) for pcall(q, $\langle e_j \rangle$, $\langle v_k \rangle$)$]\!]$

(g) Call of a parallel procedure

Syntactic mapping:
$$A'[\![\text{call } p(E_1, \ldots, E_m, v_1, \ldots, v_n)]\!] =$$
$$\text{pcall}(\text{UNIQUE}[\![p]\!], A'[\![E_1]\!]>, <\text{UNIQUE}[\![v_k]\!]>)$$

Let pca = $\text{pcall}(p, <e_j>, <v_k>)$.

Context conditions:
$p, v_1, \ldots, v_n \in \text{KNOWN}[\![\text{pca}]\!]$
$\text{KIND}[\![p]\!] = \text{prockind}(\text{tuplekind}(<n_j>), \text{tuplekind}(<r_k>))$ for some n_j, r_k
$\text{KIND}[\![\text{tuple}(<e_1>)]\!] = \text{tuplekind}(<n_j>)$
$\forall j : \text{KIND}[\![v_k]\!] = \text{varkind}(r_k)$

Let $\{v_{n+1}, \ldots, v_q\} = \text{ASSIGNED}[\![p]\!]$.
Then $\forall i, j \in \{1,\ldots,q\} : i \neq j \Rightarrow v_i \neq v_j$

Attributes:
$\text{DECLARED}[\![\text{pca}]\!] = \emptyset$
$\text{USED}[\![\text{pca}]\!] = \{p\} \cup \text{USED}[\![<e_j>]\!] \cup \{v_k\} \cup \text{USED}[\![p]\!]$
   (Note that $\text{USED}[\![p]\!]$ gives the set of identifiers used in the body of p)
$\forall i : \text{KNOWN}[\![e_j]\!] = \text{KNOWN}[\![\text{pca}]\!]$
$\text{ASSIGNED}[\![\text{pca}]\!] = \{v_k\} \cup \text{ASSIGNED}[\![p]\!]$
$\text{WAIT}[\![\text{pca}]\!] = \text{WAIT}[\![\text{BODY}[\![p]\!]]\!]$
$\text{PROTECTED}[\![x \text{ in pca}]\!] = \text{PROTECTED}[\![x \text{ in BODY}[\![p]\!]]\!] \wedge x \notin \{v_k\}$

Semantic specification:
   Every parallel statement can be made into a call of an auxiliary procedure:
   (4.10) rule :
$$\text{psq} \leftarrow\!\!\mid\!\!\mapsto <\text{system}(<d>)> \& \overline{\text{psq}}$$
$$\text{where } d = \text{pprocedure}(p, <n_j, \overline{z_j}>, \overline{<u_k>}, \overline{\text{ps}})$$
$$\{p\} \cup \{\overline{z_j}\} \cup \{\overline{u_k}\} \subseteq \text{NEW}$$
$$\{u_k\} = \text{ASSIGNED}[\![\text{ps}]\!]$$
$$\{z_j\} = \text{USED}[\![\text{ps}]\!] \setminus (\text{USEDPROCS}[\![\text{ps}]\!] \cup \text{ASSIGNED}[\![\text{ps}]\!])$$
$$\overline{\text{ps}} = \text{ps}[\![\overline{z_j} \text{ for } z_j, \overline{u_k} \text{ for } u_k]\!]$$
$$\overline{\text{psq}} = \text{psq}[\![\text{pcall}(p, <z_j>, <u_k>) \text{ for ps}]\!]$$

Note that the direction from right to left allows deleting the declaration of a procedure
that is never called.

III.2.4 The parallel language

For the next rule we need an additional predicate ("unfold-generated")

$\quad$ UG : **pstat** x **pstat** $\rightarrow$ **bool** .

UG$[\![$p **from** q$]\!]$ holds if p is generated from q by unfolding procedure calls or by applications of rules (4.1)-(4.7). Note that the specification of UG is not (and cannot be) sufficiently complete. With the help of this predicate we formulate the principle of <u>fixpoint induction</u> (see e.g. /Manna 74/):

Let p be a term of sort **pstat** that contains identifiers $\hat{q}_i$ of sort **pstat**.

(4.11) rule :

$\quad$ UG$[\![$p$[\![$pcall(q, $\langle e_{ij}\rangle$, $\langle v_{ik}\rangle$) for $\hat{q}_i]\!]$ **from** pcall(q, $\langle z_j\rangle$, $\langle u_k\rangle$)$]\!]$ $\Rightarrow$

$\quad$ psq$_1$ & $\langle$pcall(q, $\langle e_j\rangle$, $\langle v_k\rangle$)$\rangle$ & psq$_2$ $\longleftrightarrow$

$\qquad$ $\langle$system($\langle d\rangle$)$\rangle$ & psq$_1$ & $\langle$pcall($\overline{q}$, $\langle e_j\rangle$, $\langle v_k\rangle$)$\rangle$ & psq$_2$

$\quad$ where DECLARATION$[\![$q$]\!]$ = pprocedure(q, $\langle n_j, z_j\rangle$, $\langle r_k, u_k\rangle$, ps)

$\qquad$ d = pprocedure($\overline{q}$, $\langle n_j, \overline{z}_j\rangle$, $\langle r_k, \overline{u}_k\rangle$, $\overline{p}$)

$\qquad$ $\{p\}$ U $\{\overline{z}_j\}$ U $\{\overline{u}_k\}$ $\subseteq$ NEW

$\qquad$ $\overline{p}$ = p$[\![$pcall($\overline{q}$, $\langle e_{ij}\rangle$, $\langle v_{ik}\rangle$) for $\hat{q}_i]\!]$

$\qquad\qquad$ $[\![\overline{z}_j$ for z_j, $\overline{u}_k$ for $u_k]\!]$

It remains to give the specification of UG:

(i) $\quad$ UG$[\![$pblock($\langle$objects($\langle n_j, y_j\rangle$, tuple($\langle e_1\rangle$)), $\overline{ps}\rangle$) **from** pcall(p, $\langle e_1\rangle$, $\langle v_k\rangle$)$]\!]$

$\qquad$ where DECLARATION$[\![$p$]\!]$ = pprocedure(p, $\langle n_j, z_j\rangle$, $\langle r_k, u_k\rangle$, ps)

$\qquad$ $\overline{ps}$ = ps$[\![y_j$ for z_j, $\overline{u}_k$ for $u_k]\!]$

$\qquad$ $\{y_j\}$ $\subseteq$ NEW

(ii) For each of the rules (4.2)-(4.7) we add a rule

$\qquad$ P $\Rightarrow$ UG$[\![$lhs **from** ps$]\!]$ = UG$[\![$rhs **from** ps$]\!]$

$\quad$ if the rule has the form $\;$ P $\Rightarrow$ lhs $\mapsto$ rhs .

(iii) For every context K of sort **pstat** with a "hole" of sort **pstat** we add a rule

$\qquad$ UG$[\![$p **from** q$]\!]$ $\Rightarrow$ UG$[\![$K$[\![$p$]\!]$ **from** K$[\![$q$]\!]$ $]\!]$

(The reader should note that this infinite set of rules can be represented by a finite set of rules similar to the ones in (ii).)

With the help of these rules we can transform each parallel composition p = par($\langle p_u\rangle$) that meets the context conditions into a composition p' = par($\langle$call(p_u, $\langle e_{ui}\rangle$, $\langle v_{uj}\rangle$)$\rangle$) where

DECLARATION$[\![p_u]\!]$ =

$\quad$ procedure(p_u, $\langle m_{ui}, z_{ui}\rangle$, $\langle w_{uj}, x_{uj}\rangle$,

$\qquad\qquad$ guards($\langle$ $\langle c_u$, pblock($\langle s_u$, call(p_v, $\langle e_{vk}\rangle$, $\langle y_{vk}\rangle$)$\rangle$)$\rangle$) ,

$\qquad\qquad\qquad$ $\langle d_u, r_u\rangle$ $\rangle$,

$\qquad\qquad\qquad$ pmake(abort) $\qquad\qquad$) $\qquad\qquad$) ,

i.e. a tailrecursive form, where s_u is either a sequential statement, a wait-statement, or another procedure call, and r_u is either a procedure call or skip.

We now develop parallel compositions of this form further. For this purpose we consider parallel compositions

$q = par(\langle q_l \rangle) \qquad (1 \le l \le m \le |p'|)$

where each q_l has the form

$q_l = block(\langle a_k, call(p_{k_1}, \langle e_{k_1 i} \rangle, \langle v_{k_1 j} \rangle), \ldots, call(p_{k_n}, \langle e_{k_n i} \rangle, \langle v_{k_n j} \rangle) \rangle)$.

Here, a_k is either one of the statements s_u or skip.

Following /Broy 80/, we can for each of these q_l find a term t_l with $UG[\![\, t_l \text{ from } q_l\,]\!]$ that neither contains await-statements nor constituents of parallel compositions other than the q_l. Therefore, using rule (4.10) and then rule (4.11) repeatedly, we can gradually eliminate all parallel compositions. Afterwards all remaining await-statements can be transformed into guarded statements using rules (4.10) and (4.9). Finally, all **pstats** can be eliminated using rules (4.1)-(4.8).

2.5. THE CONTROL-ORIENTED LANGUAGE: LABELS AND JUMPS

When the interaction between the (control-oriented) jumps and the higher constructs of the language becomes too amalgamated, the complexity of the whole language increases considerably. For these reasons, the use of goto's has to obey certain restrictions: Jumps into blocks (resp. branches of conditionals, choices or procedures) and over declarations in the same block are forbidden; furthermore jumps out of procedures have to be avoided.

For a clear separation of language levels, the presence of goto's and labels must lead to a new class of statements. Hence, the sort **lstat** is introduced.

2.5.1. ABSTRACT SYNTAX

Let now stand **phrase** for **decl** ⊕ **lstat**. We have the following operations:

label:	**id** x **lstat** → **lstat**
goto:	**id** → **lstat**
lcondstat:	**expr** x **lstat** x **lstat** → **lstat**
lchoicestat:	**⟨lstat⟩** → **lstat**
lblock:	**⟨phrase⟩** → **lstat**

There are two more functions providing transitions between the statements of the previous section and the l-statements:

make:	**pstat** → **lstat**
elemstat:	**lstat** → **pstat**

Finally, we have the new kind

   labelkind :   → **kind**

with PROPERKIND⟦labelkind⟧ ∧ ¬ EXPRKIND⟦labelkind⟧ ∧ ¬ VALKIND⟦labelkind⟧ .

We extend the abstract syntax mapping A' to a mapping A" on labelled statements. Again we apply a UNIQUE-Operator on labels, in order to guarantee the uniqueness of a label inside its scope.

2.5.2. SPECIFICATION

(a) Elementary Statement

(i)   If the concrete statement S is a statement of the previous section, then
         A"⟦S⟧ = make(A'⟦S⟧)
      where A'⟦S⟧ is defined in the previous section.

Let ma = make(s) .

Context conditions: none

Attributes:
   DECLARED $[\![$ ma $]\!]$ = $\emptyset$
   USED $[\![$ ma $]\!]$ = USED $[\![$ s $]\!]$
   USEDLABS $[\![$ ma $]\!]$ = $\emptyset$
   KNOWN $[\![$ s $]\!]$ = KNOWN $[\![$ ma $]\!]$
   ASSIGNED $[\![$ ma $]\!]$ = ASSIGNED $[\![$ s $]\!]$

(ii) If the concrete statement LS does not contain global jumps, it can be converted into a statement of the previous section:
   A" $[\![$ LS $]\!]$ = elemstat(A" $[\![$ LS $]\!]$) .

Let el = elemstat(ls) .

Context conditions:
   USEDLABS $[\![$ ls $]\!]$ = $\emptyset$

Attributes:
   USED $[\![$ el $]\!]$ = USED $[\![$ ls $]\!]$
   KNOWN $[\![$ ls $]\!]$ = KNOWN $[\![$ el $]\!]$
   ASSIGNED $[\![$ el $]\!]$ = ASSIGNED $[\![$ ls $]\!]$
   DECLARED $[\![$ el $]\!]$ = DECLARED $[\![$ ls $]\!]$

Semantic specification:
   The semantics for elementary statements is given by the following cancellation rule:
   (5.1) rule :
      elemstat(make(s)) $\longleftrightarrow$ s

In the sequel let lsd range over **<phrase>** and lsq over **<lstat>** .

The elementary statement skip may be inserted anywhere into a sequence of l-statements:
(5.2) rule :
   lsd & lsq $\longleftrightarrow$ lsd & <make(skip)> & lsq

III.2.5 The control-oriented language

(b) <u>Labelled statement</u>

Syntactic mapping:
   $A''[\![1 : LS]\!]$ = $label(BIND[\![1]\!], A''[\![LS]\!])$

Let $lab = label(1, ls)$.

Context condition:
   $1 \notin DECLAREDLABS[\![ls]\!]$

Attributes:
   $KIND[\![1]\!]$ = labelkind
   $DECLARED[\![lab]\!]$ = $DECLAREDLABS[\![lab]\!]$ = $\{1\} \cup DECLAREDLABS[\![ls]\!]$
   $USED[\![lab]\!]$ = $USED[\![ls]\!]$
   $KNOWN[\![ls]\!]$ = $KNOWN[\![lab]\!]$

Semantic specification:
   Superfluous labels are eliminated by
   (5.3) rule:
      $USEDLABS[\![ls]\!]$ = $\emptyset$ $\Rightarrow$
      $elemstat(label(1, ls))$ $\longleftrightarrow$ $elemstat(ls)$

   In order to treat multiple labels we have
   (5.4) rule:
      lsd & $\langle label(1, ls)\rangle$ & lsq $\longleftrightarrow$ lsd & $\langle label(1, make(skip)), ls\rangle$ & lsq

   Furthermore, new labels can be introduced by
   (5.5) rule:
      lsd & $\langle ls\rangle$ & lsq $\longleftrightarrow$ lsd & $\langle label(1,ls)\rangle$ & lsq
      for $1 \in NEW$

(c) <u>Goto statement</u>

Syntactic mapping:
   $A''[\![\textbf{goto } 1]\!]$ = $goto(UNIQUE[\![1]\!])$

Let $go = goto(1)$.

Context conditions:
   $1 \in KNOWN[\![go]\!]$
   $KIND[\![1]\!]$ = labelkind

Attributes:
   DECLARED $[\![go]\!]$ = $\emptyset$
   USED $[\![go]\!]$ = {1}

Semantic specification:
   Two rules help to bring blocks of l-statements into some "normalized form":

   (5.6) rule:
       lsd & <goto(l), label(l,ls)> & lsq $\longleftrightarrow$ lsd & <label(l,ls)> & lsq

   (5.7) rule:
       Let $\langle lsd_m \rangle$ ϵ <phrase> with
       (U USEDLABS $[\![lsd_i]\!]$) = $\emptyset$ $\wedge$ (U DECLAREDLABS $[\![lsd_i]\!]$) = $\emptyset$
       and $\langle ls_n \rangle$ ϵ <lstat> . Then

       L $\cap$ (U DECLAREDLABS $[\![ls_n]\!]$) = $\emptyset$ $\Rightarrow$
       lsd & <lblock($\langle lsd_m \rangle$ & $\langle ls_n \rangle$)> & <GO(L)> & lsq
         $\longleftrightarrow$ lsd & <lblock($\langle lsd_m \rangle$ & $\langle ls_n \rangle$ & <GO(L)>)> & lsq
       where GO(L) is a term of one of the forms
         goto(l)
         lcondstat(c, goto(l_1), goto(l_2))
         lchoicestat(<goto(l_i)>)
       with l, l_1, l_2, l_i ϵ L .

(d) <u>Conditional statement with goto's</u>

   Syntactic mapping:
     A" $[\![$ **if** C **then** PP_1 **else** PP_2 **fi** $]\!]$ =
       lcondstat(A" $[\![C]\!]$, lblock(A" $[\![PP_1]\!]$), lblock(A" $[\![PP_2]\!]$))

   Let lcond = lcondstat(c, ls_1, ls_2) .

   Context condition:
     KIND $[\![c]\!]$ = bool

   Attributes:
     DECLARED $[\![lcond]\!]$ = $\emptyset$
     USED $[\![lcond]\!]$ = USED $[\![c]\!]$ U USED $[\![ls_1]\!]$ U USED $[\![ls_2]\!]$
     KNOWN $[\![c]\!]$ = KNOWN $[\![ls_1]\!]$ = KNOWN $[\![ls_2]\!]$ = KNOWN $[\![lcond]\!]$

III.2.5 The control-oriented language

Semantic specification:

If the branches of the conditional statement do not contain jumps out of the branches, the labelled conditional statement can be transformed into an elementary one according to (5.8) rule :

$$\text{USEDLABS} [\![\text{lcond}]\!] = \emptyset \Rightarrow$$
$$\text{elemstat(lcond)} \leftarrow\!\shortmid\!\mapsto \text{condstat}(c, \text{elemstat}(ls_1), \text{elemstat}(ls_2))$$

Again for "normalization" purposes the extraction of branches from conditionals is made into an rule:

(5.9) rule :

$$\text{lcond} \leftarrow\!\shortmid\!\mapsto \text{lblock}(<\text{lcondstat}(c, \text{goto}(l_1), \text{goto}(l_2))> \&$$
$$<\text{label}(l_1, ls_1), \text{goto}(l)> \&$$
$$<\text{label}(l_2, ls_2), \text{label}(l, \text{make(skip)}))>$$
$$\text{where } \{l_1, l_2, l\} \subseteq \text{NEW}$$

(e) Finite choice with goto's

Syntactic mapping:

$$A'' [\![\ulcorner PP_1 \; [\!] \; \ldots \; [\!] \; PP_n \lrcorner]\!] = \text{lchoicestat}(<\text{lblock}(A'' [\![PP_i]\!])>)$$

Let lchoice = lchoicestat($<ls_i>$) .

Context conditions: none

Attributes:

$$\text{DECLARED} [\![\text{lchoice}]\!] = \emptyset$$
$$\text{USED} [\![\text{lchoice}]\!] = \mathbf{U} \ \text{USED} [\![ls_i]\!]$$
$$\forall \ i : \text{KNOWN} [\![ls_i]\!] = \text{KNOWN} [\![\text{lchoice}]\!]$$

Semantic specification:

Analogously to (d) we need two rules:

(5.10) rule :

$$\text{USEDLABS} [\![\text{lchoice}]\!] = \emptyset \Rightarrow$$
$$\text{elemstat(lchoice)} \leftarrow\!\shortmid\!\mapsto \text{choicestat}(<\text{elemstat}(ls_i)>)$$

(5.11) rule :

$$\text{lchoice} \leftarrow\!\shortmid\!\mapsto \text{lblock}(<\text{lchoicestat}(<\text{goto}(l_i)>),$$
$$<\text{label}(l_i, ls_i), \text{goto}(l)>,$$
$$\text{label}(l, \text{make(skip)}))>$$
$$\text{where } \{l_1, \ldots, l_n, l\} \subseteq \text{NEW}$$

(f) <u>Block with goto's</u>

Syntactic mapping:
$$A"[\![\ulcorner LSD_1; \ldots ; LSD_n \lrcorner]\!] = lblock(\langle A"[\![LSD_i]\!] \rangle)$$

Let $lbl = lblock(\langle lsd_i \rangle)$.

Context conditions:

No duplicate label identifiers must be declared:
$$\forall \, i, j : i \neq j \Rightarrow DECLAREDLABS[\![lsd_i]\!] \cap DECLAREDLABS[\![lsd_j]\!] = \emptyset$$

Jumps over declarations in the same block are forbidden:
$$\forall \, i_0 : DECLAREDLABS[\![lsd_i]\!] \cup USEDLABS[\![lsd_i]\!] \neq \emptyset$$
$$\Rightarrow \forall \, j > i_0 : DECLARED[\![lsd_j]\!] \setminus DECLAREDLABS[\![lsd_j]\!] = \emptyset$$

Because of this context condition, we can assume that $lbl = lblock(\langle ds_j \rangle \,\&\, \langle ls_i \rangle)$ where the ds_j are declarations or l-statements such that $DECLAREDLABS[\![ds_j]\!] = \emptyset$ and $USEDLABS[\![ds_j]\!] = \emptyset$ and the ls_i are l-statements.

Attributes:
$$DECLARED[\![lbl]\!] = \emptyset$$
$$USED[\![lbl]\!] = ((\cup USED[\![ds_j]\!]) \cup (\cup USED[\![ls_i]\!])) \setminus$$
$$((\cup DECLARED[\![ds_j]\!]) \cup (\cup DECLARED[\![ls_i]\!]))$$
$$KNOWN[\![ds_j]\!] = KNOWN[\![lbl]\!] \cup \underset{l<j}{\cup} DECLARED[\![ds_l]\!])$$
$$KNOWN[\![ls_k]\!] = KNOWN[\![lbl]\!] \cup (\cup DECLARED[\![ds_j]\!]) \cup DL[\![\langle ls_i \rangle]\!]$$
(see below for DL)

Semantic specification:

An lblock is a block in the sense of the previous section if its body does not contain global labels:

(5.12) rule :
$$USEDLABS[\![\langle ls_i \rangle]\!] = \emptyset \Rightarrow$$
$$elemstat(lbl) \longleftrightarrow block(\langle \overline{ds_j} \rangle \,\&\, \langle elemstat(ls_j) \rangle)$$
where $\overline{ds_j} = ds_j$ if ds_j is a declaration
and $\overline{ds_j} = elemstat(ds_j)$ otherwise

Furthermore, if a given sequence of l-statements is partitioned into subsequences of the form "label - basic statement - (conditional, choice) goto" it can be converted into a system of tail-recursive procedures (cf. /McCarthy 60/). Let $L = \{l_1, \ldots, l_n, l_{n+1}\}$ be a set of labels. We say that a labelled statement is a GO(L)-statement (resp. a GO(local)-statement) if it is of one of the forms
    goto(l)
    lcondstat(c, goto(l_1), goto(l_2))
    lchoice ($\langle goto(l_i) \rangle$)

III.2.5 The control-oriented language

with $1, 1_1, 1_2, 1_i \in L$ (resp. $1, 1_1, 1_2, 1_i \notin L$) .

Consider furthermore for $i=1,...,n$ elements LS_i of $\langle lstat \rangle$ of one of the following forms:

(*) $LS_i = \langle ls_{ik} \rangle$ & $\langle go_i \rangle$ with $ls_{ik} \in lstat$ such that $USEDLABS[\![\langle ls_{ik} \rangle]\!] = \emptyset$ and $DECLAREDLABS[\![\langle ls_{ik} \rangle]\!] = \emptyset$, and with a $GO(L)$-statement go_i. Then we set

$Lab(1_i, LS_i) = \langle label(1_i, ls_{i1}), ls_{i2}, ..., ls_{in_i} \rangle$ & $\langle go_i \rangle$.

(**) $LS_i = \langle lblock(\langle ds_{ij} \rangle$ & $\langle ls_{ik} \rangle$ & $\langle go_i \rangle) \rangle$ with $\emptyset \neq USEDLABS[\![\langle ls_{ik} \rangle]\!] \subseteq L$ and a $GO(L)$-statement go_i such that all subterms of LS_i of the form $lcondstat(...)$ or $lchoicestat(...)$ are either $GO(L)$- or $GO(local)$-statements. Then we set

$Lab(1_i, LS_i) = \langle label(1_i, lblock(\langle ds_{ij} \rangle$ & $\langle ls_{ik} \rangle$ & $\langle go_i \rangle)) \rangle$.

(5.13) rule :

$lblock(\langle ds_j \rangle$ & $Lab(1_1, LS_1)$ & ... & $Lab(1_n, LS_n)$ & $Lab(1_{n+1}, make(skip)))$

$\longleftrightarrow lblock(\langle ds_j \rangle$ &

$\langle system(\langle procedure(1_1, \langle\rangle, \langle\rangle, s_1), ...,$

$procedure(1_n, \langle\rangle, \langle\rangle, s_n),$

$procedure(1_{n+1}, \langle\rangle, \langle\rangle, skip) \rangle) \rangle$ &

$\langle make(call(1_1)) \rangle)$

where s_i is defined in the following way:

If $1 \leq i \leq n$ and LS_i is of the form (*) then

$s_i = elemstat(lblock(\langle LS_i, Call_i(L) \rangle)$

where $Call_i(L) = go_i[\![make(call(1_j))$ for $goto(1_j)]\!]$.

(Now by rule (5.10) s_i can be reduced to

$block$ $(\langle elemstat(ls_{ik}) \rangle$ & $\langle elemstat(Call_i(L)) \rangle)$

where $elemstat(Call_i(L))$ again can be reduced by the rules (5.6) or (5.8).)

If $1 \leq i \leq n$ and LS_i is of the form (**) we define for $\{\bar{1}_i\} \subseteq NEW$

$LS_i' = block(\langle ds_{ij} \rangle$ & $\langle ls_{ik} \rangle$ & $\langle go_i, label(\bar{1}_i, make(skip)) \rangle)$.

Then

$s_i = elemstat(LS_i'[\![\langle Replace[\![Go]\!], goto(\bar{1}_i) \rangle$ for $Go]\!])$

where Go ranges over all $GO(L)$-statements in LS_i' that are not proper subterms of other $GO(L)$-statements and

$Replace[\![Go]\!] =$

$make(elemstat(Go[\![make(call(1_j))$ for $goto(1_j)]\!]))$.

(Now rules 5.1, 5.8 and 5.10 allow further simplification which prepares the program for the elimination of labels from inner blocks.)

As for procedural programs, it is proved in /Nickl 83/ that every program of the control-oriented language can be reduced to one of the parallel language using the rules given.

3. PROGRAMS

A program consists of a number of (possibly parameterized) components which may be types, structures, modules, or devices.

3.1. ABSTRACT SYNTAX

incl:
base: } id × ⟨id⟩ × ⟨id⟩ → inst
inst: ⟨inst⟩ → phrase

struct:
mod: } id × ⟨id⟩ × ⟨id⟩ → phrase
dev:

phr: phrase → facet

type:
structure:
module: } id × ⟨constituent⟩ × ⟨law ⊕ inst⟩ × ⟨id⟩ × ⟨facet⟩ → component
device:

program: ⟨component⟩ → system

In the sequel, let component stand for any of the operations type , structure , module , or device .

For each concrete value of component we have the additional kind
    componentkind: → kind
with the rules
    PROPERKIND ⟦ componentkind ⟧
    ¬ EXPRKIND ⟦ componentkind ⟧ .

3.2. ATTRIBUTES AND CONTEXT CONDITIONS

The following additional attributes are used:

REACHABLECOMPONENTS : id → finset id
    REACHABLECOMPONENTS ⟦ x ⟧ is the closure of USEDCOMPONENTS ⟦ x ⟧; it gives the identifiers of the components that are immediately used in the component named by x or involved in a transitive way in the definition of x.

III.3.2 Attributes and context conditions

DEFINED : **id** → **finset id**

    DEFINED⟦x⟧ gives the set of constituents that are DECLARED either in the body of x or in the list of parameters of x.

USEDCONSTITUENTS : **id ⊕ facet ⊕ constituent ⊕ term ⊕ law** → **finset id**

    USEDCONSTITUENTS⟦q⟧ =

        { y ∈ USED⟦q⟧ : KIND⟦y⟧ ∉ {typekind, structurekind, modulekind, devicekind} }

TYPECONSTS : **id ⊕ facet** → **finset id**

    TYPECONSTS gives the identifiers declared by facets which either are constituents or type instantiations.

GLOBAL : **facet ⊕ construct** → **finset id**

    GLOBAL passes on the identifiers that are available as actual parameters for local component instantiations. At the outermost level of a component these are the TYPECONSTS of the component; in inner scopes the identifiers declared in local type instantiations are added. For **construct**s the rules for propagating GLOBAL are given in 3.3.1.

3.2.1. FACETS OF COMPONENTS

First, all facets which were defined in Chapter 1 for types may also occur in all other components. This technical convenience allows an easy treatment of local instantiations. We have to define the attribute TYPECONSTS on facets:

    TYPECONSTS⟦constit(co)⟧ = {ID⟦co⟧}

    TYPECONSTS⟦law(la)⟧ = ∅

    TYPECONSTS⟦prim(f)⟧ = TYPECONSTS⟦f⟧ .

Besides these facets, we have now also phrases as facets:

Syntactic mapping:

    Let P be a phrase.

$$A⟦P⟧ = \begin{cases} phr(A''⟦P⟧) & \text{if P is a phrase of the scheme language} \\ phr(\hat{A}⟦P⟧) & \text{if P is a (system of) component instantiation(s)} \end{cases}$$

Let f = phr(p) .

Context condition:

    USED⟦f⟧ ⊆ KNOWN⟦f⟧

Attributes:
  USED$\llbracket f \rrbracket$ = USED$\llbracket p \rrbracket$
  KNOWN$\llbracket p \rrbracket$ = KNOWN$\llbracket f \rrbracket$
  DECLARED$\llbracket f \rrbracket$ = DECLARED$\llbracket p \rrbracket$
  LAWS$\llbracket f \rrbracket$ = $\emptyset$

$$\text{TYPECONSTS}\llbracket f \rrbracket = \begin{cases} \text{TYPECONSTS}\llbracket p \rrbracket & \text{if } p \text{ is an instantiation} \\ \emptyset & \text{otherwise} \end{cases}$$

  $\neg$ INSIDEPAR$\llbracket p \rrbracket$

3.2.2. DEFINITION OF PARAMETERIZED COMPONENTS

Parameterized components are used for generating parameter restrictions or facets of other components.

Syntactic mapping:
  Let **component** stand for **type**, **structure**, **module**, or **device**.
  $A \llbracket$ **component** $X = (\langle par_i \rangle : \langle restriction_j \rangle) \langle res_k \rangle : \langle facet_l \rangle$ **end of component** $\rrbracket$ =
      component$(x, \langle \hat{A} \llbracket par_i \rrbracket \rangle, \langle \bar{A} \llbracket restriction_j \rrbracket \rangle, \langle \hat{A} \llbracket res_k \rrbracket \rangle, \langle A \llbracket facet_l \rrbracket \rangle)$

Let c = component$(x, \langle p_i \rangle, \langle r_j \rangle, \langle y_k \rangle, \langle b_l \rangle)$.

Attributes:
  ID$\llbracket c \rrbracket$ = x
  KIND$\llbracket x \rrbracket$ = componentkind
  DECLARED$\llbracket x \rrbracket$ = $\bigcup$ DECLARED$\llbracket b_l \rrbracket$
  DEFINED$\llbracket x \rrbracket$ = DECLARED$\llbracket x \rrbracket$ $\cup$ {ID$\llbracket p_i \rrbracket$}
  CONSTITUENTS$\llbracket x \rrbracket$ = {y_k}
  USED$\llbracket x \rrbracket$ = ($\bigcup$ USED$\llbracket b_l \rrbracket$) \ DEFINED$\llbracket x \rrbracket$
  LAWS$\llbracket x \rrbracket$ = $\bigcup$ LAWS$\llbracket b_l \rrbracket$
  TYPECONSTS$\llbracket x \rrbracket$ = ($\bigcup$ TYPECONSTS$\llbracket b_l \rrbracket$) $\cup$ {ID$\llbracket p_i \rrbracket$}

$$\forall \, l : \text{GLOBAL}\llbracket b_l \rrbracket = \text{ID}\llbracket p_i \rrbracket \cup \begin{cases} \bigcup \text{TYPECONSTS}\llbracket x \rrbracket & \text{if component} = \text{type} \\ \bigcup_{m<l} \text{TYPECONSTS}\llbracket b_m \rrbracket & \text{otherwise} \end{cases}$$

$$\forall \, l : \text{KNOWN}\llbracket b_l \rrbracket = \begin{cases} \text{DEFINED}\llbracket x \rrbracket & \text{if component} = \text{type} \\ (\bigcup \text{DECLARED}\llbracket p_i \rrbracket) \cup (\bigcup_{m<l} \text{DECLARED}\llbracket b_m \rrbracket) & \text{otherwise} \end{cases}$$

III.3.2 Attributes and context conditions

Context conditions for c:

All visible constituents must be parameters or be declared in the component body:

$$\{y_k\} \subseteq \text{DEFINED}\,[\![x]\!]$$

A visible constituent may only be listed once:

$$k1 \neq k2 \Rightarrow y_{k1} \neq y_{k2}$$

All sorts used by visible constituents must be visible as well:

$$\forall\, y \in \{y_k\} : \text{USEDSORTS}\,[\![y]\!] \subseteq \{y_k\}$$

Definitions of identifiers must be unique:

$$\forall\, \textbf{constituent}\ w_1, w_2 : w_1 \in \{b_l\} \land w_2 \in \{b_l\} \land \text{ID}\,[\![w_1]\!] = \text{ID}\,[\![w_2]\!] \Rightarrow w_1 = w_2$$

The parameter identifiers must be distinct:

$$i1 \neq i2 \Rightarrow \text{ID}\,[\![p_{i1}]\!] \neq \text{ID}\,[\![p_{i2}]\!]$$

Parameters must not be redefined in the body:

$$\text{ID}\,[\![p_i]\!] \notin \text{DECLARED}\,[\![x]\!]$$

All sorts used by parameters must also be parameters:

$$\forall\, p \in \{p_i\} : \forall\, s \in \text{USEDSORTS}\,[\![p]\!] : \exists\, i : p_i = \text{sort}(s)$$

All identifiers mentioned in the restrictions must be parameter or type identifiers:

$$\forall\, j : \forall\, y \in \text{USED}\,[\![r_j]\!] : y \notin \{p_j\} \Rightarrow \text{KIND}\,[\![y]\!] = \text{typekind}$$

Besides laws, only instantiations of parameterized types without constituents may occur as parameter restrictions:

$$\exists\, \textbf{id}\ x_j, a_{jk}, u_{jl} : r_j = \text{incl}(x_j, \langle a_{jk}\rangle, \langle u_{jl}\rangle) \lor r_j = \text{base}(x_j, \langle a_{jk}\rangle, \langle u_{jl}\rangle) \Rightarrow$$
$$\text{KIND}\,[\![x_j]\!] = \text{typekind} \land$$
$$\text{CONSTITUENTS}\,[\![x_j]\!] = \emptyset \land \langle u_{jl}\rangle = \langle\rangle$$

If there are no parameters, there must also be no parameter restrictions:

$$\langle p_i\rangle = \langle\rangle \Rightarrow \langle r_j\rangle = \langle\rangle$$

Besides these general context conditions there are particular ones for each kind of component:

Context conditions for $t = \text{type}(x, \langle p_i\rangle, \langle r_j\rangle, \langle y_k\rangle, \langle b_l\rangle)$:

Only type instantiations may occur as phrases in types:

$$\forall\, l : \exists\, \textbf{phrase}\ p : b_l = \text{phr}(p) \Rightarrow \exists\, \langle\textbf{inst}\rangle\ \langle ib_{lj}\rangle : p = \text{inst}(\langle ib_{lj}\rangle)$$

Together with the general context conditions this ensures

$$\forall\, y \in \text{DECLARED}\,[\![x]\!] : \text{EXPRKIND}\,[\![\text{KIND}\,[\![y]\!]]\!]$$

Context conditions for $s = \text{structure}(x, \langle p_i\rangle, \langle r_j\rangle, \langle y_k\rangle, \langle b_l\rangle)$:

Statements must not be facets of a structure:

$$\forall\, l : \neg\, \exists\, \textbf{lstat}\ ls : b_l = \text{phr}(ls)$$

A structure may only declare applicative entities:

$$\forall\, y \in \text{DECLARED}\,[\![x]\!] : \text{EXPRKIND}\,[\![\text{KIND}\,[\![y]\!]]\!]$$

Device or module instantiations must not be facets of a structure:

$$\forall\, l : \neg\, \exists\, \textbf{id}\ w, \langle id\rangle\ \langle a_m\rangle, \langle id\rangle\ \langle z_n\rangle:$$
$$b_l = \text{phr}(\text{mod}(w, \langle a_m\rangle, \langle z_n\rangle)) \lor b_l = \text{phr}(\text{dev}(w, \langle a_m\rangle, \langle z_n\rangle))$$

Context conditions for m = module(x, $\langle p_i \rangle$, $\langle r_j \rangle$, $\langle y_k \rangle$, $\langle b_l \rangle$) :

  Statements must not be facets of a module:

  $\forall$ l : $\neg$ $\exists$ lstat ls : b_l = phr(ls)

  A module must not declare variables or labels:

  $\forall$ y e DECLARED$[\![x]\!]$: EXPRKIND$[\![$KIND$[\![y]\!]]\!]$ $\lor$ KIND$[\![y]\!]$ = prockind

  Device instantiations must not be facets of a module:

  $\forall$ l : $\neg$ $\exists$ id w, $\langle$id$\rangle$ $\langle a_m \rangle$, $\langle$id$\rangle$ $\langle z_n \rangle$: b_l = phr(dev(w, $\langle a_m \rangle$, $\langle z_n \rangle$))

Context conditions for d = device(x, $\langle p_i \rangle$, $\langle r_j \rangle$, $\langle y_k \rangle$, $\langle b_l \rangle$) :

  Variables and labels must not be visible constituents of device:

  $\forall$ k : EXPRKIND$[\![$KIND$[\![y_k]\!]]\!]$ $\lor$ KIND$[\![y_k]\!]$ = prockind

3.2.3. INSTANTIATION OF PARAMETERIZED COMPONENTS; TYPE BASING

(a) Component instantiation

  Syntactic mapping:

  $\hat{A}[\![$ **include** X($\langle arg_i \rangle$) as ($\langle res_j \rangle$)$]\!]$ = incl($\hat{A}[\![X]\!]$, $\langle$UNIQUE$[\![arg_i]\!]\rangle$, $\langle$BIND$[\![res_j]\!]\rangle$)

  $\hat{A}[\![$ **basedon** ($\langle res_j \rangle$) $\equiv$ X($\langle arg_i \rangle$)$]\!]$ = base($\hat{A}[\![X]\!]$, $\langle$UNIQUE$[\![arg_i]\!]\rangle$, $\langle$BIND$[\![res_j]\!]\rangle$)

  $\hat{A}[\![$ **structure** ($\langle res_j \rangle$) $\equiv$ X($\langle arg_i \rangle$)$]\!]$ = struct($\hat{A}[\![X]\!]$, $\langle$UNIQUE$[\![arg_i]\!]\rangle$, $\langle$BIND$[\![res_j]\!]\rangle$)

  $\hat{A}[\![$ **module** ($\langle res_j \rangle$) $\equiv$ X($\langle arg_i \rangle$)$]\!]$ = mod($\hat{A}[\![X]\!]$, $\langle$UNIQUE$[\![arg_i]\!]\rangle$, $\langle$BIND$[\![res_j]\!]\rangle$)

  $\hat{A}[\![$ **device** ($\langle res_j \rangle$) $\equiv$ X($\langle arg_i \rangle$)$]\!]$ = dev($\hat{A}[\![X]\!]$, $\langle$UNIQUE$[\![arg_i]\!]\rangle$, $\langle$BIND$[\![res_j]\!]\rangle$)

  Let comp e {incl, base, struct, mod, dev}, ib = comp(x, $\langle a_i \rangle$, $\langle z_k \rangle$), and let the definition of x be component(x, $\langle p_i \rangle$, $\langle r_j \rangle$, $\langle y_k \rangle$, $\langle b_l \rangle$).

  Context conditions:

  comp e {incl, base} $\Rightarrow$ KIND$[\![x]\!]$ = typekind

  comp = struct $\Rightarrow$ KIND$[\![x]\!]$ = structurekind

  comp = mod $\Rightarrow$ KIND$[\![x]\!]$ = modulekind

  comp = dev $\Rightarrow$ KIND$[\![x]\!]$ = devicekind

  $\forall$ i : a_i e GLOBAL$[\![ib]\!]$

  length($\langle a_i \rangle$) = length($\langle p_i \rangle$)

  $\langle z_k \rangle$ $\neq$ $\langle \rangle$ $\Rightarrow$ length($\langle z_k \rangle$) = length($\langle y_k \rangle$)

  k1 $\neq$ k2 $\Rightarrow$ z_{k1} $\neq$ z_{k2}

  $\forall$ i : KIND$[\![a_i]\!]$ = KIND$[\![$ID$[\![p_i]\!]]\!]$ $[\![a_j$ for ID$[\![p_j]\!]]\!]$

  Attributes:

  USED$[\![ib]\!]$ = {a_i} $\cup$ {x}

  DECLARED$[\![ib]\!]$ = $\begin{cases} \{z_k\} & \text{if } \langle z_k \rangle \neq \langle \rangle \\ \text{CONSTITUENTS}[\![x]\!] & \text{otherwise} \end{cases}$

  LAWS$[\![ib]\!]$ = $\emptyset$

III.3.2 Attributes and context conditions

$$\text{TYPECONSTS}[\![\,ib\,]\!] = \{y[\![\,a_i\ \textbf{for}\ \text{ID}[\![\,p_i\,]\!]\,]\!] : y\ e\ \text{TYPECONSTS}[\![\,x\,]\!]\,\}$$

(b) <u>System of type instantiations</u>

Syntactic mapping:

Let $IB_1,\dots,IB_n$ be type instantiations.

$$A[\![\,IB_1,\dots,IB_n\,]\!] = \text{inst}(\langle A[\![\,IB_i\,]\!]\rangle)$$

Let in = inst($\langle ib_i\rangle$) .

Context conditions: none

Attributes:

$\text{USED}[\![\,in\,]\!] = \mathbf{U}\ \text{USED}[\![\,ib_i\,]\!]$

$\text{DECLARED}[\![\,in\,]\!] = \mathbf{U}\ \text{DECLARED}[\![\,ib_i\,]\!]$

$\text{LAWS}[\![\,in\,]\!] = \emptyset$

$\text{TYPECONSTS}[\![\,in\,]\!] = \mathbf{U}\ \text{TYPECONSTS}[\![\,ib_i\,]\!]$

3.2.4. PROGRAMS

Syntactic mapping:

$$A[\![\,\langle CD_i\rangle\,]\!] = \text{prog}(\langle A[\![\,CD_i\,]\!]\rangle)$$

Let cp = prog($\langle c_i\rangle$) and $x_i = \text{ID}[\![\,c_i\,]\!]$.

Context conditions:

A component must not be defined recursively:

$$\forall\ i : x_i \notin \text{REACHABLECOMPONENTS}[\![\,x_i\,]\!]$$

The component identifiers must be pairwise distinct:

$$\forall\ i,j : i \neq j \Rightarrow x_i \neq x_j$$

The components used in the program are also defined there:

$$\text{REACHABLECOMPONENTS}[\![\,x_j\,]\!] \subseteq \{x_i\}$$

Attributes:

$\text{REACHABLECOMPONENTS}[\![\,x_i\,]\!] = \text{USEDCOMPONENTS}[\![\,x_i\,]\!]\ \mathbf{U}$
$\qquad\qquad\qquad\qquad \{\text{REACHABLECOMPONENTS}[\![\,x\,]\!] : x\ e\ \text{USEDCOMPONENTS}[\![\,x_i\,]\!]\,\}$

3.3. SEMANTICS OF PROGRAMS

3.3.1. NORMALIZATION

A program satisfying the context conditions above does not contain recursively defined components, and thus all component instantiations can be unfolded; this is effected by a family of functions whose names begin with "UF". During the unfolding, the instantiated versions of the parameter restrictions of the components are collected in a second result of the respective function. As stated in II.1.2.1, parameterized components do not possess an independent meaning; they only serve to steer the unfolding. Likewise, since modules and devices employ variables and procedures, as in the scheme language no independent meaning is given for their facets; rather they serve as auxiliaries in the definition of structures. Therefore, after the unfolding, all parameterized components as well as all modules and devices can be deleted from the program; this is done by the function REMOVE.

NORMALIZE : **program** → <component x <facet>>

$$\text{NORMALIZE} [\![\text{program}(\langle c_i \rangle)]\!] = \& \text{REMOVE} [\![\langle \overline{c_i}, ff_i \rangle]\!]$$
$$\text{where } \langle \overline{c_i}, ff_i \rangle = \text{UFC} [\![c_i]\!]$$

REMOVE : **component** x <facet> → <component x <facet>>

$$\text{REMOVE} [\![\langle \text{component}(x, \langle p_i \rangle, \langle r_j \rangle, \langle y_k \rangle, \langle b_l \rangle), ff \rangle]\!]$$

$$= \begin{cases} \langle\rangle \text{ if } \langle p_i \rangle \neq \langle\rangle \text{ or component } e \text{ \{module, device\}} \\ \\ \langle \text{component}(x, \langle\rangle, \langle\rangle, \langle y_k \rangle, \langle b_l \rangle), ff \rangle \quad \text{otherwise} \end{cases}$$

UFC : **component** → component x <facet>
UFC unfolds all local instantiations within a component.

$$\text{UFC} [\![\text{component}(x, \langle p_i \rangle, \langle r_j \rangle, \langle y_k \rangle, \langle b_l \rangle)]\!] =$$
$$\langle \text{component}(x, \langle p_i \rangle, \langle r_j \rangle, \langle y_k \rangle, ff), gg \rangle$$
$$\text{where } \langle ff, gg \rangle = \text{UFFS} [\![\langle b_l \rangle]\!]$$

UFFS : <**facet**> → <facet> x <facet>
UFFS unfolds all local instantiations within a sequence of facets.

$$\text{UFFS} [\![\langle\rangle]\!] = \langle\langle\rangle, \langle\rangle\rangle$$
$$\text{UFFS} [\![\langle f \rangle \& ff]\!] = \langle bb \& \overline{bb}, gg \& \overline{gg} \rangle$$
$$\text{where } \langle bb, gg \rangle = \text{UFF} [\![f]\!]$$
$$\langle \overline{bb}, \overline{gg} \rangle = \text{UFFS} [\![ff]\!]$$

III.3.3 Semantics

UFF : **facet** → <facet> x <facet>

   UFF unfolds all local instantiations within a facet.

   UFF $\llbracket$ constit(co) $\rrbracket$ = <<constit(co)>, <>>
   UFF $\llbracket$ law(la) $\rrbracket$ = <<law(la)>, <>>
   UFF $\llbracket$ phr(p) $\rrbracket$ = <<phr(pp$_k$)> & <f$_1$>, <g$_m$>>
      where <<phr(pp$_k$)>, <f$_1$>, <g$_m$>> = UFP $\llbracket$ <p> $\rrbracket$
   UFF $\llbracket$ prim(f) $\rrbracket$ = <<prim(b$_k$)>, <prim(f$_1$)>>
      where <<b$_1$>, <f$_1$>> = UFF $\llbracket$ f $\rrbracket$

Before we define the unfolding UFP for phrases, we need an auxiliary mapping

   UFI : **inst ⊕ phrase** → <phrase> x <facet> x <facet>

that describes the unfolding of instantiations.

Let op $\in$ {incl, base, struct, mod, dev}, ib = op(x, <a$_i$>, <z$_k$>), and let the definition of the (parameterized) component x be component(x, <p$_i$>, <r$_j$>, <y$_k$>, <b$_1$>) .

   UFI $\llbracket$ ib $\rrbracket$ = <dsq, f & fb, g & gb & fr & gr>
      where <dsq, f, g> = UFP $\llbracket$ PHRS $\llbracket$ ufb $\rrbracket$ $\rrbracket$
         <fb, gb> = UFFS $\llbracket$ $\overline{\text{ufb}}$ $\rrbracket$

$$\overline{\text{ufb}} = \begin{cases} \text{FACS} \llbracket \text{ufb} \rrbracket & \text{if op} \neq \text{base} \\ \\ <\text{prim}(f_m)> & \text{if op} = \text{base and FACS} \llbracket \text{ufb} \rrbracket = <f_m> \end{cases}$$

         ufb = < b$_1$ $\llbracket$ a$_i$ for ID $\llbracket$ p$_i$ $\rrbracket$, z$_k$ for y$_k$, $\hat{w}_r$ for w$_r$ $\rrbracket$ >
            where {w$_r$} = HIDDEN $\llbracket$ x $\rrbracket$
                  {$\hat{w}_r$} ⊆ NEW
         <fr, gr> = UFFS $\llbracket$ $\overline{\text{ufr}}$ $\rrbracket$

$$\overline{\text{ufr}} = \begin{cases} \text{FACS} \llbracket \text{ufr} \rrbracket & \text{if op} \neq \text{base} \\ \\ <\text{prim}(f_m)> & \text{if op} = \text{base and FACS} \llbracket \text{ufr} \rrbracket = <f_m> \end{cases}$$

         ufr = $\overline{<r_j>}$

$$\overline{<r_j>} = \begin{cases} \text{law}(\hat{r}_j) & \text{if } \hat{r}_j \in \textbf{law} \\ \\ \text{phr(inst}(<\hat{r}_j>)) & \text{if } \hat{r}_j \in \textbf{inst} \end{cases}$$

         $\hat{r}_j$ = r$_j$ $\llbracket$ a$_i$ for ID $\llbracket$ p$_i$ $\rrbracket$ $\rrbracket$

For all other phrases p,

   UFI $\llbracket$ p $\rrbracket$ = <<>, <>, <>> .

Here we have used two further auxiliary mappings

   PHRS : <facet> → <decl ⊕ lstat>
   FACS : <facet> → <facet>

that divide a sequence of facets into its phrases and its non-phrase facets:

$$PHRS \, [\![\, \diamond \,]\!] \; = \; \diamond$$

$$FACS \, [\![\, \diamond \,]\!] \; = \; \diamond$$

$$PHRS \, [\![\, \text{<b>} \, \& \, ff \,]\!] \; = \; \begin{cases} \text{<p>} \; \& \; PHRS \, [\![\, ff \,]\!] & \text{if } b = phr(p) \\[2mm] PHRS \, [\![\, ff \,]\!] & \text{otherwise} \end{cases}$$

$$FACS \, [\![\, \text{<b>} \, \& \, ff \,]\!] \; = \; \begin{cases} FACS \, [\![\, ff \,]\!] & \text{if } b = phr(p) \\[2mm] \text{<b>} \; \& \; FACS \, [\![\, ff \,]\!] & \text{otherwise} \end{cases}$$

UFP : <phrase> → <phrase> × <facet> × <facet>

UFP unfolds all local instatiations within a sequence of phrases.

$$UFP \, [\![\, \diamond \,]\!] \; = \; \text{<$\diamond$, $\diamond$, $\diamond$>}$$

Let pp = <inst(<ib_m>)> & dsq .

$\forall$ k : GLOBAL$[\![\, ib_k \,]\!]$ = GLOBAL$[\![\, dsq \,]\!]$ = GLOBAL$[\![\, pp \,]\!]$ **U** (**U** DECLARED$[\![\, ib_m \,]\!]$)

UFP$[\![\, pp \,]\!]$ = <(& pp_m) & $\overline{pp}$, (& ff_m) & $\overline{ff}$, (& gg_m) & $\overline{gg}$>

    where <pp_m, ff_m, gg_m> = UFI$[\![\, ib_m \,]\!]$

        <$\overline{pp}$, $\overline{ff}$, $\overline{gg}$> = UFP$[\![\, dsq \,]\!]$

Let op $\in$ {struct, mod, dev}, p = op(x, <a_i>, <z_k>), and pp = <p> & dsq .

  GLOBAL$[\![\, p_k \,]\!]$ = GLOBAL$[\![\, dsq \,]\!]$ = GLOBAL$[\![\, pp \,]\!]$

  UFP$[\![\, pp \,]\!]$ = <pq & $\overline{pq}$, ff & $\overline{ff}$, gg & $\overline{gg}$>

    where <pq, ff, gg> = UFI$[\![\, p \,]\!]$

        <$\overline{pp}$, $\overline{ff}$, $\overline{gg}$> = UFP$[\![\, dsq \,]\!]$

All other language constructs simply pass on the results of their local unfoldings. Nevertheless we give the precise definitions:

Let op $\in$ {objects, variables}, d = op(<m_i, x_i>, e), and pp = <d> & dsq .

  GLOBAL$[\![\, e \,]\!]$ = GLOBAL$[\![\, dsq \,]\!]$ = GLOBAL$[\![\, pp \,]\!]$

  UFP$[\![\, pp \,]\!]$ = <<$\overline{d}$> & $\overline{dsq}$, f & ff, g & gg>

    where $\overline{d}$ = op(<m_i, x_i>, $\overline{e}$)

        <$\overline{e}$, f, g> = UFE$[\![\, e \,]\!]$

        <$\overline{dsq}$, ff, gg> = UFP$[\![\, dsq \,]\!]$

Let prog = program(<r_i>) and pp = <prog> & dsq .

  GLOBAL$[\![\, r_i \,]\!]$ = GLOBAL$[\![\, dsq \,]\!]$ = GLOBAL$[\![\, pp \,]\!]$

  UFP$[\![\, pp \,]\!]$ = <<$\overline{prog}$> & $\overline{dsq}$, (& f_i) & ff, (& g_i) & gg>

    where $\overline{prog}$ = program(<$\overline{r_i}$>)

III.3.3 Semantics

$$\langle r_i, f_i, g_i \rangle = UFR[\![r_i]\!]$$
$$\langle \overline{dsq}, ff, gg \rangle = UFP[\![dsq]\!]$$

Here we have used the auxiliary function UFR that unfolds local instantiations in routines (see below).

Let $pp = \langle ls \rangle$ & dsq .
$\quad$ GLOBAL$[\![ls]\!]$ = GLOBAL$[\![dsq]\!]$ = GLOBAL$[\![pp]\!]$
$\quad$ UFP$[\![pp]\!]$ = $\langle\langle\overline{ls}\rangle$ & $\overline{dsq}$, f & ff, g & gg$\rangle$
$\quad\quad$ where $\langle\overline{ls}, f, g\rangle$ = UFS$[\![ls]\!]$
$\quad\quad\quad\quad$ $\langle\overline{dsq}, ff, gg\rangle$ = UFP$[\![dsq]\!]$

UFR : **routine** $\rightarrow$ **routine** x $\langle$facet$\rangle$ x $\langle$facet$\rangle$

Let $r = function(x, a)$.
$\quad$ GLOBAL$[\![a]\!]$ = GLOBAL$[\![r]\!]$
$\quad$ UFR$[\![r]\!]$ = $\langle function(x, \overline{a}), f, g\rangle$
$\quad\quad$ where $\langle\overline{a}, f, g\rangle$ = UFA$[\![a]\!]$

Let $r = procedure(p, \langle m_i, z_i \rangle, \langle w_j, x_j \rangle, s)$.
$\quad$ GLOBAL$[\![s]\!]$ = GLOBAL$[\![r]\!]$
$\quad$ UFR$[\![r]\!]$ = $\langle procedure(p, \langle m_i, z_i \rangle, \langle w_j, x_j \rangle, \overline{s}), f, g\rangle$
$\quad\quad$ where $\langle\overline{s}, f, g\rangle$ = UFS$[\![s]\!]$

UFS : **stat** $\bullet$ **pstat** $\bullet$ **lstat** $\rightarrow$ (**stat** $\bullet$ **pstat** $\bullet$ **lstat**) x $\langle$facet$\rangle$ x $\langle$facet$\rangle$
$\quad$ UFS unfolds all local instantiations within statements.

Let $s = assign(\langle x_i \rangle, e)$.
$\quad$ GLOBAL$[\![e]\!]$ = GLOBAL$[\![s]\!]$
$\quad$ UFS$[\![s]\!]$ = $\langle assign(\langle x_i \rangle, \overline{e}), f, g\rangle$
$\quad\quad$ where $\langle\overline{e}, f, g\rangle$ = UFE$[\![e]\!]$

UFS$[\![skip]\!]$ = $\langle skip, \langle\rangle, \langle\rangle\rangle$

UFS$[\![abort]\!]$ = $\langle abort, \langle\rangle, \langle\rangle\rangle$

Let $s = block(dsq)$.
$\quad$ GLOBAL$[\![dsq]\!]$ = GLOBAL$[\![s]\!]$
$\quad$ UFS$[\![s]\!]$ = $\langle block(\overline{dsq}), f, g\rangle$
$\quad\quad$ where $\langle\overline{dsq}, f, g\rangle$ = UFP$[\![dsq]\!]$

Let s = condstat(e, s_1, s_2) .

  GLOBAL $[\![\,e\,]\!]$ = GLOBAL $[\![\,s_1\,]\!]$ = GLOBAL $[\![\,s\,]\!]$

  UFS $[\![\,s\,]\!]$ = <condstat($\bar{e}$, $\bar{s}_1$, $\bar{s}_2$), f & f_1 & f_2, g & g_1 & g_2>

    where $\bar{e}$, f, g = UFE $[\![\,e\,]\!]$

       $\bar{s}_i$, f_i, g_i = UFS $[\![\,s_i\,]\!]$

Let s = choicestat(<s_i>) .

  $\forall$ i : GLOBAL $[\![\,s_i\,]\!]$ = GLOBAL $[\![\,s\,]\!]$

  UFS $[\![\,s\,]\!]$ = <choicestat($\overline{<s_i>}$), & f_i, & g_i>

    where $\bar{s}_i$, f_i, g_i = UFS $[\![\,s_i\,]\!]$

Let s = call(p, <e_i>, <v_j>) .

  $\forall$ i : GLOBAL $[\![\,e_i\,]\!]$ = GLOBAL $[\![\,s\,]\!]$

  UFS $[\![\,s\,]\!]$ = <call(p, <$\bar{e}_i$>, <v_j>), & f_i, & g_i>

    where $\bar{e}_i$, f_i, g_i = UFE $[\![\,e_i\,]\!]$

Let ps = pmake(s) .

  GLOBAL $[\![\,s\,]\!]$ = GLOBAL $[\![\,ps\,]\!]$

  UFS $[\![\,ps\,]\!]$ = <pmake($\bar{s}$), f, g>

    where $\bar{s}$, f, g = UFS $[\![\,s\,]\!]$

Let ps = pblock(dsq) .

  GLOBAL $[\![\,dsq\,]\!]$ = GLOBAL $[\![\,ps\,]\!]$

  UFS $[\![\,ps\,]\!]$ = <pblock($\overline{dsq}$), f, g>

    where $\overline{dsq}$, f, g = UFP $[\![\,dsq\,]\!]$

Let gu = guards(<c_i, ps_i>, ps) .

  $\forall$ i : GLOBAL $[\![\,c_i\,]\!]$ = GLOBAL $[\![\,ps_i\,]\!]$ = GLOBAL $[\![\,gu\,]\!]$

  GLOBAL $[\![\,ps\,]\!]$ = GLOBAL $[\![\,gu\,]\!]$

  UFS $[\![\,gu\,]\!]$ = <guards(<$\bar{c}_i$, $\overline{ps}_i$>, $\overline{ps}$), (& (f_i & $\bar{f}_i$)) & f, (& (g_i & $\bar{g}_i$)) & g>

    where $\bar{c}_i$, f_i, g_i = UFE $[\![\,c_i\,]\!]$

       $\overline{ps}_i$, $\bar{f}_i$, $\bar{g}_i$ = UFS $[\![\,ps_i\,]\!]$

       $\overline{ps}$, f, g = UFS $[\![\,ps\,]\!]$

Let aw = wait(c, ps) .

  GLOBAL $[\![\,c\,]\!]$ = GLOBAL $[\![\,ps\,]\!]$ = GLOBAL $[\![\,aw\,]\!]$

  UFS $[\![\,aw\,]\!]$ = <wait($\bar{c}$, $\overline{ps}$), f & $\bar{f}$, g & $\bar{g}$>

    where $\bar{c}$, f, g = UFE $[\![\,c\,]\!]$

       $\overline{ps}$, $\bar{f}$, $\bar{g}$ = UFS $[\![\,ps\,]\!]$

III.3.3 Semantics

Let pc = par($\langle ps_i \rangle$) .
  $\forall$ i : GLOBAL $[\![ps_i]\!]$ = GLOBAL $[\![pc]\!]$
  UFS $[\![pc]\!]$ = $\langle par(\langle \overline{ps_i} \rangle),$ & $f_i,$ & $g_i \rangle$
    where $\langle \overline{ps_i}, f_i, g_i \rangle$ = UFS $[\![ps_i]\!]$

Let s = elpstat(ps) .
  GLOBAL $[\![ps]\!]$ = GLOBAL $[\![s]\!]$
  UFS $[\![s]\!]$ = $\langle elpstat(\overline{ps}), f, g \rangle$
    where $\langle \overline{ps}, f, g \rangle$ = UFS $[\![ps]\!]$

Let ls = make(ps) .
  GLOBAL $[\![ps]\!]$ = GLOBAL $[\![ls]\!]$
  UFS $[\![ls]\!]$ = $\langle make(\overline{ps}), f, g \rangle$
    where $\langle \overline{ps}, f, g \rangle$ = UFS $[\![ps]\!]$

Let lab = label(l, ls).
  GLOBAL $[\![ls]\!]$ = GLOBAL $[\![lab]\!]$
  UFS $[\![lab]\!]$ = $\langle label(l, \overline{ls}), f, g \rangle$
    where $\langle \overline{ls}, f, g \rangle$ = UFS $[\![ls]\!]$

UFS $[\![goto(l)]\!]$ = $\langle goto(l), \langle \rangle, \langle \rangle \rangle$

Let lcond = lcondstat(e, ls_1, ls_2) .
  GLOBAL $[\![e]\!]$ = GLOBAL $[\![ls_i]\!]$ = GLOBAL $[\![lcond]\!]$
  UFS $[\![lcond]\!]$ = $\langle lcondstat(\overline{e}, \overline{ls}_1, \overline{ls}_2),$ f & f_1 & f_2, g & g_1 & $g_2 \rangle$
    where $\langle \overline{e}, f, g \rangle$ = UFE $[\![e]\!]$
       $\langle \overline{ls}_i, f_i, g_i \rangle$ = UFS $[\![ls_i]\!]$

Let lchoice = lchoicestat($\langle ls_i \rangle$) .
  $\forall$ i : GLOBAL $[\![ls_i]\!]$ = GLOBAL $[\![lchoice]\!]$
  UFS $[\![lchoice]\!]$ = $\langle lchoicestat(\langle \overline{ls}_i \rangle),$ & $f_i,$ & $g_i \rangle$
    where $\langle \overline{ls}_i, f_i, g_i \rangle$ = UFS $[\![ls_i]\!]$

Let lbl = lblock(lsq) .
  GLOBAL $[\![lsq]\!]$ = GLOBAL $[\![lbl]\!]$
  UFS $[\![lbl]\!]$ = $\langle lblock(\overline{lsq}), f, g \rangle$
    where $\langle \overline{lsq}, f, g \rangle$ = UFP $[\![lsq]\!]$

UFE : **expr** $\rightarrow$ **expr** x $\langle$**facet**$\rangle$ x $\langle$**facet**$\rangle$
  UFE unfolds all local instantiations within expressions.

UFE $[\![$ semval(u) $]\!]$ = $\langle$semval(u), $\langle\rangle$, $\langle\rangle\rangle$

UFE $[\![$ value(x) $]\!]$ = $\langle$value(x), $\langle\rangle$, $\langle\rangle\rangle$

Let e = cond(e_1, e_2, e_3) .
   GLOBAL $[\![e_i]\!]$ = GLOBAL $[\![e]\!]$
   UFE $[\![e]\!]$ = $\langle$cond($\overline{e}_1$, $\overline{e}_2$, $\overline{e}_3$), & f_i, & $g_i\rangle$
     where $\langle\overline{e}_i$, f_i, $g_i\rangle$ = UFE $[\![e_i]\!]$

Let op ϵ {tuple, finchoice} and e = op($\langle e_i\rangle$) .
   GLOBAL $[\![e_i]\!]$ = GLOBAL $[\![e]\!]$
   UFE $[\![e]\!]$ = $\langle$op($\langle\overline{e}_i\rangle$, & f_i, & $g_i\rangle$
     where $\langle\overline{e}_i$, f_i, $g_i\rangle$ = UFE $[\![e_i]\!]$

Let and e = abstract(a) .
   GLOBAL $[\![a]\!]$ = GLOBAL $[\![e]\!]$
   UFE $[\![e]\!]$ = $\langle$abstract($\overline{a}$), f, g$\rangle$
     where $\langle\overline{a}$, f, g$\rangle$ = UFA $[\![a]\!]$

Let op ϵ {apply, equal, element} and e = op(e_1, e_2) .
   GLOBAL $[\![e_i]\!]$ = GLOBAL $[\![e]\!]$
   UFE $[\![e]\!]$ = $\langle$op($\overline{e}_1$, $\overline{e}_2$), f_1 & f_2, g_1 & $g_2\rangle$
     where $\langle\overline{e}_i$, f_i, $g_i\rangle$ = UFE $[\![e_i]\!]$

Let e = fixpoint($\langle x_i\rangle$, $\langle a_i\rangle$) .
   GLOBAL $[\![a_i]\!]$ = GLOBAL $[\![e]\!]$
   UFE $[\![e]\!]$ = $\langle$fixpoint($\langle x_i\rangle$, $\langle\overline{a}_i\rangle$), & f_i, & $g_i\rangle$
     where $\langle\overline{a}_i$, f_i, $g_i\rangle$ = UFA $[\![a_i]\!]$

Let op ϵ {all, choice, comprehend} and e = op($\langle m_i$, $x_i\rangle$, c) .
   GLOBAL $[\![c]\!]$ = GLOBAL $[\![e]\!]$
   UFE $[\![e]\!]$ = $\langle$op($\langle m_i$, $x_i\rangle$, $\overline{c}$), f, g$\rangle$
     where $\langle\overline{c}$, f, g$\rangle$ = UFE $[\![c]\!]$

Let seg = segment(dsq & $\langle\rangle$, e) .
   GLOBAL $[\![e]\!]$ = GLOBAL $[\![\langle\rangle]\!]$
   UFE $[\![$ seg $]\!]$ = $\langle$segment($\overline{dsq}$, $\overline{e}$), f & ff, g & gg$\rangle$
     where $\langle\overline{dsq}$, f, g$\rangle$ = UFP $[\![$ dsq & $\langle\rangle]\!]$
        $\overline{e}$, ff, gg$\rangle$ = UFE $[\![e]\!]$

III.3.3 Semantics

UFA : **abstraction** → **abstraction** × <facet> × <facet>

Let a = abs(<m_i, x_i>, r, e) .
  GLOBAL⟦e⟧ = GLOBAL⟦a⟧
  UFA⟦a⟧ = <abs(<m_i, x_i>, r, $\bar{e}$), f, g>
    where <$\bar{e}$, f, g> = UFE⟦c⟧

3.3.2. SEMANTICS OF NORMALIZED PROGRAMS

A normalized program contains only non-parameterized types and structures, each together with a
sequence of restrictions on their facets (generated by the use of parameterized components).

(a) SEMANTICS OF TYPES

Consider a pair <t,r> where t = type(x, <>, <>, <y_k>, <b_l>) is a type and r is a sequence of
restricting facets.

The parameter type corresponding to <t,r> is $\bar{t}$ = type($\bar{x}$, <>, <>, <>, r) where $\bar{x}$ is a new
identifier.

Let Σ = (S, F, C) and $\bar{\Sigma}$ = ($\bar{S}$, $\bar{F}$, $\bar{C}$) be the signatures corresponding to x and $\bar{x}$. Then we define
Σ' = (S ∪ $\bar{S}$, F ∪ $\bar{F}$, C ∪ $\bar{C}$).

We call x consistent relative to r if for every model A of x there is a Σ'-Algebra A' such that
A is the reduct (cf. 1.3) A'|Σ and furthermore the reduct A'|$\bar{\Sigma}$ satisfies all laws of $\bar{x}$.

The semantics of <t,r> is given by all models of x provided that x is persistent and consistent
relative to r.

(b) SEMANTICS OF STRUCTURES

Consider a pair <s,r> where s = structure(x, <>, <>, <y_k>, <b_l>) is a structure and r is a
sequence of restricting facets.

The basic type t corresponding to <s,r> is defined by t = type($\bar{x}$, <>, <>, <z_m>, ff) where ff =
FACS⟦<b_l>⟧ and <z_m> is a sequence of identifiers such that {z_m} = DECLARED⟦ff⟧.

Let <$\hat{y}_n$> be the sequence of those y_k with KIND⟦y_k⟧ ≠ sortkind. Then the semantics of <s,r>
is given by the set
    { B_A⟦segment(PHRS⟦<b_l>⟧, tuple(<value($\hat{y}_n$)>))⟧ : A is a model of $\bar{x}$ } ,
where B_A is the breadth-function of 2.1 relative to the model A of the basic type $\bar{x}$, provided
that $\bar{x}$ is persistent and consistent relative to r.

REFERENCES

/ADJ 78/
J. W. Thatcher, E. G. Wagner, J. B. Wright: Data type specification: parametrization and the power of specification techniques. Proc. 10th Annual SIGACT Symposium on Theory of Computation, 1978, 119-132

/Backus 78/
J. Backus: Can programming be liberated from the von Neumann style? A functional style and its algebra of programs. Comm. ACM 21, 613-641 (1978)

/Barendregt 84/
H. P. Barendregt: The lambda calculus - its syntax and semantics (2nd rev. ed.). Studies in logic and the foundations of mathematics 103. Amsterdam: North-Holland 1984

/Bauer 71/
F. L. Bauer: Programming languages under professional and under educational aspects. Proc. Second All-Union Conference on Programming, Novosibirsk 1970. Siberian Division of the Academy of Sciences 1971. Reprinted in /Bauer, Broy 79/, 267-272

/Bauer 73/
F. L. Bauer: A philosophy of programming. A course of three lectures given at the Imperial College of Science and Technology, London, October 1973. Reprinted in /Bauer, Samelson 76/, 194-229

/Bauer 76/
F. L. Bauer: Programming as an evolutionary process. In /Bauer, Samelson 76/, 153-182. Abridged version in Proc. 2nd International Conference on Software Engineering, San Francisco 1976, 223-234

/Bauer 81/
F. L. Bauer: Programming as fulfilment of a contract. In: P. Henderson (ed.): System design. Infotech State of the Art Report 9:6. Maidenhead: Pergamon Infotech Ltd. 1981, 165-174

/Bauer, Broy 79/
F. L. Bauer, M. Broy (eds.): Program construction. Lecture Notes of the International Summer School on Program Construction, Marktoberdorf 1978. Lecture Notes in Computer Science 69. Berlin: Springer 1979

/Bauer, Gnatz 79/
F. L. Bauer, R. Gnatz: Praxis des Programmierens. Praktikum am Institut für Informatik der TU München, WS 1979/80, SS 1980

References

/Bauer, Samelson 76/

F. L. Bauer, K. Samelson (eds.): Language hierarchies and interfaces. Lecture Notes of the International Summer School on Language Hierarchies and Interfaces, Marktoberdorf 1975. Lecture Notes in Computer Science 46. Berlin: Springer 1976

/Bauer, Wössner 82/

F. L. Bauer, H. Wössner: Algorithmic language and program development. Berlin: Springer 1982

/Bauer et al. 81/

F. L. Bauer, M. Broy, W. Dosch, R. Gnatz, B. Krieg-Brückner, A. Laut, M. Luckmann, T. A. Matzner, B. Möller, H. Partsch, P. Pepper, K. Samelson, R. Steinbrüggen, M. Wirsing, H. Wössner: Programming in a wide spectrum language: a collection of examples. Science of Computer Programming 1, 73-114 (1981)

/Berghammer, Hangel 84/

R. Berghammer, E. Hangel: Die Semantik des Sprachkernes der Sprache CIP-L. Institut für Informatik der TU München, May 1984

/Brass et al. 82/

B. Brass, F. Erhard, A. Horsch, H.-O. Riethmayer, R. Steinbrüggen: CIP-S: An instrument for program transformation and rule generation. Institut für Informatik der TU München, TUM-I8211, 1982

/Broy 80/

M. Broy: Transformational semantics for concurrent programs. Information Processing Letters 11, 87-97 (1980)

/Broy, Wirsing 80/

M. Broy, M. Wirsing: Algebraic definition of a functional programming language and its semantical models. Institut für Informatik der TU München, TUM-I8008, 1980. Also in RAIRO Informatique theorique 17, 137-161 (1983)

/Broy et al. 79/

M. Broy, R. Gnatz, M. Wirsing: Semantics of nondeterministic and noncontinuous constructs. In /Bauer, Broy 79/, 553-392

/Broy et al. 80/

M. Broy, H. Partsch, P. Pepper, M. Wirsing: Semantical relations in programming languages. Proc. IFIP Congress 80, Tokyo/Melbourne. Amsterdam: North-Holland 1980, 101-106

/Broy et al. 85/

M. Broy, B. Möller, P. Pepper, M. Wirsing: Algebraic implementations preserve program correctness. Submitted for publication

/Burstall et al. 80/

R.M. Burstall, D.B. MacQueen, D.T. Sannella: HOPE : An experimental applicative language. Proc. 1980 LISP Conference, 136-143

/Clocksin, Mellish 81/

W. F. Clocksin, C. S. Mellish: Programming in PROLOG. Berlin: Springer 1981

/Dershowitz, Manna 79/

N. Dershowitz, Z. Manna: Proving termination with multiset orderings. Comm. ACM 22, 465-476 (1979)

/Dijkstra 75/

E. W. Dijkstra: Guarded commands, nondeterminacy and formal derivation of programs. Comm. ACM 18, 453-457 (1975)

/Dijkstra 76/

E. W. Dijkstra: A discipline of programming. Englewood Cliffs, N.J.: Prentice-Hall 1976

/Ershov 78/

A. P. Ershov: On the essence of compilation. In: E. J. Neuhold (ed.): Formal description of programming concepts. Amsterdam: North-Holland 1978, 391-420

/Floyd 67/

R. W. Floyd: Assigning meanings to programs. Proc. American Math. Society Symp. in Appl. Math. 19, 19-32 (1967)

/Gordon et al. 79/

M. Gordon, R. Milner, C. Wadsworth: Edinburgh LCF. Lecture Notes in Computer Science 78. Berlin: Springer 1979

/Guttag 75/

J. V. Guttag: The specification and application to programming of abstract data types. Univ. of Toronto, Comp. Syst. Research Group, Techn. Report CSRG-59, Sept. 1975

/Hennessy, Ashcroft 76/

M. Hennessy, E. A. Ashcroft: The semantics of nondeterminism. In: R. Michaelson, R. Milner (eds.): Automata, languages and programming. Edinburgh: Edinburgh University Press 1976, 479-493

References

/Hoare 69/
C. A. R. Hoare: An axiomatic basis for computer programming. Comm. ACM 12, 576-580, 583 (1969)

/Knuth 68/
D. E. Knuth: Semantics of context-free languages. Math. Syst. Theory 2, 127-145 (1968)

/Knuth 74/
D. E. Knuth: Structured programming with GOTO statements. Computing Surveys 8, 261-301 (1974)

/Kowalski 83/
R. A. Kowalski: Logic programming. Proc. IFIP Congress 83, Paris. Amsterdam: North-Holland 1983, 133-145

/Lampson et al. 77/
B. W. Lampson, J. J. Horning, R. L. London, J. G. Mitchell, G. J. Popek: Report on the programming language Euclid. SIGPLAN Notices 12, entire No.2 (1977)

/Landin 64/
P. J. Landin: The mechanical evaluation of expressions. Comp. J. 6, 308-320 (1964)

/Landin 65/
P. J. Landin: A correspondence between ALGOL 60 and Church's lambda notation: Part I. Comm. ACM 8, 89-101 (1965)

/Landin 66/
P. J. Landin: A formal description of ALGOL 60. In: T. B. Steel jr. (ed.): Formal language description languages for computer programming, Proc. IFIP Working Conf. 1964. Amsterdam: North-Holland 1966, 266-294

/Laut 78/
A. Laut: Deriving a computation structure for program trees from a context-free grammar. Institut für Informatik der TU München, Interner Bericht, Oktober 1978

/Laut 80/
A. Laut: Safe procedural implementations of algebraic types. Information Processing Letters 11, 147-151 (1980)

/Laut 82/
A. Laut: Abstrakte Syntax und Programm-Manipulation. Fakultät für Mathematik und Informatik der TU München, Dissertation, 1982

/Manna 74/
Z. Manna: Mathematical theory of computation. New York: McGraw-Hill 1974

/Markowsky 76/
G. Markowsky: Chain-complete posets and directed sets with applications. Algebra universalis $\underline{6}$, 53-68 (1976)

/McCarthy 60/
J. McCarthy: Recursive functions of symbolic expressions and their computation by machine, Part I. Comm. ACM $\underline{3}$, 184-195 (1960)

/McCarthy 62/
J. McCarthy: Towards a mathematical science of computation. Proc. IFIP Congress 62, Munich. Amsterdam: North-Holland 1963, 21-28

/McCarthy 63/
J. McCarthy: A basis for a mathematical theory of computation. In: P. Braffort, D. Hirschberg (eds.): Computer programming and formal systems. Amsterdam: North-Holland 1963, 33-69

/McCarthy et al. 65/
J. McCarthy, P. W. Abrahams, D. J. Edwards, T. P. Hart, M. J. Levin: LISP 1.5 programmer's manual. Cambridge, Mass.: MIT Press 1965

/de Millo et al. 79/
R. A. de Millo, R. J. Lipton, A. J. Perlis: Social processes and proofs of theorems and programs. Comm. ACM $\underline{22}$, 271-280 (1979)

/Möller 82/
B. Möller: Unendliche Objekte und Geflechte. Fakultät für Mathematik und Informatik der TU München, Dissertation, TUM-I8213, 1982

/Möller 84/
B. Möller (ed.): A survey of the project CIP: Computer-Aided, Intuition-Guided Programming - Wide spectrum language and program transformations. Institut für Informatik der TU München, TUM-I8406, July 1984

/Möller 85/
B. Möller: On the algebraic specification of infinite objects - ordered and continuous models of algebraic types. Acta Informatica (to appear)

References

/Nickl 83/
F. Nickl: On the semantic completeness of CIP-L. Institut für Informatik der TU München, October 1983

/Pepper 79/
P. Pepper: A study on transformational semantics. Fachbereich Mathematik der Technischen Universität München, Dissertation, 1979. Also in /Bauer, Broy 79/, 322-405

/Pepper 84/
P. Pepper (ed.): Program transformations and programming environments. NATO ASI Series. Series F: Computer and Systems Sciences 8. Berlin: Springer 1984

/Plotkin 76/
G. D. Plotkin: A powerdomain construction. SIAM J. Comp. 5, 452-486 (1976)

/Quine 60/
W. V. O. Quine: Word and object. Cambridge, Mass.: MIT Press 1960

/Requicha 77/
A. A. G. Requicha: Mathematical models of rigid solid objects. University of Rochester, N. Y., TM-28, PAP, November 1977

/de Roever 72/
W. P. de Roever: A formalization of various parameter mechanisms as products of relations within a calculus of recursive program schemes. Séminaires IRIA: Théorie des algorithmes, des langages et de la programmation, 1972, 55-88

/Scherlis, Scott 83/
W. L. Scherlis, D. S. Scott: First steps towards inferential programming. Proc. IFIP Congress 83, Paris. Amsterdam: North-Holland 1983, 199-212

/Schütte 67/
K. Schütte: Einführung in die mathematische Logik. Vorlesungsausarbeitung, Universität München 1967

/Scott 70/
D. S. Scott: Outline of a mathematical theory of computation. Proc. 4th Annual Princeton Conference on Information Sciences and Systems 1970, 169-176. Also: Oxford University Computing Laboratory, Programming Research Group, Technical Monograph PRG-2, 1970

/Scott, Strachey 71/

D. S. Scott, C. Strachey: Towards a mathematical semantics for computer languages. Oxford University Computing Laboratory, Programming Research Group, Technical Monograph PRG-6, 1971. Also in: J. Fox (ed.): Computers and automata. New York: Wiley 1971, 19-46

/Wirsing et al. 83/

M. Wirsing, P. Pepper, H. Partsch, W. Dosch, M. Broy: On hierarchies of abstract data types. Institut für Informatik der TU München, TUM-18007. Also: Acta Informatica 20, 1-33 (1983)

APPENDIX I: CONCRETE REPRESENTATION OF ABSTRACT PROGRAMS

In principle, every effective mapping from a subset of the set of character strings onto the set of abstract programs can be imagined as a concrete representation. In practice, it is advisable to use a context-free grammar (possibly further restricted for the sake of parsing efficiency) in which each production clearly corresponds to an abstract language construct as exemplified in /Laut 78/. However, notational variants may be permitted, provided they do not affect the mechanical transition from concrete to abstract syntax (parsing). A few commonly used variants are described below.

- Informal expressions
  A pair of delimiters (e.g. « and ») may be designated to enclose arbitrary text which is not (yet) formalized and stands for an expression or statement.

- Comments
  A pair of delimiters (e.g. co and oc, -- and end-of-line) may be designated to enclose arbitrary text which is not to affect the meaning of the program. Syntactic ambiguity must, of course, be avoided.
  As a special case, laws of a type may be named to ease reference to them, e.g. when they are used for transformation purposes.
  Example: laws TE: total(emptyset) ≡ zero   .

- Operator notation
  Type operations and functions may be named not only with identifiers, but also with operator symbols like +, <, -, ∧ or with arbitrary operator identifiers from a special alphabet like *conc*, *top*. Terms using such functions are usually denoted in prefix or infix notation. In order to disambiguate terms with several infix operators, each symbol may be supplied with a fixed syntactic priority conforming to conventional rules (e.g. * has higher priority than +; monadic operators have the highest priority; operators with equal priority associate to the left).
  Note that the operator symbols which denote functions of a type must not be confused with the logical connectives ∧, ∨, ⇒, ⇔ of the first-order formulas. To disambiguate formulas, infix terms that are immediate components of formulas (e.g. left and right of "=") must be parenthesized.
  Example: The function contains of the type NATSET may be denoted by ∈ (with reversed parameters). Then it could be specified as follows:
      funct(nat, natset)bool ∈ ;
      laws natset s, **nat** x, **nat** y:
          (y ∈ emptyset) ≡ **false**,
          (y ∈ incorp (s, x)) ≡ **if** x=y **then true else** x ∈ s **fi** .
  When operators are used without parameters, i.e. as operands, syntactic confusion is likely to arise; their use may therefore be restricted.

- Overloading

A function identifier or operator may be overloaded provided that for any two of its instances the tuples of parameter base modes differ (i.e. are not (submodes of) the same mode). Thus the operations in a term can be identified in a bottom-up (or inside-out) way. The use of overloaded functions as operands leads to ambiguities because there are no actual parameters identifying them uniquely; it is therefore ruled out.

If an overloaded identifier is included in the list of visible constituents of a type, all of its definitions become visible.

- Overruling

Multiple declaration of an identifier that cannot be treated as overloading is allowed provided that the identifier is not bound twice in the same scope. Binding in an inner scope overrules all the bindings of the same identifier in outer scopes. Still, as required in II.2.2, an identifier must not be used between the beginning of a section and the beginning of its scope, even if it is valid outside. This rules out confusing expressions like

$\lceil$ **nat** n $\equiv$ 7; $\lceil$ **nat** m $\equiv$ n; **nat** n $\equiv$ 8; m+n$\lrcorner$$\lrcorner$

or, even more intricate,

$\lceil$ **nat** n $\equiv$ 7; $\lceil$ **nat** n $\equiv$ n+1; n$\lrcorner$$\lrcorner$.

- Standard denotations

As long as syntactic uniqueness is maintained, frequently used constructor operators may be suppressed.

Examples:

(1) natural numbers

With   **nat** 0 $\equiv$ zero;

        nat 1 $\equiv$ succ (zero);

        nat 2 $\equiv$ 1+1;

          .
          .
          .

        nat ten $\equiv$ 5+5;

        funct $\hat{}$ $\equiv$ (**nat** x, **nat** y)**nat**: ten * x + y

it is convenient to suppress $\hat{}$ in a term like 1$\hat{}$2$\hat{}$7, yielding the term 127.

(2) character strings

It is also convenient to suppress sequences of append operations as in

append (append (append (empty, 'e'), 'n'), 'd').

To avoid confusion with identifiers, special string delimiters have to be introduced, as e.g. in "end".

APPENDIX II: BIBLIOGRAPHY OF THE PROJECT CIP

[BAUER 71]
F. L. Bauer: Programming languages under professional and under educational aspects. Proc. Second All-Union Conference on Programming, Novosibirsk 1970. Siberian Division of the Academy of Sciences 1971. Reprinted in [BAUER, BROY 79], 267-272

[BAUER 73]
F. L. Bauer: A philosophy of programming. A course of three lectures given at the Imperial College of Science and Technology, London, October 1973. Reprinted in [BAUER, SAMELSON 76], 194-229

[BAUER 76]
F. L. Bauer: Programming as an evolutionary process. In [BAUER, SAMELSON 76], 153-182. Abridged version in Proc. 2nd International Conference on Software Engineering, San Francisco 1976, 223-234

[BAUER 79a]
F.L. Bauer: Program development by stepwise transformations - The project CIP. Appendix: Programming languages under educational and under professional aspects. In [BAUER, BROY 79], 237-272

[BAUER 79b]
F.L. Bauer: Detailization and lazy evaluation, infinite objects and pointer representation. In [BAUER, BROY 79], 406-420

[BAUER 80]
F.L. Bauer: A trend for the next ten years of software engineering. In: H. Freeman, P.M. Lewis (eds.): Software Engineering. New York: Academic Press 1980, 1-23

[BAUER 81a]
F.L. Bauer: New aspects of, and new prospects for a software engineer's programming methodology. Proc. 5th COMPSAC, Chicago 1981, 315-323

[BAUER 81b]
F.L. Bauer: Programming as fulfilment of a contract. In: P. Henderson (ed.): System design. Infotech State of the Art Report 9:6. Maidenhead: Pergamon Infotech Ltd. 1981, 165-174

[BAUER 81c]
F.L. Bauer: Algorithms and algebra. In: A.P. Ershov, D. Knuth (eds.): Algorithms in modern mathematics and computer science. Lecture Notes in Computer Science 122. Berlin: Springer 1981, 421-429

[BAUER, BROY 79]
F.L. Bauer, M. Broy (eds.): Program construction. Lecture Notes in Computer Science 69. Berlin: Springer 1979

[BAUER, GNATZ 79]
F.L. Bauer, R. Gnatz: Software Engineering - Herausforderung an die Wissenschaft. Siemens data report 14, Sonderheft "Software Engineering", 2-6 (1979). Translation into English in: Siemens data report VIII, Special Issue "Software Engineering", 2-6 (1980)

[BAUER, PARTSCH 79]
F.L. Bauer, H. Partsch: "Wegweiser" für den Informatikunterricht - Funktionale Programmierung. In: K. Weinhart (ed.): Informatik im Unterricht - Eine Handreichung. Mathematik - Didaktik und Unterrichtspraxis 2. München: Oldenbourg 1979, 115-178

[BAUER, SAMELSON 76]
F.L. Bauer, K. Samelson (eds.): Language hierarchies and interfaces. Lecture Notes in Computer Science 46. Berlin: Springer 1976

[BAUER, WÖSSNER 81]
F.L. Bauer, H. Wössner: Algorithmische Sprache und Programmentwicklung. Berlin: Springer 1981, 2. Aufl. 1984

[BAUER, WÖSSNER 82]
F.L. Bauer, H. Wössner: Algorithmic language and program development. Berlin: Springer 1982

[BAUER, WÖSSNER 83]
F.L. Bauer, H. Wössner: Beispiele zur Programmentwicklung: Abgebrochener Dual-Logarithmus. Institut für Informatik der TU München, TUM-I8312, 1983

[BAUER et al. 77a]
F.L. Bauer, H. Partsch, P. Pepper, H. Wössner: Techniques for program development. In: Software engineering techniques. Infotech State of the Art Report 34. Maidenhead: Infotech International 1977, 25-50

[BAUER et al. 77b]
F.L. Bauer, M. Broy, R. Gnatz, W. Hesse, B. Krieg-Brückner: Notes on the project CIP: Towards a wide spectrum language to support program development by transformation. Institut für Informatik der TU München, TUM-INFO-7722, 1977. Revised version in: K. Alber (ed.): Programmiersprachen. Informatik-Fachberichte 12. Berlin: Springer 1978, 73-85

Appendix II: CIP Bibliography

[BAUER et al. 77c]
F.L. Bauer, H. Partsch, P. Pepper, H. Wössner: Notes on the project CIP: Outline of a transformation system. Institut für Informatik der TU München, TUM-INFO-7729, 1977

[BAUER et al. 78a]
F.L. Bauer, M. Broy, R. Gnatz, W. Hesse, B. Krieg-Brückner: A wide spectrum language for program development. In: B. Robinet (ed.): Program transformations. Proc. 3rd International Symposium on Programming, Paris, March 28-30, 1978. Paris: Dunod 1978, 1-16

[BAUER et al. 78b]
F.L. Bauer, M. Broy, R. Gnatz, W. Hesse, B. Krieg-Brückner, H. Partsch, P. Pepper, H. Wössner: Towards a wide spectrum language to support program specification and program development. SIGPLAN Notices 13:12, 15-24 (1978). Also in [BAUER, BROY 79], 543-552

[BAUER et al. 79]
F.L. Bauer, M. Broy, H. Partsch, P. Pepper, H. Wössner: Systematics of transformation rules. In: [BAUER, BROY 79], 273-289

[BAUER et al. 80]
F.L. Bauer, M. Broy, H. Partsch, P. Pepper: Das aktuelle Schlagwort: Programmtransformationen. Informatik-Spektrum 3, 192-193 (1980)

[BAUER et al. 81a]
F.L. Bauer, M. Broy, W. Dosch, R. Gnatz, F. Geiselbrechtinger, W. Hesse, B. Krieg-Brückner, A. Laut, T.A. Matzner, B. Möller, H. Partsch, P. Pepper, K. Samelson, M. Wirsing, H. Wössner: Report on a wide spectrum language for program specification and development (tentative version). Institut für Informatik der TU München, TUM-I8104, 1981

[BAUER et al. 81b]
F.L. Bauer, M. Broy, W. Dosch, R. Gnatz, B. Krieg-Brückner, A. Laut, M. Luckmann, T.A. Matzner, B. Möller, H. Partsch, P. Pepper, K. Samelson, R. Steinbrüggen, M. Wirsing, H. Wössner: Programming in a wide spectrum language: A collection of examples. Science of Computer Programming 1, 73-114 (1981)

[BERGHAMMER 84a]
R. Berghammer: Zur formalen Entwicklung von graphentheoretischen Algorithmen durch Transformation. Fakultät für Mathematik und Informatik der TU München, Dissertation, TUM-I8403, 1984

[BERGHAMMER 84b]
R. Berghammer: Zur algebraischen Charakterisierung der ganzen Zahlen. Institut für Informatik der TU München, TUM-I8407, 1984

[BERGSTRA et al. 81]
J.A. Bergstra, M. Broy, J.V. Tucker, M. Wirsing: On the power of algebraic specifications. In: J. Gruska, M. Chytil (eds.): 10th Symposium on Mathematical Foundations of Computer Science, Strbske Pleso, CSSR, September 1981. Lecture Notes in Computer Science 118, Berlin: Springer 1981, 193-204

[BERTONI et al. 79]
A. Bertoni, G. Mauri, P.A. Miglioli, M. Wirsing: On different approaches to abstract data types and the existence of recursive models. Bull. EATCS 9, 47-57 (1979)

[BRASS et al. 82]
B. Brass, F. Erhard, A. Horsch, H.-O. Riethmayer, R. Steinbrüggen: CIP-S: An instrument for program transformation and rule generation. Institut für Informatik der TU München, TUM-I8211, 1982

[BROY 77a]
M. Broy: Program development for Steinhaus type permutation generating programs. Institut für Informatik der TU München, TUM-INFO-7701, 1977

[BROY 77b]
M. Broy: Program development: The Ackermann function as an example. Institut für Informatik der TU München, TUM-INFO-7716, 1977

[BROY 78]
M. Broy: A case study in program development: sorting. Institut für Informatik der TU München, TUM-INFO-7831, 1978

[BROY 80a]
M. Broy: Transformation parallel ablaufender Programme. Fakultät für Mathematik der TU München, Dissertation, TUM-I8001, 1980

[BROY 80b]
M. Broy: Zur Spezifikation von Programmen für die Textverarbeitung. In: P.R. Wossidlo (Hrsg.): Textverarbeitung und Informatik. Fachtagung der GI, Bayreuth, 28.-30.5.1980. Informatik-Fachberichte 30. Berlin: Springer 1980, 75-93

[BROY 80c]
M. Broy: Transformational semantics for concurrent programs. Information Processing Letters 11, 87-91 (1980)

Appendix II: CIP Bibliography

[BROY 80d]
M. Broy: Transformations for reliable software. In: M.A. Hennell, L.M. Delves (eds.): Production and assessment of numerical software. London: Academic Press 1980, 151-178

[BROY 81a]
M. Broy: Are fairness-assumptions fair? Second International Conference on Distributed Computing Systems, Paris, April 1981. IEEE 1981, 116-125

[BROY 81b]
M. Broy: On language constructs for concurrent programming. In: W. Händler (ed.): CONPAR 81. Lecture Notes in Computer Science 111. Berlin: Springer 1981, 141-154

[BROY 81c]
M. Broy: Prospects of new tools for software development. In: A.J.W. Duijvestijn, C.P. Lockemann (eds.): Trends in information processing systems. Lecture Notes in Computer Science 123. Berlin: Springer 1981, 106-121

[BROY 82a]
M. Broy: A fixed point approach to applicative multiprogramming. In [BROY, SCHMIDT 82], 562-622

[BROY 82b]
M. Broy: Algebraic methods for program construction: the project CIP. SOFSEM 82. Also in [PEPPER 84a], 199-222

[BROY 83a]
M. Broy: Applicative real time programming. Proc. IFIP Congress 83. Amsterdam: Elsevier Science (North-Holland) 1983, 259-264

[BROY 83b]
M. Broy: Program construction by transformations: A family tree of sorting programs. In: A.W. Biermann et al. (eds.): Computer Program Synthesis Methodologies. Proc. NATO Advanced Study Institute, Bonas, Sept. 28 - Oct. 10, 1981. NATO Advanced Study Institute Series 95. Dordrecht: Reidel 1983, 1-49

[BROY 83c]
M. Broy: Fixed point theory for communication and concurrency. In: D. Bjørner (ed.): Formal Description of Programming Concepts II. Amsterdam: North-Holland 1983, 125-148

[BROY, KRIEG-BRÜCKNER 80]
M. Broy, B. Krieg-Brückner: Derivation of invariant assertions during program development. ACM TOPLAS 2, 321-337 (1980)

[BROY, PEPPER 80]
M. Broy, P. Pepper: Programming as a formal activity.   IEEE Transactions on Software
Engineering SE-7, 10-22 (1981). Also: Institut für Informatik der TU München, TUM-I8012, 1980

[BROY, PEPPER 82]
M. Broy, P. Pepper: Combining algebraic and algorithmic reasoning: An approach to the
Schorr-Waite-Algorithm. ACM TOPLAS 4, 362-381 (1982)

[BROY, SCHMIDT 82]
M. Broy, G. Schmidt (eds.): Theoretical foundations of programming methodology. Dordrecht:
Reidel 1982

[BROY, WIRSING 80a]
M. Broy, M. Wirsing: Programming languages as abstract data types. In: M. Dauchet (ed.): 5ème
Colloque de Lille "Les Arbres en Algèbre et en Programmation", Febr. 1980, 160-177

[BROY, WIRSING 80b]
M. Broy, M. Wirsing: Partial functions and abstract data types. Bull. EATCS 11, 34-41 (1980)

[BROY, WIRSING 80c]
M. Broy, M. Wirsing: Algebraic definition of a functional programming language and its semantical
models. Institut für Informatik der TU München, TUM-I8008, 1980. Also in RAIRO, Informatique
Théorique 17, 137-161 (1983)

[BROY, WIRSING 80d]
M. Broy, M. Wirsing: Program development: From enumeration to backtracking. Information
Processing Letters 10, 193-197 (1980)

[BROY, WIRSING 80e]
M. Broy, M. Wirsing: Initial versus terminal algebra semantics for partially defined abstract
types. Institut für Informatik der TU München, TUM-I8018, 1980

[BROY, WIRSING 81a]
M. Broy, M. Wirsing: On the algebraic specification of nondeterministic programming languages.
In: E. Astesiano, C. Böhm (eds.): 6th Colloquium on Trees in Algebra and Programming. Lecture
Notes in Computer Science 112. Berlin: Springer 1981, 162-179

[BROY, WIRSING 81b]
M. Broy, M. Wirsing: On the algebraic extensions of abstract data types. In: J. Diaz, I. Ramos
(eds.): Formalization of Programming Concepts. Lecture Notes in Computer Science 107. Berlin:
Springer 1981, 244-251

Appendix II: CIP Bibliography

[BROY, WIRSING 81c]
M. Broy, M. Wirsing: Unbounded nondeterminism - an exercise in abstract data types. In: Langages et Traducteurs. Séminaires INRIA 1981, 75-98

[BROY, WIRSING 82]
M. Broy, M. Wirsing: Partial abstract types. Acta Informatica 18, 47-64 (1982)

[BROY, WIRSING 83]
M. Broy, M. Wirsing: On the algebraic specification of finitary infinite communicating processes. In: D. Bjørner (ed.): Formal Description of Programming Concepts II. Amsterdam: North-Holland 1983, 171-198

[BROY et al. 79a]
M. Broy, R. Gnatz, M. Wirsing: Problemspezifikation - eine Grundlage für Programmentwicklung. In: P. Raulefs (ed.): Workshop on reliable software. Applied Computer Science 14. München: Hanser 1979, 235-246

[BROY et al. 79b]
M. Broy, W. Dosch, H. Partsch, P. Pepper, M. Wirsing: Existential quantifiers in abstract data types. In: H.A. Maurer (ed.): Automata, languages and programming. Lecture Notes in Computer Science 71. Berlin: Springer 1979, 73-87

[BROY et al. 79c]
M. Broy, M. Wirsing, J.P. Finance, A. Quéré, J.L. Remy: Methodical solution of the problem of ascending subsequences of maximal length within a given sequence. Information Processing Letters 8:5, 224-229 (1979)

[BROY et al. 79d]
M. Broy, R. Gnatz, M. Wirsing: Semantics of nondeterministic and noncontinuous constructs. In [BAUER, BROY 79], 553-592

[BROY et al. 80a]
M. Broy, P. Pepper, M. Wirsing: On relations between programs. In: B. Robinet (ed.): Proc. 4th International Symposium on Programming, Paris, April 1980. Lecture Notes in Computer Science 83. Berlin: Springer 1980, 59-78

[BROY et al. 80b]
M. Broy, H. Partsch, P. Pepper, M. Wirsing: Semantic relations on programming languages. Proc. IFIP Congress 80, Melbourne. Amsterdam: North-Holland 1980, 101-106

[BROY et al. 81a]
M. Broy, W. Dosch, B. Möller, M. Wirsing: GOTOs - a study in the algebraic specification of programming languages. In: W. Brauer (ed.): GI - 11. Jahrestagung. Informatik-Fachberichte 50. Berlin: Springer 1981, 109-121. Extended Version in: W.M. Lippe, F. Simon (eds.): Denotationelle und Kopierregelsemantik. Institut für Praktische Mathematik und Informatik der Christian-Albrechts-Universität Kiel, Bericht Nr. 8103, 1981, 119-138. Revised Version: University of Edinburgh, Department of Computer Science, Report CSR-89-81, 1981

[BROY et al. 81b]
M. Broy, R. Gnatz, M. Wirsing: Das aktuelle Schlagwort: Nichtdeterminismus. Informatik-Spektrum 4:2, 125-126 (1981)

[BROY et al. 81c]
M. Broy, P. Pepper, M. Wirsing: On design principles for programming languages: an algebraic approach. In: J.W. de Bakker, J.C. van Vliet (eds.): Algorithmic languages. Amsterdam: North-Holland 1981, 203-219

[BROY et al. 82a]
M. Broy, P. Pepper, M. Wirsing: On the algebraic definition of programming languages. Institut für Informatik der TU München, TUM-I8204, 1982. Also ACM TOPLAS (to appear)

[BROY et al. 82b]
M. Broy, C. Pair, M. Wirsing: A systematic study of models of abstract data types. Centre de Recherche en Informatique de Nancy, Report 81-R-042

[DELGADO KLOOS 82]
C. Delgado Kloos: Arquitectura V.L.S.I. Boletín Informativo de Telecomunicación 5:25, 9-13 (1982)

[DOSCH 83]
W. Dosch: New prospects of teaching programming languages. In: F.B. Lovis, E.D. Tagg (eds.): Informatics education for all students at university level. IFIP WG 3.2 Working Conference, Delft, June 1983. Amsterdam: North-Holland 1984, 153-169

[DOSCH 84]
W. Dosch: Zur Didaktik der Datenstrukturen. In: W. Alt, K. Haefner (eds.): Informatik als Herausforderung an Schule und Ausbildung. Informatik-Fachberichte 90. Berlin: Springer 1984, 139-144

[DOSCH, MÖLLER 83]
W. Dosch, B. Möller: An algebraic semantics for Backus' functional programming language with infinite objects. In: I. Kupka (Hrsg.): GI - 13. Jahrestagung. Informatik-Fachberichte 73.

Appendix II: CIP Bibliography

Berlin: Springer 1983, 67-85

[DOSCH, MÖLLER 84a]
W. Dosch, B. Möller: Lazy and busy FP with infinite objects. Proc. 1984 ACM Symposium on LISP
and Functional Programming, Austin, Tex., August 5-8, 1984, 282-292

[DOSCH, MÖLLER 84b]
W. Dosch, B. Möller: Impacts of functional languages on teaching and programming methodology.
In: E.D. Tagg (ed.): Proc. IFIP TC3 Working Conference on Teaching Programming, Paris, May 7-9,
1984. Amsterdam: North-Holland (to appear)

[DOSCH et al. 80]
W. Dosch, M. Wirsing, G. Ausiello, G.F. Mascari: Polynominals - The specification, analysis, and
development of an abstract data type. In: R. Wilhelm (Hrsg.): GI - 10. Jahrestagung.
Informatik-Fachberichte 33. Berlin: Springer 1980, 306-320

[DOSCH et al. 82]
W. Dosch, G.F. Mascari, M. Wirsing: On the algebraic specification of databases. Proc. 8th
International Conference on Very Large Data Bases, Mexico City, Sept. 8-10, 1982, 370-385

[ERHARD 78]
F. Erhard: Systematische Entwicklung einer Rechenstruktur für Listenverarbeitung. Institut für
Informatik der TU München, TUM-INFO-7815, July 1978

[ERHARD 81]
F. Erhard: Programmtransformation im CIP-System. Notizen zum Interaktiven Programmieren 6,
28-46 (1981)

[GNATZ 77a]
R. Gnatz: mod-Funktion und Maximumbestimmung, Entwicklung zweier Programme. Institut für
Informatik der TU München, TUM-INFO-7712, 1977

[GNATZ 77b]
R. Gnatz: Zur Konstruktion von Programmen durch Transformation. Institut für Informatik der TU
München, TUM-INFO-7741, 1977

[GNATZ 81a]
R. Gnatz: Referenzmodell für graphische Systeme - Versuch einer Axiomatik. In: J. Encarnaçao,
W. Straßer (eds.): Geräteunabhängige graphische Systeme. Drittes Darmstädter Kolloquium.
München: Oldenbourg 1981, 357-389

[GNATZ 81b]
R. Gnatz: Certification by program construction from formal specifications. Invited contribution to the International Workshop on the Certification of Graphics Software Standards, Brüssel-Rixensart, 18.-21.5.1981. Institut für Informatik der TU München, TUM-I8106, 1981

[GNATZ 82a]
R. Gnatz: Funktionelle Spezifikation interaktiver Systeme und ihre Zerlegung in Teilsysteme. In [WÖSSNER 82], 45-65

[GNATZ 82b]
R. Gnatz: Relying on abstraction to facilitate graphics programming. Computer Graphics Forum 1:3, 124-128 (1982)

[GNATZ 83a]
R. Gnatz: An algebraic approach to the standardization and the certification of graphics software. Contribution to the Workshop on the Certification of Graphics Standards, Steensel, Netherlands, June 1983. Computer Graphics Forum 2:2/3, 153-166 (1983)

[GNATZ 83b]
R. Gnatz: Graphics and education. Computers & Graphics 7:1, 101-102 (1983)

[GNATZ, PEPPER 77]
R. Gnatz, P. Pepper: fusc: An example in program development. Institut für Informatik der TU München, TUM-INFO-7711, 1977

[HESSE, SETZER 78]
W. Hesse, V.W. Setzer: The line justifier: An example of program development by transformations. Departemento de Matemática Aplicada, IME-USP, São Paulo, Report RT-04/78, 1978

[KRIEG-BRÜCKNER 78]
B. Krieg-Brückner: Concrete and abstract specification, modularization and program development by transformation. Fachbereich Mathematik der TU München, Dissertation, TUM-INFO-7805, 1978

[LAUT 80]
A. Laut: Safe procedural implementations of algebraic types. Information Processing Letters 11, 147-151 (1980)

[LAUT 81a]
A. Laut: Developing algebraic specifications of threaded data structure implementations. In: G. Goos (Hrsg.): Werkzeuge der Programmiertechnik. Informatik-Fachberichte 43. Berlin: Springer 1981, 28-40

Appendix II: CIP Bibliography

[LAUT 81b]
A. Laut: Von abstrakter Syntax zu verketteten Bäumen - Entwicklung einer abstrakten Datenstruktur für die Programm-Manipulation. Institut für Informatik der TU München, TUM-I8114, 1981

[LAUT 82]
A. Laut: Abstrakte Syntax und Programm-Manipulation. Fakultät für Mathematik und Informatik der TU München, Dissertation, 1982

[LAUT 83]
A. Laut: An algebraic specification of Pascal's file type. SIGPLAN Notices $\underline{18}$:4, 66-68 (1983)

[LAUT, MÖLLER 79]
A. Laut, B. Möller: Mutual development of the abstract computation structure TREE and the function preorder. Institut für Informatik der TU München, Internal Report, 1979

[LAUT, PARTSCH 82]
A. Laut, H. Partsch: Tuning algebraic specifications by type merging. In: M. Dezani-Ciancaglini, U. Montanari (eds.): Proc. 5th International Symposium on Programming, Turin, April 1982. Lecture Notes in Computer Science $\underline{137}$. Berlin: Springer 1982, 283-304

[LESZCZYLOWSKI, WIRSING 82]
J. Leszczylowski, M. Wirsing: A system for reasoning within and about algebraic specifications. In: M. Dezani-Ciancaglini, U. Montanari (eds.): Proc. 5th International Symposium on Programming, Turin, April 1982. Lecture Notes in Computer Science $\underline{137}$. Berlin: Springer 1982, 257-282

[MÖLLER 82]
B. Möller: Unendliche Objekte und Geflechte. Fakultät für Mathematik und Informatik der TU München, Dissertation, TUM-I8213, 1982

[MÖLLER 83]
B. Möller: An algebraic semantics for busy (data-driven) and lazy (demand-driven) evaluation and its application to a functional language. In: J. Diaz (ed.): Automata, Languages and Programming. Lecture Notes in Computer Science $\underline{154}$. Berlin: Springer 1983, 513-526

[MÖLLER 84]
B. Möller (ed.): A survey of the project CIP: Computer-Aided, Intuition-Guided Programming - Wide spectrum language and program transformations. Institut für Informatik der TU München, TUM-I8406, July 1984

[MÖLLER 85]
B. Möller: On the algebraic specification of infinite objects - Ordered and continuous models of algebraic types. Acta Informatica (to appear)

[MÖLLER et al. 84]
B. Möller, H. Partsch, P. Pepper: Programming by formal reasoning - An overview of the Munich CIP project. Submitted for publication

[PÄPPINGHAUS, WIRSING 81]
P. Päppinghaus, M. Wirsing: Nondeterministic partial logic: Isotonic and guarded truth-functions. University of Edinburgh, Dept. of Computer Science, Report CSR-83-81, 1981

[PARTSCH 79]
H. Partsch: Konstruktion effizienter Markov-Algorithmen durch Programm-Transformationen. Fachbereich Mathematik der TU München, Dissertation, TUM-INFO-7915, 1979

[PARTSCH 83a]
H. Partsch: An exercise in the transformational derivation of an efficient program by joint development of control and data structure. Science of Computer Programming 3, 1-35 (1983)

[PARTSCH 83b]
H. Partsch: On the use of algebraic methods for formal requirements definitions. In: G. Hommel, D. Krönig (eds.): Requirements engineering. Informatik-Fachberichte 74. Berlin: Springer 1983, 138-158

[PARTSCH 83c]
H. Partsch: A transformational approach to parsing and recognition. Institut für Informatik der TU München, TUM-I8314, 1983

[PARTSCH 84a]
H. Partsch: Transformational derivation of parsing algorithms executable on parallel architectures. In: U. Ammann (Hrsg.): Programmiersprachen und Programmentwicklung. Informatik-Fachberichte 77. Berlin: Springer 1984, 41-57

[PARTSCH 84b]
H. Partsch: Structuring transformational developments: A case study based on Earley's recognizer. Science of Computer Programming 4, 17-44 (1984)

[PARTSCH 84c]
H. Partsch: The CIP transformation system. In [PEPPER 84a], 305-322

Appendix II: CIP Bibliography

[PARTSCH, BROY 79]
H. Partsch, M. Broy: Examples for change of types and object structures. In [BAUER, BROY 79], 421-463

[PARTSCH, LAUT 82]
H. Partsch, A. Laut: From requirements to their formalization - A case study on the stepwise development of algebraic specifications. In [WÖSSNER 82], 117-132

[PARTSCH, PEPPER 76a]
H. Partsch, P. Pepper: A family of rules for recursion removal. Information Processing Letters 5, 174-177 (1976)

[PARTSCH, PEPPER 76b]
H. Partsch, P. Pepper: A family of rules for recursion removal related to the "Towers of Hanoi" problem. Institut für Informatik der TU München, Bericht Nr. 7612, 1976

[PARTSCH, PEPPER 77a]
H. Partsch, P. Pepper: Program transformations on different levels of programming. Institut für Informatik der TU München, TUM-INFO-7715, 1977

[PARTSCH, PEPPER 77b]
H. Partsch, P. Pepper: Beweisen durch Programmtransformation. Institut für Informatik der TU München, TUM-INFO-7719, 1977

[PARTSCH, PEPPER 83]
H. Partsch, P. Pepper: Abstract data types as a tool for requirements engineering. In: G. Hommel, D. Krönig (eds.): Requirements engineering. Informatik-Fachberichte 74, Berlin: Springer 1983, 42-55

[PARTSCH, PEPPER 84]
H. Partsch, P. Pepper: Algebraic types as a framework for program transformation. Institut für Informatik der TU München, TUM-I8408, 1984

[PARTSCH, STEINBRÜGGEN 81]
H. Partsch, R. Steinbrüggen: A comprehensive survey of program transformation systems. Institut für Informatik der TU München, Bericht TUM-I8108, 1981

[PARTSCH, STEINBRÜGGEN 83]
H. Partsch, R. Steinbrüggen: Program transformation systems. ACM Computing Surveys 15, 199-236 (1983)

[PEPPER 79]
P. Pepper: A study on transformational semantics. Fachbereich Mathematik der TU München, Dissertation, 1978. In [BAUER, BROY 79], 322-405

[PEPPER 81]
P. Pepper: On program transformations for abstract data types and concurrency. Stanford University, Computer Science Department, Technical Report STAN-CS-81-883, 1981

[PEPPER 82]
P. Pepper: Specification languages and program transformation. In: J.K. Reid (ed.): Relationship between numerical computation and programming languages. Amsterdam: North-Holland 1982, 331-346

[PEPPER 84a]
P. Pepper (ed.): Program transformations and programming environments. NATO ASI Series. Series F: Computer and Systems Sciences 8. Berlin: Springer 1984

[PEPPER 84b]
P. Pepper: Algebraic techniques for program specification. In [PEPPER 84a], p.231-243

[PEPPER 84c]
P. Pepper: Inferential techniques for program development. In [PEPPER 84a], 275-290

[PEPPER 84d]
P. Pepper: A simple calculus for program transformations (inclusive of induction). Institut für Informatik der TU München, TUM-I8409, July 1984

[PEPPER, PARTSCH 80]
P. Pepper, H. Partsch: On the feedback between specifications and implementations: An example. Institut für Informatik der TU München, TUM-I8011, 1980

[PEPPER et al. 82]
P. Pepper, M. Broy, F.L. Bauer, H. Partsch, W. Dosch, M. Wirsing: Abstrakte Datentypen: Die algebraische Definition von Rechenstrukturen. Informatik-Spektrum 5, 107-119 (1982)

[RIETHMAYER 81]
H.-O. Riethmayer: Die Entwicklung der Bedienungskomponente des CIP-Systems. Notizen zum Interaktiven Programmieren 6, 47-76 (1981)

[SANNELLA, WIRSING 82]
D. Sannella, M. Wirsing: Implementation of parametrized specifications. In: M. Nielsen, E.M. Schmidt (eds.): Automata, languages and programming. Lecture Notes in Computer Science 140. Berlin: Springer 1982, 473-488. Full version: University of Edinburgh, Dept. of Computer Science,

Appendix II: CIP Bibliography

Report CSR-103-82, 1982

[SANNELLA, WIRSING 83]
D. Sannella, M. Wirsing: A kernel language for algebraic specification and implementation. In: M. Karpinski (ed.): Foundations of Computation Theory. Lecture Notes in Computer Science 158. Berlin: Springer 1983, 413-427

[STEINBRÜGGEN 77]
R. Steinbrüggen: Equivalent recursive definitions of certain number theoretic functions. Institut für Informatik der TU München, TUM-INFO-7714, 1977

[STEINBRÜGGEN 80a]
R. Steinbrüggen: The use of nested scheme parameters in the system CIP (extended abstract). In: R. Wilhelm (Hrsg.): GI - 10. Jahrestagung. Informatik-Fachberichte 33. Berlin: Springer 1980, 106

[STEINBRÜGGEN 80b]
R. Steinbrüggen: Pre-algorithmic specifications of the system CIP. Part 1: The application, composition, and expansion of schemes for local program transformation. Institut für Informatik der TU München, TUM-I8016, 1980

[STEINBRÜGGEN 81]
R. Steinbrüggen: The composition of schemes for local program transformation. In: M. Arato, L. Varga (eds.): Proc. Third Hungarian Computer Science Conference. Budapest: Akademiai Kiado 1981, 111-124

[STEINBRÜGGEN 82]
R. Steinbrüggen: Program development using transformational expressions. Institut für Informatik der TU München, TUM-I8206, 1982

[WIRSING 82]
M. Wirsing: Structured algebraic specifications. In: B. Robinet (ed.): Proc. AFCET Symposium on Mathematics for Computer Science, Paris, March 16-18, 1982, 93-108

[WIRSING, BROY 80]
M. Wirsing, M. Broy: Abstract data types as lattices of finitely generated models. In: P. Dembinski (ed.): Mathematical Foundations of Computer Science. Lecture Notes in Computer Science 88. Berlin: Springer 1980, 673-685

[WIRSING, BROY 82]
M. Wirsing, M. Broy: An analysis of semantic models for algebraic specifications. In [BROY, SCHMIDT 82], 351-412

[WIRSING et al. 80]
M. Wirsing, P. Pepper, H. Partsch, W. Dosch, M. Broy: On hierarchies of abstract data types. Institut für Informatik der TU München, TUM-I8007. Also Acta Informatica 20, 1-33 (1983)

[WÖSSNER 82]
H. Wössner (ed.): Programmiersprachen und Programmentwicklung. Informatik-Fachberichte 53. Berlin: Springer 1982

[WÖSSNER et al. 79]
H. Wössner, P. Pepper, H. Partsch, F.L. Bauer: Special transformation techniques. In [BAUER, BROY 79], 290-321

APPENDIX III

SYNTAX DIAGRAMS FOR THE

ALGOL-LIKE AND THE PASCAL-LIKE

EXTERNAL REPRESENTATIONS

The syntax diagrams in this appendix use the following conventions: Nonterminal symbols are marked by rectangular boxes, whereas terminal symbols are marked by oval boxes. The sub-diagram belonging to a nonterminal is marked by that nonterminal in the upper left-hand corner. All paths through the diagrams must follow the direction of the arrows.

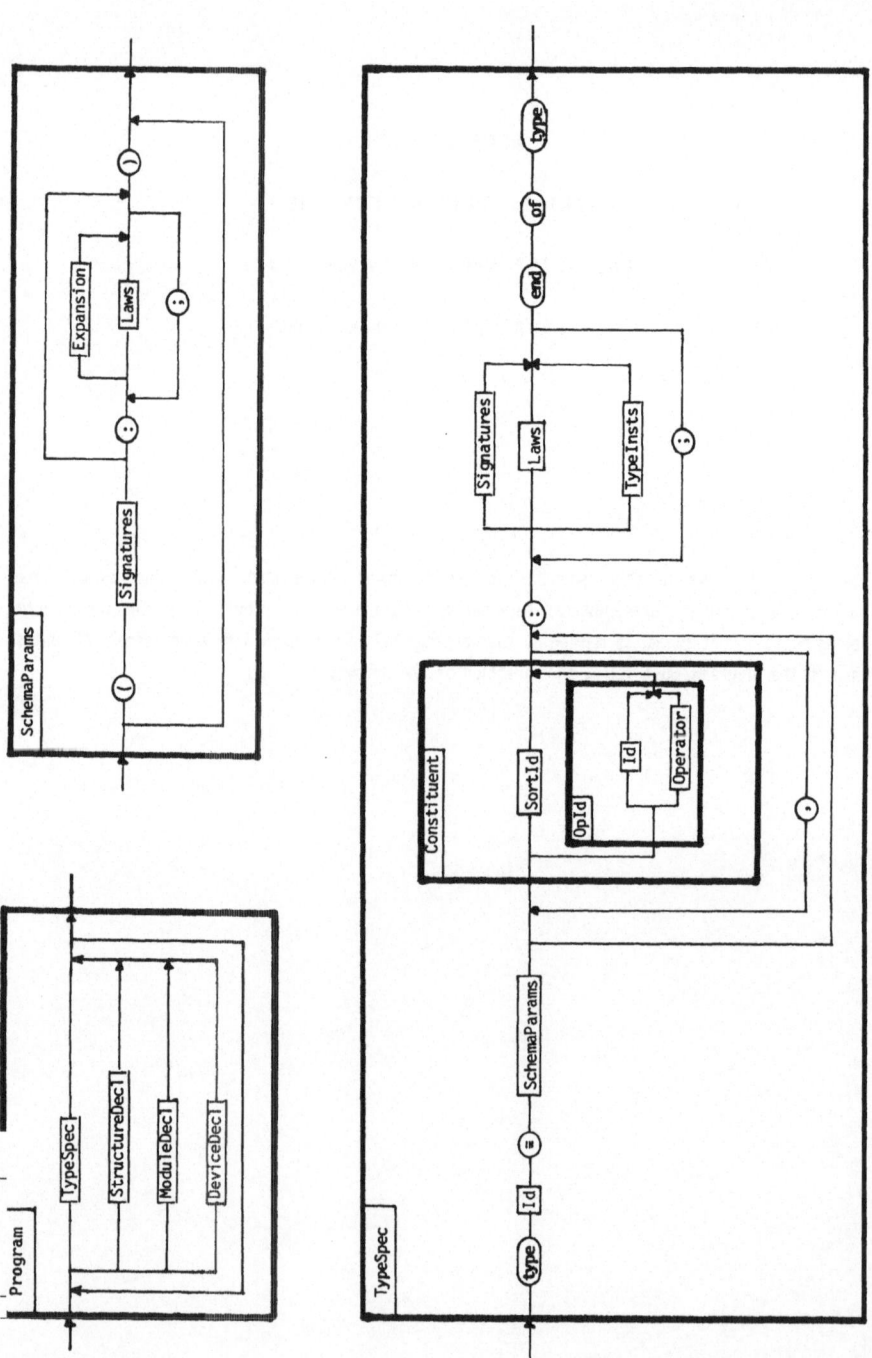

PASCAL-like Syntax

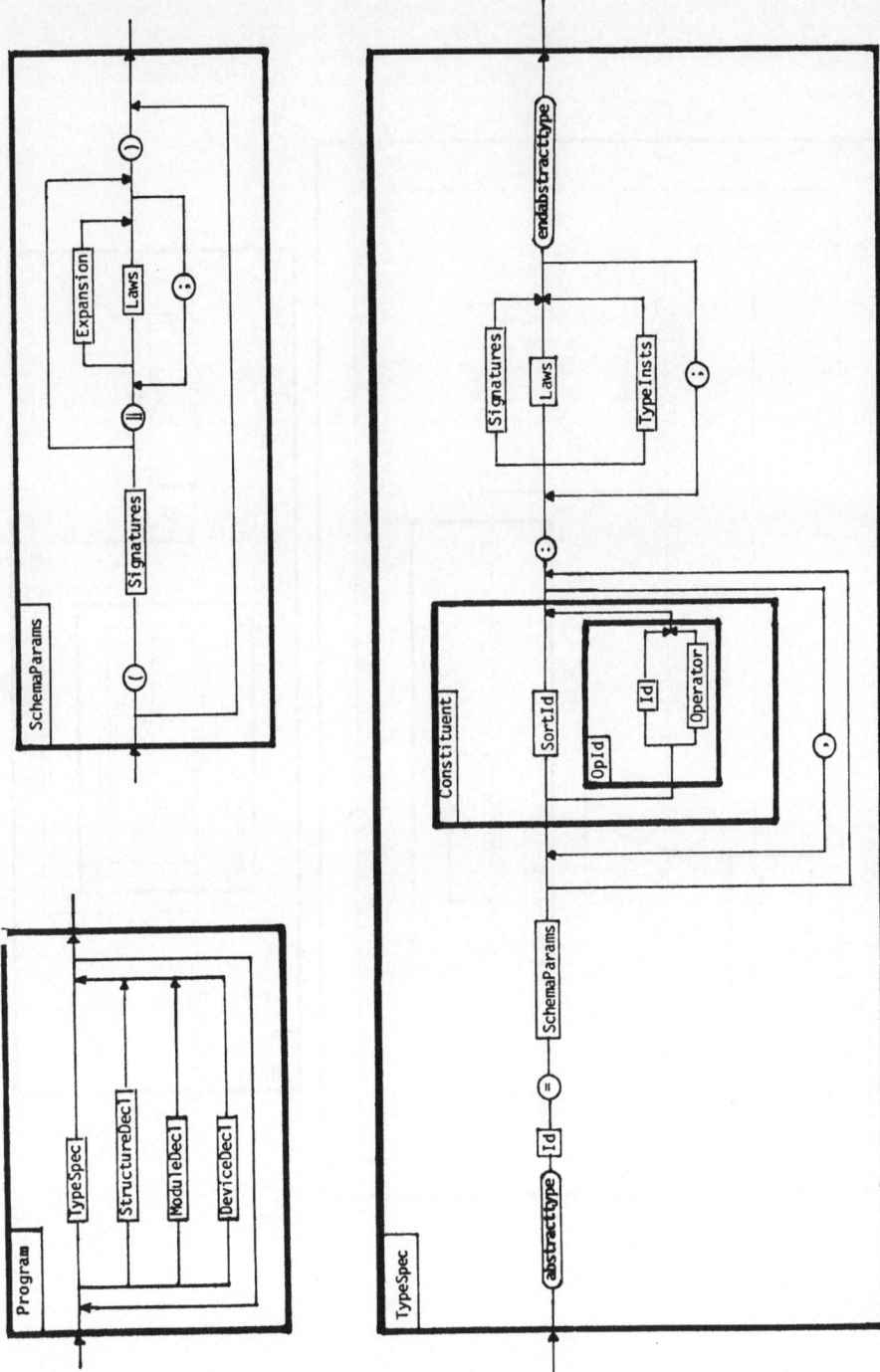

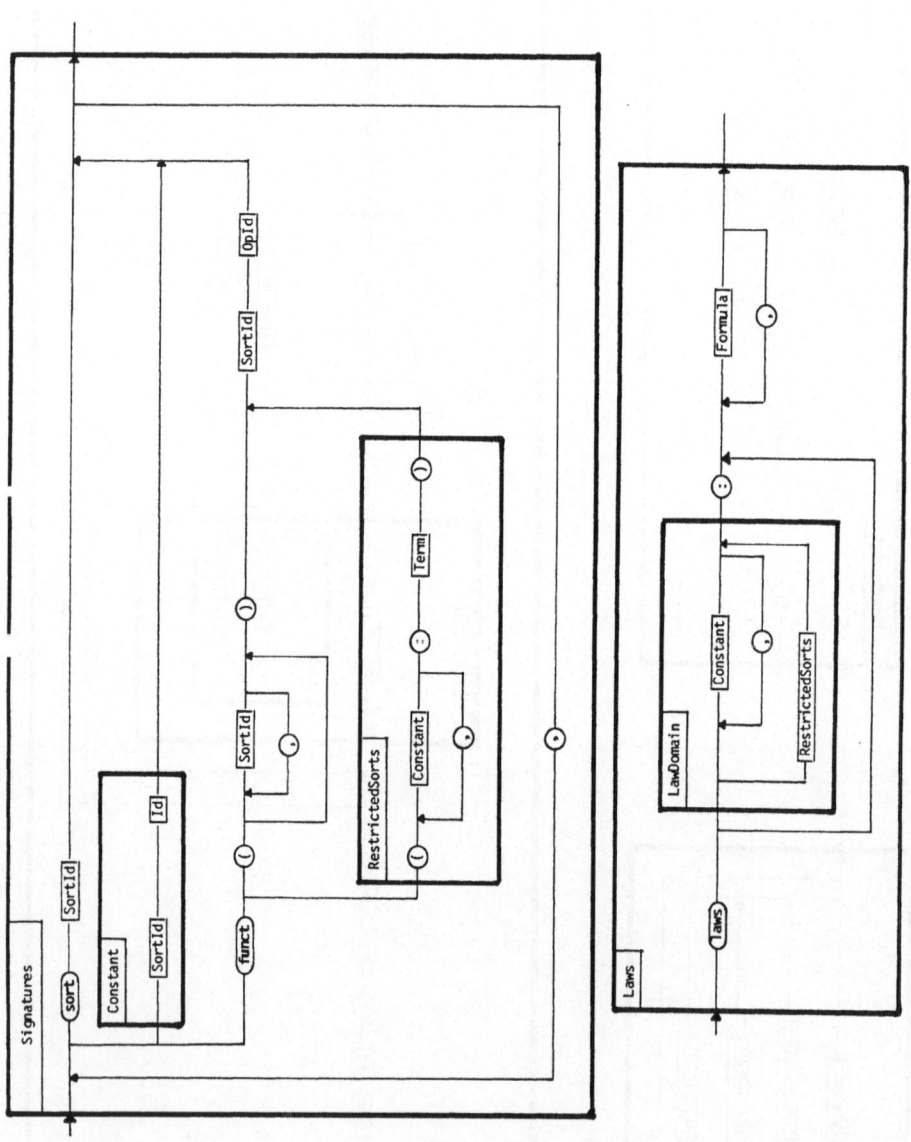

PASCAL-like Syntax

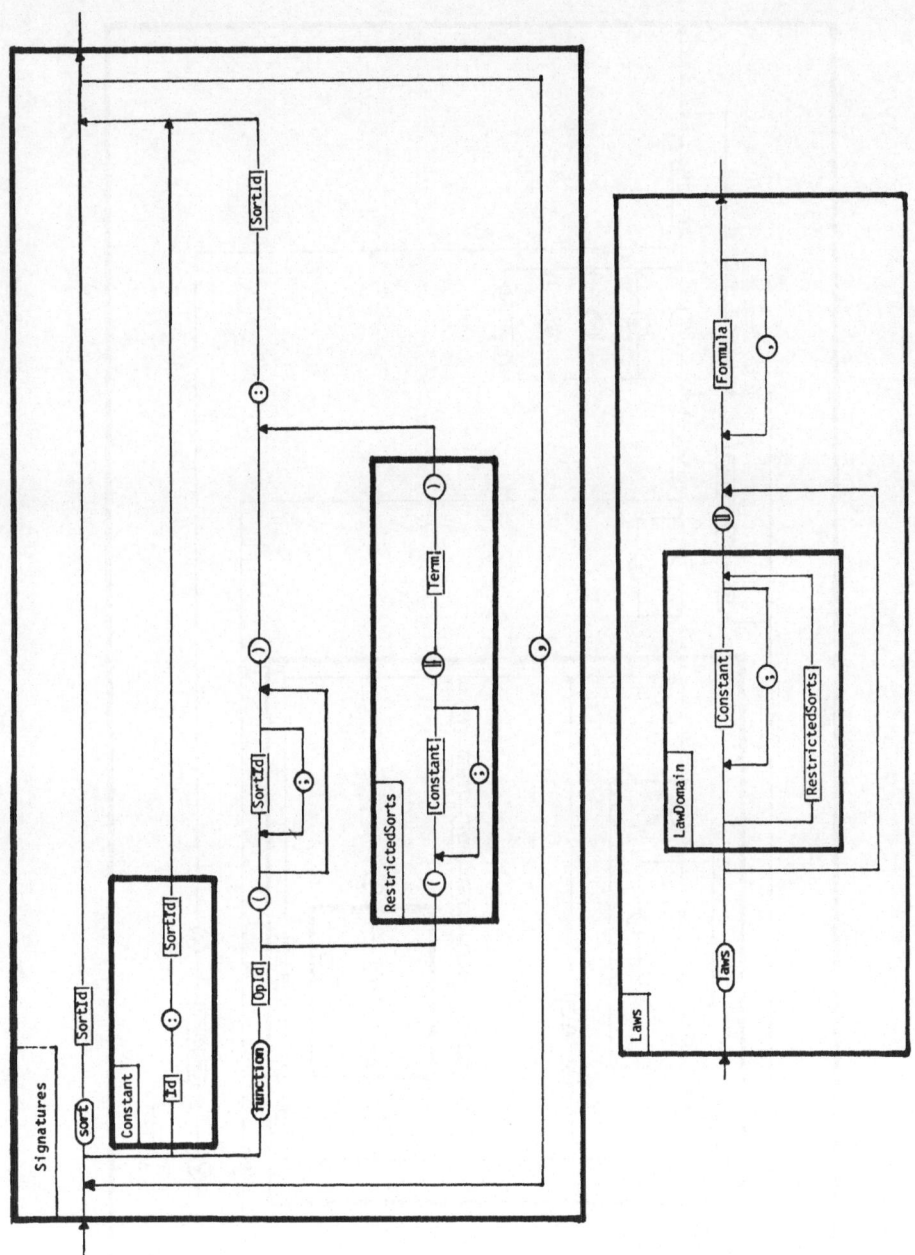

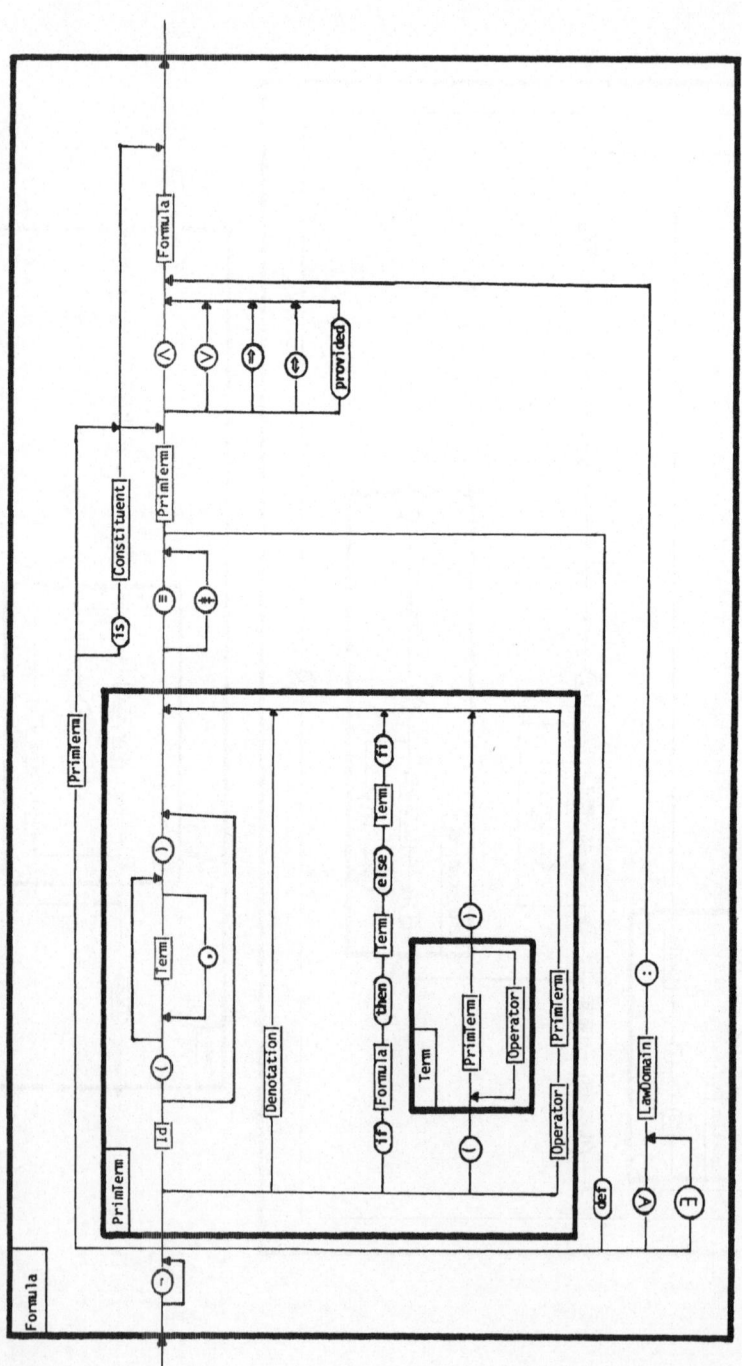

PASCAL-like Syntax

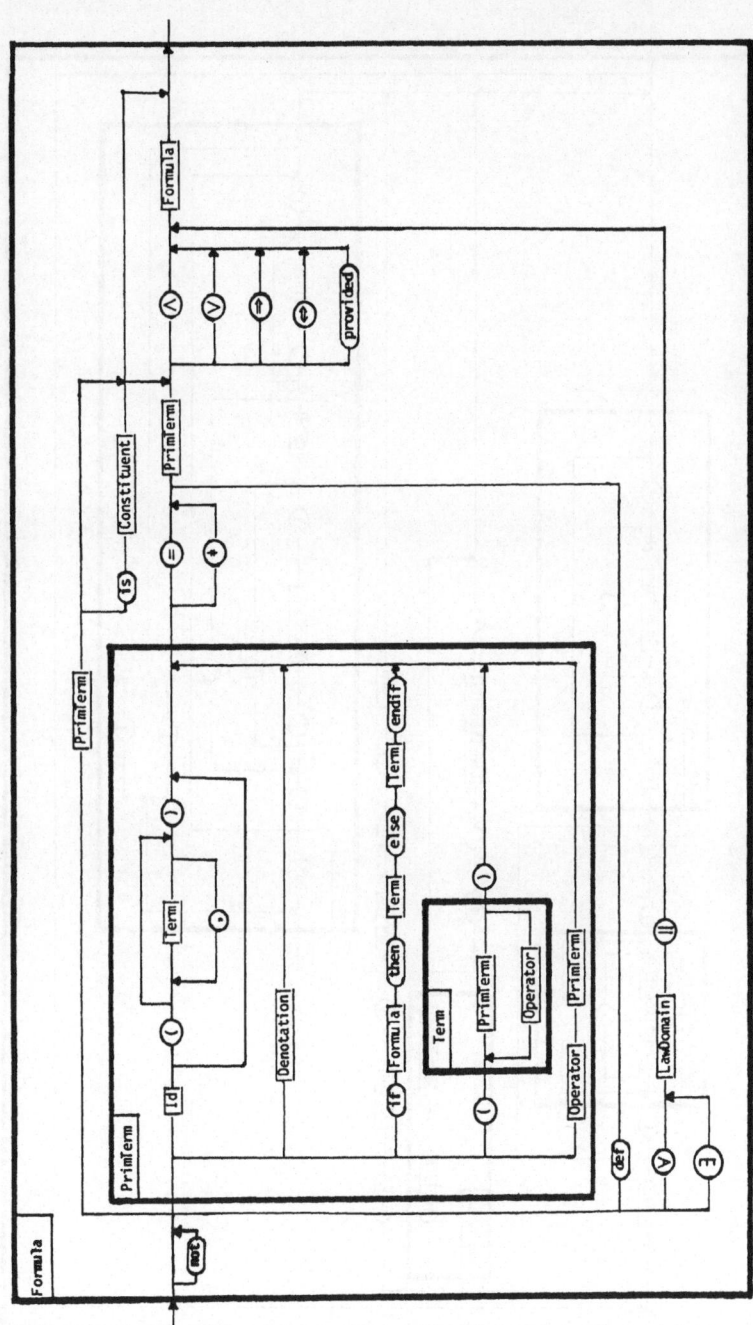

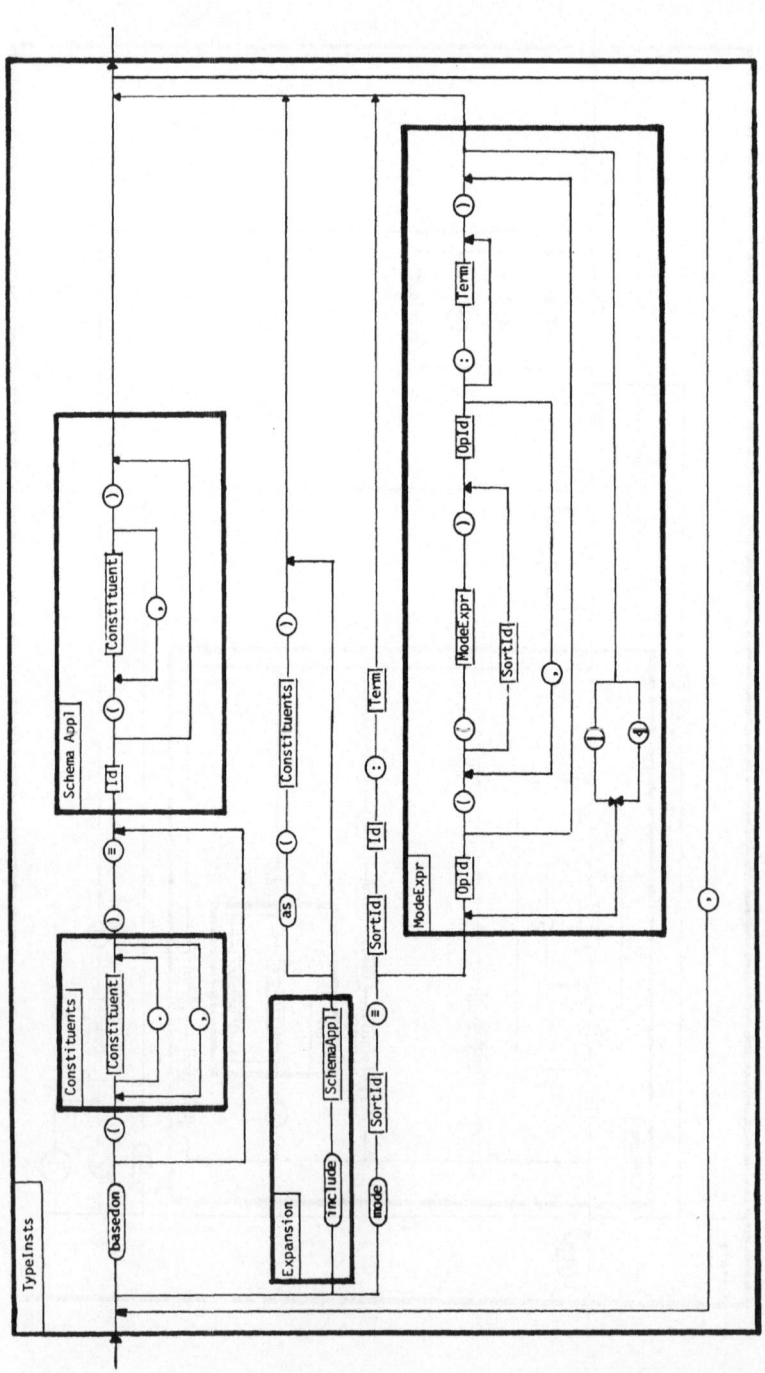

PASCAL-like Syntax

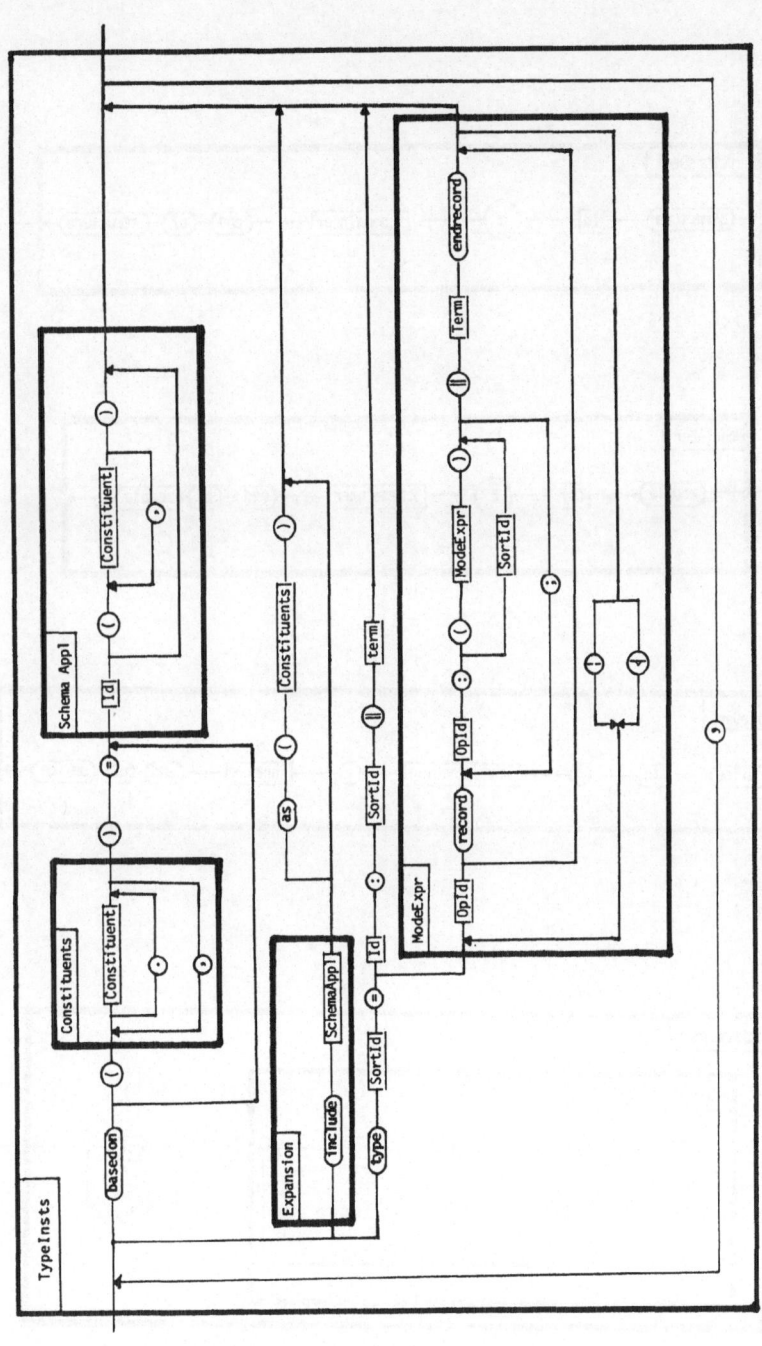

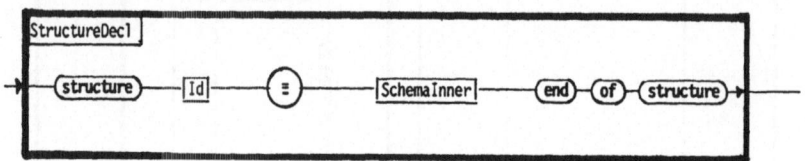

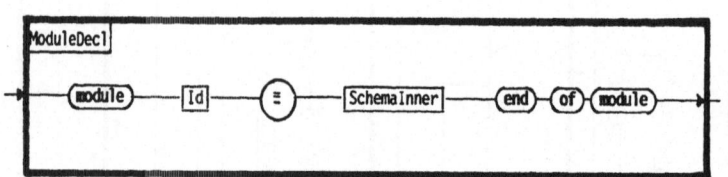

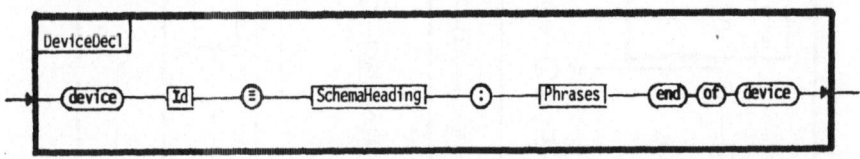

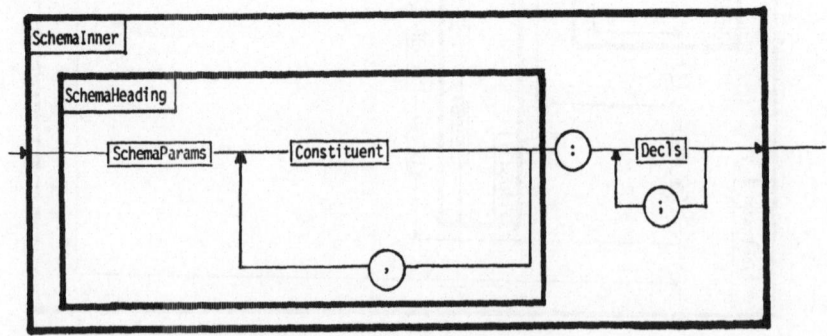

PASCAL-like Syntax

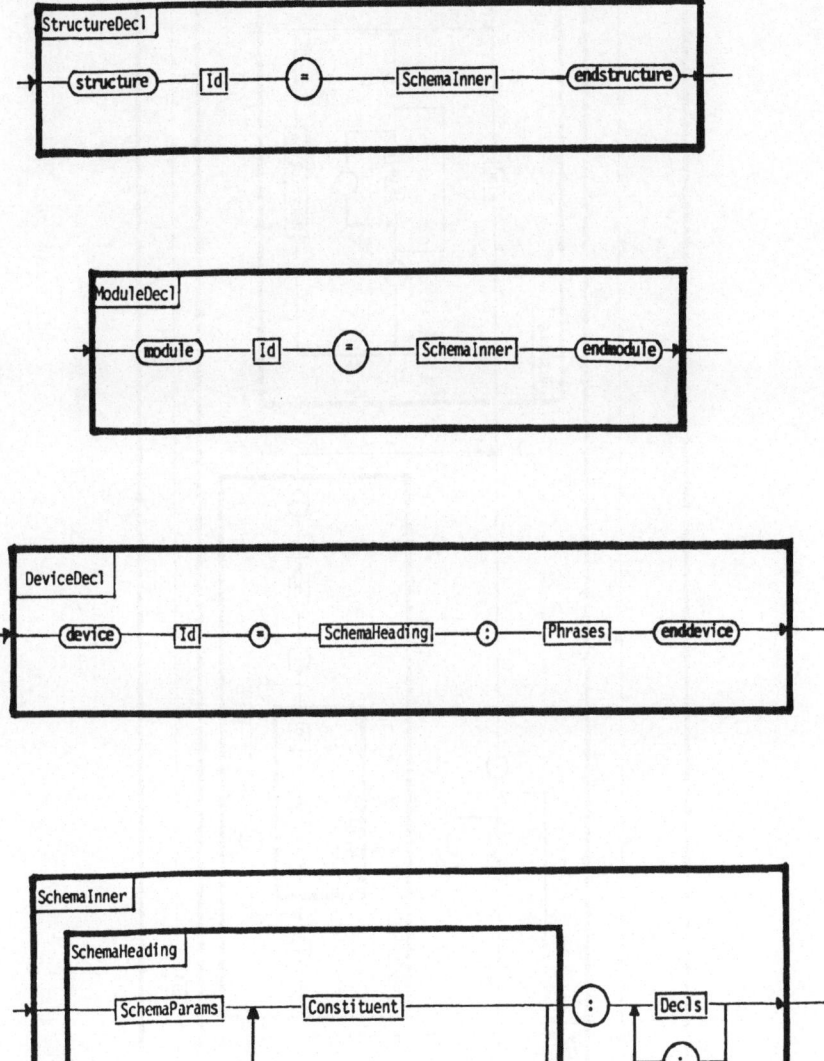

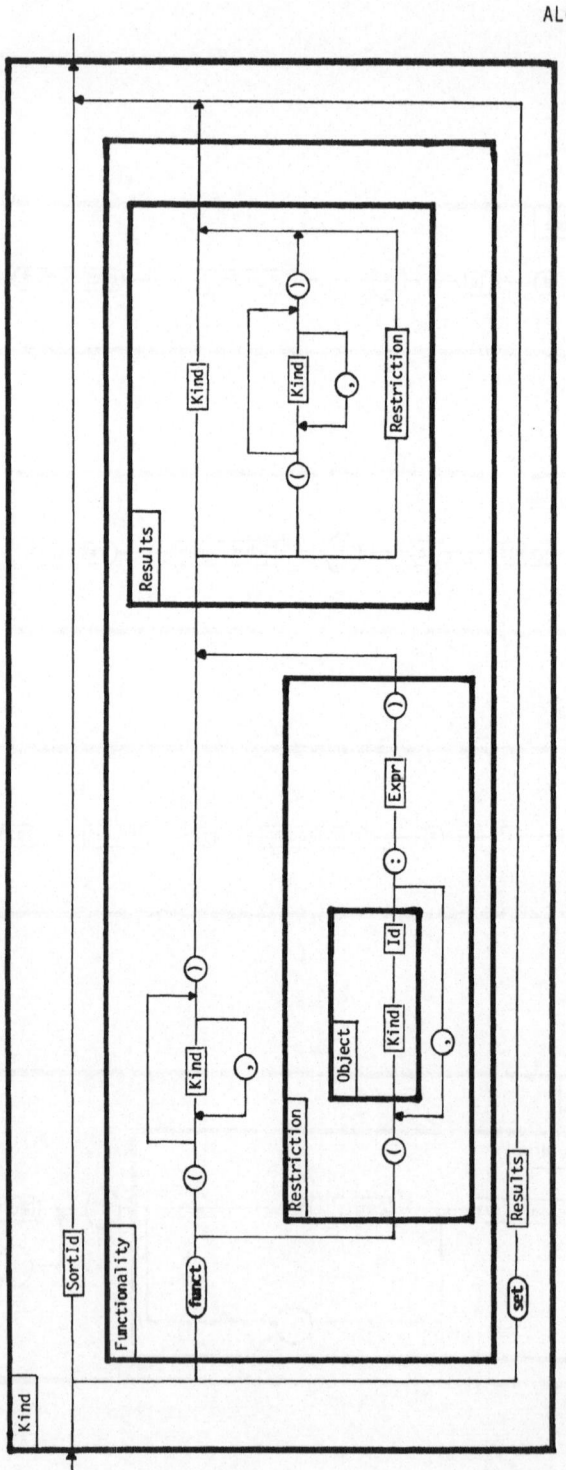

PASCAL-like Syntax

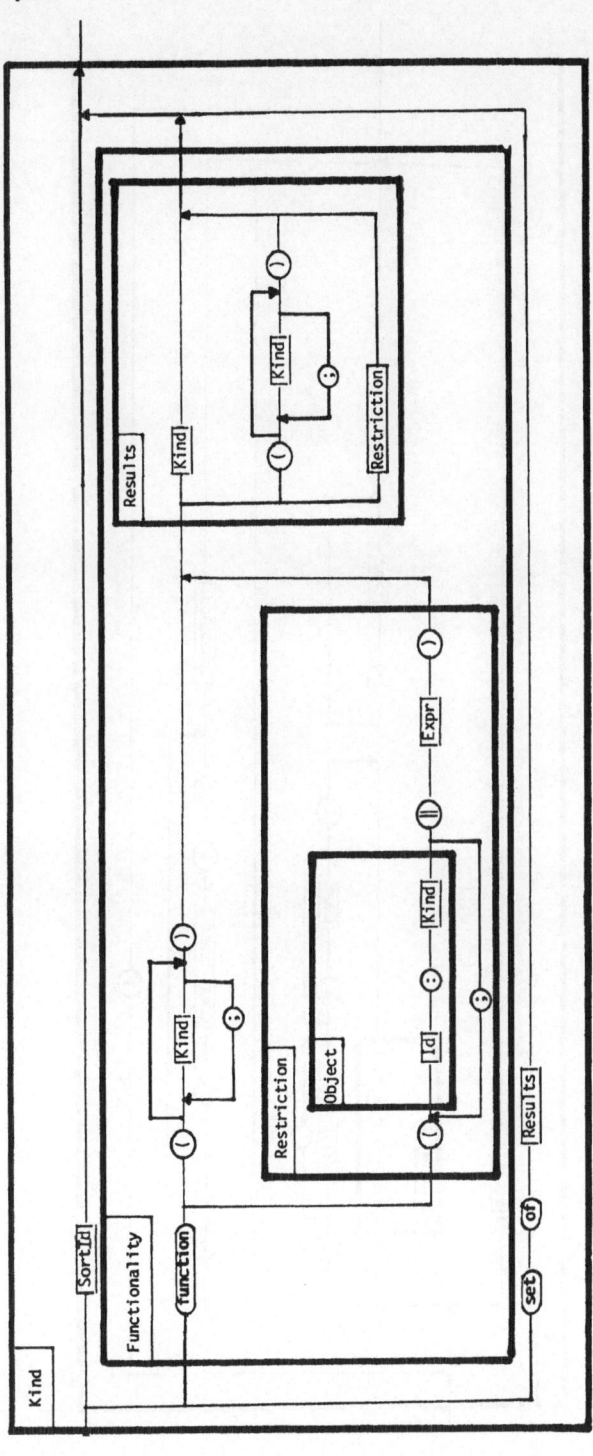

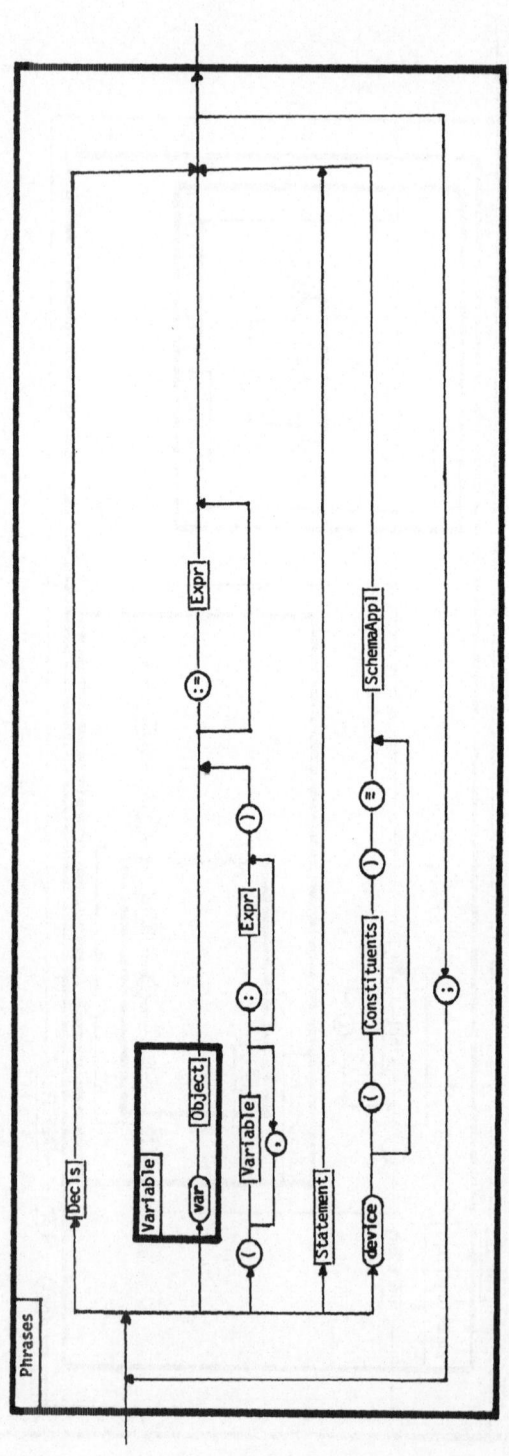

PASCAL-like Syntax

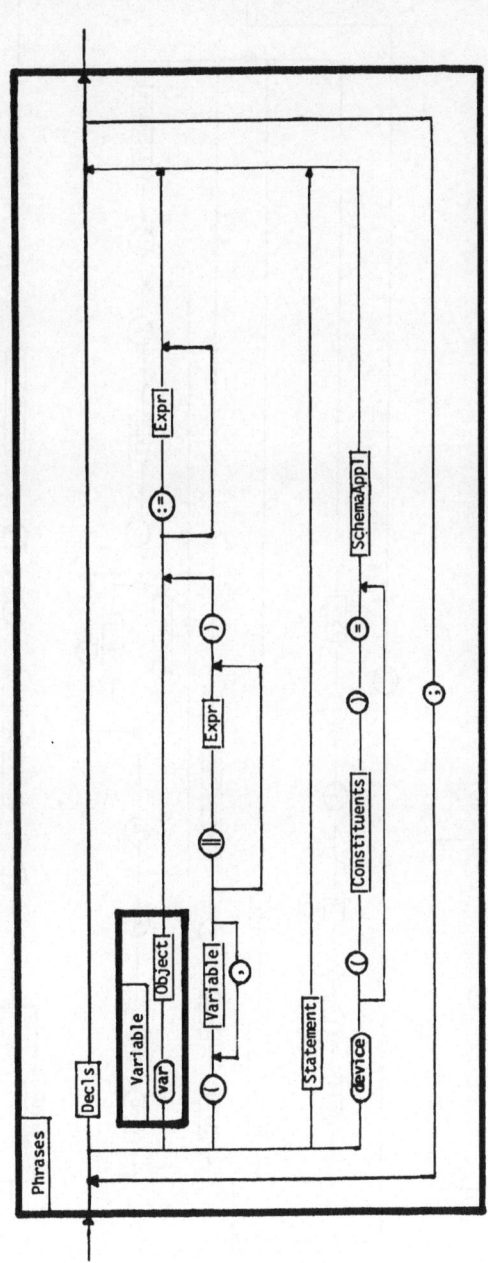

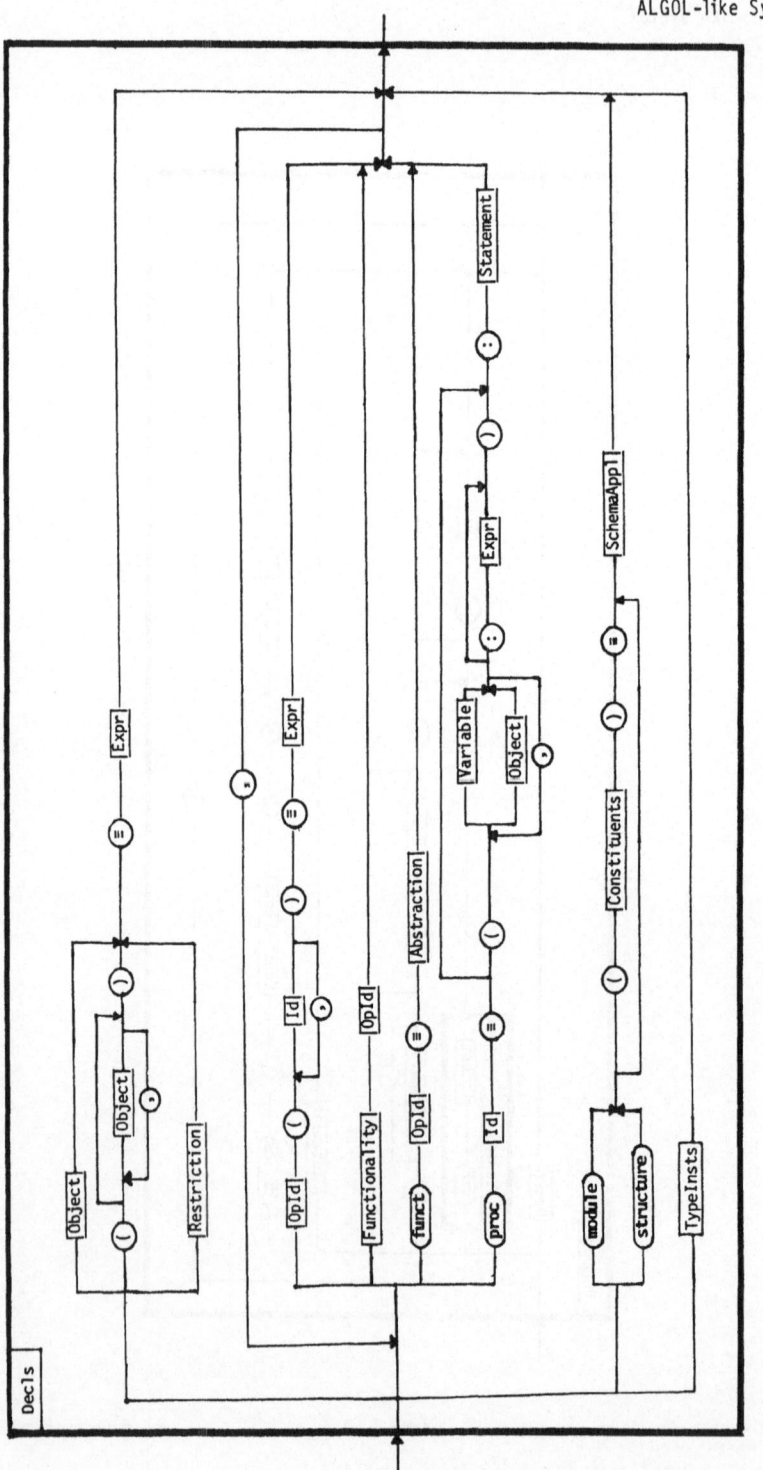

PASCAL-like Syntax

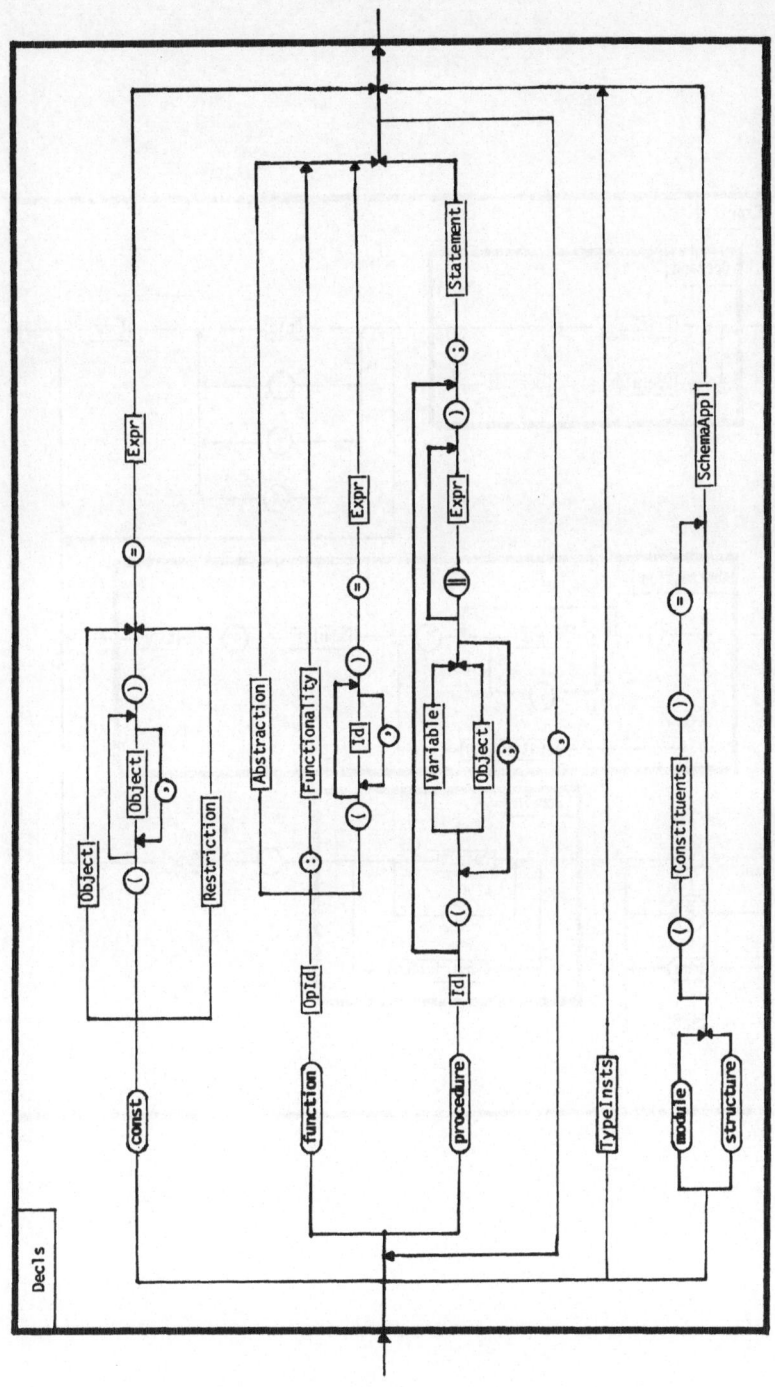

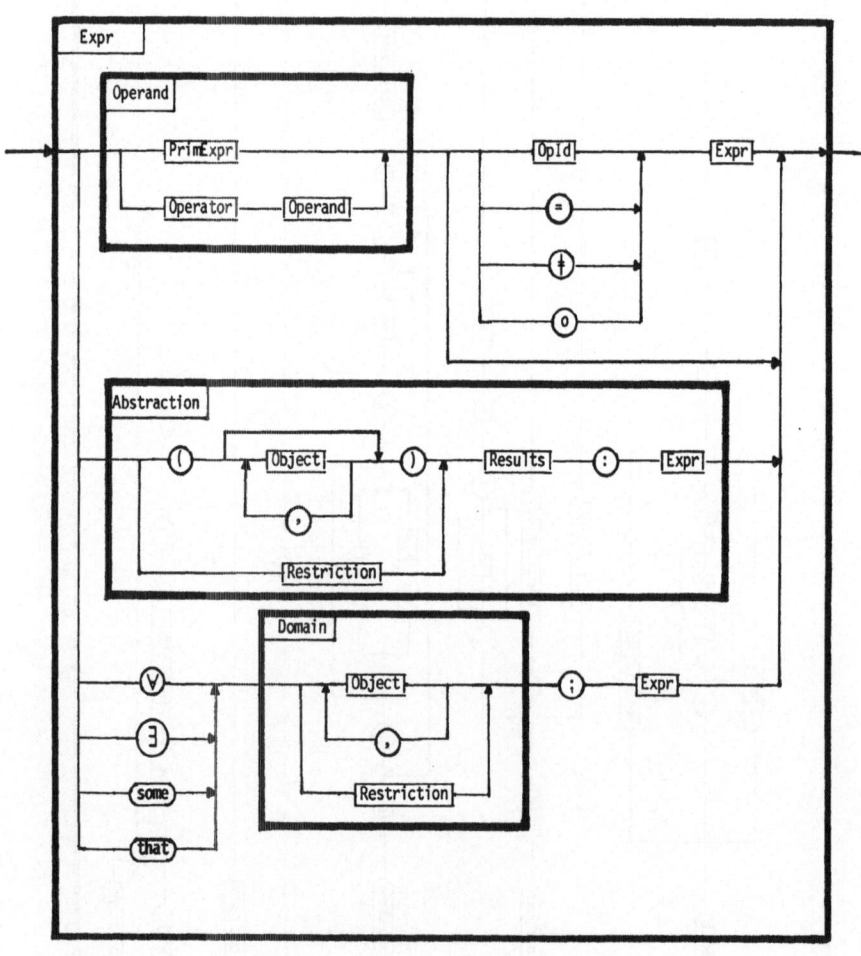

PASCAL-like Syntax

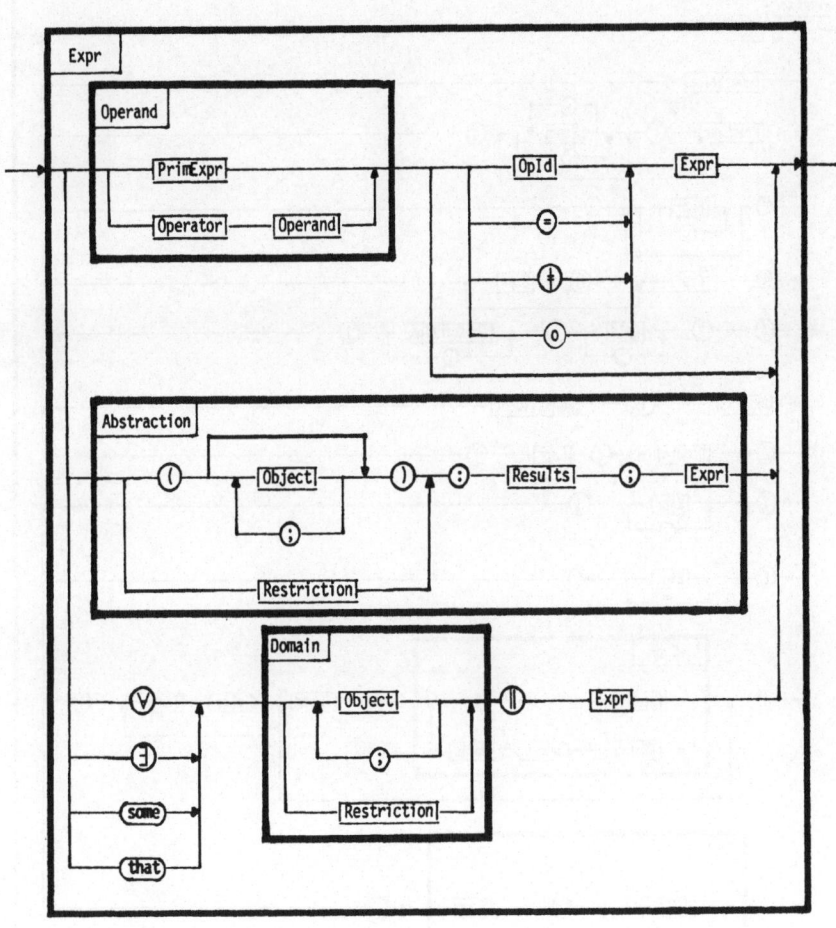

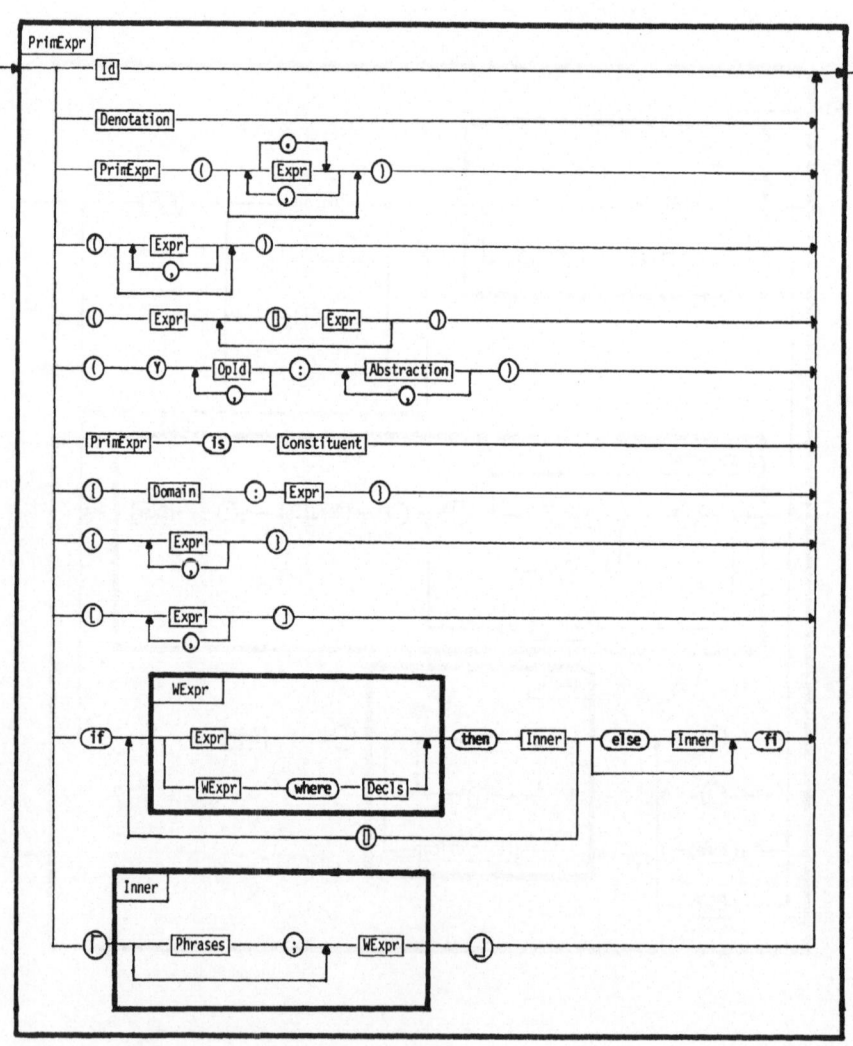

PASCAL-like Syntax

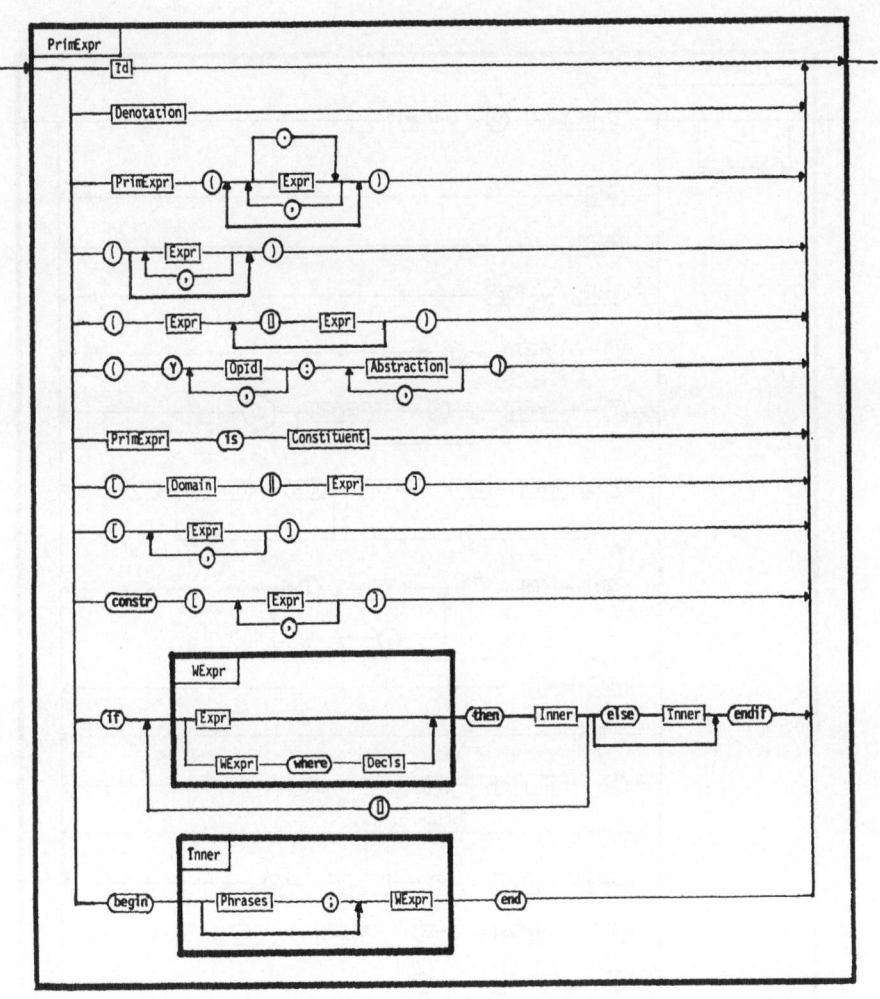

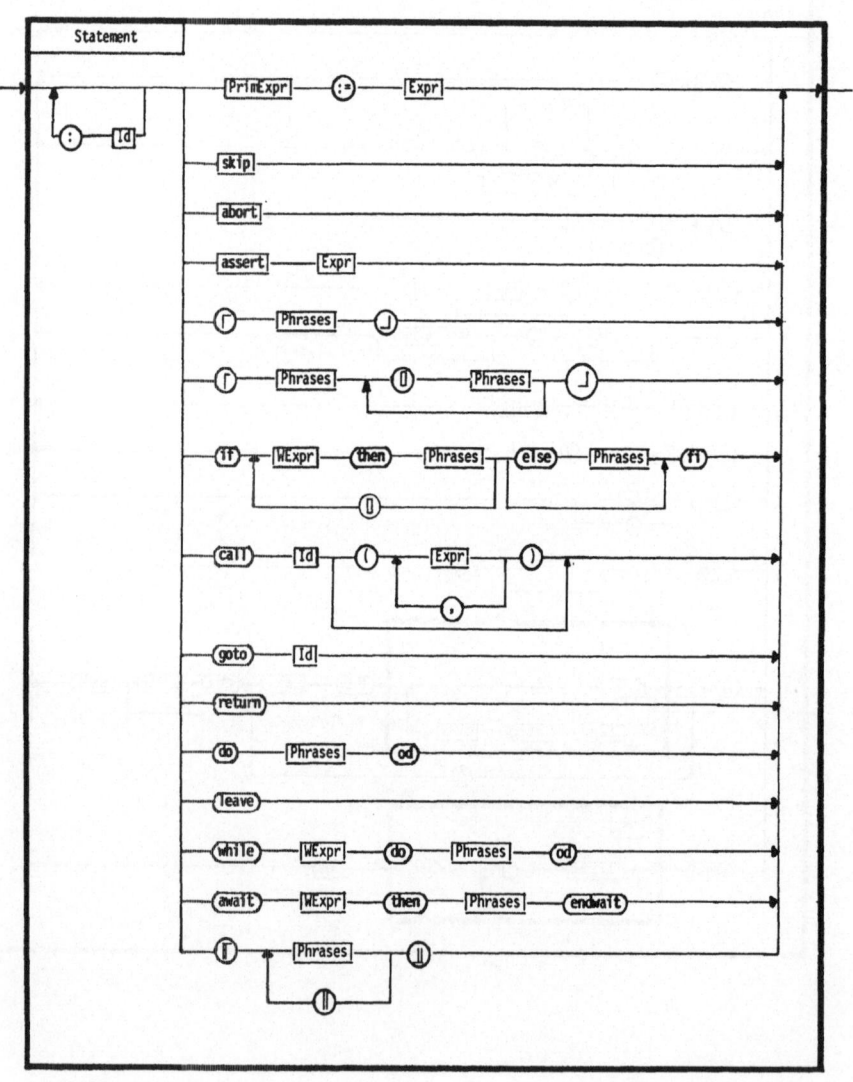

PASCAL-like Syntax

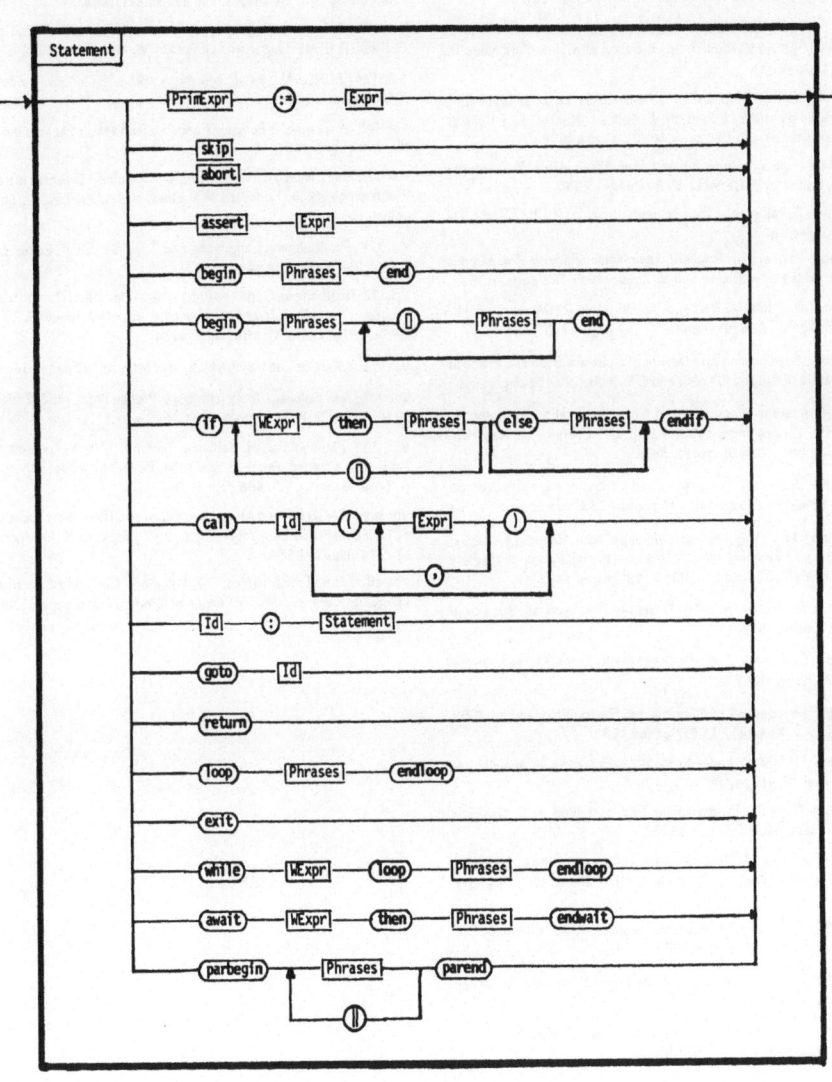